Studies in Classification, Data Analysis, and Knowledge Organization

T0189846

Titles in the Series

Maurizio Vichi · Paola Monari
Stefania Mignani · Angela Montanari

Editors

New Developments
in Classification
and Data Analysis

Proceedings of the Meeting of the Classification and
Data Analysis Group (CLADAG) of the Italian Statistical
Society, University of Bologna, September 22–24, 2003

With 92 Figures and 66 Tables

 Springer

Professor Maurizio Vichi
University of Rome "La Sapienza"
Department of Statistics,
Probability and Applied Statistics
Piazzale Aldo Moro 5
00185 Rome
Italy
maurizio.vichi@uniroma1.it

Professor Paola Monari
Professor Stefania Mignani
Professor Angela Montanari
University of Bologna
Department of Statistical Sciences
Via Belle Arti 41
40126 Bologna
Italy
paola.monari@unibo.it
stefania.mignani@unibo.it
angela.montanari@unibo.it

ISSN 1431-8814
ISBN 3-540-23809-3 Springer-Verlag Berlin Heidelberg New York

Library of Congress Control Number: 2005920314

Springer · Part of Springer Science+Business Media

springeronline.com

© Springer-Verlag Berlin · Heidelberg 2005
Printed in Germany

Softcover-Design: Erich Kirchner, Heidelberg

SPIN 11342816   43/3135 – 5 4 3 2 1 0 – Printed on acid-free paper

Preface

This volume contains revised versions of selected papers presented during the biannual meeting of the Classification and Data Analysis Group of Società Italiana di Statistica, which was held in Bologna, September 22-24, 2003.

The scientific program of the conference included 80 contributed papers. Moreover it was possible to recruit six internationally renowned invited speakers for plenary talks on their current research works regarding the core topics of IFCS (the International Federation of Classification Societies) and Wolfgang Gaul and the colleagues of the GfKl organized a session. Thus, the conference provided a large number of scientists and experts from home and abroad with an attractive forum for discussions and mutual exchange of knowledge.

The talks in the different sessions focused on methodological developments in supervised and unsupervised classification and in data analysis, also providing relevant contributions in the context of applications. This suggested the presentation of the 43 selected papers in three parts as follows:

CLASSIFICATION AND CLUSTERING
Non parametric classification
Clustering and dissimilarities

MULTIVARIATE STATISTICS AND DATA ANALYSIS

APPLIED MULTIVARIATE STATISTICS
Environmental data
Microarray data
Behavioural and text data
Financial data

We wish to express our gratitude to the authors whose enthusiastic participation made the meeting possible. We are very grateful to the reviewers for the time spent in their professional reviewing work. We would also like to extend our thanks to the chairpersons and discussants of the sessions: their comments and suggestions proved very stimulating both for the authors and the audience.

We also thank the Italian Ministero dell'Istruzione, dell'Università e della Ricerca for partially supporting the pubblication of this volume.

Special thanks are also due to the local organizing committee: G. Galimberti, L. Guidotti, A. Lubisco, S. Mignani, P. Monari, A. Montanari, M. Pillati, G. Soffritti, to the University of Bologna for financial support and hospitality, and to the many persons who, in an unofficial form, strongly contributed to the organization of the conference.

We would finally like to thank Dr. M. Bihn and her colleagues from Springer-Verlag, Heidelberg, for the excellent cooperation in publishing this volume.

Roma, Bologna
October 2004

Maurizio Vichi
Paola Monari
Stefania Mignani
Angela Montanari

Contents

Part II Multivariate Statistics and Data Analysis

Part III Applied Multivariate Statistics

Environmental Data

Microarray Data

Behavioural and Text Data

Financial Data

Classification and Clustering

Multi-Class Budget Exploratory Trees

Massimo Aria

Dipartimento di Matematica e Statistica,
Università degli Studi di Napoli Federico II, Italy
aria@unina.it

Abstract. This paper provides a new method to grow exploratory classification trees in multi-class problems. A two-stage algorithm, using recursively the latent budget model, is proposed to find ever finer partitions of objects into prior fixed number of groups. A new rule to assign the class labels to the children nodes is considered to deal with fuzzy data. Then, a software prototype namely *E.T. Exploratory Trees*, developed in the Matlab environment, is proposed to show the main features of the methodology through several interactive graphic tools [1].

1 Introduction

During the last few years, classification has shown a great success in many different fields such as medical science, customer satisfaction, pattern recognition, text mining, etc. In this context, tree methods have played an important role since the monography of Breiman et al. (1984). Later, new algorithms such as C4.5 (Quinlan, 1993), QUEST (*Quick Unbiased Efficent Statistical Tree*, Loh and Shih, 1997), Two-Stage (Mola and Siciliano, 1992), FAST (*Fast Algorithm for Statistical Trees*, Mola and Siciliano, 1997), LBT (*Latent Budget Trees for Multiple Classification*, Siciliano, 1999) have been proposed to improve classification trees.

In ordinary classification problems, each observation belongs to only one class of target (response) variable. Often, the problem concerns the analysis of fuzzy data where objects cannot be placed in distinct groups without strain, and as consequence the interest moves to the evaluation of the strength with which an observation falls into a particular class rather than another one. For example, when we classify a set of documents, the same document (i.e. a scientific paper) may be relevant to more than one topic. This kind of problem is called *multi-class problem*. There are many tree algorithms designed to handle single-class problems, but few for multi-class data (Zhang, 1998). Until now, common technique, which could be applied to the multi-class problems, consists of the decomposition of data into multiple independent binary classification problems.

---

[1]The present paper is financially supported by MIUR Funds 2001 awarded to R. Siciliano (Prot. N. 2001134928).

A segmentation procedure consists of a recursive (r-way or binary) partition of N cases into subgroups where the response variable is internally homogeneous and externally heterogeneous. In terms of methodological contributions and applications of tree-based methods, an important distinction is made between *exploratory trees* - which describes the relationships among the variables with respect to the given response that can be numerical (regression tree) or categorical (classification tree) - and *decision trees* - which allows to assign a response value or a class to a new observed case for which only the measurements of the predictors are known (Brieman et al., 1984). In our case, the main aim is to grow exploratory trees enabling to understand which iterations among predictors (and between predictors and response) are the most important to describe the classification of objects.

The principal feature of two-stage segmentation is that a predictor is not merely used as generator of splits but it plays in the analysis both a global role - evaluating the global effect on the response - and a local role - evaluating the local effect of any splitting variable that can be generated by the predictor, using statistical indexes (the τ index of Goodman and Kruskal, the conditional entropy, etc), modeling (logistic regression, latent budget model, etc) or factorial analysis (non symmetric correspondence analysis, discriminant analysis, etc)(Siciliano et al., 2000). Main goals are those one to accelerate the growing procedure by selecting the most significant predictors and to enrich the statistical interpretation within each node of the tree.

In the following, an innovative supervised classification methodology is proposed to deal with multi-class response, defining a fuzzy partitioning criterion based on a probabilistic approach, the *latent budget method*.

2 Multi-Class Budget Trees

In this paper, a new approach is introduced, namely *Multi-Class Budget Trees* (MCB), to design trees dealing with multi-class response. The idea is to use *latent budget model*, in a two-stage criteria, to define the best split to each node of the tree. Particularly, the methodology consists of a two-stage recursive algorithm. In the first stage, it selects the best predictor on the bases of a predictability measure, while in the second step, it identifies, through latent budget model, the latent typologies of observations summarizing the original groups. These are explained by the best predictor selected in the first stage.

2.1 Latent Budget Model

The Latent Budget Model (LBM) is a reduced-rank probability model to decompose a table of compositional data through a mixture of K positive factorial terms (called *latent budgets*), weighted by mixing parameters, satisfying restrictions likewise conditional probabilities (de Leeuw et al., 1991).

Notation and definition. Let (Y, X) a multivariate random variable where X is the vector of M predictors $(X_1, ..., X_m, ..., X_M)$ and Y is the criterion variable taking values in the set of prior classes $C = (1, ..., j, ..., J)$.
Let F a cross table obtained by the I modalities of a predictor X_m and the J modalities of the response Y. Let p_{ij} any relative frequency of cell (i, j) with $\sum_i \sum_j p_{ij} = 1$ for $(i = 1, ..., I)$ and $(j = 1, ..., J)$, while $\sum_j p_{ij} = p_i$. and $\sum_i p_{ij} = p_{.j}$ are the marginal row and column frequencies of F.
Let $P = D_X^{-1} F$ a $(I \times J)$ matrix of *observed budgets* attained dividing each element of F by its row marginal frequency.
The LBM approaches the observed budgets through the *theoretical budgets*

$$\pi_{i|j} = \sum_{k=1}^{K} \pi_{k|i} \pi_{j|k} \tag{1}$$

where the conditional probabilities $\pi_{j|k}$, with $(j = 1, ..., J)$, represent the k-th latent budget and where the conditional probabilities $\pi_{k|i}$, with $(k = 1, ..., K)$, are the mixing parameters of the i-th modality of the predictor X_m.
In the matrix notation the model can be written as

$$\Pi = AB' \tag{2}$$

$$A1_K = 1_I \quad 1_J'B = 1_K$$

where Π is a $(I \times J)$ matrix of theoretical budgets, A is a $(I \times K)$ matrix of mixing parameters $\pi_{k|i}$ and B is a $(J \times K)$ of latent budgets $\pi_{j|k}$.
The estimation. The model parameters can be estimated by a weighted least-squares method (Aria et al., 2003) minimizing the loss function:

$$\arg\min_{A,B} f_{WLS} \tag{3}$$

within

$$f_{WLS} = SSQ(W(P - AB')) \tag{4}$$

where W is the weight matrix used in the estimation procedure.
This estimation method has no distributional assumptions and is as well a way to generalize two different approaches to latent budget analysis: *Conditional* and *Unconditional LBM*. In the first case, when the matrix $W = I$, we have the classical approach where the parameters can be interpreted as conditional probabilities. Particularly the mixing parameter $\pi_{k|i}$ is the conditional probability of the generic element with the i-th attribute to fall into the k-th latent budget whereas the generic component $\pi_{j|k}$ is the conditional probability of the element in the k-th latent budget to assume the j-th attribute. On the contrary in the second case, when $W = D_X^{-1/2}$ in order to take into account the row marginal frequencies, we have a special case of the weighted version of mixture model presented by Mooijaart et al. (1999) that can be understood as a supervised double-layer neural network with linear

constraints.

The identification. A problem, well known in literature, is that the Latent Budget Model is not identifiable. In this case, it means that the Weighted Least-Squares estimation method produces unique solution for Π but not for A and B.

Using the matrix notation, the identifiability problem of LBM can be seen as following: $\Pi = AB' = AT^{-1}TB' = \widetilde{A}\widetilde{B}'$.

This implies that exist infinite $(K \times K)$ matrices T which give infinite different matrices $\widetilde{A}$ and $\widetilde{B}$ for the same matrix Π. In the MCB methodology, the *stabilizing algorithm* (Aria et al., 2003) is applied to identify an unique solution for the latent budget model. The key idea is to use a method based on the structure of the class of Metropolis algorithm to identify the optimal solution choosing the matrix T, which maximizes the sum of chi-square distances among the latent budgets.

2.2 Multi-Class two-stage criterion

The MCB methodology consists of a two-stage recursive partition criteria which uses conditional latent budget models to define the best split of objects in classification field when the response is multi-class. The purpose is to choose, at each node, the most explicative predictor (or a subgroup of predictors) respect to the Y variable. Then a conditional LBM is applied to find the best partition of the observations in K groups, where K represents the number of latent budgets. We can choose different strategies for the analysis from which depends the measure of K. A first way is to use $K = 2$ or $K = 3$ in order to obtain respectively a binary or a ternary tree. A second way to proceed should imply not to fix a value for K but to choose, at each node, the most parsimonious model for the data analyzed. In both cases, the methodology grows a classification tree characterized by a sequence of latent budget models assigned recursively to the internal nodes of the tree.

The partitioning algorithm, applied recursively to each internal node of the tree, is summarized in the following schema:

- *Stage 1.* **Predictors selection**
  A subset of best predictors $(X_1, ..., X_v, ..., X_V)$, with $V \leq M$, is selected from X maximizing the global relative impurity index $\gamma_{Y|X_m}$ proposed by Mola and Siciliano (1992). This measure, based on the τ index of Goodman and Kruskal, allows to consider the global role played by the predictor in the explanation of the response.

- *Stage 2.* **Split definition**
  Latent budget model is applied on the matrices obtained by the cross of each best predictor X_v and the response. The best model is chosen minimizing the *dissimilarity index* of Clogg and Shihadeh (1994) that measures the goodness of fit as the proportional distance between the

theoretical and the observed budgets:

$$\arg\min_{X_v} D(F_{Y,X_v}) \rightarrow LBM(F_{Y,X\cdot}) \tag{5}$$

with $(v = 1, ..., V)$, where $LBM(F_{Y,X\cdot})$ is the best model, and

$$D(F_{Y,X_v}) = \sum_j \sum_i \frac{p_{i\cdot}}{2}|\pi_{j|i} - p_{j|i}| \tag{6}$$

is the dissimilarity index of a LBM model for the cross table F obtained from Y and the predictor X_v.

Split interpretation. In the field of classification trees, as the LBM estimations can be seen like conditional probabilities, it allows to give a primary role to the parameters in the definition and the interpretation of the partition. Focalizing the attention on binary trees, choosing $K = 2$, the matrix A with dimensions $(I \times K)$ with $\sum_{k=1}^{2} \pi_{i|k} = 1$, the I modalities of the best predictor X^* are summarized in 2 latent budgets (representing the two children nodes). In other words the i-th modality is assigned to k-th budget which is linked to the highest mixing parameter. This means that the objects fall into the left node when they assume modalities with a $\pi_{i|k=1} \geq 0.5$ while all the other cases will fall in the right node:

$$\text{Split} \begin{cases} \pi_{i|k=1} \geq 0.5 \rightarrow t_{left} \\ \pi_{i|k=2} > 0.5 \rightarrow t_{right} \end{cases} \tag{7}$$

with $(i = 1, ..., I)$.

Assignment of class labels. The assignment of the class labels to each terminal node is given measuring the *distance of a latent budget from the independence hypothesis* represented by the mean budget of the matrix P

$$d_{j|k} = \frac{\pi_{j|k} - p_{\cdot j}}{p_{\cdot j}} \tag{8}$$

When a j modality of Y expresses a positive measure of $d_{j|k}$ this means that it will play an important role in the definition of the k-th child node. On the contrary, when $d_{j|k}$ measure is not positive, the j modality does not take place in the explanation of the k-th child node. In other words, a general rule to assign class labels to a node can be so defined:
let the j class label of the response (with $j = 1, ..., J$):

- if $d_{j|k=1} > 0$ then the j class label is assigned to the left node;
- if $d_{j|k=2} > 0$ then the j class label is assigned to the right node.

Differently from the classical methodologies which force the informative structure of the data giving to each terminal node only one class label (in multiclass problems too), the MCB method overcomes this matter assigning, to each node, one or more class labels, specifying also the strength with which each of them contributes to describe the identified pattern.

3 E.T. software and application

The primordial role and advantage of segmentation can be associated to the use of a tree graph to describe relations among variables (exploratory tree) as well as later on to classify new cases (decision tree). General purpose and specialized statistical software have been implementing numerical procedures and standard interfaces to get and describe the results of the analysis. But a lack of attention has been paid on the visualization aids associated to a tree graph and also to the numerical results obtained by a segmentation routine within each node of the tree. To fill in this empty, it has been proposed an interactive software, namely E.T. *Exploratory Trees* (see fig. 2), developed in MATLAB environment and characterized by an intensive use of graphical tools and computational procedures in order to apply two-stage segmentation routines in a new fashion. E.T., described by Aria (2003) and Aria and Siciliano (2003), can be seen as an ideal software for learning from trees, allowing an interactive exploration of data by discovering patterns using colors (see fig. 1), by clicking within the node to describe local results (see fig. 2), by merging modeling and trees[2] .

To show an applicative example of the Multi-Class Budget Tree methodology with the E.T. software, a dataset taken from a Survey of the Bank of Italy about Family Budgets at the year 2000 is considered[3]. This consists of 1998 observations where interest pertains to the study of the kind of investment preferred by the head of the family. The response variable summarizes five variables concerning the different forms of investment preferred: banking, postal, bond, share, cash or none preferred form. Several different typologies of investors correspond to this response, such as *classical investor* (banking, postal, bond), *modern investor* (share) and investor without preferences. 25 categorical predictors have been considered, 11 of them are about the social-demographical condition (age, education, etc.) while 14 concern the economical situation (salary, save, properties, etc.) of the head of the family.

The results of the analysis are shown in the following figure. Particularly, figure 1 contains the multi-class exploratory tree explaining the iterations among the predictors and the response. To give an example of the ability of E.T. to browse the graph, figure 2 shows a description of the node 13 obtained by a simple *click* of the mouse. Figure 3 clarify how the split and the class labels are defined through the MCB methodology. We can see that the modalities of the best predictor *Region* (with 5 modalities: North-West, North-East, Middle, South, Islands) fall into the left or into the right node on the bases of the measure of mixing parameters linked to them. Looking at the table of latent budgets, the label classes 1,2,6 are joined to the left node instead of the 3,4,5 which are associated to the right node. It means that, the left node is characterized by all the families which prefer to invest

---

[2]The latest version of the E.T. software can be required to the author by email.
[3]http://www.bancaditalia.it/statistiche/ibf

by banking and postal systems (*old style family from the South and Islands*). On the contrary, the right node is characterized by all the other families that invest their money by share and bond (*modern style family from the North and Middle*).

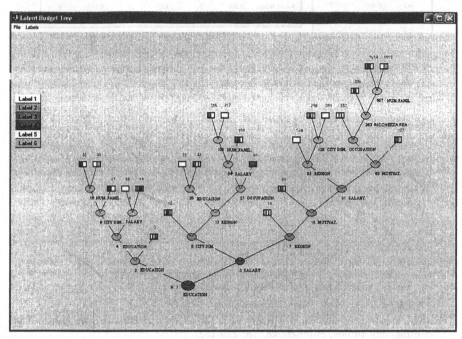

Fig. 1. The Multi-Class Budget Exploratory Tree (*Family Budget Survey*)

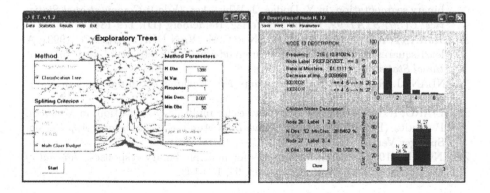

Fig. 2. The GUI of E.T. software and the description of node 13 (*Family Budget Survey*)

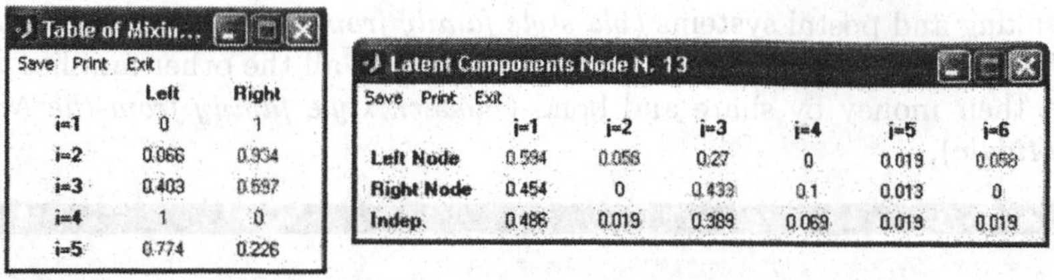

	Left	Right
i=1	0	1
i=2	0.066	0.934
i=3	0.403	0.597
i=4	1	0
i=5	0.774	0.226

	j=1	j=2	j=3	j=4	j=5	j=6
Left Node	0.594	0.058	0.27	0	0.019	0.058
Right Node	0.454	0	0.433	0.1	0.013	0
Indep.	0.486	0.019	0.389	0.069	0.019	0.019

Fig. 3. The mixing parameters and the latent component matrices of the node 13 (*Family Budget Survey*)

References

ARIA, M. (2003): *Un software fruibile ed interattivo per l'apprendimento statistico dai dati attraverso alberi esplorativi. Contributi metodologici ed applicativi.* Tesi di dottorato in Statistica Computazionale ed Applicazioni, XVI ciclo, Napoli.

ARIA, M., MOOIJAART, A., SICILIANO, R., (2003): Neural Budget Networks of Sensorial Data, in M. Schader et al.: *Studies in Classification, Data Analysis, and Knowledge Organization, Between Data Science and Applied Data Analysis*, Springer-Verlag, XIII, 369-377.

BREIMAN L., FRIEDMAN J.H., OlSHEN R.A., STONE C.J. (1984): *Classification and regression trees*, Belmont C.A. Wadsworth, 1984.

CLOGG, C.C., SHIHADEN E.S. (1994): *Statistical Models for Ordinal Variables*, Thousand Oaks, CA.: Sage Publications.

DE LEEUW, J., VAN DER HEIJDEN, P.G.M. (1991): Reduced-rank models for contingency tables, *Biometrika*, 78, 229-232.

LOH, W.Y., SHIH., Y.S., (1997): Split selection methods for classification trees. *Statistica Sinica*, 7(4), October 1997.

MOLA, F., SICILIANO, R. (1997): A Fast Splitting Procedure for Classification and Regression Trees, *Statistics and Computing*, 7, Chapman Hall, 208-216.

MOLA, F., SICILIANO, R. (1992): A two-stage predictive splitting algorithm in binary segmentation, in Y. Dodge, J. Whittaker. (Eds.): *Computational Statistics: COMPSTAT 92*, 1, Physica Verlag, Heidelberg (D), 179-184.

MOOIJAART, A., VAN DER HEIJDEN, P.G.M., VAN DER ARK, L.A.(1999): A least-squares algorithm for a mixture model for compositional data, *Computational Statistics and Data Analysis.*

QUINLAN, J. R. (1993): *C4.5: Programs For Machine Learning.* Morgan Kaufmann, Los Altos.

SICILIANO, R. (1999): Latent budget trees for multiple classification, in M. Vichi, P. Optitz (Eds.): *Classification and Data Analysis: Theory and Application*, Springer Verlag, Heidelberg (D).

ZHANG, H., (1998): Classification trees for multiple binary responses. *Journal of the American Statistical Association*, 93, 180-193.

Methods to Compare Nonparametric Classifiers and to Select the Predictors

Simone Borra[1] and Agostino Di Ciaccio[2]

[1] Dipartimento SEFEMEQ,
Università di Roma "Tor Vergata", Italy
borra@economia.uniroma2.it
[2] Dipartimento di Statistica, Probabilità e Statistiche Applicate,
Università di Roma "La Sapienza", Italy
agostino.diciaccio@uniroma1.it

Abstract. In this paper we examine some nonparametric evaluation methods to compare the prediction capability of supervised classification models. We show also the importance, in nonparametric models, to eliminate the noise variables with a simple selection procedure. It is shown that a simpler model usually gives lower prediction error and is more interpretable. We show some empirical results applying nonparametric classification models on real and artificial data sets.

1 Introduction

In this article we examine evaluation methods of supervised classification models in a nonparametric context. More precisely, we are addressing two fundamental tasks:

- examine some nonparametric evaluation methods to compare the prediction capability of classification models;
- show that the use of a selection procedure in order to eliminate the noise variables can provide a more capable and interpretable model.

These tasks have particular relevance in a Data Mining problem. Often in this case, objective of the analysis is to predict correctly the class of new observed cases and consequently we are interested in the models having the greatest prediction capability. With this respect, we have to evaluate the prediction capability of each classification model, ensuring the evaluation comparability with other concurrent models. We are also interested to obtain reliable and interpretable models, which can be obtained removing the noise variables. This could be a difficult task with non-parametric classification models and in particular with aggregate predictors.

We deal with these specific evaluation problems in the following paragraphs using a simulation approach with well known machine-learning and artificial data-sets.

2 Nonparametric estimators of predictive performance

The most used measure of prediction capability of a nonparametric classification model is the *error-rate*, defined as the ratio between the number of misclassified cases, given by the classifier, and the total number of cases examined. The error-rate of the classifier on the entire population is named *"true error-rate"*. It is usually unknown because we can observe the true class of the cases only on a sample. In a sample, the error-rate of a classifier obtained considering the same data used to estimate the model is named *"apparent error-rate"* or *"re-substitution error-rate"*.

The apparent error-rate is a poor estimator of future performance. Usually the apparent error-rate is an optimistic estimator of the true error-rate: using Neural Networks or Aggregated Classification Trees (for example AD-ABOOST), often it is possible to obtain a null apparent error-rate. This situation is named over-fitting and usually leads to disastrous results on new data.

To obtain a more realistic value of the true error-rate we have to obtain an estimate on independent data-sets. Given a complete data-set with one classification variable Y and s predictors $X_1, X_2, ..., X_s$, we split it in two parts: a training set with N cases and a test set with H cases.

$$Training - set = \{(y_i, x_{i1}, x_{i2}, \dots, x_{is})\} \quad i = 1, 2, ...N \qquad (1)$$

$$Test - set = \{(y_h^*, x_{h1}^*, x_{h2}^*, \dots, x_{hs}^*)\} \quad h = 1, 2, ...H \qquad (2)$$

Fixed a classification model M, the predicted class for the i-th case is:

$$\hat{y}_i = M(x_i) \qquad (3)$$

Using the test-set, an estimate of the prediction error can be obtained as the misclassification rate:

$$P_e(M) = \frac{1}{H} \mid \{h : M(\mathbf{x}_h^*) \neq y_h^*\} \mid \qquad (4)$$

When the data-set is very large, we can split randomly in two data-sets (training and test set) without loss of information, obtaining both a stable classifier and a reliable estimation $P_e(M)$ of the prediction error. On the contrary, when data-set is of small-medium size, we have to use the same data for the model building and its assessment.

In this situation, we can consider several different methods to estimate the prediction error:

- Using all data-set we obtain the apparent error (AE).
- Splitting the data set in several folds we can calculate cross-validation (CV) estimators, for example, Leave-one-out or K-fold CV. In the last approach the cases are randomly split into a partition of K mutually exclusive test-sets of approximately equal size. The model is estimated

K times, excluding each time one tests-set and testing the model on the excluded cases, obtaining K error-rates. Averaging these values we obtain the k-fold cross-validation error-rate.

- We can achieve a more stable cross-validation estimator, the Replicated CV (RCV), averaging CV estimates obtained starting from different random partitions of the data set.
- The Holdout (H) estimator is obtained splitting randomly the data-set in 2 parts: one part (for example 2/3 of data-set) used as training data while the other part used as an independent test-set on which calculate the error-rate estimation.
- The Holdout Random Resampling (HRR) is calculated averaging different Holdout estimates obtained from repeated random splits ($\geq$ 100) of the data set.
- Bootstrap estimators (B) (for example 0,632 Bootstrap) are obtained averaging estimates calculated on several bootstrapped data-sets.

All previous methods (except AE) could be stratified, i.e. the same percentage of cases in each class is maintained into the test-set as observed in the data-set. This procedure usually reduces the estimator's variability. In presence of classes with very small frequencies of cases, we could consider the opportunity to introduce a cost function which weights differently the error-rate of each class. In this paper we will not analyse this possibility.

3 Comparison of predictive performance estimators

To compare several estimators of the predictive performance of a classifier, we could evaluate their bias and variability. Several authors have considered this problem and many empirical results are reported in literature.

Kohavi (1995) reviewed some methods, including H, CV and B, comparing these approaches on a variety of real data-sets. He showed that k-fold CV with moderate k (10-20) reduces the variance while increasing the bias; greater values of k give less biased estimator but higher variability. With small sample size, reducing the value of k increases bias and variability. Bootstrap has low variance but extremely large bias on some problems, while H usually performs worse than CV.

We conducted a large number of simulations on real and simulated data-sets, to compare the variability and the bias of the methods introduced in the previous paragraph.

For example, in Figure 1 we show the whisker plots of stratified 10-fold CV estimator replicated 50 times changing randomly the partition. The model used is the classifier ADABOOST C4.5 applied to the well known SPAM data-set (UCI repository: 4601 e-mail messages, 57 predictors, 1 dummy = spam/no spam). The range of the 10-fold CV is (4.97-5.95). We can note that the 10-fold CV, which correspond to the means (indicated with squares) of

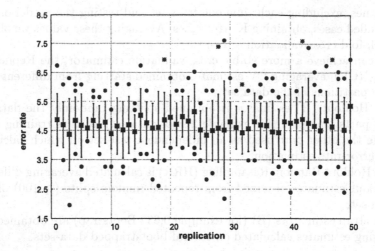

Fig. 1. 10-fold CV replicated 50 times for ADABOOST-C4.5 (Spam Data-set).

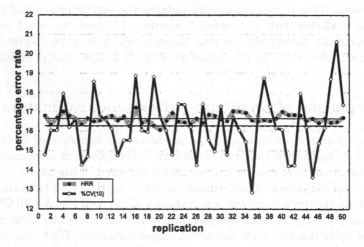

Fig. 2. 10-fold CV and HRR replicated 50 times for ADABOOST-C4.5 (Hepatitis Data-set).

10 values, are slightly influenced by the sample variability. Figure 2 shows a comparison between stratified HRR (66% training-34% test, replicated 200 times) and stratified 10-fold CV, both replicated 50 times, using the classifier ADABOOST C4.5 applied to Hepatitis-data (155 cases, 19 predictors, 1 dummy). The HRR variability is smaller than 10-fold CV. In this case the value of the apparent error is 0 and the Leave-one-out error is 14.19. We used also a simulated data-set with 10000 cases, 7 predictors, 5 classes. We drew 500 times a sample of 200 cases. On each sample we estimated the

classifier, the true error-rate (as the performance of the estimated classifier on the complete data-set), the 10-fold CV, the 10-fold R-CV, the HRR. In this simulation we have observed that stratified HRR and 10-fold R-CV give always better results than simple CV. Moreover the estimates of HRR and R-CV are quite similar in terms of bias and variance. From these results it is clearly inadequate to compare classifiers on the basis of a simple method as CV or H, because the conclusion about the predictive performance of a classifier could depend strongly on the sample drawn. With medium-small size data-set, we suggest to use an estimation method based on a sufficiently large number of replications (as HRR or R-CV).

4 Methods for variable selection in nonparametric classification models

It is not pointed out, in the machine-learning literature, that eliminating the noise variables it can be obtained a more capable and interpretable model. In this literature the prevalent approach consists of including all the variables in the model and then using a pruning procedure to reduce its complexity.

On the contrary, our aim is to investigate if removing the "noise" variables it is possible to increase the prediction capability of nonparametric classifiers. This objective requires a strategy for the selection of the variables to discard, in order to individuate the model with the best predictive performance. We can choose essentially between two different approaches:

- consider indexes built from the observed joint distribution of each predictor with the class, independently from the choice of a classifier;
- consider the contribution of each variable to the prediction capability of the classifier.

In the first approach we can use, for example, indexes based on the entropy (see Yao et al. 1999). A well known index is the Information Gain which evaluates the worth of a predictor X by measuring the information gain with respect to the class Y. Another common index is the Gain Ratio. Both these indexes increase their value when the partition induced by the predictor X reduces the entropy. Moreover, these indexes are usually calculated over all cases of the data set.

In the second approach we consider indexes which compare the prediction performance of classifiers on different groups of variables. Such indicators are generally specific for every single method and they make difficult the comparison among different methods. On the other hand, to be able to compare several models, as usually requested in a Data Mining context, it is necessary to individuate measures applicable to several types of classifiers.

As starting point in the definition of such measure, it is possible to consider the effect obtained, dropping a single variable X_j, on the classification error of a test sample. Such effect can be measured by the difference between the classification error-rate for the model without the predictor X_j and the classification error-rate for the full model. For example, we can consider the following index to evaluate the irrelevance of a predictor:

$$\delta_j = err(X_j) - err \qquad (5)$$

The index depends on the method used to estimate the true error-rate and a high value of δ_j indicates a great influence of the predictor X_j on the classification error. Negative values of δ_j point out noise predictors, whose elimination increases the predictive capability of the model.

We can build another index based on the *margins* calculated by the model. The margin for the i-th case on the test sample, m_i, is defined as the difference between the probability to belong to the true class and the maximum of the probabilities to belong to another class (see Hastie et al. 2001).

$$m_i = \Pr\,(true\ class) - \max\ \Pr\,(other\ class) \qquad (6)$$

With aggregated classifiers based on majority vote criterion, for instance Adaboost and Bagging, the margin is defined as the difference between the proportion of votes for the true class and the maximum proportion of votes among the other classes. The relevance of this notion in classification problems is evident, for example, if we search a bound for the true error using aggregated classifiers (Schapire et al., 1998) or if we look for the optimal separating hyperplanes in the Support Vector Machines theory.

We can start with some initial considerations: when the margin is negative, the case is misclassified. Keeping fixed the classification error, a model can be preferred to another one if it has a lower sum, in absolute terms, of negative margins and an higher sum of positive margins (in fact, in this case, the probability of allocation of a case to the wrong class decreases). The classification error outlines only the number of misclassified cases without any information about the ambiguousness of the assignment of the cases to the classes. We can consider different indices based on the margins calculated on the test sample cases: the sum of all margins; the sum of negative margins; the sum of positive margins; the sum of the probabilities of the misclassified cases. We observed the relation between the error-rate and indices based on the margins analysing an artificial data-set replicated 200 times. When the percentage of error rate increases on the test set, the sum of the total margins, positive margins and negative margins decrease while the sum of probabilities of the misclassified cases rises.

An index to evaluate the irrelevance of a predictor is:

$$mr_j = \frac{\sum_i m_i - \sum_i m_i(X_j)}{n} \qquad (7)$$

where $m_i(X_j)$ is the margin corresponding to the i-th case of the test set, obtained by the model excluding variable X_j while m_i corresponds to the full model.

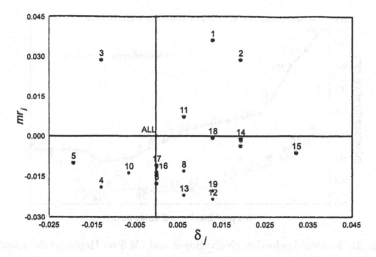

Fig. 3. Comparison between mr_j and δ_j (ADABOOST-C4.5 on Hepatitis data-set).

This index assumes high values when, dropping the variable X_j, the sum of margins $\sum_i m_i(X_j)$ is small. When the reduced model performs better than the full model we have $mr_j < 0$ and there is a strong indication to drop the variable X_j if jointly $mr_j < 0$ and $\delta_j < 0$.

The joined analysis of the two indicators gives some information on the relative contribution of the single variables to the prediction capability. In Figure 3 we show the comparison between the indices mr_j and δ_j applied to Hepatitis-data using ADABOOST C4.5. Each point represents the relevance of one predictor. It can be noted that also fixing the value of δ_j we can have very different values of mr_j. Moreover, in the plot we can individuate the predictors which downgrade the performance of the model as the points with lower coordinates (in our example, variables 5, 4 and 10).

5 Relevance of variable selection in prediction accuracy

Sometimes the data-set includes a very large number of variables and few cases, for example in microarray data analysis. In this case, having a small number of variables improves the interpretability of the model and furthermore, eliminating noise variables, produces a more stable and accurate classifier. In the machine learning literature this aspect is undervalued and it is supposed that for nonparametric classifiers there is no need to select the variables (only procedures of tuning and pruning are studied to avoid overfitting problems). Nevertheless often it is possible to obtain better results in terms of prediction capability using only a subset of variables. For example, considering Hepatitis-data and classifier C4.5, we have found that

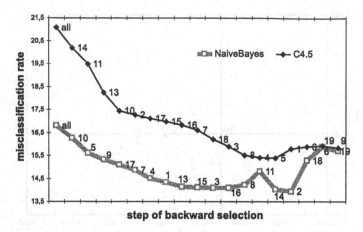

Fig. 4. Backward selection (NaiveBayes and C4.5 on Hepatitis data-set).

$P_e^H (C4.5) = 20.94$ when we use all variables and $P_e^H (C4.5) = 15.41$ using only 5 selected variables.

To individuate and drop the noise variables for a classifier, we could observe if the prediction error decreases in the reduced model ($\delta_j < 0$). In our analysis we have used a backward selection procedure to eliminate the variables.

We used the Hepatitis data-set, in which 155 hepatitis patients are classified as "survival" or "non survival" (19 covariates, 6 quantitative, include missing values). In the original study of the Stanford Medical School it was used a logistic model with only 4 covariates. The same data set has been analysed by Breiman (2001): using a Random Forest model with all variables he achieves an error-rate of 12.3, while a higher error-rate of 17.4 was obtained using the logistic regression with all variables. Is the error-rate estimator accurate? Is it possible to obtain a better result using a subset of the variables?

Using a stratified HRR replicated 200 times we obtain the following estimates of the error-rate: 18.9 for logistic regression and 17.2 for Random Forest. Then, we have not a significative difference about their prediction capability. These results are definitively more reliable than the Breiman's results, considering what we have shown in par. 3.

We have applied two other models, Naïve Bayes and C4.5, to the same data set, and we have adopted a backward procedure for the variable selection based on the index δ_j. In Figure 4 we show the trend of the classifier's error-rate (estimated with stratified HRR) when we drop recursively one variables at a time.

In both cases we can note that the backward procedure selects a better model than the full model. Adopting as index of predictor irrelevance mr_j we do not find better results, as it is shown in the table 1, where we consider the selected C4.5 models on Hepatitis data, because high margins do not imply low error-rate.

Index	Number of included variables	Prediction Error	Sum of margins
δ_j	6	15.38	28.77
mr_j	10	18.53	28.52

Table 1. Selected C4.5 models on Hepatitis data, using mr_j and δ_j.

6 Conclusions

We can expose some final considerations about the previous results. We point out that stratified R-CV and stratified HRR are very effective methods to estimate the prediction capability of the nonparametric classifier for small/medium data-sets. We can also strongly suggest to consider a selection procedure to individuate the most accurate and interpretable model. With this respect, the use of an index based on the error-rate seems preferable to an index based on margins and this selection procedure could improve greatly the predictive capability of the classifier.

References

BREIMAN, L. (2001): *Looking inside the black box*, Wald Lecture 2, Berkeley University.

HASTIE, T., TIBSHIRANI, R., FRIEDMAN, J. (2001): *The elements of statistical learning*. Springer Series in Statistics. Springer-Verlag, New York.

KOHAVI, R. (1995): A study of Cross-Validation and Bootstrap for Accuracy Estimation and Model Selection, in Proceedings of the *14th IJCAI*, CA:Morgan Kaufmann, San Francisco, 338–345.

SCHAPIRE, R.E., FREUND, Y., BARTLETT, P., LEE, W.S. (1998): Boosting the Margin: A new explanation for the effectiveness of voting methods, *The Annals of Statistics, 26, 1651–1686*.

YAO, Y.Y., WONG, S.K.M., BUTZ, C.J. (1999): On Information-Theoretic Measures of Attribute Importance, proceedings of *Pacific-Asia Conference on Knowledge Discovery and Data Mining, 133–137*.

Variable Selection in Cell Classification Problems: A Strategy Based on Independent Component Analysis

Daniela G. Calò, Giuliano Galimberti, Marilena Pillati, and Cinzia Viroli

Dipartimento di Scienze Statistiche,
Università di Bologna, Italy
{calo,galimberti,pillati,viroli}@stat.unibo.it

Abstract. In this paper the problem of cell classification using gene expression data is addressed. One of the main features of this kind of data is the very large number of variables (genes), relative to the number of observations (cells). This condition makes most of the standard statistical methods for classification difficult to employ. The proposed solution consists of building classification rules on subsets of genes showing a behavior across the cells that differs most from that of all the other ones. This variable selection procedure is based on suitable linear transformations of the observed data: a strategy resorting to independent component analysis is explored. Our proposal is compared with the nearest shrunken centroid method (Tibshirani *et al.* (2002)) on three publicly available data sets.

1 Introduction

The recent advances in biotechnology have yielded an ever increasing interest in genome research. The novel cDNA microarray technology allows for the monitoring of thousands of genes simultaneously and it is being currently applied in cancer research. The data from such experiments are usually in the form of large matrices of expression levels of p genes under n experimental conditions (different times, cells, tissues . . .), where n is usually less than 100 and p can easily be several thousands. Due to the large number of genes and to the complex relations between them, a reduction in dimensionality and redundancy is needed in order to allow for a biological interpretation of the results and for subsequent information processing.

In this paper the problem of supervised classification of cells is addressed. The particular condition $p \gg n$ makes most of the standard statistical methods difficult to employ from both analytical and interpretative points of view. For example, including too many variables may increase the error rate in classifying units outside the training set and make the classification rules difficult to interpret. The inclusion of irrelevant or noisy variables may also degrade the overall performances of the estimated classification rules. There is a vast literature on gene selection for cell classification; a comparative study of several discrimination methods in the context of cancer classification based on filtered sets of genes can be found in Dudoit *et al.* (2000). Variable selection in this context has also biological foundations: most of the abnormalities in cell behavior are due to irregular gene activities. It is then important to employ tools that allow to highlight these particular genes.

The proposed solution consists of building classification rules on genes selected by looking at the tails of the distributions of gene projections along suitable directions. Since gene expression profiles are typically non-gaussian, it seems relevant to catch not only the linear (second-order) aspects of the data structure but also the non-linear (higher-order) ones. For this reason, our proposal focuses on searching the less statistically dependent projections. These directions are obtained by independent component analysis (Hyvärinen *et al.* (2001)).

2 Independent component analysis

Independent component analysis is a recently developed method originally proposed in the field of signal processing, as a solution to the so called "blind source separation" problem. In this context the purpose is to recover some independent sources by the observation of different signals, that are assumed to be linear mixtures of these unknown sources.

Subsequently this method has been applied to image analysis, time series analysis and gene expression data analysis. In this latter context, much emphasis has been posed on the ability of ICA in finding so-called functional genomic units, each of which contains genes that work together to accomplish a certain biological function.

Denote by $x_1, x_2, ...x_m$ the m observed variables which are supposed to be modelled as linear combinations of k latent variables $s_1, s_2, ..., s_k$:

$$x_i = a_{i1}s_1 + a_{i2}s_2 + ... + a_{im}s_k \quad \text{for all} \quad i = 1, ..., m \tag{1}$$

where the a_{ij} $(j = 1, ..., k)$ are real coefficients. The s_j are assumed to be *mutually statistically independent*.

The ICA transformation can be put in the following compact notation:

$$\mathbf{X} = \mathbf{AS}. \tag{2}$$

Since it describes how the observed data are generated by a mixing process of hidden components, the matrix $\mathbf{A}$ is often called *mixing matrix*. The only requirement on $\mathbf{A}$ is that it is a full column rank matrix. However, it is easy to verify that if the data are supposed to be sphered, the mixing matrix must be an orthogonal one.

The estimation of the independent latent sources is performed by searching for a linear transformation of the observed variables

$$\hat{\mathbf{S}} = \mathbf{WX}. \tag{3}$$

such that the mutual statistical dependence between the estimated sources is minimized.

The statistical dependence between k variables $s_1, \ldots, s_k$ can be quantified by the mutual information $I(s_1, \ldots, s_k)$. Restricting the attention to sphered data, minimizing $I(s_1, \ldots, s_k)$ is equivalent to maximizing the sum of the marginal negentropies $J(s_j)$ since:

$$I(s_1, \ldots, s_k) = J(s_1, \ldots, s_k) - \sum_{j=1}^{k} J(s_j), \qquad (4)$$

and the joint negentropy $J(s_1, \ldots, s_k)$ is a constant (see Hyvärinen *et al.* (2001) for details). As negentropy is the Kullback-Leibler divergence between a probability density function and a gaussian one with the same covariance matrix, the less dependent directions are the most non-gaussian ones. This implies that it is not sufficient to take into account the information in the covariance matrix, but it is necessary to consider also higher-order relations. For this reason, ICA allows to explore not only the linear structure of the data, but also the non-linear one. It should be stressed that the core assumption of ICA is the existence of mutual independent components. However, it is interesting to note that even if this assumption does not hold, the method can be interpreted as a particular projection pursuit solution.

3 Gene selection in cell classification: a solution based on ICA

As already mentioned above, the aim of this paper is to propose a method to select subsets of genes that could be relevant for cell classification. This selection is performed by projecting the genes onto the directions obtained by ICA: thus, the p genes are considered as units and the n cells as variables. In practice, any other linear transformation method, such as singular value decomposition (SVD) (Wall *et al.* (2003)), could be employed. The use of ICA is consistent with the fact that gene expression profiles usually exhibit non-gaussianity. In particular, the distribution of gene expression levels on a cell is "approximately sparse", with heavy tails and a pronounced peak in the middle. Due to this particular feature, the projections obtained by ICA should emphasize this sparseness. Highly induced or repressed genes, that may be useful in cell classification should lie on the tails of the distributions of $\hat{s}_j$ $(j = 1, \ldots, k)$. Since these directions are as less dependent as possible, they may catch different aspects of the data structure that could be useful for classification tasks.

The proposed solution is based on a ranking of the p genes. This ranking is obtained as follows:

- k independent components $\hat{s}_1, \ldots, \hat{s}_k$ with zero mean and unit variance are extracted from the training set;

- for gene l ($l = 1, \ldots, p$), the absolute score on each component $|\hat{s}_{lj}|$ is computed. These k scores are synthesized by retaining the maximum one, denoted by g_l: $g_l = \max_j |\hat{s}_{lj}|$;
- the p genes are sorted in increasing order according to the maximum absolute scores $\{h_1, \ldots, h_p\}$ and for each gene the rank $r(l)$ is computed.

We suggest to use the subset of genes located in the last m positions of this ranking (with $m \ll p$) to build any classification rule, that is $\{l : r(l) \geq m\}$. The rationale behind this is that these m genes show, with respect to at least one of the components, a behavior across the cells that differs most from that of the bulk of the genes.

The proposed strategy relies on the choice of suitable values for both the number of components and the number of genes. If the goal is to build a classification rule on a manageable set of genes that accurately classifies the cells, a plausible criterion to select the optimal number of components consists in selecting the value of k which yields the smallest estimated error rate with the smallest number of genes (in this way the value of m is chosen implicitly). In practice, this criterion may be implemented by considering several values for the number k of components. For each value of k the ranking is computed and a sequence of classification rules is built for several values of m (with $m \ll p$). For each of these classification rules the error rate is estimated, and the minimum is determined. Finally, the value of k is chosen such that it achieves this minimum rate with the smallest number of genes. (in case that more than one value is selected, the smallest one is obviously preferred).

4 Applications to real data sets

In this section the proposed strategy is applied to three publicly available data sets: the lymphoma data set of Alizadeth et al. (2000), the small round blue cell tumor data set of Khan et al. (2001) and the leukemia data set of Golub et al. (1999).

We run our gene selection procedure (both ICA and SVD based ones) for k ranging from 1 to 10. For each value of k, we tried 30 different values of the number m of selected genes, ranging from p to 1.

The performances of classification rules based on subsets of genes selected according to our proposal are compared with those obtained by the nearest shrunken centroid (SC) method (Tibshirani et al. (2002)). This method is based on an enhancement of the nearest centroid classifier and its main feature is that the class centroids are shrunken toward the overall centroid in order to reduce the effect of noisy genes. Classification is made to the nearest shrunken centroid. This shrinkage procedure performs automatic gene selection. In particular, if a gene is shrunken to zero for all classes, then it is dropped from the prediction rule. In order to compare the results of our gene selection procedure with those obtained through the shrunken centroids, the nearest centroid method is used in class prediction, but any other postprocessing classifier could be applied.

We implemented our procedure in R code, resorting to the libraries pamr and fastICA to perform nearest shrunken centroid classification and independent component analysis, respectively.

Given the small number of cells in each data set, the classification error rates are estimated by balanced cross-validation for each of the compared procedures. However, when comparing the estimated error rate curves, the following difference should be taken into account. In our procedure (both the ICA and the SVD version) each cross-validation training set is used to extract k components, according to which the sequence of nested gene subsets of given sizes is created (therefore, this sequence may vary from one training set to another); the cells in the corresponding cross-validation test set are finally classified on the basis of these subsets of variables. Differently, in pamr the sequence of nested gene subsets is unique, being based on the whole training set, and each cross-validation training set differs from the others only with respect to the class centroids. Therefore, the variability in gene ranking due to training set perturbations is not taken into account when evaluating the SC method performances.

4.1 Lymphoma data set

The data set contains gene expression levels for $p =4026$ genes in 62 cells and consists of 11 cases of B-cell chronic lymphocytic leukemia (B-CLL), 9 cases of follicular lymphoma (FL) and 42 cases of diffuse large B-cell lymphoma (DLBCL). The gene expression data are summarized by a 4026×62 matrix. Missing data were imputed by a 15 nearest-neighbors algorithm.

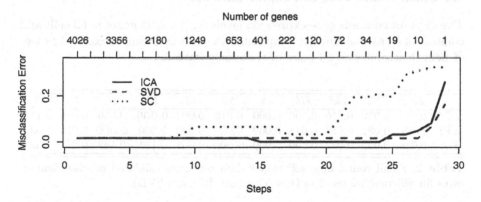

Fig. 1. Lymphoma data set: cross-validated misclassification rates. The axis at the top of the plot indicates the number of genes retained at each step.

	4026	1817	1522	1249	519	401	72	26	19	10	5
ICA	0.016	0.016	0.016	0.016	0.016	0.000	0.000	**0.000**	0.032	0.048	0.081
SVD	0.016	0.016	0.016	0.016	0.016	0.016	0.016	0.016	0.016	**0.016**	0.065
SC	0.016	**0.016**	0.032	0.065	0.065	0.065	0.097	0.210	0.194	0.306	0.323

Table 1. Lymphoma data set: cross-validated misclassification rates for different values of m ($k = 7$ for ICA, $k = 2$ for SVD).

Figure 1 displays the results obtained with $k=7$ components for ICA and for $k=2$ components for SVD. The graph shows that gene selection by suitable projections gives better performances than those achievable by the nearest shrunken centroid method, which is based on marginal gene selection. Moreover, the ICA-based procedure performs better than the SVD one, since it allows to achieve a zero cross-validated error rate by reducing the number of genes from 4026 to just 26. For this number of genes the shrunken centroids estimated error rate is dramatically higher (0.210, as shown in Table 1).

In order to understand the reason why the SC method is outperformed, we focused our attention on the last 5 genes surviving the elimination procedure. As far as the SC method is concerned (Figure 2), it seems that this procedure may not always be able to identify genes that discriminate between all of the classes; it also tends to select genes that are highly correlated (correlations between these genes range between 0.70 and 0.98). On the other hand, the ICA based solution in this case selects genes that make the class structure more evident (Figure 3). It is interesting to remind that the information about class membership is not taken into account in extracting the components (and hence in building the gene ranking).

4.2 Small round blue cell tumor data set

The data set contains gene expression levels for $p =2038$ genes in 63 cells and consists of 8 cases of Burkitt lymphoma, 23 cases of Ewing sarcoma, 12 cases of neuroblastoma and 20 cases of rhabdomyosarcoma.

	2308	761	423	310	38	33	21	16	15	13	9
ICA	0.048	0.032	0.016	0.000	0.000	0.016	0.000	**0.000**	0.016	0.016	0.111
SVD	0.048	0.032	0.016	0.016	0.000	0.000	0.000	0.000	**0.000**	0.016	0.032
SC	0.048	0.032	0.032	0.000	0.000	**0.000**	0.095	0.111	0.143	0.254	0.333

Table 2. Small round blue cell tumor data set: cross-validated misclassification rates for different values of m ($k = 6$ for both ICA and SVD).

As Table 2 shows, all the three methods are able to accurately predict the classes, but the ones based on ICA and SVD achieve this result with a lower number of genes (16 and 15 respectively, against 33 for SC method).

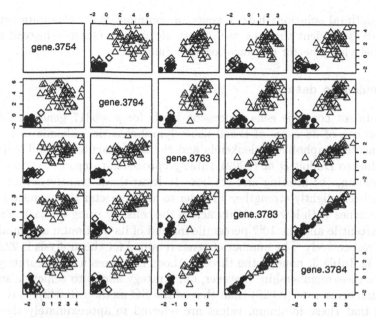

Fig. 2. Lymphoma data set: scatter plot matrix of the last 5 genes surviving the shrinkage procedure (△=DLCL, ●=FL, ◇=CLL).

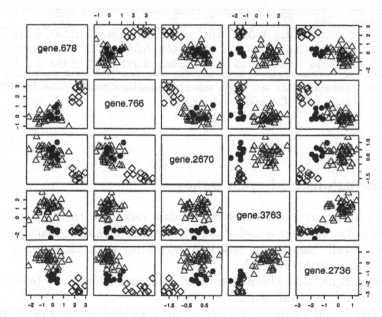

Fig. 3. Lymphoma data set: scatter plot matrix of the last 5 genes of the ranking obtained by ICA (△=DLCL, ●=FL, ◇=CLL).

These optimal solutions have 7 genes in common. With this data set it is particularly evident that the use of suitable subsets of genes instead of the whole set yields better classification performances.

4.3 Leukemia data set

The data set contains gene expression levels for p =6817 genes in 72 cells and consists of 38 cases of B-cell acute lymphoblastic leukemia, 9 cases of T-cell acute lymphoblastic leukemia and 25 cases of acute myeloid leukemia. According to Dudoit *et al.* (2002), three preprocessing steps were applied: (a) thresholding, (b) filtering and (c) base 10 logarithmic transformation. Step (b) has been slightly strengthen in order to make stricter the exclusion criterion for genes with low variability across the cells, by using for each gene the 90th percentile and the 10th percentile instead of its maximum and minimum values respectively. The number of genes retained for the analysis is 2226. As shown in Table 3, none of the three methods is successful in accurately predict the class membership. However, our strategy allows to achieve a smaller minimum error rate (0.028) than that of the SC method (0.042). It is worth noting that these minimum values are referred to approximately the same number of selected genes.

	2226	262	37	29	27	20	17	13	10	6	3
ICA	0.042	0.042	0.028	**0.028**	0.042	0.042	0.056	0.111	0.194	0.333	0.528
SVD	0.042	0.042	0.042	0.042	**0.028**	0.056	0.083	0.153	0.153	0.306	0.403
SC	0.042	0.056	0.056	**0.042**	0.056	0.083	0.097	0.167	0.194	0.194	0.333

Table 3. Leukemia data set: cross-validated misclassification rates for different values of m ($k = 7$ for ICA and $k = 5$ for SVD).

5 Conclusions and open issues

As the preliminary results on these real data sets show, the proposed strategy seems to represent a useful tool to detect subsets of relevant genes for supervised cell classification based on microarray data. However, some aspects deserve further research.

For example, some alternatives to the proposed criterion for building the ranking could be investigated.

Firstly, in the proposed strategy all the k estimated components are assumed to be equally important, since the definition of ICA implies no ordering of the independent components. It is possible, however, to introduce an order among them: Hyvärinen *et al.* (2001) suggest as ordering criteria the norm of the columns of the mixing matrix or the value of suitable non-gaussianity measures on the estimated components. These criteria could be adopted to weight each component during the construction of the gene ranking (for example, by increasing the importance of the most non-gaussian ones).

Secondly, it can be noted that g_l is equivalent to the distance of gene l from the (zero) mean vector in the space of the k components in terms of the Minkowski metric

$$g_l = \left\{ \sum_{j=1}^{k} |\hat{s}_{lj}|^\lambda \right\}^{1/\lambda} \tag{5}$$

with $\lambda \to \infty$. It could be interesting to evaluate the sensitivity of the procedure and the robustness of the gene ranking to the choice of different values for λ or of different distance measures.

Moreover, the issues concerning the choice of both the number k of the components and the number m of retained genes should be examined in more depth.

Finally, the interaction between the proposed selection method and other classifiers could be explored.

References

ALIZADEH, A.A., EISEN, M.B., DAVIS, R.E. *et al.* (2000): Distinct Types of Diffuse Large B-cell Lymphoma Identified by Gene Expression Profiling. *Nature*, 403, 503-511.

DUDOIT, S., FRIDLYAND, J. and SPEED, T.P. (2002): Comparison of Discrimination Methods for the Classification of Tumors using Gene Expression Data. *Journal of the American Statistical Association*, 457, 77-87.

GOLUB, T.R., SLONIM, D.K., TAMAYO, P. *et al.* (1999): Molecular Classification of Cancer: Class Discovery and Class Prediction by Gene Expression Monitoring. *Science*, 286, 531-537.

HYVÄRINEN, A., KARHUNEN, J. and OJA, E. (2001): *Independent Component Analysis*, Wiley, New York.

KHAN, J., WEI, J., RINGNER, M. *et al.* (2001): Classification and Diagnostic Prediction of Cancers Using Gene Expression Profiling and Artificial Neural Networks. *Nature Medicine*, 7, 673-679.

TIBSHIRANI, R., HASTIE, T., NARASIMHAN, B. and CHU, G. (2002): Diagnosis of Multiple Cancer Types by Shrunken Centroids of Gene Expression, *Proceedings of the National Accademy of Sciences*, 99, 6567-6572.

VIROLI, C. (2003): Reflections on a Supervised Approach to Independent Component Analysis, *Between Data Science and Applied Data Analysis*, (M. Schader, W. Gaul e M. Vichi eds.), Studies in Classification, Data Analysis, and Knowledge Organization, Springer Berlin, 501-509.

WALL, M.E., RECHTSTEINER, A. and ROCHA, L.M. (2003): Singular Value Decomposition and Principal Component Analysis, in: *A Practical Approach to Microarray Data Analysis*, Berrar D.P., Dubitzky W. and Granzow M. (Eds.), Kluwer, Norwell, 91-109.

Simplifying Classification Trees Through Consensus Methods

Rossella Miglio and Gabriele Soffritti

Dipartimento di Scienze Statistiche
Università di Bologna, Italy
miglio@stat.unibo.it, soffritt@stat.unibo.it

Abstract. Methods for comparing and combining classification trees based on proximity measures have been proposed in the last few years. These methods could be used to analyse a set of trees obtained from independent data sets or from re-sampling methods like bootstrap or cross validation applied to the same training sample. In this paper we consider, as an alternative to the pruning techniques, a modified version of a consensus algorithm we have previously proposed that combines trees obtained by bootstrap samples. This consensus algorithm is based on a dissimilarity measure recently proposed. Experimental results are provided to illustrate, in two real data sets, the performances of the proposed consensus method.

1 Introduction

Classification trees represent non parametric classifiers that exploit the local relationship between the class variable and the predictors (Breiman et al. 1984). Tree-based methods are notoriously unstable: small perturbations in their training sets may result in large changes in the constructed classifier. This is due to the hierarchical structure of those methods; furthermore, a multiplicity of structures can also derive from different greedy search algorithms used for identifying trees, or from different pruning methods.

Model uncertainty is a problem common to many data analyses. In the literature there are two approaches to the model uncertainty problem: combine model predictions or choose a single model. Several authors have shown that combining multiple versions of unstable classifiers, such as trees, results in reduced test set error rate: these include bagging, boosting and Bayesian model averaging (Breiman 1996, Freund and Schapire 1996, 1999). The main effect of these techniques is to reduce the variance of the classifier even if they do not allow interpreting and exploring the data structure through an alternative tree. A different solution consists in exploring a set of plausible models in order to select good models which may reveal different aspects of the data (Chipman et al. 2001).

Furthermore, some methodologies have been introduced to identify a consensus of different classification trees. The purpose of the different consensus methods proposed in literature has been either to recover an hypothetical true classification or to summarize at best the set of classifications obtained from the analysis of different data sets.

Given a set of binary trees $T = \{T_i, \; i = 1, \ldots, m\}$, a consensus tree can be obtained for instance by combining those parts of the considered trees about which there is general agreement. Starting with the root node labelled $k = 1$, the node k $(k \geq 1)$ of the consensus tree can be splitted on the variable that occurred most frequently at node k among the set T. If the most frequent event at node k is not to split, then the consensus tree will not split at k. If two or more variables tie for the most frequent split, then one solution is to pick a tied variable at random or, alternatively, ties can be broken by conditioning on previous splitting variables in the path (Shannon and Banks, 1999). Alternatively, Shannon and Banks (1999) derive a single tree that is central with respect to a group of trees and propose an algorithm for combining a sample of classification trees using maximum likelihood estimation which results in a single, interpretable tree.

Another way to obtain a consensus tree is to grow a tree which results similar as much as possible to the trees of T according to specific proximity measures between classification trees (Miglio and Soffritti 2003, 2004).

In this paper we study the performance of a modified version of an algorithm proposed by Miglio and Soffritti (2003) to identify a consensus tree when the set of classification trees is obtained by using resampling methods like bootstrap or cross-validation, in order to detect if such tree can represent a valid alternative to the ones obtained through pruning techniques.

In Section 2 we describe the consensus algorithm proposed by Miglio and Soffritti (2003) together with some modifications that have been introduced to robustify this procedure. Section 3 reports the results of applications to two real data examples and concluding remarks.

2 Proximity-based consensus methods

The consensus algorithm we consider in this paper is based on the dissimilarity measure proposed by Miglio and Soffritti (2004). This measure takes into account the partitions associated to the trees, their predictive power and the predictors used at each split. When two classification trees have to be compared, all these aspects (the structure, the partition and the predictive power) should be simultaneously considered. In fact, trees having the same distance with respect to their structures can show a very different predictive power. On the other hand, trees with the same predictive power can have very different structures. The proposed measure is defined as follows:

$$\delta\left(T_i, T_j\right) = \sum_{h=1}^{H} \alpha_{ih}(1 - s_{ih})\frac{m_{h0}}{n} + \sum_{k=1}^{K} \alpha_{jk}(1 - s_{jk})\frac{m_{0k}}{n}, \qquad (1)$$

where m_{h0} and m_{0k} denote the number of units which belong to the h-th leaf of T_i and to the k-th leaf of T_j, respectively; the introduction of the relative frequency of each leaf weights the discrepancies proportionally to the number of their observations. α_{ih} and α_{jk} measure the dissimilarities between the paths of the two trees; they can be defined to penalize structural differences between trees based on where these occur (for more details see Miglio and Soffritti 2004). s_{ih} and s_{jk} are similarity coefficients whose values synthesize the similarities s_{hk} between the leaves of T_i and those of T_j, defined so as to take into account the partitions and the predictive powers of the trees; for instance, a possible definition for s_{ih} is $s_{ih} = max\{s_{hk}, k = 1, \ldots, K\}$, where

$$s_{hk} = \frac{m_{hk} c_{hk}}{\sqrt{m_{h0} m_{0k}}}, \; h = 1, \ldots, H, \; k = 1, \ldots, K; \qquad (2)$$

m_{hk} is the number of objects which belong both to the h-th leaf of T_i and to the k-th leaf of T_j; $c_{hk} = 1$ if the h-th leaf of T_i has the same class label as the k-th leaf of T_j, and $c_{hk} = 0$ otherwise.

The maximum value of $\delta(T_i, T_j)$ can be reached when the difference between the structures of T_i and T_j is maximum and the similarity between their predictive power is zero. The normalizing factor for $\delta(T_i, T_j)$ is equal to

$$\max \delta (T_i, T_j) = \sum_{h=1}^{H} \alpha_{ih} \frac{m_{h0}}{n} + \sum_{k=1}^{K} \alpha_{jk} \frac{m_{0k}}{n}, \qquad (3)$$

and the normalized version of the proposed dissimilarity is thus:

$$\Delta (T_i, T_j) = \frac{\delta (T_i, T_j)}{\max \delta (T_i, T_j)}. \qquad (4)$$

Miglio and Soffritti (2003) proposed a procedure to identify a tree T_c which summarizes as much as possible the information contained in the observed set of trees $T = \{T_i, i = 1, \ldots, m\}$. This purpose has been pursued by searching for the tree T_c which minimizes the following objective function:

$$V(T_c) = \sum_{i=1}^{m} W_i \Delta(T_c, T_i), \qquad (5)$$

where $\Delta(T_c, T_i)$ is the proximity between the consensus tree and a generic tree of T computed according to measure (4). The W_i ($i = 1, \ldots, m$) are researcher-supplied, nonnegative weights such that they sum to 1; two possible ways to choose W_i are: (i) give trees the same weight ($W_i = 1/m$ for $i = 1, \ldots, m$); (ii) use an inverse function of the error rate of T_i.

Generally, finding the tree T_c which minimizes $V(T_c)$ is computationally intensive; accordingly, a numerical algorithm has to be used. The following algorithm searches for the consensus tree among the trees belonging to T and to those that can be obtained by deleting nodes from the trees of T. Specifically, the proposed algorithm is composed of three main steps.

1. For each tree $T_i \in T$, the sub-trees obtained considering only the paths of length r (starting with $r = 1$) and the corresponding leaves are identified; let $T^r = \{T_j^r, j = 1, \ldots, z_r\}$ be the set of trees obtained in this way.
2. For each tree $T_j^r \in T^r$, $V(T_j^r)$ is computed, where

$$V(T_j^r) = \sum_{i=1}^{m} W_i \Delta(T_j^r, T_i) \qquad (6)$$

   is the weighted sum of the dissimilarities between the generic sub-tree of length r, T_j^r, and the trees of T.
3. The tree of T^r for which the value of $V(T_j^r)$ results minimum is selected; this tree is T_c^r, the consensus tree of length r; r is set equal to $r + 1$; if this value is not greater than r_{max}, the length of the longest path present in trees of T, then the algorithm will return to step 1; otherwise it will stop.

The output of this algorithm is a sequence of consensus trees and of values of the objective function $\{T_c^r, V(T_c^r) \; r = 1, \ldots, r_{max}\}$. The value of $V(T_c^r)$ indicates the dissimilarity between T_c^r and the observed set of trees T; the tree T_c^r with the minimum value of $V(T_c^r)$ will be the consensus tree T_c.

The number of trees considered in this search depends on m and r_{max}, so the solution identified by the algorithm will be optimal only if the number of observed trees is high and/or their paths are long.

For this reason, we have modified the algorithm previously proposed to extend the search to more trees. This purpose can be pursued in different ways. In this paper we analyse the following solution: whenever a sub-tree T_j^r evaluated by the algorithm is composed by more than one path of length r, the analysis is extended by examining not only T_j^r but also every tree obtained from T_j^r considering separately each single path of length r.

Another solution, not analysed in detail in the following, which is similar to the one proposed by Miglio (1996), is to consider all the split defining questions involved in the m trees of T as possible splits for the identification of T_c. Furthermore, in order to robustify the search of the consensus tree, the objective function defined by equation (5) has been modified by considering the median dissimilarity instead of the mean. Finally we propose to determine the consensus trees T_c^r, for $r = 1, \ldots, r_{max}$, using only those instances that are classified in the same way by at least the 70% of the trees; in this way we exclude those instances that probably lie on the boundaries of the decision rules. This threshold value could be changed according to the researcher's aims and/or to the properties of the analysed data set.

3 Experimental results and concluding remarks

In this section we show the performance of the proposed algorithm studying two real classification problems. In the first the objective is to correctly identify benign from malignant breast tumors (Mangasarian and Wolberg 1990).

It is a two-class problem. Each of the 699 instances consists of 9 cell attributes each of which is measured on a 1-10 scale plus the class variable. The class labels 1 and 2 denote benign and malignant breast tumors respectively; high predictor values correspond to worse health conditions. The Wisconsin Breast Cancer Database is in the UCI repository (ftp.ics.uci.edu/pub/machine-learning-databases) of machine learning databases and was obtained from the University of Wisconsin Hospitals.

The second data set analysed through the proposed algorithm concerns with the classification of radar returns from the ionosphere (Sigillito et al. 1989). The targets of this radar database, collected by a system in Goose Bay, Labrador, were free electrons in the ionosphere: good radar returns are those showing evidence of some type of structure in the ionosphere, while bad returns are those that do not; this is the class variable. Each of the 351 instances in the data base is described by 34 continuous attributes corresponding to the complex values returned by the system for a given complex electromagnetic signal. The ionosphere database is in the UCI repository of machine learning databases and was obtained from the Johns Hopkins University.

For the breast cancer problem we generated 60 training sets of 600 observations, bootstrapping a reduced data set (we considered only 683 observations without missing values). In the second real data set we used 300 observations to obtain bootstrap samples while the remaining observations were used as test set to evaluate the performance of the proposed consensus method. The bootstrap trees were fit using a procedure like CART (Breiman et al. 1984) implemented in GAUSS, with the Gini criterion for splitting.

As previously described, the consensus trees were determined by using only those instances that were classified in the same way by at least the 70% of the trees; in this way we excluded the 5% of the observations in the first example and the 1% in the second one.

The algorithm was applied using two different systems of weights: giving the trees the same weight ($W_i = 1/m$ for $i = 1, \ldots, m$) and with weights inversely related to their error rates. We considered also two different objective functions V: the mean and the median dissimilarity.

The results are summarized in Table 1 and Table 2. In the first example, the different choices of weights and of objective functions led to the same results. The tree with the minimum mean and median dissimilarity from the 60 trees of T among 131 possible consensus trees is also the one with the minimum test set error rate (see Table 1). This tree shows a performance similar to the ones obtained through a bagging procedure applied to the bootstrap trees: its test set error rate is slightly lower than the mean value of the test set error rates associated to these trees.

In the second example the results were the same by using the two systems of weights, while changed if the mean or the median objective function was considered; they are summarized in Table 2. Thus, for this second example, a different choice of the objective function lead to a slightly different consensus tree. From the bootstrap trees and following the proposed algorithm we

r z_r Consensus measure	Test set error rate (%)
1 6 0.058	7.30
2 69 0.053	5.10
3 37 0.050	5.10
4 14 0.060	5.80
5 5 0.075	7.30

Table 1. Values of the consensus measure and of the error rate for the consensus trees identified by the algorithm for the breast cancer example.

		Consensus measure		
r z_r	T_c^r	Mean	Median	Test set error rate (%)
1 6	T_1, T_2	**0.1857**	0.1750	0.157
	T_3	0.1858	**0.1540**	0.137
2 24	T_1, T_2	0.0897	**0.0750**	0.118
	T_6	**0.0888**	0.0755	0.098
3 65	T_6	**0.1062**	0.0815	0.118
	T_{39}	0.1120	**0.0565**	0.118
4 39	T_{13}	0.1277	**0.0780**	0.118
	T_{37}	**0.1274**	0.0800	0.118
5 1	T_1	0.1292	0.0820	0.118

Table 2. Values of the consensus measure and of the error rate for the consensus trees identified by the algorithm for the ionosphere example.

identified 136 possible consensus trees. The minimum test set error rate is related to the tree with the longest path (level) equal to 2 and the minimum value of the mean objective function. It is important to underline that these different results depend on only one of the 51 observations belonging to the test set. The three consensus trees identified at the second level differ only on the value of the variable involved in the first split, while the consensus trees identified at the next level are extensions of the second tree of the previous one. Table 3 shows some descriptive measures of the dissimilarity values between pairs of trees computed between bootstrap trees and consensus trees within each level and using a set of constant weights. Also this information could be used, with the test set error rate, to evaluate the preferable consensus tree. In this example we could use the best consensus tree of the second or third level (T_6 and T_{39} respectively). Furthermore, the consensus tree T_6 at the second level shows performances similar to the bagging procedure and error rates lower than the mean test set error rate of bootstrap trees.

From the comparison between the consensus tree identified by the procedure and the ones obtained through pruning methods, the first one has a more simple structure and a better accuracy than the others. So, when trees obtained from bootstrap samples are available, the illustrated strategy could represent an alternative to pruning techniques. The obtained results

r	T_c^r	Minimum	Maximum	Median	Mean	St. dev.
1	T_1, T_2	0.0850	0.4410	0.1750	0.1857	0.0981
	T_3	0.0830	0.3950	0.1540	0.1858	0.0791
2	T_1, T_2	0.0000	0.3480	0.0750	0.0897	0.0939
	T_6	0.0000	0.3480	0.0755	0.0888	0.0928
3	T_6	0.0000	0.3780	0.0815	0.1062	0.1027
	T_{39}	0.0000	0.3460	0.0565	0.1120	0.0876
4	T_{13}	0.0080	0.3610	0.0780	0.1277	0.0861
	T_{37}	0.0000	0.3450	0.0800	0.1274	0.0856
5	T_1	0.0000	0.3350	0.0820	0.1293	0.0771

Table 3. Some descriptive measures of the dissimilarity values computed between bootstrap trees and consensus trees for the ionosphere example.

seem promising, but more real and simulated data sets should be analysed to obtain a wider evaluation of the performances of the considered algorithm. Further investigation should regard also the choice of the instances to be considered by the algorithm in the search of the consensus tree, which seems a crucial aspect of the proposed strategy.

References

BREIMAN L.(1996): Bagging predictors. *Machine learning, 24, 123-140.*

BREIMAN L., FRIEDMAN J.H., OLSHEN R.A. and STONE C.J. (1984): *Classification and Regression Trees.* Wadsworth, Belmont, California.

CHIPMAN H. A., GEORGE E. I. and McCULLOCH R. E. (2001): Managing multiple models. In: T. Jaakola and T. Richardson (Eds.): *Artificial Intelligence and Statistics 2001.* ProBook, Denver, 11-18.

FREUND Y. and SHAPIRE R. (1996): Experiments with a new boosting algorithm. In: Saitta L. (Ed.): *Machine Learning: Proceedings of the Thirteenth International Conference.* San Francisco, 148-156.

FREUND Y. and SHAPIRE R.(1999): A short introduction to boosting. *Journal of Japanese Society for Artificial Intelligence, 14, 771-780.*

MANGASARIAN O. L. and WOLBERG W. H. (1990): Cancer diagnosis via linear programming. *SIAM News, 23, 1-18.*

MIGLIO R. (1996): *Metodi di partizione ricorsiva nell'analisi discriminante.* PhD Thesis, Dipartimento di Scienze Statistiche, Bologna.

MIGLIO R. and SOFFRITTI G. (2003): Methods to combine classification trees. In: M. Shader, W. Gaul and M. Vichi (Eds.): *Between data science and applied data analysis.* Springer-Verlag, Heidelberg, 65-73.

MIGLIO R. and SOFFRITTI G. (2004): The comparison between classification trees through proximity measures. *Computational Statistics and Data Analysis, 45, 577-593.*

SHANNON W. D. and BANKS D. (1999): Combining classification trees using MLE. *Statistics in Medicine, 18, 727-740.*

SIGILLITO V. G., WING S. P., HUTTON L. V., and BAKER K. B. (1989): Classification of radar returns from the ionosphere using neural networks. *Johns Hopkins APT Technical Digest, 18, 262-266.*

Selecting the Training Set in Classification Problems with Rare Events

Bruno Scarpa[1] and Nicola Torelli[2]

[1] Dipartimento di Statistica ed Economia Applicata
   Università di Pavia, Italy
   bruno.scarpa@unipv.it
[2] Dipartimento di Scienze Economiche e Statistiche,
   Università di Trieste, Italy
   nicola.torelli@econ.units.it

Abstract. Binary classification algorithms are often used in situations when one of the two classes is extremely rare. A common practice is to oversample units of the rare class when forming the training set. For some classification algorithms, like logistic classification, there are theoretical results that justify such an approach. Similar results are not available for other popular classification algorithms like classification trees. In this paper the use of balanced datasets, when dealing with rare classes, for tree classifiers and boosting algorithms is discussed and results from analyzing a real dataset and a simulated dataset are reported.

1 Introduction

In the application of statistical classification algorithms it is supposed that a set of information is available and it is used to obtain a rule for classifying new units. This dataset, the training set or design set, contains, for each unit, information about the class to which it belongs and some relevant attributes. It is reasonable to expect that a good selection of the training set could have a role in obtaining a good classification algorithm.

A critical situation occurs when in a two class problem it is *a priori* known that the probability that a unit belongs to a class is close to zero (*i.e.*, it is a rare class). When this happens, a popular choice is to include in the training set more units that belong to the rare class in order to have a balanced sample where the number of units in the two classes are similar, *i.e.*, a disproportionate stratified sample is selected with strata defined by the categories of the variable of interest. This is the solution recommended in applying classification algorithms to data mining problems: Berry & Linoff (2000, p. 197), for instance, in their book suggest "oversampling [...] by taking more of the rare outcomes and fewer of the common outcome". A similar suggestion is in Sas (1998). In many practical instances this suggestion corresponds to including in the training set all the units of the rare class and getting a sample including roughly the same number of units from the other class. This strategy of dealing with rare classes seems to be the standard one among data mining practitioners.

In the machine learning literature there have been recently some studies aimed to develop new and more efficient strategies to deal with imbalance in the two classes. Some promising procedures suggest using re-sampling from the rare class or sampling specific units from the frequent class (for a review, see Japkowicz (2000)). We will not consider here these techniques, since the main aim of the paper is to discuss the appropriateness of the simple strategy of stratifying the training sample with respect to the classification variable, when events are rare. We then will compare this solution with even simpler alternative strategies that can be basically derived by ignoring the imbalance in the two classes and using standard random sampling from the available dataset.

Oversampling the rare class has sound theoretical justifications at least in the case of regression models for binary dependent variables (*i.e.*, logistic regression). These results will be reviewed in section 2. Similar theoretical results are not available for other classification algorithms. In section 3, we will compare the simple strategy of oversampling the rare class with other simple strategies for the selection of the training set in order to evaluate their effects on the performances of some popular classification algorithms, *i.e.*, tree classifiers and the boosting algorithm (by combining prediction from several weak classifiers). Finally, some preliminary results from the analysis of real and simulated datasets will be presented (section 4).

2 The effect of stratifying the sample by the classification variable in logistic classification

The aim of logistic regression is to model the response variable Y that, for the i_{th} unit, takes the value 1 with probability π_i and 0 with probability $1 - \pi_i$, and it is assumed that

$$\text{logit}\,(\pi_i) = \log\left(\frac{\pi_i}{1 - \pi_i}\right) = x_i^T \beta$$

where x_i is a vector of characteristics of the i_{th} unit and β is a parameter vector.

The parameters can be estimated using the available data by maximizing the appropriate likelihood function. The classification of new units could be achieved by estimating the probability π_i by

$$\frac{1}{1 + e^{x_i^T \hat{\beta}}}$$

where $\hat{\beta}$ are the parameter estimates, and by classifying as $Y = 1$ those units which have estimated π_i greater than a threshold (typically 0.5).

When data are obtained by a disproportionate stratification of the sample by the Y variable (e.g., a larger sample from the rare stratum $Y = 1$) maximum likelihood leads to inconsistent estimates of the β vector. More specifically, the first element of this vector, β_0 (the intercept), is biased while the other components of the vector β are estimated consistently. Including in the sample a higher proportion of cases with $Y = 1$ can affect estimates of π and consequently the ability of correctly classifying new units.

This problem has been faced by Prentice and Pyke (1979) in the context of case-control studies and by Cosslett (1981) in econometric applications of qualitative dependent variable models. The main results of these papers can be summarized as follows:

1. the bias of β_0 is

$$\log \left(\frac{1 - \eta}{\eta} \frac{\bar{y}}{1 - \bar{y}} \right).$$

Where η is the proportion of $Y = 1$ in the population and $\bar{y}$ is the proportion of $Y = 1$ in the sample. If η is known then one can get unbiased estimates of β. Note that in classification problems this correction implies the use of a corrected threshold to classify new units on the basis of estimated π;

2. data on rare events are more informative (*i.e.*, the variance of $\hat{\beta}$ gets smaller if there are more data for which $Y = 1$); hence collecting more $Y = 1$ is a good strategy;

3. balancing the sample ($\bar{y} = 0.5$) is very often a good strategy (close to the optimal, see, Cosslett (1981)).

At least in the case of logistic classification there are theoretical results to justify balancing the sample when ones and zeros are not balanced in the population but it is important to bear in mind that the classification algorithm must be adjusted to take into account possible bias in the estimates.

3 Training set selection with tree classifiers and boosting algorithms

In this section, we will evaluate the performance of some binary classification algorithms used in data mining, *i.e.* classification trees and combination of weak tree classifiers by the boosting algorithm, under alternative strategies to deal with a rare class. Unlike the case of logistic classification, for these algorithm theoretical results are not available. We will draw some preliminary and tentative evidence from the analysis of two examples evaluating different strategies of sampling for each of the two family of models considered.

To this aim, a real dataset and a simulated example with a (relatively) rare class will be analyzed. In both cases alternative strategies for selecting (or weighting) the training set will be used.

The first dataset is the one proposed for the CoIL Challenge 2000 (see the web site http://www.liacs.nl/ putten/library/cc2000/). The goal is to predict whether a customer is interested in buying a caravan insurance policy using 86 variables on customer characteristics which include product usage data and socio-demographic information. The training set contains 5822 records (and the test set contains 4000 records), including the information about whether or not they have a caravan insurance policy. The percentage of events, *i.e.* of customers, that have insurance policy in the training set is about 6%.

The second dataset is a simulated one; it consists of 10000 records (5000 to train the algorithm and 5000 to test it) with three variables, $X = [x_1, x_2]^T$ and y. The two x's are generated from a bivariate normal distribution with

$$\text{mean}(X) = \begin{bmatrix} 35 \\ 3 \end{bmatrix} \qquad \text{cov}(X) = \begin{bmatrix} 10 & -0.3 \\ -0.3 & 0.9539 \end{bmatrix},$$

and the y takes on the value 1 for the positive elements of a normal distribution with

$$\text{mean}(y) = -5.5 + 0.1x_1 - 0.5x_2 \qquad \text{var}(y) = 0.1$$

and zero otherwise. In this case, the training set contains about 3% of ones (events).

Both the datasets are split randomly in two sub-samples (the training set and the test set) and here we assume that the quality of alternative algorithms are to be judged by their performances in the test set. This choice is possible and reasonable in our example because of the large size of the dataset; but note that availability of large datasets are typical when applying classification algorithms to data mining problems.

When using classification tree algorithms (Hastie, Tibshirani and Friedman (2001)) we will adopt the usual strategy of randomly partitioning the training set into two subsets, the first subset is used for the splitting algorithm, the second one for the pruning algorithm.

Evaluation of prediction accuracy of a classification is usually done by the overall error, defined as the number of misclassified records over the number of records in the test set. However, especially in the case of rare events, this indicator can be misleading if not useless. In fact, if the percentage of events is very low, we can get a low overall rate by simply predicting every single record as a non-event, and this is, clearly, meaningless.

It can be worth introducing alternative criteria to evaluate the performance of the classifiers, to take into account the different propensity toward false positive errors (predicting an event when the unit is actually a non event) and false negative errors (predicting a non event when the unit is an event); in data mining literature, those errors are evaluated using different measures, for instance Precision (P) which is the proportion of well predicted events over the total number of predicted events and Recall (R) which is the proportion of events well predicted over the total number of events in the test set. Let us consider the confusion matrix

	Predicted		
Actual	Events	Non events	Total
Events	n_{00}	n_{01}	$n_e = n_{00} + n_{01}$
Non-Events	n_{10}	n_{11}	$n_e = n_{10} + n_{11}$
Total	$n_0 = n_{00} + n_{10}$	$n_1 = n_{01} + n_{11}$	n

overall error, Precision and Recall are defined by

$$\text{overall error} = \frac{n_{10} + n_{01}}{n} \qquad P = \frac{n_{00}}{n_{00} + n_{10}} \qquad R = \frac{n_{00}}{n_{00} + n_{01}}.$$

A more general measure, F, has been introduced (Joshi (2002)) to combine Precision and Recall defined as the armonic mean of the two measures:

$$F = 2 \left(\frac{PR}{R + P} \right).$$

Another tool for evaluating performances of a classification algorithm, widely used in data mining applications, is the Lift curve. The Lift curve is built as follows : (a) sort the test set by the estimated scores, *i.e.*, the estimated probability of being in one of the two classes, using all the available records (also those in the test set: for classification trees such a measure is, for each terminal node, the proportion of events predicted correctly in the training set); (b) split all the units into groups defined by the percentiles of the distribution of the scores; (c) for each percentile calculate the proportion of events predicted to be in the class defined by each percentile. Plotting this measure against the percentiles gives a function that should theoretically be monotone decreasing (empirically one can observe some exception to this pattern). Interpretation of the Lift curve is quite simple since it measures how the classification algorithm improves over a prediction made without any classification model. Therefore, when comparing alternative classifiers by the Lift curve, the higher the curve the better the performance of the algorithm.

We will use different strategies to select the training set for two different classification algorithm.

The first family of algorithm considered are classification trees and the selection of the training set is as follows:

(i) the entire training set is used for training the classifier; in this case the training sample is a simple random sample and events and non-events are not balanced (T not-bal);

(ii) a random sub-sample of non-events (zeros in our examples) is selected in order to obtain a balanced training set, with the same number of events and non-events; in this case the size of the training set used to estimate the tree is smaller than the size used in (i) but the proportion of events (which are the more informative data) is higher (T bal);

(iii) the selection is as in (ii), but a correction is applied in order to take into account the different ratio between the probability (assumed to be known) of being a member of the rare class and the proportion of units from the rare class in the sample. This correction, in principle similar to that one suggested by the theoretical results for logistic classification, consists of not using the level 0.5 as a threshold to classify the units into one of the two classes in the validation set. The new threshold will be the proportion of events in the original data set (T bal-corr).

A second family of classification models used, is a combination of classification trees by the boosting algorithm (Hastie, Tibshirani and Friedman (2001)). Boosting is an iterative procedure that, at each step, estimates on the same data a new classifier (in our case we use trees), but in each iteration the algorithm puts more weight on observation that at the previous iteration were misclassified. At the end the new classifier will be a weighted average of the single classifications (giving more weight to the classifiers with lower error).

As we have done for trees, we implemented different strategies of sampling, in particular it seems reasonable to rely upon a more general definition of misclassification errors. The standard boosting algorithm uses the overall error as a measure of wrong classification of records. In our case, with a small number of events, it seems reasonable to consider other measures of misclassification error. We have used the following strategies:

(iv) use of a standard boosting algorithm, starting from a not balanced training set, and using the overall misclassification error for each iteration of the algorithm. The choice of a not balanced training set is based on the observation that at each iteration of the algorithm the effect of possible poor classification of the (rare) events will lead to a training set, at the next step, that will include more events, and it could therefore implicitly take into account imbalance in the training sets (B not-bal);

(v) use of a new boosting algorithm that takes into account rare classes. In this case, the misclassification error used for the algorithm is no longer the overall error, but we consider two different kinds of error taking into account either false positive or false negative at each iteration, and the weight of each record at each iteration is a weighted average of the two errors (B rare);

(vi) use of the standard boosting algorithm starting from a balanced training set, using the same correction as in (iii) for the prediction of the classes for the units in the training set at each iteration. For each tree we correct the threshold used to get events classified in the validation set, by multiplying it by an estimate of the proportion of non-events. As we have seen in (ii) and in (iii) this strategy uses a larger but not balanced training set (B bal-corr).

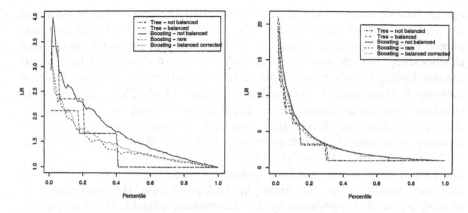

Fig. 1. Lift functions from alternative training set selection for caravan data (left) and simulated data (right)

4 Results and conclusions

Table 1 shows the overall error, Recall, Precision and F for the best model obtained using the 6 strategies. The first part of the Table refers to the Caravan dataset, while the second part to the simulated dataset. The missing elements in the table, refer to non defined values: the Precision is not defined when the prediction classifies all the record as non-events, therefore neither F is defined.

		caravan dataset				simulated dataset			
		overall	recall	precision	F	overall	recall	precision	F
(i) T	not-bal.	0.0595	0.0000	—	—	0.0232	0.4666	0.3153	0.3763
(ii) T	balanced	0.3837	0.0989	0.6723	0.1725	0.0818	0.1882	0.8108	0.3056
(iii) T	bal. corr.	0.0595	0.0000	—	—	0.0234	0.4347	0.1801	0.2548
(iv) B	not-bal.	0.0705	0.2105	0.0672	0.1019	0.0236	0.4340	0.2072	0.2805
(v) B	rare	0.0967	0.1366	0.1176	0.1264	0.0286	0.3400	0.3063	0.3223
(vi) B	bal. corr.	0.0597	0.0000	—	—	0.0256	0.3924	0.2793	0.3263

Table 1. Different measures of prediction accuracy for 6 algorithms in the two datasets. T=tree, B=boosting

Figure 1 presents the Lift function for the two datasets considered. It is worth noting that for balanced tree with or without correction the lift function is exactly the same, because the difference between the two models consists only in the choice of the threshold.   Results shown in Table 1 and Figure 1 can lead to some preliminary and very cautionary conclusions and can suggest some directions for future work.

As expected, the overall prediction accuracy is not a good measure of performance; it is easy to get a low error rate by classifying all the units as members of the more frequent class. The results show that, at least for the Caravan dataset, if one only focus on overall error, we can see that there are no models with an overall error lower than the proportion of events in the test set and we could improve the classifier by classifying all the units as non events. Note that F and the Lift function will suggest instead using the boosting. For the simulated dataset, the overall error leads to a model obtained using the strategy (i). As we have already noted, to select the best strategy is more sensible to consider the value of F. This will lead us to conclude that a classification tree using balanced dataset and correcting the threshold is the best choice. But note that, instead, if we select the best strategy by looking at the Lift curve we would select the boosting algorithm.

The results from the analysis of the two datasets presented does not allow us to clarify which approach should be preferred over the others, and the main conclusion is that, unlike in the logistic case, the simple strategy of sampling with stratification by the classification variable is not as good as expected and its possible benefits are still unclear even after applying reasonable corrections. Suggesting the use of balanced sample as a panacea when a class is extremely unfrequent, as is often done in data mining applications of classification algorithms, has no theoretical foundation nor empirical support.

The role of boosting when classes are not balanced should be clarified by further analysis: it seems that its use can lead to better classifiers, but note that we base our conclusions only upon the analysis of two datasets where, by the way, the predictive power of the algorithms is very low. A more thorough analysis of the problem here considered by using also other classification techniques to be applied to larger and more complex datasets can be fruitful. Also considering the impact of data quality when selecting the training set deserve further investigation.

Moreover, in future work, strategies proposed in the machine learning literature, which are based on resampling the rare (or the frequent) class, deserve more attention and a comparison between them and strategies suggested by sound statistical theory can be extremely useful.

References

BERRY, M. J. A. and LINOFF, G. S. (2000): *Mastering Data Mining*, Wiley, New York.

COSSLETT, S. R. (1981): Maximum likelihood estimator for choice based models, *Econometrica, 49, 1289–1316*.

HASTIE, T., TIBSHIRANI, R. and FRIEDMAN, J. (2001): *The Elements of Statistical Learning*, Springer, New York.

JAPKOWICZ, N. (2000): The class imbalance problem: Significance and strategies, *Proceedings of the 2000 International Conference on Artificial Intelligence* pp. 111–117.

JOSHI, M. (2002): On evaluating performance of classifiers for rare classes, url:www-users.cs.umn.edu/ mjoshi/papers/icdm02sub.ps.

PRENTICE, R. L. and PYKE, R. (1979): Logistic disease models in case-control studies, *Biometrika, 66, 403–411*.

SAS (1998): SAS Institute Best Practice Paper, Data Mining and the Case for Sampling, URL:http//nas.cl.uh.edu/boetticher/ML-DataMining/SAS-SEMMA.pdf.

A Classification and Discrimination Integrated Strategy Conducted on Symbolic Data for Missing Data Treatment in Questionnaire Survey

Maria Gabriella Grassia

Dipartimento di Matematica e Statistica,
Università di Napoli "Federico II", Italy
mgrassia@unina.it

Abstract. In a statistical survey, the treatment of missing data needs the adoption of particular precautions considering that each decision has an impact on the analysis results. In this paper we propose a strategy based on Classification and Discrimination methods conducted on symbolic data and it enables us to extract both compatibility rules and to impute data in order to reconstruct the information. The strategy makes use of tools developed in statistical methods fields for the analysis of complex structures named symbolic objects. The starting point is the use of the Symbolic Marking for the determination of the rules (complex units) for the construction of the Edit plane. The following phase is the construction of the symbolic matrix and the last phase will be the reconstruction of the missing data by comparing symbolic objects through the application of a suitable dissimilarity measure based on "Minkowski L_1" weighted distance. The proposed strategy has been applied to a real case of 100 manufacturing enterprises located in the South Italy.

1 Introduction

The treatment of missing data needs the adoption of particular precautions considering that each decision has an impact on the analysis results. In a statistical survey, we can have Total (MRT) or Partial (MRP) missing data.

In this paper we will refer to MRP. In order to correctly consider the possible solutions for the reconstruction of missing information, it is necessary to separate the missing data characterization criteria (by using the Edit of the compatibility plane, that is to say association rules among variables) from the information reconstruction criteria (by using the more effective Imputation methods).

The proposed strategy is based on Classification and Discrimination methods conducted on symbolic data and it enables us to extract both compatibility rules and to impute data in order to reconstruct the information.
The innovative parts of the strategy concern two aspects. The first one shows

the possibility to extract from data the necessary rules for the construction of the Edit plane; the second one concerns the possibility to impute data comparing complex units (not elementary units), extracted for the construction of the plane. It is so possible to reduce the computational weight of the donor imputation. The strategy makes use of tools developed in statistical methods fields for the analysis of complex structures named symbolic objects, meaning with this label both the definition of the characteristics of the constitutive elements and the connections able to link each unit with the related object. The starting point is the use of the Symbolic Marking (Gettler-Summa, et al. 1998) for the determination of the rules (complex units) in order to construct the Edit plane. The following phase is the creation of the symbolic matrix of a modal generic element and the last phase will be the reconstruction of the missing data by comparing symbolic objects through the application of a suitable dissimilarity measure (Bruzzese, Davino, 2002) based on "Minkowski L_1" weighted distance. The proposed strategy has been applied to a real case; we have reconstructed the missing data related to a survey conducted on a manufacturing enterprises. A sample formed by 100 units has been interviewed about a very important topic: how the most important economic factors influence the efficiency of the enterprises located in the South Italy.

2 Symbolic objects for missing data treatment

The limits of the methodologies usually used in a classical context for the imputation of missing answers are the computational weight with $2^n * (n-1)$ comparisons for each single variable and the discriminating choice of the variables minimum set. It is possible to overcome these limits by defining the compatibility plane through the construction of conceptual models described in symbolic object terms. These objects can be built by using expert opinion (Balbi & Verde, 1998), or by using acquired knowledge on surveys done in several editions (Grassia &Muratore 2001).

In this paper our aim is to build symbolic objects from the current data survey.

A symbolic object s is defined by a triplet (a,R,d) (Diday, 1998), where:

- $d=(d_1,..., d_j,..., d_p)$ is the description of the object, formed by the values assumed by a set of p descriptors, $Y=(Y_1,...,Y_j,...,Y_p)$;
- a is an identification function;
- $R=(R_1,..., R_j,..., R_p)$ is the relation used for the comparison between the description given at a conceptual level, (in purpose) from d and the individual observations.

The descriptors of a symbolic object can be *interval, categorical, multi-modal variables* and they can show several modalities in the description of each object. The boolean function a assumes values {0, 1} and allows to determine those elements that are included by the description d and to build the extension of the object s (*ext(s)*).

X	....	Y_j y_{jl} ,...., y_{jmj}	....	Σ
...	....	...	....	...
k	....	$(n_{k_{jl}}$,...., $n_{k_{jm}})$	....	$n_{k\cdot\cdot}$
...	....	...	....	...
k'	....	$(n_{k'_{jl}}$,...., $n_{k'_{jm}})$	....	$n_{k'\cdot\cdot}$
...	....	...	....	....
Σ	....	$(n_{\cdot_{jl}}$,...., $n_{\cdot_{jm}})$	....	$n_{\cdot\cdot\cdot}$

Table 1. A symbolic data array with integer frequency distributions

Therefore, we start from the identification of the structural characteristics that allow to divide the observed sample and to build the related symbolic objects.

Let's consider a set of units obtained from a questionnaire $E = \{1,2,\ldots.Q\}$ consisting of a unit subset with complete answers $E_1 = \{1,2,\ldots.N\}$ and by a subset made up of incomplete units $E_2 = \{N+1,N+2.\ldots Q\}$ with $E_1, E_2 \subseteq E$ and $E_1 \cap E_2 = \emptyset$.

E_1 and E_2 are both answer categories. It is important to specify that in this context the continuous variables are transformed in intervals and the word "category" is extended to these intervals. If from the E dataset we build some symbolic objects (case clusters), the elementary units of the set E are no more single observations but a collection of them built by considering common characteristics. Thus, the symbolic data matrix will be:

Therefore, the generic symbolic object *assertion* built by the database will be described by modal variables (Bock & Diday 2000):

$$s = \wedge_{j=1}^{R} \left[Y_j = \{y_{jm}, p_{jm}\}_{m=1,2\ldots m_j} \right] \tag{1}$$

where $p_{jm} = \frac{n_{k_j m_j}}{n_{k\cdot\cdot}}$ is the related weight of y_{jm} (relative frequency or probability), m-th modality of Y_j.

If we also consider the implications inside the object, assuming *if-then* logical rules (Agrawal et al., 1993), the symbolic *assertion* will be:

$$s = \underbrace{\wedge_{a=1}^{A} \left[Y_a = \{y_{am}, p_{am}\}_{m=1,2\ldots m_a} \right]}_{(A)} \rightarrow \underbrace{\wedge_{c=1}^{C} \left[Y_c = \{y_{cm}, p_{cm}\}_{m=1,2\ldots m_c} \right]}_{(B)}$$

$$\rightarrow \tag{2}$$

with $A, C \subseteq Y$ and $A \cap C = \emptyset$ where A is the set of the antecedent categories (possible, independent and exclusive) and C is the set of consequent categories. Objects belonging to E_1 show values in comparison with the descriptors of the (A) *expression* and of the (C) *consequence*, while the objects in E_2 show values only in comparison with (A). Therefore, the *extension* in

E_1 of a generic symbolic object s is a case cluster whose behaviour can be used for the case answers imputation (or case clusters) of the E_2 dataset.

3 Imputation procedure steps

In this section, we are going to show how to build symbolic objects and how to impute the answers. Selection of those descriptors able to define the expression and the consequence of the objects. For the objects construction we will use a clustering strategy, while for the selection of descriptors able to define the expression and the consequence we will use the symbolic marking technique (Gettler-Summa, et al. 1998). This method was conceived as an help to the interpretation of the most important Multidimensional Data Analysis techniques (factorial and clustering), and it gives a description of the characteristics of the partition clusters in k, considering the logical relationships (and, or, if-then) among the categories of the clusters descriptors. The procedure determines some *marking cores*, in other words some cores of identical observations related to a set of "characterising" variables:

$$mc_g : [Y_1 = y_{1m}] \wedge ..... \wedge [Y_r = y_{rm'}]$$

with $r \leq P$

The union of G *marking cores* mc_g (expressed as logical AND), based on the disjunction element OR , is the description of the k group:

$$k : mc_1 \vee mc_2 \vee ...... \vee mc_g \vee ...... \vee mc_G$$

By using the MGS algorithm, that is based on a supervised algorithm (this uses a step by step selection procedure with ascending strategy), it is possible to evaluate the discriminating power of each descriptor and then to obtain rules expressed in *if-then* form. This can be obtained thanks to the maximization of the two indexes:

1. $\text{Rec} = Card[ext_k(mc_g)]$
2. $\text{Deb} = Card[ext_{\bar{k}(mc_g)}]$

where mc_g is a generic marking that is a subset k belonging to E_1 characterised by the same categories of one or more descriptors. The *Rec* index is the percentage of elements belonging to k able to satisfy the conditions defined by the marking; the *Deb* index is the percentage of elements able to satisfy the marking, but it does not belong to k.

3.1 The imputation of missing data

In order to impute to (single cases or clusters) E_2 objects some values for the missing records, it is necessary to determine, through a suitable symbolic distance, the E_1 object with *minimum* distance. This object has to be the most similar in the (A) *expression* to E_2 objects. In the literature on the subject, many symbolic dissimilarity measures among objects have been proposed (Bock and Diday, 2000; Bocci and Rizzi, 2000); it is important to consider in this case a measure able to assume a maximum value when two objects have no characteristic in common. In the following, we use a proper dissimilarity measure based on the "Minkowski L?" weighted distance, giving an equal weight to all the variables. The distance between two objects is given by the distance between the expressions and the *consequences*. Objects having missing records have values only related to the descriptors of the *expression*. Therefore, it is necessary to calculate all the distances between the objects in E_1 and in E_2 in order to impute to the objects in E_2 the values of the consequence descriptors of those objects that are the most similar in E_1. Let's consider two generic objects $s = A \to C$ of E_1 and $s' = A'$ of E_2 characterised by the same variables in A *expression*. The distance between s and s' calculated according to (A) and (A') is given by:

$$d(s, s') = \frac{\sum_{a=1}^{\#[A]} d(Y_j, Y_j')}{\#[A]} \text{ with } s \neq s' \tag{3}$$

where ($\#\,A$) is the number of variables in A and the distance between Y_j and Y_j' is based on the comparison between frequency distributions as follows:

$$d(Y_j(s), Y_j(s')) = \frac{\sum_{m=1}^{m_j} |p_{yj}(s) - p_{yj}(s')|}{\max\{p_{yj}(s); p_{yj}(s')\}} / m_j \tag{4}$$

where m_j is the number of categories of Y_j.

The distance between the two objects vary from 0 and 1. The distance is zero if the two objects have the same probability distribution and it is 1 if they are completely different. To the missing records will be imputed the values assumed by the descriptors in the *consequence* of the *donor* object with minimum distance.

If S are the objects of E2 = {N+1,N+2....Q}, a relative measure of the loss of information in data reconstruction is given by:

$$\sum_{j=1}^{S} d_j w_j n_s \text{ with } w_j = \frac{r_j}{\sum_{j=N+1}^{Q} r_j} \tag{5}$$

where d_j is the distance between the object that has missing data (s') and the "donor" object (s), $n_{s..}$ is the cases number in the object and r_j is the records number to impute for each object on the total number of record to impute. If each object is formed by a single case it (5) will be:

$$\sum_{j=N+1}^{Q} d_j w_j \tag{6}$$

This index changes from 0 and 1.

N°	Variable	N°	Variable
1	Line of business	10	Auditing
2	Juridical form	11	Intermediate product
3	Year of beginning	12	Number of Customers
4	Type of enterprise	13	Revenues
5	Participation at pool	14	The Trend of proceeds
6	Participation at industrial zone	15	Interest rate on loans (short term)
7	Other office	16	Interest rate on loans (long term)
8	Number of employees	17	Request for credit not obtained from the banks
9	Trademark	18	Availability to pay higher rates in order to obtain credit

Table 2. The variables

						N°	%
var_8						1	2,9
var_11						1	2,9
var_18						1	2,9
var_16						4	11,4
var_15	var_16					14	40,0
var_17	var_18					1	2,9
var_13	var_14	Var_16				1	2,9
var_12	var_13	Var_14				1	2,9
var_13	var_15	Var_16				1	2,9
var_15	var_16	Var_17	var_18			1	2,9
var_13	var_14	Var_15	var_16			2	5,7
var_12	var_13	Var_14	var_15			1	2,9
var_12	var_13	Var_14	var_15	var_18		2	5,7
var_13	var_15	Var_16	var_17	var_18		2	5,7
var_12	var_13	Var_14	var_15	var_16	var_18	2	5,7
Total						35	100,0

Table 3. The possible combinations of the missing fields

Cluster 1 (N=13) Market 1	N.	%	V-Test	Mod.	Variable
	5	7,69	3,605		
			3,021	NO	Var_11
Rec	5	38,46	2,727	€ 15.000.000	Var_13
Deb	0	0,00	0,870	NO	Var_17

Table 4. The first marking of the class 1

4 An example of imputation on real data

The proposed strategy has been implemented in order to impute the missing data in a dataset coming from a survey conducted on a sample of 100 manufacturing enterprises of the Naples province and related to the lend on usury topic.

As shown in the following (Table 2), we have 18 variables, where the last six are very important questions (Revenues, Rate of interest, etc.)

Of 100 records, 65 are complete records e 35 are missing records.

For the missing fields we have done a frequency distribution of the possible combinations of the missing fields.

After having done a cluster analysis on units having full field, from the 8 classes we have extracted 22 marking cores characterised by the same descriptors modality with missing fields. For example we show the first marking on the class number 1:

If we consider the characteristics of the first class, we can assume that:

IF

Line of business= *canning industry* **OR** *textile industry* **OR** *tan industry*

Table 5. The symbolic data matrix

AND Juridical form = *Srl* **OR** *Spa*, **AND** Year of beginning= 8-15 ......
THEN

Intermediate product   = NO **AND** Revenues=15.000.000 Ä AND Request for credit not obtained from the banks=NO

We have extracted the marking and built the symbolic objects matrix expressed in modal form composed by 22 rows (modal objects) and 18 columns (Tab.4).

For each record showing missing data, using the formula (4), we have calculated the distance from the 22 objects for the variables having full fields, by choosing as donor the object having minimal distance. The imputation has been done both for the reconstruction of the symbolic matrix, giving to the receiving unit the distribution of the donor object and in the traditional data matrix, giving to the receiving unit the modality of the donor object with higher frequency.

The loss of information index is 0,132 and it can be considered a good result.

5 Conclusions and future developments

The proposed strategy has the following advantages:

1. The minimum distance is not calculated between the receiving unit and each donor unit, but it is calculated only between the receiving objects

(single units or clusters) and the donor objects. In computational terms the weight is reduced.

2. The choice of *matching* variables is not optional but it is an analysis result.
3. The variables distribution form is well kept by assigning more than a value with the related weights (relative frequencies or probability).
4. It can be used for naturally complex data.

Future developments concern the possibility to treat, at the same time, several types of variables (multi-nominal, modals, continuous and interval variables) without making transformations on them and the possibility to match *a-priori* knowledge with knowledge mined by extracted rules.

Further important aspects to develop are the construction of a multiple text for the evaluation of the marking union, the validation of the robustness method and the application of other distances (not symbolic even) for the choice of the donor object.

References

ARKHIPOFF O. (1996): *La qualité de l'information et sa precision*, Colloque de l'ISEOR.

BALBI, S., GRASSIA M.G. (2003): Meccanismi di accesso al mercato del lavoro degli studenti di Economia a Napoli – Profili dei laureati attraverso tre indagini ripetute in *Transizione Università- Lavoro: la definizione delle competenze*, Cleup.

BALBI S., VERDE R. (1998): Structuring Questionnaires as Symbolic Objects: a New Tool for Improving Data Quality in Surveys, *III International Seminar on New Techniques and Technologies - NTTS*, Sorrento.

BARCAROLI G. (1993): *Un approccio logico formale al problema del controllo e della correzione dei dati statistici*, Quaderni di Ricerca, n.9, ISTAT.

BOCK H., DIDAY E. (2000): *Analysis of Symbolic Data*, Springer – Verlag,.

BOCCI L., RIZZI A. (2000): Misure di prossimità nell'analisi dei dati simbolici, in *Atti della XL Riunione Scientifica della società Italiana di Statistica, Sessioni Plenarie e specializzate*, Firenze 26-28 aprile 2000, 91-102.

BRUZZESE D., DAVINO C. (2003): Post Analysis of Association Rules in a Symbolic Framework, *Atti della XLI Riunione Scientifica della società Italiana di Statistica*, Milano 5-7 giugno 2003, 63-66.

GRASSIA, M.G., MURATORE, M.G. (2001): The contribution of symbolic objects theory to errors prevention in CATI questionnaires, *IV International Seminar on New Techniques and Technologies* – NTTS, Creta

GETTLER-SUMMA M. (1998): *MGS in SODAS: Marking and Generalization by Symbolic Objects in the Symbolic Official Data Analysis Software*, Cahier9935, Université Dauphine LISE CEREMADE – Paris.

LITTLE, R.J.A., RUBIN, D.B. (1987): *Statistical analysis with missing data*, New York, Wiley &Sons.

MASSRALI M., GETTLER-SUMMA M., DIDAY E. (1998): *Extracting knowledge from very large databases*, Kesda '98, Luxembourg.

A Collinearity Based Hierarchical Method to Identify Clusters of Variables

Annalisa Laghi[1] and Gabriele Soffritti[2]

[1] Servizio Controllo di Gestione e Sistemi Statistici
  Regione Emilia-Romagna, Bologna, Italy
  alaghi@regione.emilia-romagna.it
[2] Dipartimento di Scienze Statistiche
  Università di Bologna, Italy
  soffritt@stat.unibo.it

Abstract. The most frequently used hierarchical methods for clustering of quantitative variables are based on bivariate or multivariate correlation measures. These solutions can be unsuitable in presence of uncorrelated but collinear variables. In this paper we propose a hierarchical agglomerative algorithm based on a similarity measure which takes into account the collinearity between two groups of variables. Its main theoretical features are described and its performance is evaluated both on simulated and real data sets.

1 Introduction

Hierarchical clustering methods can be used to identify groups of either statistical units or variables, or both (Anderberg (1973), Hartigan (1975), Nicolau and Bacelar-Nicolau (1998), Gordon (1999), Soffritti (1999), Soffritti (2003)). Many methods for clustering of units have been proposed and widely discussed in the statistical literature but only few solutions deal with identifying groups of variables.

Aiming at clustering variables, the starting point of most of the agglomerative algorithms is a symmetric proximity (similarity or dissimilarity) $m \times m$ matrix $\mathbf{P} = [p_{ij}]$, where p_{ij} is the proximity between the i-th and j-th variables to be classified, and m is the number of variables observed on n units. When all the variables are quantitative the most frequently used hierarchical methods implement some of the classical algorithms (e.g. single linkage, average linkage between groups (UPGMA), complete linkage), using a suitable transformation of Pearson's correlation coefficient r_{ij} to measure the similarity between X_i and X_j: usually $|r_{ij}|$ or r_{ij}^2, which allow to take into account only the magnitude of the linear relationship and not its direction. A strategy recently proposed by Vigneau and Qannari (2003) allows to cluster variables taking into consideration also the sign of the correlation coefficients; their solution is suitable when negative correlations indicate disagreement between variables.

As described in Soffritti (1999), most of these methods seem not to be completely satisfactory. In fact, they take into consideration only bivariate correlations; besides, some of them (e.g. single, UPGMA and complete link-age) ignore the correlations existing within each group of variables. The use of multivariate association measures between two sets of variables can over-come these drawbacks. Soffritti (1999) considered hierarchical methods based on some multivariate association measures already proposed in the statisti-cal literature, and introduced a new measure which resulted more suitable to identify hierarchical groupings of variables. However, since all those mea-sures are functions of the squared canonical correlations between two groups of variables, they can't detect, for instance, non linear relationships and fail also in identifying properly collinearity relations.

In this paper we focus our attention on the analysis of the collinear re-lations existing among a set of m variables in a data matrix $n \times m$ $\mathbf{X}$; in fact, since collinear variables contain similar and redundant information, they should be classified together. Furthermore, as it is stressed by Belsley (1991), collinearity is concerned with numerical or geometric characteristics of a given data matrix $\mathbf{X}$ whether or not it is used in a regression context. After a short description of the main differences between collinearity and correlation, we propose a hierarchical agglomerative algorithm based on a similarity measure which takes into account the collinearity between two groups of variables. We discuss the main theoretical features of the proposed solution and illustrate the results obtained from the analysis of some simulated and real data sets.

2 An association measure based on collinearity

It is well known from the statistical literature (Belsley 1991) that collinear-ity and correlation are not the same thing. Considering, for simplicity, the bivariate case, two variables are collinear if they lie almost on the same line, that is, if the angle between them is small or, equivalently, the cosine of this angle is high. But a small angle between two vectors is not equivalent to a high correlation between them: a high correlation surely implies a low angle, but the converse need not be true (Belsley 1991, p. 20). In fact the geometric interpretation of the statistical concept of correlation between two vectors is simply the cosine of the angle between the two corresponding mean-centred variables. Therefore the use of an association measure among variables based on collinearity instead of correlation seems particularly suitable whenever the comparison with the mean values for each variable is not proper or relevant, for instance in the analysis of relative variations or binary variables. It can also be shown that in some cases (see Section 3) two vectors can become arbitrarily collinear while remaining completely uncorrelated.

Among the several approaches proposed to diagnose the presence of colli-nearity relations and to measure their degree, the one that resulted more successful and can also be formulated out of a regression context is based on the eigensystem of $C = Y'Y$ (Belsley 1991), where Y is the $n \times m$ matrix obtained by scaling each column of X to have unit length, and thus C contains the cosines of the angles between each pair of variables.

Suppose the m variables are now divided in two groups G_1 and G_2, composed by m_1 and m_2 variables respectively ($m_1 + m_2 = m$), and let Y_1 and Y_2 be the submatrices of Y (respectively $n \times m_1$ and $n \times m_2$) referred to G_1 and G_2. The following partition of the matrix C can thus be introduced:

$$C = \begin{bmatrix} C_{11} & C_{12} \\ C_{21} & C_{22} \end{bmatrix}, \tag{1}$$

where $C_{11} = Y_1'Y_1$ and $C_{22} = Y_2'Y_2$ are the matrices (respectively $m_1 \times m_1$ and $m_2 \times m_2$) of the cosines of the angles between each pair of variables within the two groups, and $C_{12} = Y_1'Y_2$ is the $m_1 \times m_2$ matrix of the cosines of the angles between each variable in G_1 and each one in G_2.

Assuming without loss of generality that $m_1 \geq m_2$, a similarity measure between G_1 and G_2 based on the amount of the collinearity between the two groups of variables can be obtained by applying the multivariate association measure already proposed by Soffritti (1999) to the matrix of the cosines C considered in its partitioned form, as follows:

$$s(G_1, G_2) = \frac{tr(C_{11}^{-1}C_{12}C_{22}^{-1}C_{21})}{tr(C_{11})tr(C_{22})} = \frac{\sum_{k=1}^{m_2} c_k^2}{m_1 m_2}, \tag{2}$$

where c_k^2 denotes the k-th eigenvalue of $C_{11}^{-1}C_{12}C_{22}^{-1}C_{21}$; c_k^2 also represents the squared cosine of the angle between the k-th pair of variables obtained from a modified version of canonical correlation analysis, in which linear combinations of the variables belonging to each group are identified in such a way that cosines of the angles are maximized instead of correlations, and with the constraints of unit length instead of unit variance.

The theoretical properties of this measure are analogous to the ones of the measure proposed by Soffritti (1999); it lies in the $[0, 1/m_1]$ interval, and takes into account both the overall collinearity between groups of variables (expressed by means of the sum of the squared cosines of the angles between pairs of the quasi-canonical variables identified as previously described) and the numbers of variables within the two groups. In this way the association between G_1 and G_2 is set equal to a mean squared cosine for each pair of variables, one from G_1 and one from G_2. Furthermore, when groups composed by single variables are examined ($m_1 = m_2 = 1$), measure (2) gives the squared cosine of the angle between pairs of starting variables; when $m_1 > m_2 = 1$, it reduces to the uncentered multiple squared correlation coefficient of the variable belonging to G_2 on the ones present in G_1 (Belsley 1991, p. 29).

The proposed measure also allows a different definition, based on the links between canonical correlation and principal component analysis (Muller 1982) slightly modified so as to take into account collinearity relations among variables instead of correlation ones. In fact, every variable belonging to G_1 and G_2 can be transformed to produce zero cosines within the two groups, and reproduce all the collinearity relations between groups by means of a modified version of principal component analysis, in which linear combinations of the variables from each group are identified in such a way that lengths are maximized instead of variances, with the constraints of orthogonality instead of incorrelation. If the m_1 variables in G_1 are substituted by the m_1 corresponding quasi-principal components obtained as just described, and the same is made for the m_2 variables in G_2, the new cosine matrix computed with respect to the so obtained $m_1 + m_2$ quasi-principal components will have the following form:

$$C^* = \begin{bmatrix} I_{m_1} & C^*_{12} \\ C^*_{21} & I_{m_2} \end{bmatrix}, \tag{3}$$

where I_{m_1} and I_{m_2} are identity matrices of order m_1 and m_2 respectively, and C^*_{12} is the $m_1 \times m_2$ matrix of the cosines k_{ij} of the angles between pairs of quasi-principal components, one from G_1 and one from G_2. It can be demonstrated (Soffritti 1999) that measure (2) is also equal to the average of the $m_1 m_2$ squared cosines of the angles between each quasi-principal component obtained from the set G_1 and each one from G_2:

$$s(G_1, G_2) = \frac{\sum_{i=1}^{m_1} \sum_{j=1}^{m_2} k_{ij}^2}{m_1 m_2}. \tag{4}$$

Measure (2) can be used to identify hierarchical groupings of variables. At the first step of the hierarchical process, when equation (2) is computed between pairs of variables, it gives the square of the cosine of the corresponding angles. At the other steps, when the groups are composed by more than one variable, equation (2) is used to measure the amount of collinearity between groups.

3 Examples of applications to real and simulated data

The proposed method has been applied to simulated data matrices X, with $n = 500$ and $m = 9$, generated so as to contain two groups of variables. The first four variables have been obtained, as described in Soffritti (1999), in such a way to have given values for Pearson's correlation coefficient. Matrices R_1 and C_1 contain the correlation coefficients and the cosines of the angles between each pair of variables, respectively:

$$R_1 = \begin{bmatrix} 1.000 & .796 & .135 & .399 \\ & 1.000 & .348 & .250 \\ & & 1.000 & .788 \\ & & & 1.000 \end{bmatrix}, \quad C_1 = \begin{bmatrix} 1.000 & .797 & .137 & .401 \\ & 1.000 & .349 & .251 \\ & & 1.000 & .787 \\ & & & 1.000 \end{bmatrix}.$$

As all the mean values of these variables are very close to zero, every correlation coefficient assumes a value which is very similar to the corresponding cosine. The remaining five variables have been generated so as to be collinear but not correlated. This result has been obtained by considering five orthonormal vectors ($\mathbf{u}_k$, $k = 1, ..., 5$) belonging to the orthogonal complement of $\mathbf{i}$ in R^n, where $\mathbf{i}$ is the vector of n ones (Belsley 1991, p. 20); then, five variables have been defined as linear combinations of $\mathbf{i}$ and one orthonormal vector: $\mathbf{x}_k = \mathbf{i} + \alpha_k \mathbf{u}_k$, $k = 1, ..., 5$. These variables have unit mean value; they are also perfectly uncorrelated: in fact, as $\mathbf{x}_k' \mathbf{x}_h = (\mathbf{i} + \alpha_k \mathbf{u}_k)'(\mathbf{i} + \alpha_h \mathbf{u}_h) = n$ for every $k \neq h$, the covariance between $\mathbf{x}_k$ and $\mathbf{x}_h$ is zero. The angle between $\mathbf{x}_k$ and $\mathbf{x}_h$, a_{kh}, depends on n and on the values of the coefficients α_k and α_h by the following relation: $a_{kh} = cos^{-1}[n(n + \alpha_k^2)^{-0.5}(n + \alpha_h^2)^{-0.5}]$; thus in this way it is possible to define variables becoming arbitrarily collinear while remaining absolutely uncorrelated, depending on the values of n and of the coefficients α_k. For instance, when $n = 500$, if $\alpha_k = 0.2$ for every k, the angle a between each pair of variables will be 0.725, and $cos(a) = 0.999$; if $\alpha_k = 50$ for every k, $a = 80.4$, and $cos(a) = 0.17$.

Several data matrices have been generated as just described by controlling the collinearity within the second group through different values of α_k, $k = 1, ..., 5$ while keeping constant the correlations among the first four variables. Specifically, each data matrix has been obtained fixing a value for α_1 and computing the remaining coefficients as multiple of α_1, in this way: $\alpha_k = k\alpha_k$ for $k = 2, ..., 5$. This procedure has been repeated for increasing values of α_1, starting from 4 up to 38, step 2.

All the methods based on simple and canonical correlations described in Section 1 always failed in recovering the cluster structure present in all these data matrices because of the zero correlations within the second group, while the proposed procedure succeeded in all the considered situations.

The proposed procedure has been applied also to a real data matrix, which contains the relative variations between 1996 and 1997 of six variables for the twenty Italian regions; the variables are: X_1 = gross domestic product; X_2 = gross value added; X_3 = expenditure for final domestic consumptions; X_4 = internal demand; X_5 = present population; X_6 = resident population. The data are taken from the ISTAT (Italian National Statistical Institute) web site (www.istat.it), where many other indicators can be downloaded. Matrices $\mathbf{R}$ and $\mathbf{C}$ contain the correlation coefficients and the cosines of the angles between each pair of variables, respectively:

$$\mathbf{R} = \begin{bmatrix} 1.00 & .77 & -.02 & -.08 & -.15 & -.14 \\ & 1.00 & -.19 & .11 & -.27 & -.32 \\ & & 1.00 & -.00 & .41 & .42 \\ & & & 1.00 & -.58 & -.51 \\ & & & & 1.00 & .96 \\ & & & & & 1.00 \end{bmatrix}, \quad \mathbf{C} = \begin{bmatrix} 1.00 & .92 & .76 & .74 & .32 & .31 \\ & 1.00 & .78 & .82 & .29 & .25 \\ & & 1.00 & .94 & .58 & .56 \\ & & & 1.00 & .37 & .37 \\ & & & & 1.00 & .97 \\ & & & & & 1.00 \end{bmatrix}$$

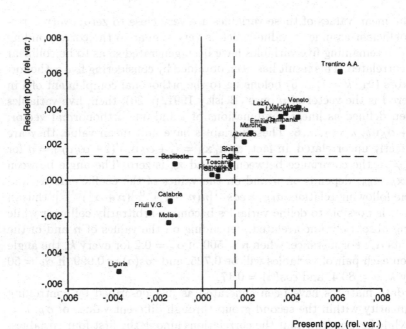

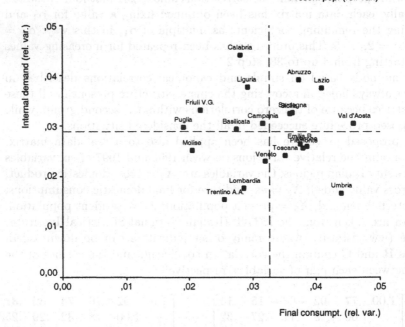

Fig. 1. Scatter plots of (X_5, X_6) and of (X_3, X_4) for the twenty Italian regions.

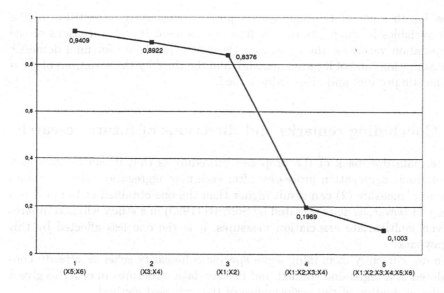

Fig. 2. Values assumed by measure (2) at the five steps of the aggregation process (groups of variables in brackets) for the real data example.

From the comparison between the values of each correlation coefficient and the corresponding angle it emerges that on one hand X_5 and X_6 are highly correlated and collinear ($r_{5,6} = .96$; $c_{5,6} = .97$), while on the other hand X_3 and X_4 are uncorrelated but almost collinear ($r_{5,6} = -.00$; $c_{3,4} = .94$). The reasons of this difference are well explained by the scatter plots in Fig. 1; the first is referred to X_5 and X_6, and clearly shows a linear dependence between the relative variations of the two variables (dashed lines identify the centroid of the data, while straight lines crossing in $(0,0)$ the absence of variation for both variables); in the second scatter plot, referred to X_3 and X_4, the relative variations result to be clearly uncorrelated, but at the same time they are also positive for each region, thus giving a high value of the cosine $c_{3,4}$. Therefore every measure based on correlation does not identify any cluster structure between these two variables, while the measure defined in equation (2) does. The correlation coefficient seems to be inadequate in the analysis of the considered data matrix as it is not correct to evaluate the arithmetic mean values of the relative variations computed for the Italian regions.

The results obtained by applying the proposed procedure to this real data matrix are synthesized in Fig. 2: the variables which have been aggregated at each step of the hierarchical process and the corresponding values of measure (2) are indicated on X and Y axes, respectively. The similarity measure assumes decreasing values with maximum variation between the third and the fourth steps of the aggregation process, suggesting a partition of the six variables in three groups: the first is composed by the variations of the population variables, the second by those of expenditure for final domestic consumptions and of internal demand, and the third by the variations of gross domestic product and gross value added.

4 Concluding remarks and directions of future research

The main drawback of the proposed procedure is that it can produce non monotonic aggregation processes: after each new aggregation, the maximum value of measure (2) can result higher than the one obtained at the previous step. However, as demonstrated by Soffritti (1999) in a study which compares seven multivariate association measures, it is the one less affected by this drawback.

We are currently examining some specific collinearity schemes already considered in a regression context and further data structures in order to give a wider evaluation of the performance of the proposed method.

Finally, we are studying an objective criterion to establish the number of clusters and further ways of measuring the similarity between groups of variables based on collinearity.

References

ANDERBERG, M.R. (1973): *Cluster Analysis for Applications*. Academic Press, New York.

BELSLEY, D.A. (1991): *Conditioning Diagnostics*. John Wiley and Sons, New York.

GORDON, A.D. (1999): *Classification*. Chapman and Hall/CRC, London.

HARTIGAN, J.A. (1975): *Clustering Algorithms*. John Wiley, New York.

NICOLAU, F.C. and BACELAR-NICOLAU, H. (1998): Some trends in the classification of variables. In: C. Hayashi, N. Ohsumi, K. Yajima, Y. Tanaka, H. Bock and Y. Baba (Eds.): *Data Science, Classification and Related Methods*. Springer, Berlin, 89-98.

MULLER, K.E. (1982): Understanding canonical correlation through the general linear model and principal components. *The American Statistician, 36, 342-354*.

SOFFRITTI, G. (1999): Hierarchical clustering of variables: a comparison among strategies of analysis. *Communications in Statistics - Simulation and Computation, 28, 977-999*.

SOFFRITTI, G. (2003): Identifying multiple cluster structures in a data matrix. *Communications in Statistics - Simulation and Computation, 32, 1151-1177*.

VIGNEAU, E. and QANNARI, E.M. (2003): Clustering of variables around latent components. *Communications in Statistics - Simulation and Computation, 32, 1131-1150*.

On the Dynamic Time Warping for Computing the Dissimilarity Between Curves

Isabella Morlini

Dipartimento di Economia, Sezione di Statistica,
Università di Parma, Italy
isabella.morlini@unipr.it

Abstract. Dynamic time warping (DTW) is a technique for aligning curves that considers two aspects of variations: horizontal and vertical, or domain and range. This alignment is an essential preliminary in many applications before classification or functional data analysis. A problem with DTW is that the algorithm may fail to find the natural alignment of two series since it is mostly influenced by salient features rather than by the overall shape of the sequences. In this paper, we first deepen the DTW algorithm, showing relationships and differences with the curve registration technique, and then we propose a modification of the algorithm that considers a smoothed version of the data.

1 Introduction

Functional data analysis involves the extension of classical statistical procedure to data where the raw observation x_i is a curve. In practice, these curves are often a consequence of a preliminary interpolating process applied to discrete data sequences. In calculating the dissimilarity between curves the main problem is that the starting time for each sequence may be arbitrary or there may be a sort of physiological or meteorological timescale that relates non linearly to physical time. More abstractly, the values $x_i(t_j)$ of sequences $i = 1, \ldots, N$ at time t_j $(j = 1, \ldots, T_i)$ may differ because of two types of variation. The first is the *range variation* due to the fact that the values of two series x_1 and x_2 may simply differ at points of time at which they can be compared. The second is the less familiar domain variation which is exhibited when x_1 and x_2 should not be compared at a fixed value of t but at times t_1 and t_2 at which the two values are essentially in comparable states. Fig. 1 shows two examples in which domain variation occurs. Fig. 1a illustrates 6 recordings of the X-axis position of a subject's right hand while signing one of the 95 words in Australian Sign Language (Bay, 1999). The starting time for each record is arbitrary, so it is essential to find a common timescale to combine information across records. Fig. 1b shows the rainfall intensity measured by 5 raingauges in the Cortina d'Ampezzo area (Morlini and Orlandini, 2001). These five raingauge stations are distributed over a rectangular area of about 19 km × 8 km and have a different elevation. In comparing these

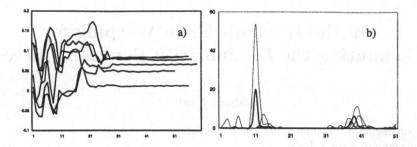

Fig. 1. Examples of curves in which domain variation occurs. (a) Recordings of the X-axis position of a subject's right hand while signing the word *alive* in Australian Sign Language. (b) Rainfall intensity measured by 5 rain gauges in the Cortina d'Ampezzo area (Northern Italian Alps).

curves we need to consider that weather is driven by factors that are timed differently for different spatial locations.

The problem of transforming the arguments of curves before functional data analysis is referred to by Silverman (1995) and Ramsay and Li (2003) as curve registration, while in the engineering literature as time warping. In particular, dynamic time warping (DTW) is a technique for computing a dissimilarity measure between two warped series which has been applied in many different fields like data mining, finance and manufacturing. Although DTW has been successfully used, especially in speech recognition (Rabiner and Juang, 1993), it can produce incorrect results when aligning, for example, two values which are identical but the first is a part of a rising trend in series 1 and the second is a part of a falling trend in series 2. An additional problem is that the algorithm may fail to find the natural alignment of two sequences simply because a salient feature (i.e. a peak, a valley, an inflection point, a plateau) in one series is slightly higher or lower than its corresponding feature in the other sequence. This may rise when the overall shapes of the series are identical, but data are noisy. Both these problems occur since DTW only considers the single values of each sequences and since the algorithm has few constrains. In this paper, rather then imposing constrains (as, among others, in Myers *et al.*, 1980) we introduce a modification of DTW which considers smoothed estimates of the values of the series. These estimates are obtained by smoothing each sequence with splines and are aimed to find new points which are less noisy and depend on the overall shape of the series. For a different approach to measure the dissimilarity among series and methodological problems related to this task, we refer to Piccolo (1990).

2 Dynamic time warping and curve registration

To align two sequences $x_i(t_j)$ and simultaneously measure the dissimilarity between them, the DTW algorithm first implies the construction of a $T_1 \times T_2$

matrix $\mathbf{M}$ in which the generic element (r, c) is the distance $d(x_1(t_r), x_2(t_c))$ between the value of sequence 1 at time t_r and the value of sequence 2 at time t_c. Note that the series $x_i(t)$ may be vector valued, as would be the case, for example, if they indicate position in two or three dimensional space or simultaneous aspects of a single phenomenon. At this stage of DTW any distance may be used in the construction of the matrix $\mathbf{M}$. Each element (r, c) corresponds to the alignment between points $x_1(t_r)$ and $x_2(t_c)$. The dissimilarity between x_1 and x_2, also called dynamic time warping cost (DTWC) is defined as follows:

$$\text{DTWC} = \min \sqrt{\sum_{k=1}^{K} d_k \Big/ K} \tag{1}$$

where $\max(T_1, T_2) \leq K \leq T_1 + T_2 - 1$ and d_k $(k = 1, \ldots, K)$ are elements of $\mathbf{M}$ subject to:

1. Boundary conditions for $k = 1$ and $k = K$: $d_1 = d(x_1(t_1), x_2(t_1))$ and $d_K = d(x_1(T_1), x_2(T_2))$. This requires the first and the last addends in the sum to be diagonally opposite corner elements of $\mathbf{M}$.
2. Continuity constrains for $k = 2, \ldots, K - 1$: given $d_k = d(x_1(t_r), x_2(t_c))$ then $d_{k-1} = d(x_1(t_\rho), x_2(t_\gamma))$ where $r - \rho \leq 1$ and $c - \gamma \leq 1$. This condition restricts two successive elements d_k in the summation to be adjacent (including diagonally) elements in $\mathbf{M}$.
3. Monotonicity constrain for $k = 2, \ldots, K - 1$: given $d_k = d(x_1(t_r), x_2(t_c))$ then $d_{k-1} = d(x_1(t_\rho), x_2(t_\gamma))$ where $0 \leq r - \rho$ and $0 \leq c - \gamma$. This forces the couple of points for which the distance is taken into account in (1) to be monotonically spaced in time.

Note that if $T_1 = T_2$, any distance between $x_1(t)$ and $x_2(t)$, with no warping, can be seen as a special case of (1), where each $d_k = d(x_1(t_r), x_2(t_c))$ is constrained such that $r = c$. Without this constrain, the DTWC is a dissimilarity measure, since the triangular inequality property does not hold. While finding this measure of dissimilarity, the DTW algorithm indirectly solves the alignment problem between each pair of sequences. The curve registration problem, as referred by Ramsay and Li (1998), is somehow different, since the aim is to align a family of curves $x_i(t_j)$ to a target function y, by minimizing a fitting criterion between the $x_i(t_j)$ and y. For this aim, a time warping strictly increasing function is defined. As shown in Fig. 2a, by finding the elements d_k of $\mathbf{M}$ which minimize the dissimilarity (1) between x_1 and x_2 we find a warping path, instead. From this path we cannot draw the two warping functions to align x_1 to x_2 and to align x_2 to x_1, since a single point on one time series may map onto a large subsection of the other series (see Fig. 2b). In order to find two monotonic - not strictly increasing - warping functions one could eliminate the boundary condition $d_K = d(x_1(T_1), x_2(T_2))$ and restrict the continuity constrain such that $r - \rho = 1$ for aligning x_1 to x_2 and such that $c - \gamma = 1$ for aligning x_2 to x_1 (the pictorial representation of the resulting steps in the path is reported in Fig. 3b). With this restriction,

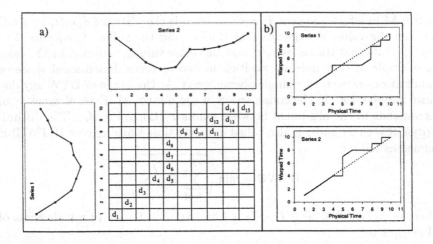

Fig. 2. (a) Example of distances included in the DTWC. (b) The warping path.

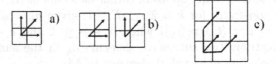

Fig. 3. Pictorial representations of step-paths (a) The DTW step (b) Step with restrictions on the continuity constrains. (c) Step without the continuity constrains.

however, the DTWC turns asymmetric. So we cannot define at the same time a dissimilarity measure and a warping function without eliminating the continuity constrain of the warping path (as illustrated in Fig. 3c). One could reduce the number of *singularities*, that is the number of points of one series mapping onto a plurality of points of the other series, by imposing other constrains on the DTW (Rabiner and Juang, 1993). Yet the weakness of this algorithm should be not ascribed to the number of singularities but to the fact that, especially when the data are noisy, these singularities may be due to range rather than to domain variation. In order to affect the reason of singularities rather than simply their number, we propose a different approach which is aimed to smooth the data before applying DTW and to obtain points which are less noisy and depend on the overall shape of the series. These new points are obtained by smoothing each sequence by a piecewise linear or cubic spline. For a different approach, but with similar aims, we refer to Keogh and Pazzani (1998). An open problem remains the choice of the smoothing parameter λ or the number of knots k. Since as λ and k increase, the number of singularities gets larger, one should keep these values as small as possible consistent with obtaining a reasonable degree of smoothing for the data and for the problem at hand. In the following section we design two experiments

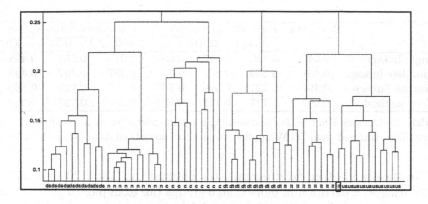

Fig. 4. Dendrogram of the group average cluster analysis (excluded the last 3 levels) for the Synthetic Control Chart Data Set.

for clustering series on the basis of their DTWC and we indirectly measure the validity of our approach and find reasonable values for λ and k on the basis of the clustering results.

3 Experimental results

The validity of the smoothing step before applying the DTW algorithm is studied in this section by means of a synthetic and a real data set taken from the UCI KDD archive (Bay, 1999). The first is the Synthetic Control Chart data set consisting of 600 time series of control charts synthetically generated. There are 100 series of length 60 for each of the following classes: normal (n), cyclic (c), increasing trend (it), decreasing trend (dt), upward shift (us), downward shift (ds). Without warping, both the k-means and the hierarchical cluster analyses aren't able to distinguish class n from c, class it from us and dt from ds. We wrote a Matlab program for randomly choosing 10 series for each class, smoothing each series, implementing the DTW algorithm and successively clustering the series on the basis of the DTWC between each pair of sequences. Fig. 4 shows the dendrogram (excluded the last 3 levels) obtained with the group average hierarchical cluster analysis and a cubic spline smoother with $\lambda = 0.10$. For exactly 6 groups there is only one misclassified series. For the same data, dendrograms are similar, but slightly worse in that for exactly 6 groups there is more than 1 misclassified sequence, for cubic splines with 10 equally spaced knots and for different values of λ ranging from 0.20 to 0.02. A simulation study changing 100 times the series to be classified, using a smoothing spline with $\lambda = 0.10$ and obtaining dendrograms with different hierarchical methods, shows that the aggregation steps may vary remarkably and, in some instances, cyclic series remain isolated until the upper levels.

	Raw data	Piecewise linear spline			Cubic smoothing spline		
		$t = 0.01$	$t = 0.10$	$t = 0.20$	$\lambda = 0.02$	$\lambda = 0.04$	$\lambda = 0.07$
Single linkage	0.047	0.800	0.727	0.050	0.047	0.556	0.498
Complete linkage	0.497	0.556	0.800	0.800	0.497	0.497	0.498
Average linkage	0.497	0.727	0.560	0.556	0.497	0.727	0.560
Ward method	0.497	0.727	0.727	0.727	0.497	0.727	0.560

Table 1. Correct Rand index between the actual partition in 3 groups and the partitions obtained with DTW applied to raw and smoothed data (ASL Data Set).

In these and other dendrograms, the optimal cut (Zani, 2000, pp. 218-222) achieves a partition in more than 6 groups (for example, 10 groups with a unique series belonging to class c and 5 homogeneous groups with series belonging to the other classes). The comparison of the dendrograms achieved with raw data shows that for fixed cuts corresponding to 10 and 15 clusters, the groups achieved with previous smoothing are more homogeneous (the average number of different series in each group being smaller). For 6 groups, the averages of the correct Rand index (Hubert and Arabie, 1985) between the correct partition and the partitions obtained with DTW applied to raw data and DTW applied to smoothed data show that the last partitions are more similar to the actual one.

The second data set is the Australian Sign Language (ASL), consisting of the x, y, and z positions of a volunteer naive Auslan signer's right hand (there are more measurements in the database which we do not consider in this work). The positions are captured by using position trackers and instrumental gloves. For each word, 27 records are present. Here we consider the 81 records relative to the words *alive* (E), *all* (L) and *answer* (R). Records have different lengths (the average being 57), so Euclidean distance cannot be a benchmark in this example. We compare DTW in its original formulation with DTW applied to smoothed data. We consider raw variables and gridded data estimates obtained with tensor product splines. Since we are dealing with spatial data, rather than smoothing each dimension of the records separately, we use vector valued splines. Table 1 reports the correct Rand index between the partition in 3 groups obtained with different splines and different hierarchical clustering methods and the actual partition in 3 groups. The parameter t in the piecewise linear splines is the given tolerance (De Boor, 1999).

With cubic splines with too much flexibility results are identical to those obtained with no smoothing while with $\lambda = 0.07$ or $\lambda = 0.02$ results are better or at least identical. All piecewise linear splines lead to more homogeneous partitions, with respect to those obtained with raw data. With the complete linkage, the best values for t are 0.1 and 0.2 while for the single and the average linkage the value leading to the most homogeneous partition is 0.01. The original Rand index (Rand, 1971) confirms these results. Besides, as shown in Fig. 5b e Fig. 5c for the average linkage method, the aggregation

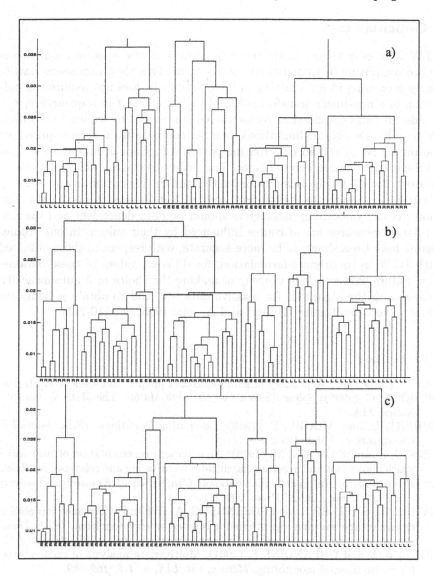

Fig. 5. Dendrograms of the average linkage method (excluded the last 3 levels) for the ASL data set. (a) Raw data. (b) Smoothed data with piecewise linear spline ($t = 0.2$). (c) Smoothed data with piecewise linear spline ($t = 0.1$).

steps lead to partitions in more than 5 groups in which in each cluster all series belong to the same class. This is verified for more than 6 clusters for DTW applied to original data (Fig. 5a).

4 Conclusions

DTW is an easy to implement technique which allows registration of curves before computing dissimilarities between them. This algorithm seems particularly promising in data mining problems, since it does not require the definition of a non-linear transformation of the argument t in sequences $x_i(t_j)$. Besides, it can be applied to vector valued curves and to sequences of different lengths. Despite its limitations, like the computational time required for computing M, it should be a routine part of a functional data analysis that combines information across curves. The main objective of this work was to improve the DTW algorithm in order to limit the distortion in the warping of curves and moderate the importance of salient features in noisy data. The choice of the smoothing parameters should be data dependent and the dissimilarity measures are of course influenced by their values. In our studies results have been shown to be more accurate, with respect to those obtained with DTW in its original formulation, for different values of these parameters. Future works include the way of making the choice of λ automatically, to speed up the algorithm for massive data sets and to obtain p-values for the modified Rand index (Hubert and Arabie, 1985, pp. 210-211).

References

BAY, S. (1999): UCI Repository of Kdd Databases [http://kdd.ics.uci.edu]. Irvine.

DE BOOR, C. (1999): *Spline Toolbox For Use with Matlab*, The Math Works Inc., Natick, MA.

HUBERT, L. and ARABIE, P. (1985): Comparing Partitions, *IEEE Journal of Classification, Vol.2, 193-218.*

KEOGH, E. and PAZZANI, M. (1998): An enhanced representation of time series which allows fast and accurate classification, clustering and relevance feedback, *Proceedings of the Fourth International Conference of Knowledge Discovery and Data Mining*, AAAI Press, 239-241.

MYERS, C., RABINER, L. and ROSENBERG, A. (1980): Performance tradeoffs in dynamic time warping algorithms for isolated word recognition, *IEEE Transactions on Acoustics, Speech and Signal Processing, Vol. ASSP- 28, 623-635.*

MORLINI, I. and ORLANDINI, S. (2001): Multivariate analysis of radar images for environmental monitoring, *Metron, vol. LIX, n. 1-2, 169-189.*

PICCOLO, D. (1990): A distance measure for classifying ARIMA models, *Journal of Time Series Analysis, 5, 3, 183-204.*

RABINER, L. and JUANG, B. (1993): *Fundamentals of Speech Recognition*, Englewood Cliffs, N.J., Prentice Hall.

RAMSAY, J.O. and LI, X. (1998): Curve registration, *J.R.S.S., Series B, 60, 351-363.*

RAND, W.M. (1971): Objective criteria for the evaluation of clustering methods, *Journal of the American Statistical Association, 66, 846-850.*

SILVERMAN, B.W. (1995): Incorporating parametric effects into functional principal components analysis, *J.R.S.S, Series B, 57, 673-689.*

ZANI, S. (2000): *Analisi dei dati statistici*, vol. II, Giuffrè, Milano.

Metrics in Symbolic Data Analysis

Luciano Nieddu and Alfredo Rizzi*

Dipartimento di Statistica, Probabilità e Statistiche Applicate
Università degli Studi di Roma "La Sapienza"
luciano.nieddu@uniroma1.it, alfredo.rizzi@uniroma1.it

Abstract. The Authors consider the general problem of similarity and dissimilarity measures in Symbolic Data Analysis. First they examine the classical definitions of *elementary event, assertion object, hierarchical dependences and logical dependences*, then they consider some well-known measures resemblance measures between two objects (Sokal-Michener, Roger-Tanimoto, Sokal-Sneath, Dice-Czekanowski-Sorenson, Russel-Rao). For resemblance measures based on aggregation functions, the authors consider the proposals of Gowda-Diday, De Baets et al., Malerba et al., Vladutu et al., and Ichino-Yaguchi.

1 Introduction

The analysis of symbolic data has led to a new branch of Data Analysis called Symbolic Data Analysis (SDA) where the objects considered are new entities for which the representation as point in $S = Y_1 \times Y_2 \times \cdots \times Y_n$ (which usually reduces to $\Re^n$) no longer holds. In SDA features characterizing symbolic objects may take more than one value, or may be in the form of interval data or be qualitative data or subsets of qualitative data. Symbolic data can also be used after clustering in order to summarize a huge set of data to describe, for exploratory purposes, the obtained clusters and their internal variation. Another important source of symbolic objects comes from relational databases in order to study a set of units whose description needs the merging of several relations.

A crucial issue in the adaptation of standard statistical techniques to symbolic data lays in the specification of resemblance measures between objects. Various techniques that have been developed for exploratory data analysis and multidimensional classification manage to handle almost exclusively numerical variables. In the last decade there has been a flurry of activity aimed at extending these techniques to symbolic data (Nagabhushan et al. 1995), (Lauro et al., 2000) (Périnel and Lechevallier, 2000), (Mali and Mitra 2003).

This paper presents a series of well-established similarity and dissimilarity indexes for binary symbolic objects. Some distance measures will be suggested

---

*This paper is common job of both the Authors. Paragraphs 1 and 4 are referred to A. Rizzi, while paragraphs 2 and 3 to L. Nieddu

for binary symbolic objects that could also be useful for probabilistic symbolic objects. In section 2 the definition of symbolic data will be recalled, while in section 3 several resemblance measures will be considered. In section 4 the due conclusions will be drawn.

2 Symbolic data analysis

2.1 A symbolic object is defined as a description that is expressed as a conjunction of statements regarding the values assumed by the variables. Let Ω be the set of observed objects, each one characterized by p variables $y_i, i = 1, \ldots, p$. Formally a variable $y_i : \Omega \to O_i$ can be considered as a function, where O_i is the observation set of y_i. The variable y_i may be measured on a nominal, ordinal, interval, ratio or absolute scale.

An **elementary event** is an event of the type $e = [y_i \in V_i]$ indicating that variable y_i takes values in $V_i \subseteq O_i$. The elementary event e can be true or false, therefore a mapping of the type $e = \Omega \to \{true, false\}$ can be associated to the elementary event e. An **assertion object** is composed by the logical conjunction of elementary events: $a = \wedge_i [y_i \in V_i]$. Again a mapping of the type $a = \Omega \to \{true, false\}$ will be associated to the assertion object a. Boolean assertion objects can be used to provide, via the logical conjunction of elementary events, a precise description of a concept. The **extension** of each assertion object a on the set Ω is defined as the subset of Ω for which the assertion a is true. To actually represent data, the description of concepts by Boolean assertions must take into account various types of logical dependencies between variables, such as *Hierarchical dependences* (mother-daughter) and *Logical dependences* (cfr. section 3).

3 Similarity and dissimilarity measures

3.1 A dissimilarity measure D on a set of elements E is a real valued function $D : E \times E \to \Re$ such that $D(a, a) \leq D(a, b) = D(b, a) < \infty \ \forall a, b \in E$. Usually $D(a, a) = 0$ and $D(a, b) \in [0, 1]$. A dissimilarity measure for which $D(a, a) = 0$ and that fulfils the triangle inequality is called a metric or distance[2]. Furthermore it is called an ultrametric if it fulfils the condition: $D(a, b) \leq \max \{D(a, c), D(c, b)\} \ \forall a, b, c \in E$. Obviously an ultrametric it is also a metric. Analogously a similarity measure S on a set of elements E is a real valued function $S : E \times E \to \Re$ such that $0 \leq S(a, b) = S(b, a) \leq S(a, a)$ $\forall a, b \in E$ and usually $S(a, b) \in [0, 1]$.

If a resemblance measure fulfils an inequality dual to the ultrametric condition (i.e. $S(a, b) \geq \min \{S(a, c), S(c, b)\}$ $\forall a, b, c \in E$) it is named an ultraminima.

---

[2]Sometimes it is named a semi-metric or semi-distance, and the terms "metric" and "distance" are left for those dissimilarities fulfilling the definiteness condition (see for instance, Rizzi, 1985 or Esposito et al. 2000)

Given a similarity measure S on $E \times E$, and a strictly decreasing function ξ in $[0,1]$ then the mapping $D(a,b) = \xi[S(a,b)]$ is a dissimilarity index. Conversely, if ξ is also non-negative in $[0,1]$, then the quantity $S(a,b) = \xi[D(a,b)]$ is a similarity index. Usual transformations are $\xi(x) = \max(x) - x$ or $\xi(x) = \sqrt{\max(x) - x}$ or $\xi(x) = \cos(90x)$.

3.2 Given two symbolic objects, $a = \wedge_i [y_i \in a_i]$ and $b = \wedge_i [y_i \in b_i]$ the dissimilarity between these two objects can be computed aggregating the *comparison functions*, which are dissimilarities measures computed independently for each variable. The usually applied *aggregation function* is the generalized Minkowski metric. To compute comparison functions for each variable, agreement-disagreement indices can be used (De Carvalho 1994) according to the following table: Where $\dot{b}$ is the complementary set of b_k in the domain

	Agreement	Disagreement
Agreement	$\alpha = \pi(a_k \cap b_k)$	$\beta = \pi\left(a_k \cap \dot{b}\right)$
Disagreement	$\gamma = \pi(\dot{a})$	$\delta = \pi(\dot{a})_k$

Table 1. agreement-disagreement table

O_k and $\pi(a_k)$ is a function that accounts for the description potential (DP) of a_k and that can be defined as:

$$\pi(a_k) = \begin{cases} |a_k| & \text{if the variable is integer, nominal or ordinal} \\ |\overline{a}_k - \underline{a}_k| & \text{if the variable is a continuous interval.} \end{cases}$$

where the symbols $\overline{a}$ and $\underline{a}$ represent the upper and the lower bounds of an interval of the real line. According to the previous definitions, classical similarity and dissimilarity indexes have been extended for symbolic data. Namely, some similarity measures are:

Sokal-Michener	$S = \frac{\alpha+\delta}{\alpha+\beta+\gamma+\delta}$	Sokal-Sneath	$S = \frac{\alpha}{\alpha+2(\beta+\gamma)}$
Jaccard	$S = \frac{\alpha}{\alpha+\beta+\gamma}$	Dice-Czekanowski-Sorenson	$S = \frac{2\alpha}{2\alpha+\beta+\gamma}$
Roger-Tanimoto	$S = \frac{\alpha+\delta}{\alpha+\delta+2(\beta+\gamma)}$	Russel-Rao	$S = \frac{\alpha}{\alpha+\beta+\gamma+\delta}$
Kulczynski	$S = \frac{1}{2}\left(\frac{\alpha}{\alpha+\beta} + \frac{\alpha}{\alpha+\gamma}\right)$	Occhiai-Driver-Kroeber	$S = \frac{\alpha}{\sqrt{(\alpha+\beta)(\alpha+\gamma)}}$

Russel-Rao similarity index is peculiar, since in all the other indexes when the DP of $(a_k \cap b_k)$ (i.e. the DP of what is not in a_k or in b_k) is considered in the index then it is present both at the numerator and at the denominator of the fraction. Roger-Tanimoto and Sokal-Sneath indexes double weight mismatches (i.e. $a_k \cap \dot{b}$ and $\dot{a}$) and the former ignores conjoint absence (i.e. $\dot{a}$).

On the other hand Dice-Czekanowski-Sorenson index double weights conjoint presence without considering conjoint absence.

Kulczynski and Occhiai-Driver-Kroeber can be considered, respectively, as the arithmetic and geometric mean of the quantities $\alpha/(\alpha+\beta)$ and $\alpha/(\alpha+\gamma)$ which represent the proportion of agreements on the marginal distributions.

It is worth noticing that, except for Sokal-Michener, Roger-Tanimoto and Russel-Rao, all the other indexes are indeterminate if $\alpha = \beta = \gamma = 0$, which could occur even if in very special cases, such as, for instance, when a_k and b_k are two degenerate intervals.

Analogous dissimilarity measures can be obtained from the previous one simply considering the dissimilarity index $D = 1 - S$.

Another class of resemblance measures for symbolic objects is based on the notion of DP of a symbolic object a and do not require a variable-wise function and an aggregation function to obtain an aggregate resemblance measure.

Gowda and Diday have proposed various types of similarity and dissimilarity measures (see Gowda and Diday 1992). To overcome some disadvantages of the previous measure, Ravi and Gowda (1999) have proposed modified resemblance measures which can be used on symbolic data composed of qualitative and quantitative values. Dissimilarity between two symbolic objects, a and b, can be computed, variable-wise, considering the contributions of three components which incorporate different types of dissimilarities due to:

position, (defined for quantitative data): represents the relative positions of the two features values on the real line and can be computed, for interval data, as $D_p(a_k, b_k) = \cos\left[90\left(1 - |\underline{a}_k - \underline{b}_k|/u_k\right)\right]$ where u_k is the length of the maximum interval for the k-th feature;

span, is due to the relative dimensions of the feature values without taking into account their intersection and is calculated, for interval data and for qualitative data as $D_s(a_k, b_k) = \cos\left\{45\left[\pi\left(a_k\right) + \pi\left(b_k\right)\right]/\pi\left(a_k \oplus b_k\right)\right\}$ where $\oplus$ is the Cartesian join operator;

content, takes into account the common part of the two features and can be calculated as $D_c(a_k, b_k) = \cos\left[90\pi\left(a_k \cap b_k\right)/\pi\left(a_k \oplus b_k\right)\right]$.

Dissimilarity is then computed, for quantitative interval data as $D(a_k, b_k) = D_p(a_k, b_k) + D_s(a_k, b_k)$ while for qualitative data as $D(a_k, b_k) = D_s(a_k, b_k) + D_c(a_k, b_k)$.

De Baets et al. (2001) have examined twenty-eight measures of similarity between crisp subsets of a finite universe proposing a class of rational similarity measures based on the cardinality of the sets involved that, according to the notation used in Table 1, can be written as:

$$S(a,b) = \frac{r \min\{\beta, \gamma\} + s \max\{\beta, \gamma\} + t\alpha + u\delta}{r' \min\{\beta, \gamma\} + s' \max\{\beta, \gamma\} + t'\alpha + u'\delta} \quad r,r',s,s',t,t',u,u' \in \{0,1\}.$$

To obtain a reflexive similarity index the conditions $t = t'$ and $u = u'$ must hold[3]. Indeterminacy cases are handled setting the index to 1. Besides the usual properties that should be verified by a similarity index, De Baets et al. suggest three other boundary conditions, regarding similarity to the empty set, similarity to the universe and similarity between complementary sets. The only two indexes that verify all the three boundary conditions are obtained for $r = s = r' = 0$, $s' = t = t' = u = u' = 1$ and $r = s = 0$, $r' = s' = t = t' = u = u' = 1$, the second one being the well known Sokal-Michener simple matching coefficient.

3.4 An effort to empirically compare dissimilarity measures for Boolean symbolic objects has been carried out by Malerba et al. (2001). The data set considered for testing is the well-known Abalone Fish dataset, available from the Machine Learning Repository (University of California at Irvine), contains 4177 records of Abalone fishes described by nine mixed attributes. This dataset is usually used to predict the age of an abalone fish using attributes like sex, weight, shell weight etc (see Malerba et al. 2001)[4]. The argument sustained in the paper of Malerba et al. is that, considered that the performance of techniques such regression-tree on the abalone fish dataset is quite high, the eight attributes are sufficient to predict the age of an abalone. They then "expect that the degree of dissimilarity between crustacean computed on the independent attributes do actually be proportional to the dissimilarity in the dependent attribute" (Malerba et al 2001). Abalone data have been aggregated into nine symbolic objects using SODAS software[5] and the performance of ten dissimilarity indexes (including De Carvalho's, Ichino and Yaguchi's and Gowda and Diday's) have been compared. It is not clear, however, how the proportionality of the degree of dissimilarity stated above should still hold when the 4177 abalone fishes have been grouped into symbolic objects.

Vladutu et al (2001) have proposed a distance for symbolic data in the context of Generalized Radial Basis Function networks. The proposed distance is tailored only for discrimination purposes, i.e. a training set where data have previously been assigned to one of N classes is assumed to be available. The use of this type of distance even if proved useful on a number of test-sample (Vladutu et al 2001) is restricted to supervised learning where it reduces to a distance between row profiles in a matrix where the rows are the possible values of the character and the columns are the classes.

Let a be a symbolic object: the definition of DP varies according to the type of symbolic object considered (constrained or unconstrained). For an unconstrained symbolic object the DP is given by $\pi(a) = \Pi_{j=1}^{p} \pi(a_j)$ while

---

[3]Some of the measures that can be obtained for particular choices of the coefficients are well known in the literature: for instance, the choice $r = s = u = u' = 0$, $r' = s' = t = t' = 1$ gives the Jaccard's index, while the choice $r = s = u = 0$, $r' = s' = t = t' = u' = 1$ yields the Russel-Rao

[4]Detailed information on the dataset are also available at ftp://ftp.ics.uci.edu/pub/machine-learning-databases/abalone/abalone.names

[5]http://www.cisia.com/download.htm

for a constrained Boolean symbolic object the definition needs to be slightly modified in order to take into account hierarchical and logical dependences. For dependences of the type *if* $(y_j \in s_j)$ *then* $(y_i \in s_i)$ the DP becomes $\pi(a) = \Pi_{j=1}^P \pi(a_j) - \pi(a')$ where $\pi(a')$ is the DP of the incoherent restriction of a which includes all the description vectors fulfilling a and are incoherent.

For a hierarchical dependence of the type *if* $(y_j \in s_j)$ *then* $(y_i \in \{NA\})$, the DP becomes $\pi(a) = \pi(a_j \cup NA)\Pi_{j=1, j\neq i}^P \pi(a_j) - \pi(a') - \pi(a'')$ where y_i takes values in an enlarged domain containing, as a category, the label "NA", $\pi(a')$ is the DP including all description vectors where $y_i \notin NA$ even if the assumption of the relation is true, and $\pi(a'')$ is the DP including all vectors where $y_i \in NA$ even if the "if" part of the relation is false. This extended definition of DP can be applied to the determination of dissimilarity measures which are a trivial extension of Ichino & Yaghuchi's (Ichino and Yaguchi 1994) distance such as $D(a, b) = (\pi(a \oplus b) - \pi(a \cap b) + \gamma[2\pi(a \cap b) - \pi(a) - \pi(b)])/R$ $\gamma \in [0, 0.5]$ where R can be equal to 1, or be the potential of the entire domain of the p variables or $\pi(a \oplus b)$. For the first two choices of the dissimilarity measures are equivalent and the triangular inequality does not hold. The third choice for ends up in a metric.

It is worth noticing that the previous dissimilarities are closely related to the concept of symmetric difference between two sets. Indeed an interesting class of distances based on the idea of symmetric difference can be applied to the computation of dissimilarity for symbolic data. Let μ be a measure for a set, a possible distance between two sets a_k and b_k could be $D(a_k, b_k) = \mu(a_k - b_k)$ where $a_k - b_k$ denotes the symmetric difference, and if μ coincides with the DP then the previous quantity, for qualitative datasets, reduces to $D(a_k, b_k) = \pi(a_k \oplus b_k) - \pi(a_k \cap b_k)$ which is also a liable option for a dissimilarity measure for interval data, for it is equivalent to Ichino and Jaguchi's distance when $\gamma = 0$. This distance is easily extended to compare two functions f_{a_k} and f_{b_k} (which could be, for instance, two density functions for probabilistic symbolic objects) defined over an interval O_k: $D(a_k, b_k) = \int_{O_k} |f_{a_k} - f_{b_k}| d\mu$

A distance assuming values in $[0,1]$ is:

$$D(a_k, b_k) = \begin{cases} \frac{\mu(a_k - b_k)}{\mu(a_k \cup b_k)} & \text{if } \mu(a_k \cup b_k) > 0 \\ 0 & \text{if } \mu(a_k \cup b_k) = 0 \end{cases}$$

that, when applied to functions defined over the same set, reduces to: $D(a_k, b_k) = \int_{O_k} |f_{a_k} - f_{b_k}| d\mu / \int_{O_k} \max(f_{a_k} - f_{b_k}) d\mu$.

The previous distance can be slightly modified, taking into account the measure of the domain O of the sets

$$D(a_k, b_k) = \begin{cases} \frac{\mu(a_k - b_k)}{\mu(O) - \mu(a_k \cap b_k)} & \text{if } \mu(O) - \mu(a_k \cap b_k) > 0 \\ 0 & \text{if } \mu(O) - \mu(a_k \cap b_k) = 0 \end{cases}$$

All the quantities proposed can be used on single features of symbolic data or on the whole symbolic object considering the notion of DP, which, for a boolean symbolic object $a = \wedge_{i=1}^p [y_i \in a_i]$ can be considered a measure of the volume of the Cartesian product $\times_{i=1}^p a_i$. Another way to compute dissimilarity between symbolic objects as dissimilarity between sets is to use the Hausdorff distance, which was initially defined to compare two sets. Given the function $h(A, B) = \sup_{a \in A} \inf_{b \in B} \|b - a\|$, the Hausdorff distance between two sets A and B both in $\Re^p$ is defined as $\max \{h(A, B), h(B, A)\}$. In the particular case of vectors of intervals this distance can be computed as $D(a, b) = \sum_{i=1}^p \max \left\{ |\underline{b}_i - \underline{a}_i|, |\overline{b}_i - \overline{a}_i| \right\}$, that, reduces to the city-block distance for degenerate intervals corresponding to points in $\Re^p$.

4 Conclusions

Symbolic data analysis has been introduced by E. Diday in the late 80's. In the last decade we have had many papers, national and international research groups and specific international research to implement adequate software. The well-known SODAS project has produced a prototype software for SDA implemented by 17 institutions of 9 European countries. All these researches have a common ground: a resemblance measure between two or more symbolic objects. The measure of resemblance is different for Booleans objects and for different kinds of variables or probabilistic objects. The choice of the methods to synthesize different resemblance measures is another crucial point in SDA.

The problem of data codification is open particularly with regard to the stability of the conclusions that can be deduced from the data set.

Often the objects are characterised by different kinds of variables many of which have been studied for the first time in Statistics just with reference to this type of analysis (for instance algebra of intervals).

We believe that SDA can improve the approach to explain data. We need to process these data to reduce our information and to gain some understanding of the phenomenon under consideration. SDA has specific applications in Data mining and, particularly, in the elaboration of large data sets. In these researches the stability of the conclusions is very important when new revisions of the data are considered or the data are slightly changed.

SDA has had many kinds of applications but it is still not very well known by scholars, particularly in the Anglo-Saxon academic world, and the applications are generally done in academic circles and refer to classical data, such as Fisher's Iris. It is very complicated to obtain data from firms because of privacy issues and it is also very complicated to codify large data sets in the logic of SDA.

It is our specific opinion that SDA can find very important applications in different sectors of the economy, social sciences, technology and in many other important branches of research. The Software is not yet well known to different people in firms. The heavy formalization of SDA can limit the use by scholars not specifically expert in mathematics and particularly in abstract algebra.

References

BOCCI L.,RIZZI A.,(2000): Misure di prossimità nell'analisi dei dati simbolici, *Società Italiana di Statistica, Atti della XL riunione scientifica*, Firenze,2000

DE BAETS B., DE MEYER H., NAESSENS H.,(2001): A class of rational cardinality-based similarity measures, *Journal of Computational and Applied Mathematics*, 132, 51-69

DE CARVALHO F.A.T.,(1994): Proximity Coefficients between Boolean Symbolic Objects in: *New Approaches in classification and Data Analysis*, Diday, E. & Lechevallier, Y. & Schader, M. and

ESPOSITO F., MALERBA D., TAMMA V., BOCK H. H.,(2000): Classical Resemblance Measures, in *Analysis of Symbolic Data. Exploratory Methods for extracting statistical information from complex data*, Bock, H.H., and Diday E., (Eds.), Series: studies in classification, data analysis and Knowledge Organization, Vol. 15, Springer-Verlag, Berlin, ISBN 3-540-66619-2

GOWDA K. C., DIDAY E.,(1992): Symbolic Clustering using a new similarity measure. *IEEE Transaction on Systems, Man and Cybernetics* 22 (2), 368-378,

ICHINO M., YAGUCHI H., (1994): General Minkowski metrics for mixed type data analysis, *IEEE Transaction on System, Man and Cybernetics*, 24, 4, pp. 698-708

LAURO N.C., VERDE R., PALUMBO F.,(2000): Factorial Discriminant Analysis on Symbolic Objects, in *Analysis of Symbolic Data. Exploratory Methods for extracting statistical information from complex data*, Bock, H.H., and Diday E., (Eds.), Vol. 15, Springer-Verlag, Berlin, ISBN 3-540-66619-2

MALERBA D., ESPOSITO F., GIOVIALE V. & TAMMA V.,(2001): Comparing dissimilarity measures in Symbolic Data Analysis. *Proceedings of the Joint Conferences on New Techniques and Technologies for Statistics and Exchange of Technology and Know-how (ETK-NTTS'01)*, 473-481

MALI K., MITRA S.,(2003): Clustering and its validation in a symbolic framework, *Pattern Recognition Letters* 24, 2367-2376

NAGABHUSHAN P.,GOWDA K.C., DIDAY E.,(1995): Dimensionality reduction of symbolic data, *Pattern Recognition Letters*, 16, 219-223

PÉRINEL E., LECHEVALLIER Y.,(2000): Symbolic Discrimination Rules, in *Analysis of Symbolic Data. Exploratory Methods for extracting statistical information from complex data*, Bock, H.H., and Diday E., (Eds.), Vol. 15, Springer-Verlag, Berlin, ISBN 3-540-66619-2

RAVI T.V., GOWDA K.,(1999): An ISODATA clustering procedure for symbolic objects using a distributed genetic algorithm, *Pattern Recognition Letters* 20, 659-666.

RIZZI, A.,(1998): Metriche nell'analisi dei dati simbolici, *Statistica*, 4, 577-588

VLADUTU L.,PAPADIMITRIOU S., MAVROUDI S., BEZERIANOS A.,(2001): Generalised RBF Networks Trained Using and IBL Algorithm for Mining Symbolic Data, in *Advances in Knowledge Discovery and Data Mining*, 5th *Pacific-Asia Conference*, 2001, Hong Kong, China, Cheung D., G. J. Williams and Q. Li (Eds.) Series, Lecture Notes in Artificial Intelligence Volume 2035, pp. 587-593, Springer-Verlag Heidelberg.

Constrained Clusterwise Linear Regression

Antonella Plaia

Dipartimento di Scienze Statistiche e Matematiche "S. Vianelli",
Università di Palermo, Italy
plaia@unipa.it

Abstract. In market segmentation, Conjoint Analysis is often used to estimate the importance of a product attributes at the level of each single customer, clustering, successively, the customers whose behavior can be considered similar. The preference model parameter estimation is made considering data (usually opinions) of a single customer at a time, but these data are usually very few as each customer is called to express his opinion about a small number of different products (in order to simplify his/her work). In the present paper a Constrained Clusterwise Linear Regression algorithm is presented, that allows simultaneously to estimate parameters and to cluster customers, using, for the estimation, the data of all the customers with similar behavior.

1 Introduction

Conjoint analysis (CA) is one of many techniques for handling situations in which a decision maker has to deal with options that simultaneously vary across two or more attributes. By CA we can estimate the structure of a consumer's preference (i.e., estimate preference parameters such as part-worths, importance weights, ...), given his or her overall evaluations of a set of alternatives that are prespecified in terms of levels of different attributes (Green and Srinivasan (1990)). Let's think, for example, to a new product to be introduced in an existing competitive array, or to possible changes in current product: how consumers might react? The product can be described by K *attributes* (characteristics), which can assume a certain number of levels each. Each combination of these attribute levels represents a particular product, that, here, is called *profile* or *stimulus*. In the full profile technique for data collection, a sample of respondents is asked to judge (for example to rate on a 0 - 10 scale) a complete set of alternative products, usually obtained considering a factorial design of the attribute levels. In the data analysis step, the importance weight for each attribute of the products is analytically determined, according to one of the possible conjoint preference model. If a vector model is assumed, the *l-th* respondent's preference for the *j-th* stimulus, y_{lj}, is given by:

$$y_{lj} = \sum_{k=1}^{K} w_{lk} x_{jk}. \tag{1}$$

where w_{lk} denotes the l-th respondent's importance weight for each of the K attributes and x_{jk} is k-th attribute level in the j-th stimulus.

Ordinary Least Squares (OLS) applied to the data of each respondent allow to estimate the importance weights w_{lk}, and the estimation is as much better as much greater the number of "observations" (that is stimuli) is. But the greater the number of stimuli, that is the number of products to judge, the less reliable the judges. So the problem is: how these estimates can be improved, in terms of degrees of freedom, that is in terms of number of "observations", without increasing the number of stimuli each respondent has to judge? A way could be to estimate parameters for groups rather than individuals, by pooling together data from "similar" respondents. That is, if we could cluster "similar" respondents we could use all the data corresponding to clustered units to estimate the parameters of a single model. The homogeneity inside clusters has to concern model parameters and not data themselves. Therefore, we should, on one side, estimate each single model parameters in order to cluster similar respondents, but, on the other, we should find similarity among respondents before estimating model parameters. How to solve for this problem?

2 Conjoint analysis versus constrained clusterwise linear regression

As far as the final goal of CA is market segmentation, by clusterwise linear regression (CLR) (Spath (1979)) we can simultaneously solve for the optimal feasible partition of respondents, and the parameters of the respondent's preference model in each group.

Generally, when we speak about classification of linear relationships we think to a model of the type:

$$y_i = \sum_{c=1}^{C} \sum_{k=1}^{K} a_{ic} \beta_k^c x_{ik} + \varepsilon. \tag{2}$$

where:
y_i is the ith observation of the dependent variable, $i = 1, 2, \cdots, n$;
x_{ik} is the ith observation of the kth regressor, $i = 1, 2, \cdots, n, k = 1, 2, \cdots, K$;
β_k^c is the kth regression coefficient in cluster c, $k = 1, 2, \cdots, K$, $c = 1, 2, \cdots, C$;

$a_{ic} = \begin{cases} 1 \text{ if unit } i \text{ belongs to cluster } c \\ 0 \text{ otherwise} \end{cases}$

$\varepsilon \sim N(0, \sigma^2)$.

In such a model the parameters to be estimated are: the number of clusters C, the coefficients of regression in each cluster and the membership of each unit to clusters. Starting from a $K+1$-dimensional n-sample, (do not confuse n, that is the total number of observations, with L, number of respondents, or J, number of stimuli; of course, $n = J * L$) and considering a random starting partition of units, the "All Substitution at a the Same Time" (ASST) algorithm proposed in Plaia (submitted) moves, at each iteration, from a cluster to another, all the units that, changing cluster, reduce the objective function (3):

$$Z = \sum_{c=1}^{C} \sum_{i=1}^{n_c} \left(y_i - \sum_{k=1}^{K} b_k^c x_{ik} \right)^2 = \sum_{c=1}^{G} SSE_c. \tag{3}$$

that is reduce the sum of the squares of errors over the C clusters.

For example in Fig. 1, unit P moves from cluster 2 to cluster 1 if this reduces the objective function (3). In particular, differently from Spath's exchange algorithm, the ASST one considers, at each iteration, *all the exchanges* which cut down the objective function (3), respecting the constraint on the minimum number per cluster: this constraint guarantees for parameters estimability inside each cluster (the estimation is repeated at the end of each iteration).

The procedure stops as soon as the solution becomes stable, that is when no more exchanges can reduce (3).

This algorithm improves Spath's Exchange algorithm as the number of iterations to converge is less than 1/60 of Spath's, as shown in Plaia (submitted).

In order to be applied instead of CA, a contiguity constrain has to be added to ASST algorithm: that is, while trying to improve the partition according to (3), each group of J observations which represent the opinion of a single respondent has to remain in the same cluster. This represents a considerable reduction in the number of feasible partitions from the unconstrained case. The proposed methodology has been tested by means of a number of Monte-Carlo simulations, as it will be better explained in the following sections.

3 Constrained clusterwise linear regression

Given an n-sample with a generic $(K+1)$-dimensional element $(y_i, x_{i1}, x_{i2}, \ldots, x_{iK})$, where $x_{i1}, x_{i2}, \ldots, x_{iK}$ are independent variables and y_i is the dependent variable, we can say that the problem of "constrained clusterwise linear regression" (CCLR) consists in finding an appropriate number of clusters of the observations, say C, such that respondents inside each cluster are homogeneous in the sense that their preference model, and therefore its parameters are similar.

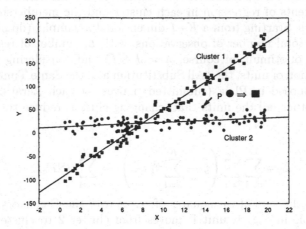

Fig. 1. Exchange algorithm.

The procedure can be summarized as follow:

STEP 1

    I Set $C = 1$ and estimate model (2) parameters.

    II Compute sample coefficient of determination $R^2_{1,1}$. If $R^2_{1,1} \geq \delta$, we conclude that a single preference model is common to all respondents. If $R^2_{1,1} < \delta$ go to STEP 2 (δ is a threshold for the coefficient of determination, for example $\delta = 0.8$).

STEP 2

    I Set $C = 2$ and choose an initial random bipartition respecting the contiguity constraints: that is all the data corresponding to a respondent must belong to the same cluster.

    II Estimate the two preference model parameters.

    III Apply ASST algorithm in order to optimize the bipartition, while respecting the contiguity constraint.

    IV Compute the two coefficients of determination $R^2_{2,1}$ and $R^2_{2,2}$. If both of them are greater than or equal to δ, we conclude that $C = 2$ is the most appropriate number of clusters: the optimal partition has been found. If at least one of the two coefficients of determination is lower that δ, go on to STEP 3.

STEP 3

    I Choose an initial random bipartition, respecting the contiguity constraints, for the cluster whose coefficient of determination is lower than δ (if there are more than one, consider only the first cluster).

    II Estimate preference model parameters in each cluster.

III Apply ASST algorithm in order to optimize the C-partition ($C = 3$ the first time we pass through STEP 3), while respecting the contiguity constraint.

IV Compute the coefficients of determination $R^2_{C,1}$, $R^2_{C,2}$, ..., $R^2_{C,C}$. If these are all greater than or equal to δ, we conclude that C is the most appropriate number of clusters: the optimal partition has been found. If at least one of the coefficients of determination is lower that δ, go back to the beginning of STEP 3.

As a result we have estimated both the number of clusters C, that is the number of preference model, the membership of each respondent to clusters, and the preference model parameters.

4 Simulations and results

In order to study the performances of the proposed methodology, Monte-Carlo simulation has been used, according to the parameters in Table 4.

Considering a product described by 6 attributes ($K = 6$), 4 2-level and 2 3-level, a 16 trials orthogonal main effect factorial design (Addelman (1962)) has been considered (Table 4); the design defines the 16 stimuli each of the 1,000 respondents has to judge (n=16,000), on a 0-10 scale. We also suppose that the actual number of clusters can be 2, 3 or 4: these looks like a sensible number of clusters with only 1,000 respondents, but can be changed without compromising CCLR.

Variables	Levels
N. of respondents	1,000
N. of attributes	6
	4 2-level, 2 3-level
N. of stimuli	16
N. of clusters	2, 3, 4

Table 1. Simulation parameters

Algorithm outline:

1. Generate data for a given number of clusters (2, 3, or 4), that is generate ε from a Normal$(0, 1)$ and vector β from Uniform, get y according to model (2), and rescale y on a $0 - 10$ scale.
2. Generate a random starting size-2 partition, respecting the contiguity constrain.
3. Estimate model parameters inside each cluster, by OLS.
4. Redefine the partition by applying ASST algorithm, respecting the contiguity constrain.

x_1	x_2	x_3	x_4	x_5		x_6	
-1	-1	-1	-1	-1	1	-1	1
-1	1	1	1	-1	1	0	-1
1	-1	1	1	-1	1	1	1
1	1	-1	-1	-1	1	0	-1
-1	1	1	-1	0	-1	-1	1
-1	-1	-1	1	0	-1	0	-1
1	1	-1	1	0	-1	1	1
1	-1	1	-1	0	-1	0	-1
1	-1	1	1	1	1	-1	1
1	1	-1	-1	1	1	0	-1
-1	-1	-1	-1	1	1	1	1
-1	1	1	1	1	1	0	-1
1	1	-1	1	0	-1	-1	1
1	-1	1	-1	0	-1	0	-1
-1	1	1	-1	0	-1	1	1
-1	-1	-1	1	0	-1	0	-1

Table 2. Orthogonal main effect factorial design

5. Repeat steps 3-4 until the partition becomes stable.
6. Increase the number of groups if at least one of the coefficients of determination (of regression model inside clusters) is lower than a predefined level ($R^2 < 0.8$), with a new starting partition obtained dividing randomly, in two groups, the group whose coefficient of determination is lower than 0.8 and go to step 3, otherwise, go to the next step.
7. Repeat steps 2-6 for 5 times (in order to verify if a different starting point can lead to a different solution).

At the end of step 6 an "optimal" partition is gained. The algorithm is applied with all the considered cluster sizes (2, 3 and 4).

The results reported in Table 4 refer to 750 runs of the outlined algorithm: that is, 50 runs (steps 1-6), each replicated with 5 random starting size-2 partition (step 7) for each of the considered cluster sizes (2, 3, 4). The estimated "optimal" partition is compared with the true one by means of the index proposed by Rand (1971), bounded between 0 and 1 (0 means two completely different partitions, 1 two identical partitions).

Table 4 also shows the percentage of success of the procedure, that is the number of times the right number of clusters is found, and the ratio between the mean (over all the clusters) coefficient of determination for the "optimal" partition and the true mean coefficient of determination. With the true number of clusters equal to 2, the percentage of success is total, as the obtained partition is identical to the true one, and therefore parameter estimate is the best. With the true number of clusters equal to 3, the percentage of success is 88.66%, with an obtained partition identical to the true one; in the 11.34% of cases the estimated number of clusters is 2 (underestimate), but with an

True number of clusters		Estimated Number of Clusters		
		2	3	4
2	% success	100%		
	Rand index	1		
	Mean coefficient of determination rate	1		
3	% success	11.34%	88.66%	
	Rand index	0.89	1	
	Mean coefficient of determination rate	0.94	1	
4	% success		22.40%	77.60%
	Rand index		0.91	1
	Mean coefficient of determination rate		0.96	1

Table 3. Percentage of success and mean values of the indices for the comparison of partitions

"optimal" partition that is always very similar to the true one (Rand index is about 0.9); the ratio between the mean coefficient of determination for the "optimal" partition and the true mean coefficient of determination is very high as well, so the procedure underestimates the number of clusters because two groups in the simulated data were very similar.

To better understand this underestimation, let us consider Fig. 2. The 1000 respondents should correctly be partitioned in four clusters, as four regression lines are present (Fig. 2 a). Actually, two regression lines fit well too, as the two regression coefficients, $R_1^2 = 0.8434$ and $R_2^2 = 0.8394$ show (Fig. 2 b). Of course, even if with just two regression lines we reach our aim (a good fit), the Rand index cannot have a high value (close to 1), as many couples of units belonging to different clusters according to the first partition will be in the same cluster in partition 2 (all the couples made by one unit of cluster 1 (or 3) and one of cluster 2 (or 4)).

With the true number of clusters equal to 4, the percentage of success is 77.60%, with an obtained partition identical to the true one; in the 22.40% of cases the estimated number of clusters is 3 (underestimate), but with an "optimal" partition that is always very similar to the true one (Rand index is about 0.9); the ratio between the mean coefficient of determination for the "optimal" partition and the true mean coefficient of determination is very high as well, so again, the procedure underestimates the number of clusters because two groups in the simulated data were very similar. Finally, it is important to highlight that only an overestimate of the number of clusters represents a real fault for the algorithm, but this never happens.

So we can conclude that, if the objective is to find the partition with the fewest number of clusters, that provides a satisfactory fit to the data, the Constrained Clusterwise Linear Regression always gets it.

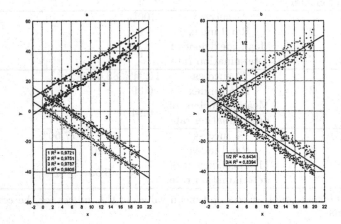

Fig. 2. Example of misclassification?

5 Conclusions

This paper proposed a new method, based on ASST algorithm proposed in Plaia (submitted), called Constrained Clusterwise Linear Regression, to be used instead of Conjoint Analysis. Differently from CA, CCLR allows to find, simultaneously, both the optimal feasible partition of respondents and the parameters of respondent's preference model in each cluster of the partition.

Simulation results have shown the algorithm good performance for an example consisting in a 1,000 respondent sample who have to express their opinion about a 6 attribute product. Of course, CCLR can be applied to different sample sizes and to product described by a diverse number of attributes, without loosing its potentiality.

References

ADDELMAN S. (1962): Orthogonal main-effect plans for asymmetrical factorial experiments. *Technometrics, 4, 21-26.*

GREEN P. E. and SRINIVASAN V. (1990): Conjoint analysis in marketing: new developments with implication for research and practice. *Journal of Marketing, 25, 3-19.*

PLAIA, A. (2003): New Algorithms for Clusterwise Linear Regression. *submitted to Computational Statistics and Data Analysis.*

RAND, W. L. (1971):Objective criteria for the evaluation of clustering methods. *Journal of the American Statistical Association, 66(336), 846-850.*

SPATH, H. (1979): Clusterwise Linear Regression. *Computing, 22:367-373.*

Crossed Clustering Method on Symbolic Data Tables

Rosanna Verde[1] and Yves Lechevallier[2]

[1] Seconda Università di Napoli - Italy
rosanna.verde@unina2.it
[2] INRIA - Rocquencourt, Domaine de Voluceau - France
Yves.Lechevallier@inria.fr

Abstract. In this paper a crossed clustering algorithm is proposed to partitioning a set of symbolic objects in a fixed number of classes. This algorithm allows, at the same time, to determine a structure (taxonomy) on the categories of the object descriptors. This procedure is an extension of the classical simultaneous clustering algorithms, proposed on binary and contingency tables. It is based on a dynamical clustering algorithm on symbolic objects. The optimized criterion is the ϕ^2 distance computed between the objects description, given by modal variables (distributions) and the prototypes of the classes, described by marginal profiles of the objects set partitions. The convergence of the algorithm is guaranteed at a stationary value of the criterion, in correspondence of the best partition of the symbolic objects in r classes and the best partition of the symbolic descriptors in c groups. An application on web log data has allowed to validate the procedure and suggest it as an useful tool in the Web Usage Mining context.

1 Introduction

In Symbolic Data Analysis (SDA) framework, a generalization of clustering dynamic algorithm (Diday, 1971, Celeux et al. 1989) has been proposed (Chavent, 1997; Chavent et al., 2003; De Carvalho et al., 2001; Verde et al., 2000) in order to partition a set E of symbolic objects (hereafter denoted SO's), described by multi-valued variables (interval, multi-categorical, modal), in a predefined number k of homogeneous clusters. Like in the classical clustering algorithm, the optimized criterion is a measure of the best fitting between the partition and the classes representation of such partition. The first phase of the clustering process consists of choosing a suitable clusters representation. Due to the nature of the symbolic data, we propose to represent the classes by means of *prototypes* which summarize the whole information of the SO's belonging to each class. Each prototype is even modelled like a SO. Furthermore, depending on the type of the cluster representation, every object of E is assigned to a class according its proximity to prototype. In SO clustering methods, several distances and dissimilarity measures have been proposed as allocation (or assignment) functions. In particular, whereas both SO's and prototypes are described by interval variables, the most suitable distance, defined between intervals, seems to be the Hausdroff distance (Chavent et al., 2003); while, if they are described by modal variables, the dissimilarity measure can be chosen among classical distances between distributions (e.g. ϕ^2) or, applying to context dependent measures (De Carvalho et al., 2001). Finally, if the SO descriptors are symbolic variables of different nature (interval, multi-categorical, modal) it possible to homogeneize them in modal ones.

The convergence of the algorithm to a stationary value of the criterion is guaranteed by the consistency between the type representation of the classes and the properties of the allocation function. Different algorithms, even referring to the same scheme, have been proposed depending on the nature of the SO descriptors and on the allocation function.

Generalized dynamic algorithm on symbolic objects has already found interesting applications in different contexts of analysis, for instance in: clustering archaeological data, described by multi-categorical variables; looking for typologies of waves, characterized by intervals values; analyzing similarities between the different shapes of micro-organism, described by both multi-categorical and intervals; comparing social-economics characteristics in different geographical areas with respect to the distributions of some variables (e.g.: economics activities; income distributions; worked hours; etc).

The main advantage of using a symbolic cluster algorithm is surely in comparing and clustering aggregated and structured data. In this perspective, a generalization of crossed clustering algorithm (Govaert, 1977, 1995) to symbolic data can appear interesting in this context of analysis and it is here proposed too. Such algorithm performs iteratively a cluster on the rows and on the variables of a symbolic data table.

2 General scheme of dynamical clustering algorithm

Let E a set of symbolic objects s described by p symbolic variables y_j ($j = 1, \ldots, p$) and a weight $\mu_s > 0$. According to the standard dynamic clustering algorithm (Celeux et al.,1989) we look for the partition $P \in P_k$ of E in k classes, among all the possible partitions P_k, and the vector $L \in L_k$ of k prototypes $(g_1, \ldots, g_i, \ldots, g_k)$ representing the classes in P, such that, a criterion Δ of fitting between L and P is minimized:

$$\Delta(P^*, L^*) = Min\{\Delta(P, L) \mid P \in P_k, L \in L_k\}$$

This criterion is defined as the weighted sum of the dissimilarities $\delta(x_s, g_i)$ between the descriptions of the SO's of E collected in a vector x_s and the prototype g_i representing the cluster C_i, for all the clusters C_i ($i = 1, ..., k$) and for all the objects s of C_i:

$$\Delta(P, L) = \sum_{i=1}^{k} \sum_{s \in C_i} \mu_s . \delta^2(x_s, g_i) \text{ where: } C_i \in P, g_i \in \Lambda$$

The dynamic algorithm is performed in the following steps:

a) *Initialization*: a random partition $P = (C_1, \ldots, C_k)$ of E is performed.
b) *representation step*:

      for j=1 to k, find g_h associated to C_h such that:
$$\sum_{x_s \in C_h} \mu_s . \delta^2(x_s, g_h) \text{ is minimized}$$

c) *allocation step*:

      test $\longleftarrow$ 0
      for all x_s do
        find m such that C_m is the class of s of E
        find l such that: $l = \arg\min_{h=1,\ldots,k} \delta(x_s, g_h)$
        if $l \neq m$
          test $\longleftarrow$ 1; $C_l \longleftarrow C_l \cup \{x_s\}$ and $C_m \longleftarrow C_m - \{x_s\}$

d) if $test = 0$ then stop, else go to b)

Then, the first choice concerns with the representation structure by prototypes $(g_1, \ldots, g_k)$ for the classes $\{C_1, \ldots, C_k\} \in P$.
The criterion $\Delta(P, L)$ is an additive function on the k clusters and the N elements of E. Therefore, Δ decreases under the following conditions:

- *uniqueness* of the affectation cluster for each element of E;
- *uniqueness* of the prototype g_h which minimizes the criterion Δ for all the cluster C_h (for $h = 1, \ldots, k$) of the partition P of E.

3 Crossed dynamical clustering algorithm

The proposed crossed dynamical clustering algorithm aims at finding a structure in the symbolic data. The data are collected in a symbolic data table $\mathbf{X}=[X^1, \ldots, X^v, \ldots, X^p]$. Along the rows of $\mathbf{X}$ we find the descriptions of the SO's x_s ($s = 1, ..., N$) of E, while the columns of X^v contain the distributions of the symbolic variables y_v ($v = 1, ..., p$). We assume all the y_v's are multi-categorical ones. We denote with V_v and $V = \bigcup_{v=1}^{p} V_v$ the set of categories of the symbolic variable y_v and the complete set of the several categories of the p variables, respectively.

The general scheme of the dynamical algorithm, described above, is followed to cluster the rows of the symbolic data table $\mathbf{X}$ in a set of homogeneous classes, representing typology of SO's and to group categories of the symbolic variables. According to the aim of obtaining rows partition, a classification of the symbolic descriptors is accomplished. Some authors (Govaert, 1977, Govaert and Nadif, 2003) proposed the maximization of the χ^2 criterion between rows and columns of a contingency table. In our context we extent the crossed clustering algorithm to look for the partition P of the set E in r

classes of objects and the partitions Q in c column-groups of V, according to the Φ^2 criterion on symbolic modal variables:

$$\Delta(P, (Q^1, \ldots, Q^p)) = \sum_{v=1}^{p} \Phi^2(P, Q^v | Q)$$

where: Q^v is the partition associated to the modal variable y_v and $Q = (Q_1, \ldots, Q_c) = (\bigcup_{v=1}^{p} Q_1^v, \ldots, \bigcup_{v=1}^{p} Q_k^v, \ldots, \bigcup_{v=1}^{p} Q_c^v,)$. It worth to notice that the optimized criterion Δ is additive.

The cells of the crossed tables can be modelled by marginal distributions (or profiles) summarizing the classes descriptions of the rows and columns.

$\Delta(P, Q, G)$ is consistent with the criterion of the clustering algorithm. Such that it allows to optimize iteratively the two partitions P and Q, as well as the related representation $\mathbf{G}$.

$$(\mathbf{X^1}, \ldots, \mathbf{X^v} = \begin{pmatrix} x_{1v_1} & \cdots & x_{1v_j} & \cdots & x_{1v_m} \\ \vdots & \vdots & \vdots & \vdots & \vdots \\ x_{sv_1} & \cdots & x_{sv_j} & \cdots & x_{sv_m} \\ \vdots & \vdots & \vdots & \vdots & \vdots \\ x_{Nv_1} & \cdots & x_{Nv_j} & \cdots & x_{Nv_m} \end{pmatrix} \ldots, \mathbf{X^P}) \Rightarrow \mathbf{G} = \begin{pmatrix} g_{11} & \cdots & g_{1c} \\ \cdots & g_{ik} & \cdots \\ g_{r1} & \cdots & g_{rc} \end{pmatrix}$$

The value g_{ik} of the matrix $\mathbf{G}$, counting in the set of rows belonging to the class P_i and the set of columns belonging to the class Q_k, is computed by the following formula:

$$g_{ik} = \sum_{v=1}^{p} \sum_{s \in P_i} \sum_{j \in Q_k^v} x_{sj} = \sum_{s \in P_i} \sum_{j \in Q_k} x_{sj} \tag{1}$$

The marginal profiles of $\mathbf{G}$ matrix is denoted as:

$$g_{.k} = \sum_{i=1}^{r} g_{ik} = \sum_{i=1}^{r} \sum_{s \in P_i} \sum_{j \in Q_k} x_{sj} = \sum_{j \in Q_k} \sum_{s=1}^{N} x_{sj} = \sum_{j \in Q_k} x_{.j}$$

The ϕ^2 distance between a row vector of $\mathbf{X}$ and the row vector $g_i = (g_{i1}, \ldots, g_{ic})$ of $\mathbf{G}$ is computed with respect to the aggregated $\tilde{x}_s$'s rows $\tilde{x}_s^v = (\tilde{x}_{s1}^v, \ldots, \tilde{x}_{sc}^v)$ belonging to the partition Q^v, for each variable y_v, where:

$$\phi^2(\tilde{x}_s^v, g_i) = \sum_{k=1}^{c} \frac{1}{g_{.k}} \left(\frac{\tilde{x}_{sk}^v}{\tilde{x}_{s.}^v} - \frac{g_{ik}}{g_{i.}} \right)^2 \qquad \text{with} \tag{2}$$

$$g_{i.} = \sum_{k=1}^{c} g_{ik} \qquad \tilde{x}_{sk}^v = \sum_{j \in Q_k^v} x_{sj} \qquad \tilde{x}_{s.}^v = \sum_{j=1}^{c} \sum_{j \in Q_k^v} x_{sj}$$

$$d^2(\tilde{x}_s, g_i) = \sum_{v=1}^{p} \phi^2(\tilde{x}_s^v, g_i) \tag{3}$$

The ϕ^2 distance between a column vector of $\mathbf{X}$ and the column vector $g^k = (g_{1k}, \ldots, g_{rk})$ of $\mathbf{G}$ is computed with respect to the aggregated $\tilde{x}^j$'s columns $\tilde{x}^j = (\tilde{x}^{1j}, \ldots, \tilde{x}^{rj})$ belonging to the partition P, where:

$$\phi^2(\tilde{x}^j, g^k) = \sum_{i=1}^{r} \frac{1}{g_{i.}} \left(\frac{\tilde{x}^{ij}}{\tilde{x}^{\cdot j}} - \frac{g_{ik}}{g_{.k}} \right)^2 \quad \text{with} \tag{4}$$

$$g_{.k} = \sum_{i=1}^{r} g_{ik} = \sum_{s=1}^{N} \sum_{j \in Q_k} x_{sj} \qquad \tilde{x}^{ij} = \sum_{s \in P_i} x_{sj} \qquad \tilde{x}^{\cdot j} = \sum_{i=1}^{r} \sum_{s \in P_i} x_{sj} = x_{\cdot j}$$

The Crossed Dynamic Algorithm is performed in the following steps:

a) *Initialization*; a random partition $P = (P_1, \ldots, P_r)$ of E and p random partitions $(Q^v = (Q_1^v, \ldots, Q_c^v), v = 1, \ldots, p)$ are chosen.
b) *Block model representation step:*
   The prototype table G is computed by the formula (1).
c) *Row allocation step:*
   test_row ⟵ 0;
   for all objects s of E do
       Such that P_i is the class of s, find i^* which verifies :
       $i^* = \arg \min_{i=1,\ldots,r} d(\tilde{x}_s, g_i)$ where d is defined by (3)
       if $i^* \neq i$
           test_row ⟵ 1; $P_{i^*} \longleftarrow P_{i^*} \cup \{s\}$ and $P_i \longleftarrow P_i - \{s\}$
d) *Block model representation step:*
   The prototype table G is computed by the formula (1).
e) *Column allocation step:*
   test_column ⟵ 0
   for all variables y_v do
   for all categories j of V^v do
       Such that Q_k^v is the class of j, find j^* which verifies :
       $j^* = \arg \min_{k=1,\ldots,c} \phi(\tilde{x}^j, g^k)$ where ϕ is defined by (4)
       if $j^* \neq j$ test_column ← 1; $Q_{k^*}^v \leftarrow Q_{k^*}^v \cup \{j\}$ and $Q_j^v \leftarrow Q_k^v - \{j\}$
f) if *test_row* = 0 and *test_column* = 0 then stop, else go to b)

According to the inertia decomposition theorem we obtain the relations :

$$\Phi^2(E, Q) = \Delta(P, Q, G) + \Phi^2(P, Q) \tag{5}$$
$$\Phi^2(P, V) = \Delta(P, Q, G) + \Phi^2(P, Q) \tag{6}$$

In row allocation step b) the partition Q and the prototype block model stay fixed, while the criterion $\Delta(P, Q, G) = \sum_{i=1}^{r} \sum_{s \in P_i} x_{s..} d^2(\tilde{x}_s, g_i)$ decreases. By the relation (5) the criterion $\Phi^2(P, Q)$ increases.

In column allocation step e) the partition P and the prototype block model stay fixed, while the criterion $\Delta(P, Q, G) = \sum_{k=1}^{c} \sum_{j \in Q_k^v} x_{.j} \phi^2(\tilde{x}^j, g^k)$ decreases. By the relation (6) the criterion $\Phi^2(P, Q)$ increases. Therefore, globally, the criterion $\Phi^2(P, Q)$ increases in each step of the process.

4 Application

An application of the dynamical algorithms on symbolic data is here shown in the context of the Web Usage Mining (Sauberlich and Huber, 2001). It has been performed on the Web Logs Data, coming from the HTTP log files by the INRIA web server (Lechevallier et al., 2003). This study aims to detect the behavior of the users and, at the same time, to check the effectiveness of the structure of the site. Behind the research of typologies of users, we have defined a hierarchical structure (taxonomy) over the web pages, at different levels of the directories. The data set concern the set of *page views* by visitors which visited the INRIA site from the 1st to the 15th of January, 2003. Globally, the database contained 673.389 clicks (like *page views* in an user session), which were already filtered from robot/spider entries and accesses of graphic files. An important aspect in the analyzing of logfiles is the *navigation* which is a set of clicks relative to the same user.

A further cleaning of the analyzed logfile has been performed in order to keep only the navigations on both URL: *www.inria.fr* and *www-sop.inria.fr*. Moreover, only *long navigations* (duration $\geq$ 60s, the ratio duration/number of clicks $\geq$ *4sec.* and number of visited pages $\geq$ 10) has been taken into account for the analysis. The selected navigations were 2639, corresponding to 145643 clicks. For sake of brevity, we have restrained our analysis just to two web sites at the highest level. The visited pages were collected in semantic topics according to the structure of the two web sites. In particular the clicks on the web site *www.inria.fr* were referred to 44 topics; while the clicks on the web site *www-sop.inria.fr*, to 69 topics. Thus, we have considered the 2639 as symbolic objects described by two symbolic multi-categorical variables: *www.inria.fr* and *www-sop.inria.fr* having 44 and 69 categories respectively. The data have been collected in a symbolic tables where each row contains the descriptions of a symbolic object (navigation), the distribution of the visited topics on the two websites. Following our aim to study the behavior of the INRIA web users, we have performed a symbolic clustering analysis to identify homogeneous typology of users according to the sequence of the visited web pages or, better, according to the occurrences of the visited pages of the several semantic topics.

The results of the navigation set partition in 12 classes and of the topics one in 8 classes, constituted by the two partitions Q^1 and Q^2, are shown in the Table 1.

Topic_1	Topic_2	Topic_3	Topic_4
/www/partenaires	/www/projets	/www/presse	/www/dias
/www/agos-sophia	/www/rrrt	/www/actualites-siege	/sop/dias
/www/modeles	/www/w3c	/www/multimedia	
/sop/partenaires	/www/manifestations	/www/icons	
/sop/agos-sophia	/sop/projets	/www/fonctions	
/sop/color	/sop/sophia	/sop/chir	
/sop/interne-sophia	/sop/site-eng	/sop/direction	
/sop/wiki	/sop/externe		
/sop/modeles	/sop/colloquium	Topic_7	Topic_8
/sop/sapr	/sop/horde		
/sop/didacticiel	/sop/manifestations	/www/recherche	/www/sophia
/sop/ctime	/sop/international	/www/accueil-siege	/www/site-old
/sop/freesoft		/www/personnel	/sop/cgi-bin
		/www/intro-inria	/sop/commun
		/www/publications	/sop/accueil-sophia
Topic_5	Topic_6	/www/cgi-bin	/sop/intro-sophia
		/www/ra	/sop/actualites-sophia
/www/travailler	/www/rapports	/www/interne-siege	/sop/rev
/www/formation	/www/semir	/www/international	/sop/intech
/www/valorisation	/sop/rapports	/www/site-beta	/sop/services
/sop/formation	/sop/semir	/www/sophia-antipolis	/sop/challengeTV
/sop/recherche	/sop/rmi	/www/thesauria	/sop/xml

Table 1. Topic descriptions groups

For example, the *Topic_5* associated to the group Q^5 is composed by two subgroups, one for each website, $Q_1^5=\{travailler, formation, valorisation\}$ for the website *www* and $Q_1^5=\{formation, recherche\}$ for the website *sop*.

It is worth to notice as the 8 topics groups correspond to different typology of information. In particular, the 8 groups can be identified as follows:

T-group 1 → *INTRANET*; T-group 2 → *Scientific information: Conferences, project activities*; T-group 3 → *Dissemination*; T-group 4 → *dias*; T-group 5 → *Training*; T-group 6 → *Research activity*; T-group 7 → *Headquarter (www.inria.fr)*; T-group 8 → *Headquarter - Sophia research activity*.

From the classification, Table 2, we can remark that: the topics-group 2 represents the set of the most visited topics by the users; the users of the class 8 have visited this group attentively more than the others; the topics-group 1 represents the set of topics specially visited by the users of the class 3; the topic group 1 contains the internal internet users of INRIA. Therefore, analyzing the classes of navigations, we note that: the class 3 contains the navigations with an high number of visited pages; the users of this class have visited different topic groups (1,2,6 and 7); the class 4 contains the navigations which have been visited only the topics group 5. This topics group represents the general topics of INRIA (training, researchers, scientific meetings, etc.)

This application on real data must be considered as a brief example of an automatic clustering on structure complex data aiming to perform simultaneously typologies of navigations and groups of topics, homogenous from a semantic point of view.

An extension of our approach to more web sites or to several symbolic variables would be able to take into account a hierarchical structure of complex data descriptors. According to our example, in the clustering process, if

	Topic_1	Topic_2	Topic_3	Topic_4	Topic_5	Topic_6	Topic_7	Topic_8	pages
Navigation_ 1	222	1470	587	34	611	80	18757	143	21904
Navigation_ 2	78	2381	254	7	3094	80	2055	249	8198
Navigation_ 3	8578	7767	425	309	448	2749	2091	1386	23753
Navigation_ 4	29	280	115	7	3387	7	347	91	4263
Navigation_ 5	209	242	9	26	23	2544	221	55	3329
Navigation_ 6	29	1185	3204	28	1247	19	2670	82	8464
Navigation_ 7	43	140	22	795	39	47	218	636	1940
Navigation_ 8	288	35742	920	90	594	308	2174	1101	41217
Navigation_ 9	186	1040	136	106	283	72	370	3739	5932
Navigation_10	24	39	6	2786	2	25	49	210	3141
Navigation_11	175	7630	606	87	574	326	10227	257	19882
Navigation_12	4	231	3088	4	96	8	179	10	3620
Total pages	9865	58147	9372	4279	10398	6265	39358	7959	145643

Table 2. Contingence table of the navigations and topic groups

rubriques at lower level of the web architecture are grouped in homogeneous topics, their belonging to a higher level of the web site must be made save.

In conclusion, the most relevant difference of the crossed clustering algorithm on complex data with respect to the one on classical data, is surely in its extension to multi-valued categorical variables with an associated hierarchical structure.

References

CELEUX, G., DIDAY, E., GOVAERT, G., LECHEVALLIER, Y., RALAM-BONDRAINY, H. (1989): *Classification Automatique des Données, Environnement statistique et informatique.* Bordas, Paris.

CHAVENT, M., DE CARVALHO, F.A.T., LECHEVALLIER, Y., VERDE, R. (2003): Trois nouvelles méthodes de classification automatique de données symboliques de type intervalle. *Revue de Statistique Appliquées,* n. 4.

DE CARVALHO, F.A.T, VERDE, R., LECHEVALLIER, Y. (2001): Deux nouvelles méthodes de classification automatique d'ensembles d'objets symboliques décrits par des variables intervalles. *SFC'2001,* Guadeloupe.

DIDAY, E. (1971): La méthode des Nuées dynamiques *Revue de Statistique Appliquée, 19, 2, 19–34.*

GOVAERT, G. (1977): Algorithme de classification d'un tableau de contingence. In Proc. of *first international symposium on Data Analysis and Informatics,* INRIA, Versailles, 487–500.

GOVAERT, G. (1995): Simultaneous clustering of rows and columns. *Control Cybernet.,* 24, 437–458

GOVAERT, G., NADIF M. (2003): Clustering with block mixture models. *Pattern Recognition,* Elservier Science Publishers, 36, 463-473

LECHEVALLIER, Y., TROUSSE, B., VERDE, R., TANASA, D. (2003): *Classification automatique: Applications au Web-Mining.* In: Proceeding of SFC2003, Neuchatel, 10–12 September.

SAUBERLICH, F., HUBER K.-P. (2001) : A Framework for Web Usage Mining on Anonymous Logfile Data. In : Schwaiger M. and Opitz O.(Eds.): *Exploratory Data Analysis in Empirical Research,* Springer-Verlag, Heidelberg, 309–318.

VERDE, R., DE CARVALHO, F.A.T., LECHEVALLIER, Y. (2000) : A Dynamical Clustering Algorithm for Multi-Nominal Data. In : H.A.L. Kiers, J.-P. Rasson, P.J.F. Groenen and M. Schader (Eds.): *Data Analysis, Classification, and Related Methods,* Springer-Verlag, Heidelberg, 387–394.

Part II

Multivariate Statistics and Data Analysis

Some Statistical Applications of Centrosymmetric Matrices

Estela Bee Dagum[1], Laura Guidotti[2], and Alessandra Luati[1]

[1] Dipartimento di Scienze Statistiche
Università di Bologna, Italy
beedagum@stat.unibo.it, luati@stat.unibo.it
[2] Dipartimento di Matematica,
Università di Bologna, Italy
guidotti@dm.unibo.it

Abstract. Centrosymmetric matrices have been recently studied on an algebraic point of view: properties like the existence of the inverse, the expression of the determinant and the eigenspaces characterisation in the case of square matrices have been object of interest. The theoretical results obtained for this class of matrices find applications in many fields of statistics.
In this study, we introduce two classes of centrosymmetric matrices that are used in probability calculus and time series analysis, namely, the transition matrices for the classification of states of periodic Markov chains and the smoothing matrices for signal extraction problems.

1 Introduction

A matrix $\mathbf{C} \in \mathbb{R}^{m \times n}$ of generic element c_{ij}, $i = 1, \ldots, m$ and $j = 1, \ldots, n$, is *rectangular centrosymmetric* (Weaver, 1985), if

$$c_{ij} = c_{m+1-i, n+1-j}.$$

A centrosymmetric matrix is symmetric with respect to its geometric center and can be equivalently defined as the matrix $\mathbf{C} \in \mathbb{R}^{m \times n}$ satisfying the relation

$$\mathbf{C} = \mathbf{E}_m \mathbf{C} \mathbf{E}_n$$

where $\mathbf{E}_k \in \mathbb{R}^{k \times k}$ is the permutation matrix with ones on the cross diagonal (bottom left to top right) and zeros elsewhere, *i.e.* of generic element $e_{ij} = 1$ if $i + j = k + 1$ and $e_{ij} = 0$ otherwise, for $i, j = 1, \ldots, k$.

Centrosymmetric matrices can be found in many applications in statistics and time series analysis. The most commonly known are: the symmetric Toeplitz matrices $\mathbf{R} \in \mathbb{R}^{m \times m}$ of generic element $r_{ij} = r_{i+k, j+k} = r_{ji}, i, j = 1, \ldots, m, k = 1, \ldots, m - 1$ for the autocorrelation of stationary time series (see Trench, 1997); the commutation matrix $\mathbf{K}_{mn} \in \mathbb{R}^{mn \times mn}$ such that $\mathbf{K}_{mn} vec\mathbf{A} = \mathbf{K}_{mn} vec\mathbf{A}^{\prime}$, where $vec\mathbf{A}$ is the vector obtained by stacking the column of the matrix $\mathbf{A}$ one underneath the other (see Magnus and Neudecker, 1979). Furthermore, Iosifescu (1980) and Kimura (1957) transition matrices for some Markov chain in genetic problems are centrosymmetric. Recently, (rectangular) centrosymmetric matrices also can be viewed as a particular case of (generalized) reflexive matrices whose properties have been recently employed in linear least-squares problems (Chen, 1998).

In this study we derive some properties of centrosymmetric matrices which find application in two different statistical problems, that are the classification of the states of a finite Markov chain, and the filtering of time series in a process of signal extraction.

2 Properties of centrosymmetric matrices

Centrosymmetric matrices inherit desirable properties from the properties of the permutation matrices $\mathbf{E}_k$ which are: (a) symmetric (b) orthogonal and (c) reflections, $i.e.$

$$\mathbf{E}_k \overset{(a)}{=} \mathbf{E}_k^T \overset{(b)}{=} \mathbf{E}_k^{-1} \text{ and } \mathbf{E}_k^2 \overset{(c)}{=} \mathbf{I}_k$$

where $\mathbf{I}_k$ is the identity matrix of order k and $\mathbf{E}_k^T$ and $\mathbf{E}_k^{-1}$ stand for the transpose and the inverse of $\mathbf{E}_k$, respectively. Useful references concerning the properties of centrosymmetric matrices can be found in Andrew (1998). However, the main characteristic of the set

$$\mathcal{C}_n = \left\{ \mathbf{C} \in \mathbb{R}^{n \times n}, c_{ij} = c_{n+1-i,n+1-j}, \forall i,j = 1, \ldots, n < \infty \right\},$$

of square centrosymmetric matrices of order n is that it is an **algebra** (Weaver, 1985). In fact, let $\mathbf{C}, \mathbf{C}_1, \mathbf{C}_2, \mathbf{C}_3 \in \mathcal{C}_n$ and $\alpha \in \mathbb{K}$. Then, the following properties characterising $\mathcal{C}_n$ as an algebra hold:

1. $\mathbf{C}_1 + \mathbf{C}_2 \in \mathcal{C}_n$.
2. $\mathbf{C}_1 + \mathbf{C}_2 = \mathbf{C}_2 + \mathbf{C}_1$.
3. $\mathbf{C}_1 + (\mathbf{C}_2 + \mathbf{C}_3) = (\mathbf{C}_1 + \mathbf{C}_2) + \mathbf{C}_3$.
4. $\exists \mathbf{O} \in \mathcal{C}_n, \mathbf{C}_1 + \mathbf{O} = \mathbf{C}_1$.
5. $\exists - \mathbf{C}_1 \in \mathcal{C}_n, \mathbf{C}_1 + (-\mathbf{C}_1) = \mathbf{O}$.
6. $\mathbf{C}_1 \mathbf{C}_2 \in \mathcal{C}_n$.
7. $\mathbf{C}_1 (\mathbf{C}_2 \mathbf{C}_3) = (\mathbf{C}_1 \mathbf{C}_2) \mathbf{C}_3$.
8. $\mathbf{C}_1 (\mathbf{C}_2 + \mathbf{C}_3) = \mathbf{C}_1 \mathbf{C}_2 + \mathbf{C}_1 \mathbf{C}_3$.
9. $(\mathbf{C}_1 + \mathbf{C}_2) \mathbf{C}_3 = \mathbf{C}_1 \mathbf{C}_3 + \mathbf{C}_2 \mathbf{C}_3$.
10. $\alpha (\mathbf{C}_1 \mathbf{C}_2) = (\alpha \mathbf{C}_1) \mathbf{C}_2 = (\mathbf{C}_1 \alpha) \mathbf{C}_2 = \mathbf{C}_1 (\alpha \mathbf{C}_2) = (\mathbf{C}_1 \mathbf{C}_2) \alpha \in \mathcal{C}_n$.

A further relevant property of centrosymmetric matrices is their **invariance with respect to the linear transformation** (Dagum and Luati, 2003) $t : \mathbb{R}^{m \times n} \rightarrow \mathbb{R}^{m \times n}$, such that $c_{ij} \mapsto c_{m+1-i,n+1-j}$, for $i = 1, \ldots, m$ and $j = 1, \ldots, n$ or equivalently, $\mathbf{C} \mapsto \mathbf{E}_m \mathbf{C} \mathbf{E}_n$.

The property of square centrosymmetric matrices of being an algebra is crucial both on an *algebraic* and on a *statistical* point of view. Purely algebraically speaking, centrosymmetric matrices are the most general structured matrices, respect to some symmetry, to constitute an algebra. In fact, neither the spaces of symmetric ($\mathbf{C} \in \mathbb{R}^{n \times n}$, $c_{ji} = c_{ij}$) or squared persymmetric ($\mathbf{C} \in \mathbb{R}^{n \times n}$, $c_{ji} = c_{n+1-i,n+1-j}$) matrices are closed respect to the row-column matrix product, *i.e.* they do not satisfy **6**. Nevertheless, matrices that are both persymmetric and symmetric, so-called bisymmetric, constitute a proper subalgebra of $\mathcal{C}_n$. On a statistical point of view, we will show that the property of being an algebra is relevant in the convergence theory for periodic Markov chains that describe problems of gambler ruin in the case of fair play. At the same way, invariance under the t-transformation is crucial for smoothing matrices associated to linear estimators of the non stationary mean of time series.

3 Statistical applications of centrosymmetric matrices

Markov chains. Markov chains are stochastic processes $\{X_t\}_{t=1,...,T}$ that describe systems evolving among various states in a probabilistic manner. The probability of the system to be in a state $i = 1, \ldots, k$, at time t, depends only on the state of the system at time $t - 1$, *i.e.*

$$P(X_t = i \mid X_1, X_2, \ldots, X_{t-1}) = P(X_t = i \mid X_{t-1}).$$

Usually, Markov chains are represented by transition matrices $\mathbf{P} \in \mathbb{R}^{k \times k}$ whose generic elements p_{ij} are the probabilities of moving from the state i, to the state j in one time, *i.e.*

$$p_{ij} = P(X_t = j \mid X_{t-1} = i).$$

According to the nature of such probabilities, many kinds of Markov chains can be defined, each with different characteristics. We are interested here to a particular class of Markov processes, namely random walks with absorbing or reflecting barriers that are of the form $X_t = X_{t-1} + \varepsilon_t$, $\varepsilon_t \sim NID(0, \sigma^2)$ with states, say b, that are *absorbing barriers* if $P(X_t = b \mid X_{t-1} = b) = 1$ or superior/inferior ($\pm$) *reflecting barriers* if $P(X_t = b \pm 1 \mid X_{t-1} = b) = 1$.

These processes are often associated to gambler ruin problems where it is of interest to understand how transition probabilities modify in the long run. To give an example, let $k - 1$ be the number of coins between two players, A and B, each having a coin in their hand. They simultaneously reveal wether the coins are head or tails. If both are head or tails, then A wins both coins, if they are different, the two coins are won by B. The game stops when one player possesses all the coins and the other nothing (absorbing barriers) and start again if the looser is somehow refunded (reflecting barriers).

The $k \times k$ transition matrix associated to a random walk with **absorbing barriers** is

$$P = \begin{bmatrix} 1 & 0 & 0 & \dots & 0 & 0 & 0 \\ q & 0 & p & \dots & 0 & 0 & 0 \\ 0 & q & 0 & \dots & 0 & 0 & 0 \\ \dots & \dots & \dots & \dots & \dots & \dots & \\ 0 & 0 & 0 & \dots & q & 0 & p \\ 0 & 0 & 0 & \dots & 0 & 0 & 1 \end{bmatrix}$$

where $p = p_{i,i+1}$, $q = 1 - p = p_{i,i-1}$ and there are two absorbing states such that, once entered, they cannot be left. These are the state corresponding to zero coins and that corresponding to all the $k - 1$ coins. In this way, the rows and columns of P are the states corresponding to the number of coins possessed by A, and therefore $i, j = 0, 1, \dots, k - 1$. For $p = q = \frac{1}{2}$ (fair game with equal probability of winning, p, or loosing, q), the matrix P is centrosymmetric and, by **6**, so is P^n, whose generic element $p_{ij}^{(n)} = P(X_{t+n} = j \mid X_t = i)$ represents the probability of passing from the state i to the state j after n steps. Denoting by $\lim\limits_{n \to \infty} P^n$ the matrix of generic element $\lim\limits_{n \to \infty} p_{ij}^{(n)}$, the following holds (Doob, 1990)

$$\lim_{n \to \infty} P^n = \begin{bmatrix} 1 & 0 & 0 & \dots & 0 & 0 & 0 \\ \pi_1 & 0 & 0 & \dots & 0 & 0 & 1 - \pi_1 \\ \pi_2 & 0 & 0 & \dots & 0 & 0 & 1 - \pi_2 \\ \dots & & \dots & \dots & \dots & & \\ \pi_{k-2} & 0 & 0 & \dots & 0 & 0 & 1 - \pi_{k-2} \\ 0 & 0 & 0 & \dots & 0 & 0 & 1 \end{bmatrix}$$

where $\pi_0 = \pi_{k-1} = 1$ and each remainder $\pi_i \in (0, 1)$, representing the probability of winning $i - 1$ coins, depends on the starting state i. In other words, playing to the infinite certainly leads to the ruin of one gambler.

If P is centrosymmetric, then it follows by **6** and by the elementwise convergence that the limit matrix is centrosymmetric as well. This implies that, starting from i coins, in the case of fair game the long-time average probability of ruin is equal to that of winning, $i.e.$

$$P^{(n)}(X_t = 0 \mid X_{t-1} = i) \underset{n \to \infty}{=} P^{(n)}(X_t = k - 1 \mid X_{t-1} = k - 1 - i).$$

One may ask how many steps are needed for the game to stop. To this purpose, the matrix P is usually studied through three matrices obtained after rearranging the matrix P such that the r absorbing states are in the first rows: in our examples, $r = 2$ and the states are ordered as $0, k-1, 2, \dots, k-2$. Hence

$$P^* = \begin{bmatrix} I_r & O \\ R & Q \end{bmatrix}$$

where $I_r \in \mathbb{R}^{r \times r}$ is the identity matrix representing the probability of transition from the r absorbing states, $O \in \mathbb{R}^{r \times k-r}$ is the null matrix of the transition probabilities from an absorbing to a non absorbing state, $R \in \mathbb{R}^{k-r \times r}$

gives the probabilities of moving from a non absorbing state to an absorbing one, and the elements of $\mathbf{Q} \in \mathbb{R}^{k-r \times k-r}$ are the transition probabilities among non absorbing states. If $\mathbf{P}$ is centrosymmetric, then it is easy to see that $\mathbf{Q}$ and $\mathbf{R}$ are centrosymmetric and (from **6, 8** and using the properties of **E**) so are: the fundamental matrix $\mathbf{N} = (\mathbf{I}_{k-r} - \mathbf{Q})^{-1}$, the vector $\mathbf{m} = \mathbf{Nw}$, where $\mathbf{w}$ is a vector of ones and the matrix $\mathbf{A} = \mathbf{NR}$, that are employed in the study of the properties of the Markov chain associated to $\mathbf{P}$. In fact, n_{ij} is the expected number of transitions in the state j before an absorbing state is reached, starting from the state i; $m_i = \sum_{j=1}^{k-r}$ is the expected number of transitions in the state i before an absorbing state is reached; a_{ij} is the probability of being absorbed in the state j starting from a non absorbing state i.

The centrosymmetric structure of the fundamental matrix $\mathbf{N}$ and equivalently of $\mathbf{Q}$ and $\mathbf{P}$ reveals to be very helpful when the theoretical properties of the process are studied in a purely algebraic way, by means of the eigenvalues of the associated transition matrix (Feller, 1950). In fact, the spectrum of centrosymmetric matrices has been widely studied and many results have been obtained based on a decomposition of any centrosymmetric matrix in a block matrix orthogonally similar to a block-diagonal matrix whose eigenvalues can be immediately calculated (see Cantoni and Butler, 1976).

The transition matrix associated to a random walk with **reflecting barriers**, describing a gambler ruin problem when the looser is refunded and can start playing indefinitely, has the following form

$$\mathbf{P} = \begin{bmatrix} 0 & 1 & 0 & \dots & 0 & 0 & 0 \\ q & 0 & p & \dots & 0 & 0 & 0 \\ 0 & q & 0 & \dots & 0 & 0 & 0 \\ \dots\dots\dots\dots\dots\dots\dots\dots\dots \\ 0 & 0 & 0 & \dots & q & 0 & p \\ 0 & 0 & 0 & \dots & 0 & 1 & 0 \end{bmatrix}.$$

and, as in the preceding case, for $p = q = \frac{1}{2}$ (fair game case) $\mathbf{P} \in \mathcal{C}_k$. It follows from **1, 6, 7** and **10** that the matrix $\frac{1}{n}\left(\mathbf{P} + \mathbf{P}^2 + \dots + \mathbf{P}^n\right)$ is centrosymmetric and for $n \to \infty$ it converges to a centrosymmetric matrix with rows all equal and elements strictly positive (see Doob, 1990). Each row is the *equilibrium vector* which gives the long-run probabilities of each state after n steps. The centrosymmetric structure of the limit matrix $\lim_{n\to\infty} \frac{1}{n} \sum_{m=1}^{n} \mathbf{P}^m$, as well as that of the matrices $\mathbf{I}_n + \frac{1}{n} \sum_{n=1}^{n} \mathbf{P}^h$, representing the average amount of time spent in each state during the first n transitions, is preserved by virtue of the fact that the set $\mathcal{C}_n$ is an algebra.

Time series. In time series analysis, a useful way to estimate the trend underlying the data is by fitting locally a polynomial function, such that any fitted value at a time point t depends only on the observations corresponding to time points in some specified neighborhood of t. Such a fitting curve is smooth by construction. Let us denote a time series as the set $\{(t_j, y_j), j = 1, \cdots, N\}$ where each target point t_j is the time the observation y_j is taken. Any transformation s acting on the time series to produce smooth estimates is a *smoother*. Usually s depends on a smoothing parameter, say η, which is selected according to the variability of the data and the amount of smoothing desired. The value of the smoothing parameter determines the number of observations averaged to obtain each estimate. In particular, if $\eta \to 0$, then the neighborhoods are made of only one observation and the result of the smoothing is an interpolation, whereas if $\eta \to \infty$, then all the observations are considered and smoothing produces a constant line corresponding to the mean of the series. Once that the smoothing parameter is fixed, any smoother becomes linear and can be represented by a squared matrix, let us call it $\mathbf{S}$, in such a way that $s : \mathbb{R}^N \to \mathbb{R}^N$, $\mathbf{y} \longmapsto \widehat{\mathbf{y}} = \mathbf{S}\mathbf{y}$, where $\mathbf{y} \in \mathbb{R}^N$ is an N-dimensional vector corresponding to the input data and $\widehat{\mathbf{y}} \in \mathbb{R}^N$ is the N-dimensional vector representing the smoothed values. Let now $w_{hj}, h, j = 1, \cdots, N$, denote the generic element of the *smoothing matrix* $\mathbf{S}$. The w_{hj}'s are the weights to be applied to the observations $y_j, j = 1, ..., N$, to get the estimate $\widehat{y}_h$, for each $h = 1, ..., N$, i.e. $\widehat{y}_h = \sum_{j=1}^{N} w_{hj} y_j$. These weights depend on the shape of the weight function associated to any smoother. Once the smoothing parameter has been selected, the w_{hj}'s for the observations corresponding to points falling out of the neighborhood of any target point are null, such that the estimates of the $N - 2m$ central observations are obtained by applying $2m + 1$ symmetric weights to the observations neighboring the target point. The estimates of the first and last m observations can be obtained by applying asymmetric weights of variable length to the first and last m observations respectively:

$$\widehat{y}_h = \sum_{j=-m}^{m} w_{h,h-j} y_{h-j} \, , \, h = m+1, \ldots, N-m \qquad \text{(central observations)}$$

$$\widehat{y}_p = \sum_{r=1}^{m_p} w_{pr} y_r \, , \, p = 1, \ldots, m \qquad \text{(initial observations)}$$

$$\widehat{y}_q = \sum_{z=1}^{m_q} w_{q,N+1-z} y_{N+1-z} \, , \, q = N-m+1, \ldots, N \qquad \text{(final observations)}$$

where $2m + 1$ is the length of the time invariant symmetric filter and m_p and m_q are the time-varying lengths of the asymmetric filters. Hence, the smoothing matrix $\mathbf{S}$ has the following structure,

$$
\mathbf{S} = \begin{bmatrix} \underset{(m \times 2m)}{\mathbf{W}^a} & \underset{(m \times N - 2m)}{\mathbf{O}} \\ & \underset{(N - 2m \times N)}{\mathbf{W}^s} & \\ \underset{(m \times N - 2m)}{\mathbf{O}} & \underset{(m \times 2m)}{\mathbf{W}^{a'}} \end{bmatrix}
$$

where $\mathbf{O}$ is a null matrix and $\mathbf{W}^a$, $\mathbf{W}^s$, $\mathbf{W}^{a'}$ are submatrices whose dimensions are shown in parentheses. In particular, $\mathbf{W}^s$ is a $(2m + 1)$-diagonal matrix (in the same sense of a tridiagonal matrix) and its row elements are the symmetric weights of the moving average to be applied to central observations while the rows of the matrices $\mathbf{W}^a$ and $\mathbf{W}^{a'}$ are the sets of asymmetric weights for the first and last observations, respectively. Smoothing matrices are centrosymmetric and their submatrices of symmetric weights are rectangular centrosymmetric. Furthermore, the submatrices of asymmetric weights for the first and last observations are the t-transform of each other $\mathbf{W}^a = t\,(\mathbf{W}^{a'})$.

The relevant properties in time series filtering are 6 and 7, since matrix product is equivalent to linear filters convolution. In particular, 6 assures that if $\mathbf{A}$ and $\mathbf{B}$ are smoothing matrices, then $\mathbf{AB}$ is a smoothing matrix as well. The same holds when repeatedly smoothing a vector of observations by the same filter; in this case, property 7 is applied. These properties are crucial for the construction and study of filters resulting from the convolution of well-known systems of weights.

4 Concluding remarks

We illustrated some applications of centrosymmetric matrices in statistics. Particularly, the emphasis was in the classification of states of finite Markov chains and in the filtering of time series.

We showed that random walk with absorbing or reflecting barriers describing gambler ruin problems in the case of fair game are represented by transition matrices $\mathbf{P} \in \mathcal{C}_k$. Since $\mathcal{C}_k$ is an algebra, the centrosymmetric structure of $\mathbf{P}$ is preserved when taking its power, limit and linear combinations. This allows an easy study of the theoretical properties of the process based on the spectral analysis of $\mathbf{P}$ and gives information on the characteristics of the equilibrium distribution contained in the (centrosymmetric) limit matrix.

Concerning time series, we showed that smoothing matrices $\mathbf{S}$ are centrosymmetric and invariant respect to a linear transformation t that consists in reverting the order of the row and columns of the matrix. The role of this transformation in time series filtering is crucial since the two submatrices of $\mathbf{S}$ whose rows represent the asymmetric weights for the first and last observations are one the t-transform of the other. The consequences of this relation are important from both computational and theoretical viewpoints. In fact, on a computational point of view, it allows to halve the dimension of any smoothing problem by considering only m instead of $2m$ asymmetric filters. In particular, this reduction is substantial, especially when dealing with long filters that asymmetrically weight a considerable number of initial and end observations. On the other hand, theoretically, it becomes significant when asymmetric weights are derived on the basis of assumptions that are different from those corresponding to symmetric weights.

In further research, we intend to investigate the statistical properties of classes of matrices which are somehow related to centrosymmetric matrices, such that: centro-antisymmetric matrices ($\mathbf{C} \in \mathbb{R}^{m \times n}$, $-c_{ij} = c_{m+1-i,n+1-j}$), centro-Hermitian matrices ($\mathbf{C} \in \mathbb{C}^{m \times n}$, $\overline{c_{ij}} = c_{m+1-i,n+1-j}$), persymmetric matrices ($\mathbf{C} \in \mathbb{R}^{m \times n}$, $c_{ji} = c_{m+1-i,n+1-j}$), centro-orthogonal matrices ($\mathbf{C} \in \mathbb{R}^{n \times n}$, $\mathbf{C}^{-1} = c_{n+1-i,n+1-j}$).

References

ANDREW A.L. (1998): Centrosymmetric matrices. *SIAM Rev.* 40, 3, 697-698.

CANTONI A., BUTLER P. (1976): Eigenvalues and Eigenvectors of Symmetric Centrosymmetric Matrices. *Linear Algebra and its Applications.* 13, 275-288.

CHEN H.C. (1998): Generalized Reflexive Matrices: Special Properties and Applications. *SIAM. J. Matrix. Anal. Appl.* 19, 1, 140-153.

DAGUM E.B., LUATI A. (2003): A Linear Transformation and its Properties with Special Applications in Time Series Filtering, *Linear Algebra and its Applications*, forth.

DOOB J.L. (1990): *Stochastic Processess*, Wiley.

FELLER W. (1966): *An Introduction to Probability Theory and its Applications*, Wiley.

IOSIFESCU M. (1980): *Finite Markov Processes and their Applications*, Wiley.

KIMURA M. (1957): Some Problems of Stochastic Processes in Genetics. *Annals of Mathematical Statistics*, 28,82-901.

MAGNUS J.R. and NEUDECKER H. (1979): The Commutation Matrix: Some Properties and Applications. *The Annals of Statistics*, 7, 381-394.

TRENCH W. F. (1997): Numerical Solution of the Inverse Eigenvalue Problem for Real Symmetric Toeplitz Matrices. *SIAM, J. Sci. Comput.*18, 1722-1736.

WEAVER J.R. (1985): Centrosymmetric (Cross-symmetric) Matrices, their Basic Properties, Eigenvalues, Eigenvectors. *Amer. Math. Monthly.* 92,711-717.

Selection of Structural Equation Models with the PLS-VB Programme

Giuseppe Boari[1] and Gabriele Cantaluppi[2]

[1] Istituto di Statistica,
   Università Cattolica del S. Cuore di Milano, Italy
   giuseppe.boari@unicatt.it
[2] Istituto di Statistica,
   Università Cattolica del S. Cuore di Milano, Italy
   gabriele.cantaluppi@unicatt.it

Abstract. Parameter and latent score estimates of structural equation models with latent variables may be obtained by the use of the PLS (Partial Least Squares) algorithm. The program PLS-VB, developed in Visual Basic Application as an Excel add-in for this purpose, is presented. Its use for the selection among competing models is also considered.

1 The reference model, preliminary analysis and PLS

Structural equation models with latent variables are typically used when the main attention is given to the analysis of the relationship among p latent variables Y_j, $j = 1, \ldots, p$, (unobservable conceptual constructs) and to the evaluation of their scores (the unknown values for each of the n individual cases). To this purpose the observations on the so-called manifest variables are available; it is assumed that these proxy variables are measured on a common scale and are connected to the corresponding latent variables by a linear function, following the classical Factor Analysis approach with oblique (non-orthogonal) latent factors. This situation typically arises in the analysis of questionnaire data, collected for psychological or socio-economical surveys. The reference model consists of two fundamental relations: the first one concerning the relationships among latent variables, the second being the so-called measurement model, relating each latent variable to the corresponding p_j ($j = 1, \ldots, p$) manifest indicators X_{jh} ($h = 1, \ldots, p_j$).
The $q < p$ ($q \geq 1$) latent variables depending on no other variable are called "exogenous", while the remaining $(p - q)$ latent variables, which at least depend on another one, are called "endogenous".
The PLS-VB programme considers "recursive" models of the following type

$$Y_j = \sum_{k=1}^{j-1} \beta_{jk} Y_k + \zeta_j, \qquad j = q+1, \ldots, p, \tag{1}$$

where the generic endogenous Y_j may depend only on the previous endogenous or exogenous variables; the covariance matrix of the equation errors ζ_j

is assumed to be diagonal. We will also consider measurement models of the so-called "reflective" type, where the manifest variables are functions of the latent and not vice-versa, that is

$$(X_{jh} - \bar{x}_{jh}) = \lambda_{jh} Y_j + \varepsilon_{jh}, \qquad j = 1, \ldots, p, \ h = 1, \ldots, p_j, \qquad (2)$$

where $\bar{x}_{jh}$ are the average reference values and ε_{jh} the measurement errors. Distributional hypotheses concern null-average and no mutual correlation of the random variables Y_j, ε_{jh} $(j = 1, \ldots, p, h = 1, \ldots, p_j)$, ζ_j $(j = q + 1, \ldots, p)$. Preliminary to the inference stage is the exploratory analysis, which regards the so-called scale reliability study, to verify whether the measurement models are correctly specified. To this aim, as suggested in the psychometric literature, despite some criticism, both Cronbach α index is used, in order to evaluate the internal coherence of each scale describing each latent concept Y_j $(j = 1, \ldots, p)$, as well as the α *if item deleted* index, to evaluate the marginal contribution of each observable variable X_{jh} to the latent $Y_j, h = 1, \ldots, p_j$. When these indices give evidence that the internal coherence of each scale is not achieved or that some observable variable X_{jh} is redundant then the measurement model should be reformulated. In particular, let s_{jh}^2 and s_j^2 be the variance estimates respectively of the manifest variables X_{jh} and of the group totals $T_j = \sum_{h=1}^{p_j} X_{jh}$ (with values $t_{ij} = \sum_{h=1}^{p_j} x_{ijh}$); the reliability indices are then evaluated as:

$$\alpha_j = \frac{p_j}{p_j - 1} \left(1 - \frac{\sum_{h=1}^{p_j} s_{jh}^2}{s_j^2} \right) \quad \text{and} \quad \alpha_{jh} = \frac{p_j - 1}{p_j - 2} \left(1 - \frac{\sum_{k \neq h} s_k^2}{s_{j(h)}^2} \right),$$

where $s_{j(h)}^2 = s_j^2 + s_{jh}^2 - 2 \left[\sum_{i=1}^n t_{ij} x_{ijh} - \left(\sum_{i=1}^n t_{ij} \right) \left(\sum_{i=1}^n x_{ijh} \right) / n \right] / (n - 1)$ and $j = 1, \ldots, p, h = 1, \ldots, p_j$.

Once the exploratory study has been performed, the estimation of model (1) is considered. It is well known that models described by equations (1) and (2) usually depend on several parameters and moreover the involved manifest variables are typically highly correlated (quasi collinearity); for these main reasons, the PLS algorithm, first proposed in Wold (1985) and further extended by Lohmöller (1989), seems to be the most appropriate, also considering the predictive character of this approach, which gives a solution proposal to the problem of score indeterminacy.

Following the PLS approach, our programme first estimates the scores of the latent variables then the β_{jk} parameters $(j = q + 1, \ldots, p, \ k = 1, \ldots, j - 1)$ and performs tests of hypotheses on these parameters making it possible to select only significant relationships. In other words, the parsimonious final model may be selected by considering those models containing also redundant relationships, which empirical evidence will show not significant.

In order to introduce the PLS algorithm, the causal relationships among latent variables may be specified by the following matrix notation, corresponding to (1)

$$[Y_{q+1} \ldots Y_p]' = [\mathbf{\Gamma} | \mathbf{B}] [Y_1 \ldots Y_q Y_{q+1} \ldots Y_p]' + [\zeta_{q+1} \ldots \zeta_p]'$$

where the elements of the sub-matrices Γ and $\mathbf{B}$, of dimensions $(p - q) \times q$ and $(p - q) \times (p - q)$, are the coefficients β_{jk} $(j = q+1, \ldots, p,\ k = 1, \ldots, j-1)$. To describe causal relationship among the p latent variables, the square matrix $\mathbf{T} = \{t_{jk}\}$, with values $t_{jk} = 1$ if Y_j depends on Y_k and $t_{jk} = 0$ otherwise, can be defined.

Since we consider models of the recursive type, the elements on the diagonal and in the upper triangular part of $\mathbf{T}$ are zeroes, as well as those in the first q rows (corresponding to the exogenous variables) though belonging to the lower triangular part. Note that the matrix $[\Gamma | \mathbf{B}]$ corresponds to the last $(p - q)$ rows of $\mathbf{T}$.

For any specified causal structure of the model and starting from the initial vector of weights $\mathbf{w}_j^{(0)} = (1, 0, \ldots, 0)'$, the PLS-VB programme loops through the following steps:

- latent score computation $Y_j = \sum_h w_{jh}^{(r-1)} (X_{jh} - \bar{x}_{jh})$ (with manifest variables)
- instrumental variable definition $Z_j = \sum_{k=1}^{p} \tau_{jk} Y_k$ (by adjacent variables; $\tau_{jk} = \pm 1$)
- weight vector $\mathbf{w}_j^{(r)}$ updating, according to the following formula

$$w_{jh}^{(r)} = \text{sign} \left\{ \sum_h \text{sign} \left[\text{Cov} (X_{jh}, Y_j) \right] \right\} \frac{\text{Cov} (X_{jh}, Z_j)}{\sum_h \text{Cov} (X_{jh}, Z_j)}, \qquad r = 1, 2, \ldots$$

and where $\tau_{jk} = \max(t_{jk}, t_{kj}) \cdot \text{sign} \left[\text{Cov} (Y_j, Y_k) \right]$, see Lohmöller (1989). Observe that the computation of the latent scores Y_j produces non standard latent values as a linear combination, with normalized weights, of the corresponding manifest variables, in a way analogous to the Lohmöller (1989) proposal, pp. 29-30.

This procedure ensures the model identifiability, since, as observed also in Lohmöller (1989), p. 222, fixing the scale of the latent variables is sufficient to assure their unique definition. In the PLS-VB programme, here introduced, only manifest variables measured on the same scale are considered.

The iterations continue until weight convergence is achieved; the parameters β_{jk}, λ_{jh} are then estimated via Ordinary Least Squares, according to the relations (1) and (2). The scores Y_j^*, expressed in the original scale, can be obtained (cp., for example, Zanella et al., 2002), remembering that $Y_j = Y_j^* - \bar{y}_j$, as $y_{ij}^* = \bar{y}_j + \sum_h w_{jh} x_{ijh}$, where $\bar{y}_j = \sum_h w_{jh} \bar{x}_{jh}$ are the latent means.

Finally, to allow an easier reading, the program expresses the scores and their mean values in centesimal units, by the following transformation $\hat{y}_{ij} = 100 \left(y_{ij}^* - x_{\min} \right) / \left(x_{\max} - x_{\min} \right)$, where $x_{\min}$ and $x_{\max}$ are the limit values of the common scale of measurement adopted for the manifest variables.

2 Model selection

As previously mentioned, for any assigned model structure the PLS-VB programme computes the β_{jk} parameters, once the latent scores have been calculated. We will choose the model which, among all competing structural models, is characterized by the scores given by the PLS procedure and best describes the linear relationship between exogenous and endogenous variables. It may be identified by the following selecting procedure. In order to identify the most parsimonious model, you need to specify first the r "target" variables, which are assumed, among the $(p - q)$ endogenous, to be of primary interest with regard to the problem under investigation.

These variables, which correspond, for simplicity sake, to the last r equations of the model (1), will be considered as basic reference in the criterion adopted to evaluate the model performance. Note that the model is substantially expressed by means of the β_{jk} coefficients, estimated, via OLS regression, considering the latent scores being observed values.

In particular, the adopted criterion suggests to choose, among the models with significant non zero β_{jk} coefficients, the one which attains the minimum of the following function:

$$G\left(g_{p-r+1}, \ldots, g_p\right) = \sum_{j=p-r+1}^{p} \left(\ln \hat{\sigma}_j^2 + g_j \frac{\ln n}{n}\right) = \sum_{j=p-r+1}^{p} G_j \qquad (3)$$

where $\hat{\sigma}_j^2$ $(j = p - r + 1, \ldots, p)$ are the residual variances of the regression models relating the r "target" variables Y_j to the corresponding regressors, amounting to $g_j \geq 0$; note that when $g_j = 0$ we have $\hat{\sigma}_j^2 = \mathrm{Var}\left(Y_j\right)$.

It can be pointed out that (3) resembles the BIC criterion structure (Schwarz, 1978), reformulation of the well known AIC by Akaike, which takes into account a penalty term depending on the model complexity; moreover, it is also equivalent to compare the residual variance proportions.

In Boari, Cantaluppi (2003) a complete example, regarding the Customer Satisfaction analysis of a public railway service, is shown.

3 Programme description

Once installed the `plsvb.xla` add-in tool, the application may be started with a new job referring to a data set previously loaded or typed in the Excel sheet (see Figure 1). Note that the first line data range should include the variable names, which the program will use in the subsequent phases, while the first column is (not necessarily) devoted to contain an individual identification field (case or number name).

The current job may be resumed at the point where we decided to hide the dialog box in each of the following steps. Furthermore, whenever a step has been completed, one may press the "Next" Button to advance to the next available step.

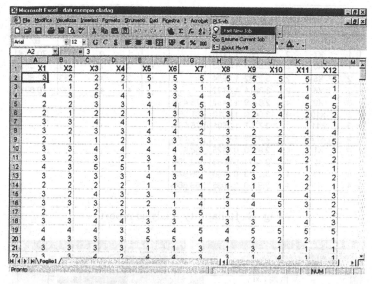

Fig. 1. Starting a new job.

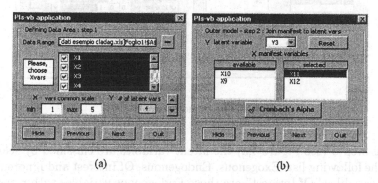

(a)   (b)

Fig. 2. Input step and outer model definition.

Step 1 defines the data range, the manifest variables to be considered in the analysis, the extent of their scale (assumed to be common to all the X observable variables) and the number of Y latent variables, see Figure 2(a). As displayed in Figure 2(b), Step 2 describes the so-called outer (or measurement) model, expressing the reflective relationships between the latent and the corresponding observable variables. Cronbach's Alpha Button produces a report (see Figure 3) concerning the reliability analysis of the single scales (the groups of observable variables linked to each latent variable); the "α if" statistic (alpha if item deleted) is also printed for all the scales containing more than two proxy variables.

The next two steps are devoted to the inner (causal or path) model specification.

α if deleted					
Yver	Xver	Num	Avg	Var	α if
1	X7	2	3.1862	1.1460	
1	X8	2	2.5315	1.3943	
2	X5	2	3.2132	1.1984	
2	X6	2	3.3514	1.3732	
3	X9	4	2.8709	1.2453	78.46%
3	X10	4	3.0420	1.4018	81.58%
3	X11	4	2.7207	1.2501	75.59%
3	X12	4	2.3123	1.4323	77.89%
4	X1	4	2.9850	0.4425	58.43%
4	X2	4	2.4234	0.6063	62.98%
4	X3	4	3.3273	0.5160	66.97%
4	X4	4	2.9730	0.8095	69.88%

Cronbach α			
Yver	Num	Count	α
1	2	333	70.79%
2	2	333	78.37%
3	4	333	82.89%
4	4	333	70.80%

Fig. 3. Reliability analysis report.

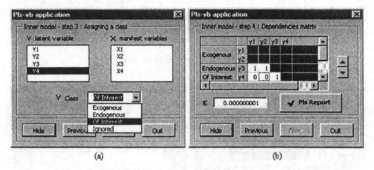

(a)   (b)

Fig. 4. Inner model definition.

During Step 3 (see Figure 4,a) the latent variables are classified by selecting from the following list: Exogenous, Endogenous, Of Interest and Ignored. The latent variables "Of Interest" are those Endogenous variables with respect to which the G statistic, see (3), is computed (by summing up the G_j statistics referring to the corresponding linear regression sub-models), whereas an "Ignored" latent variable will be excluded (together with all its corresponding observables) from the subsequent analyses.

In Step 4 (see Figure 4,b) relationships among the latent variables are defined, by filling the **T** matrix of dependencies: a unitary value means that the corresponding column variable is connected to the corresponding row variable through an oriented arrow, while a null value means no relationship (a double click toggles between these values).

The fixed constant ε, used by the program to terminate the iteration procedure of the PLS algorithm, can also be redefined.

The "PLS Report" Button produces the final reports (see Figure 5 for a comprehensive view) displaying model parameter estimates as well as all statistics needed to check model fitting (see Bayol *et al.*, 2000 and Lohmöller, 1989,

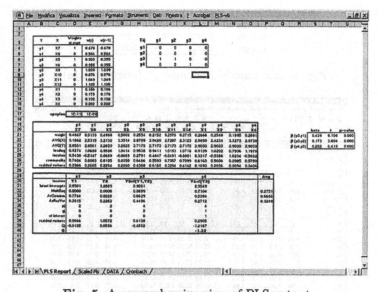

Fig. 5. A comprehensive view of PLS output.

| | y1 | y1 | y2 | y2 | y3 | y3 | y3 | y3 | y4 | y4 | y4 | y4 |
	X7	X8	X5	X6	X9	X10	X11	X12	X1	X2	X3	X4
weight	0.4867	0.5133	0.4998	0.5002	0.2554	0.2152	0.2578	0.2715	0.2666	0.2548	0.1895	0.2891
AVG(X)	3.1862	2.5315	3.2132	3.3514	2.8709	3.0420	2.7207	2.3123	2.9850	2.4234	3.3273	2.9730
AVG(Y)	2.8501	2.8501	3.2823	3.2823	2.7173	2.7173	2.7173	2.7173	2.9033	2.9033	2.9033	2.9033
loading	0.9274	1.0688	0.9586	1.0414	0.9538	0.9411	1.0193	1.0718	0.9139	1.0202	0.7938	1.1970
location	0.5430	-0.5147	0.0669	-0.0669	0.2791	0.4847	-0.0491	-0.6001	0.3317	-0.5386	1.0234	-0.5022
communality	0.7404	0.8083	0.8105	0.8350	0.6466	0.5593	0.7357	0.7099	0.6163	0.5606	0.3985	0.5780
residual variance	0.2968	0.2665	0.2264	0.2260	0.4388	0.6160	0.3294	0.4142	0.1693	0.2856	0.3094	0.3406

Fig. 6. Outer model estimates.

	y1	y2	y3	y4	Avg
location	Y1	Y2	Y3=f(Y1,Y2)	Y4=f(Y3)	
latent intercepts	2.8501	3.2823	0.9261	2.3549	
MultRsq	0.0000	0.0000	0.3899	0.7104	0.2751
AvCommun	0.7744	0.8228	0.6629	0.5384	0.6666
AvResVar	0.2815	0.2262	0.4496	0.2712	0.3249
pi	2	2	4	4	
qi	0	0	2	1	
of interest	0	0	0	1	
residual variance	0.9866	1.0572	0.6138	0.2905	
Gi	-0.0135	0.0556	-0.4532	-1.2187	
G				-1.2187	

Fig. 7. Inner model estimates.

for an in-depth description), assuming normally distributed scores.

The various reports will be stored in proper worksheets automatically created by the programme. The last one produced (as displayed in Figure 9) contains the latent score estimates, expressed in the original scale, as well as in centesimal and standard units.

The following technical requirements are at least necessary for PLS-VB programme properly run: Win95/98 or Windows NT and Microsoft Excel 2000.

	beta	t	p-value
ß(y3,y1)	0.429	9.108	0.000
ß(y3,y2)	0.173	3.804	0.000
ß(y4,y3)	0.202	6.419	0.000

Fig. 8. Inner model relationships (original scale).

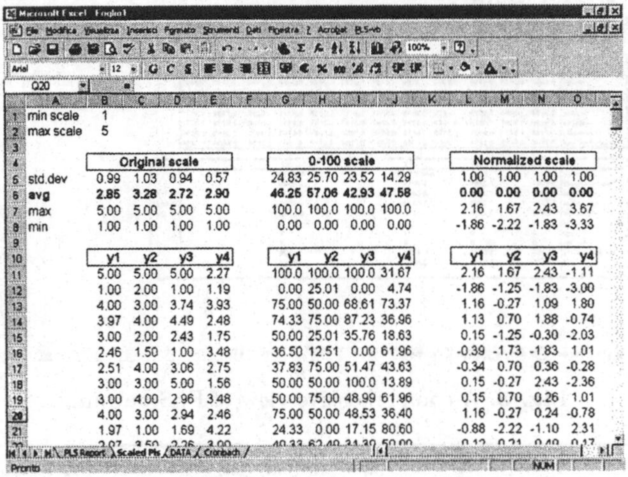

Fig. 9. Latent score estimates in different scales.

The authors wish to thank Dr. Riccardo Martiradonna, chairman of Mediasoft Srl, Milan, Italy, for his contribution to the realization of the programme, that we believe to be of great interest to the scientific community.

References

BAYOL, M.P., DE LA FOYE, A., TELLIER, C. and TENENHAUS, M. (2000): Use of the PLS Path Modelling to estimate the European Customer Satisfaction Index (ECSI) model. *Statistica Applicata, 12, 361–375*.

BOARI, G. and CANTALUPPI, G. (2003): Reperimento di modelli ad equazioni strutturali parsimoniosi con il programma PLS-VB. *Serie E.P. 115*, Istituto di Statistica, Università Cattolica del S. Cuore, Milano.

LOHMÖLLER, J.-B. (1987): *LVPLS Program Manual, Version 1.8*. Zentralarchiv für Empirische Sozialforschung, Köln.

LOHMÖLLER, J.-B. (1989): *Latent Variable Path Modeling with Partial Least Squares*. Physica-Verlag, Heidelberg.

SCHWARZ, G. (1978): Estimating the dimension of a model. *Annals of Statistics, 6, 461–464*.

WOLD, H. (1982): Soft modeling: the basic design and some extensions. In: K.G. Joreskog, H. Wold (Eds.): *Systems under indirect observations, vol. 2*. North Holland, 1–54.

ZANELLA, A., BOARI, G. and CANTALUPPI, G. (2002): Indicatori statistici complessivi per la valutazione di un sistema per la gestione della qualità: esame del problema ed un esempio di applicazione. In: *Atti della Riunione Satellite della XLI Riunione Scientifica SIS*. Cleup, Padova, 1–26.

Web Robot Detection - Preprocessing Web Logfiles for Robot Detection

Christian Bomhardt[1], Wolfgang Gaul[1], and Lars Schmidt-Thieme[2]

[1] Institut für Entscheidungstheorie und Unternehmensforschung
University of Karlsruhe, Germany
[2] Institute for Computer Science
University of Freiburg, Germany

Abstract. Web usage mining has to face the problem that parts of the underlying logfiles are created by robots. While cooperative robots identify themselves and obey to the instructions of server owners not to access parts or all of the pages on the server, malignant robots may camouflage themselves and have to be detected by web robot scanning devices. We describe the methodology of robot detection and show that highly accurate tools can be applied to decide whether session data was generated by a robot or a human user.

1 Introduction

The first web robots appeared in 1993 (The Web Robots Pages): "MOMspider" by Roy T. Fielding (indexing, statistics), "Wanderer" by Matthew Gray (measuring web growth), and "JumpStation" by J. Fletcher (indexing). At these times, most problems of robot deployment appeared in the area of overloaded web servers or waste of bandwidth. Although, in 1993, the web community was "small" compared to nowadays, the increasing use of robots led to the standard for robot exclusion (Koster (1994)). Cooperative robots follow these guidelines and are - in general - easy to detect. Malignant robots ignore these guidelines and may even apply stealth technologies.

Today, one of the most important concerns in web robot detection is unethical content usage (e.g., unauthorized usage of US Government's National Weather Service (NWS) forecast data (Anaconda), extraction of mail addresses for spamming (Ipaopao.com)), and other forms of unexpected usage (bots that sign up email accounts for spamming (Captcha)). Additionally, robot requests decrease web server speed, may distort logfiles (at least 16% of the web traffic originates from robots (Menascé et al. (2000))), and thereby influence serious web mining.

Today's most widely used technologies for robot detection can be divided into four major categories: *Simple methods* (checking the [agent] and [IP address] fields in logfile entries, checking of requests for `robots.txt` (Arlitt et al. (2001)), *traps* (embedding of HTML code that looks like a link, but indeed is invisible for a real user (Mullane (1998))), *web navigation behavior analysis* (trying to find implicate log characteristics based on the objectives of the different robots (Almeida et al. (2001))) and - as an improvement - *navigational pattern modeling* (defining session attributes and applying data/web mining algorithms that decide in favor of the absence/presence of robot visits based on the calculated attribute values (Tan and Kumar (2000,2001)))). With the simple methods cooperative robots can be detected. The only problem is the actuality of the robot lists as the number of web robots increases and changes of the identification information can occur and have to be updated. This technology is unable to detect malignant robots. Traps can detect malignant robots because trapfile lists can be created with files that would never be requested by human users. If there are such requests they originate from a robot - if not - one cannot be sure whether site visits of robots have occurred. If files from the trapfile list have been requested by an unidentified robot a malignant robot has been found. Web navigation behavior analysis can detect robots - malignant ones as well as new and/or known but modified ones - based on the different ways how human beings and robots access information contained in web sites. A robot detection tool RDT (Bomhardt (2002)) - a specialized web data preprocessing software enabling the researcher to effectively work with and understand large logfile data - one of the main requirements to build accurate prediction models - combines web navigational behavior analysis with navigational pattern modeling.

In the following the robot detection process will be divided into two main phases: *Web Data Preprocessing* with the substeps sessionizing, session labeling, and calculation of session attributes (feature vector) and *Robot Mining* with the substeps robot detection model development and deployment. The robot mining phase is well supported by different software systems like the SAS Enterprise Miner. With the robot detection tool RDT we fill the preprocessing gap and enable researchers to quickly gain accurate input for the robot mining phase. With this support, they can focus on model developing.

2 Web data preprocessing for robot detection

Every webserver can at least write a logfile that lists all HTTP-requests in the order they occur. Each HTTP-request is represented by a single line in the logfile using the combined logfile format (Apache) which most HTTP servers can create. Each logfile entry consists of the following nine fields: [IP address] [name] [login] [date] [request] [status] [size] [referrer] [agent] with [IP address] as client IP address, [name] as name of the user (usually unused), [login] as login-name of the basic HTTP-authentication, [date] as date and time of the request, [request] as HTTP-request containing the request method, the URL of the requested resource (page), and the desired HTTP-protocol, [status] as 3-digit status code returned by the server, [size] as number of bytes actually returned by the server, [referrer] as URL of the referencing page and [agent] as name of the client agent (e.g., "Mozilla/4.75[en](WinNT;U)"). Request, referrer and agent are provided by the client and are unreliable for analysis. The other fields are generated by the web server and, therefore, trustworthy. The structure of the examined web site is another source of information. It is used for the calculation of advanced session attributes in the later model.

2.1 Sessionizing

The first step - sessionizing - combines single requests (=logfile entries) into user sessions. Berendt et al. (2001) give an overview over the different types of sessionizers and their performance. We use a timeout based heuristics where requests with the same agent and IP address are grouped together as long as the maximum idle time between two requests is smaller than 30 minutes (according to Catledge and Pitkow (1995)). Here, navigation path construction (Gaul and Schmidt-Thieme (2000)) can also be applied. For a common user session, requests can be divided into two groups: main requests as a result of an user action and auxiliary requests automatically issued by browsers to retrieve objects referenced by the main request (images, java applets). The set of requests of one pageview span one main request and its auxiliary requests. We define every requested HTML resource as main request and assign the remaining requests to the main requests corresponding to their referrers. Requests without suitable main request contained in the session are treated as main requests.

2.2 Session labeling

Session labeling describes the operation of assigning a session to a human user or a robot. Robots issued by unregistered users are unable to login into a website as they do not know the necessary username and password. So every session with a login name can be classified as user session. This has to be considered if you run your own administrative robots that use HTTP authentication.

Some files are known to be never requested by real users. These may be some hidden linked files from traps (Mullane (1998)), robots.txt requested by robots following the robot guidelines (Koster (1994)) or typical files from worm attacks (e.g., cmd.exe for Nimbda (Heng)). All these files are stored in the *trapfile list* and as requests for such files normally originate from a robot, they are used to reliably identify robots.

Cooperative robots that obey to the robot exclusion standard (Koster (1994)) identify themselves with their own agent tag. These tags are contained in the *robot agent list*. The agent field in the request line is sent by the client and malignant robots could use it to camouflage themselves by sending a well known browser agent tag instead of their own. It is therefore impossible to build a "true" user agent list. But it is useful to have a *common agent list* that contains user agents to differentiate between known robot tags, common agent tags or unknown tags.

Some IP addresses are known to be the home of spiders - for example the IP addresses used by the google bots. These IPs can be saved in the *robot IP list* and so requests from those IPs can be identified as robots.

There is a list of known robots available from `http://www.robotstxt.org/wc/robots.html` (The Web Robots Pages). Among other things, it contains the robot name, IP and agent tag. For easier updates, this list is stored separately but used identically to the robot agent and robot IP lists.

You may consider all traffic originating from some special IPs to consist of user sessions (for example, your department's computer room). To achieve this, the tool checks the IP against known IPs from the *user IP list*. We used the session labeling heuristics from figure 1. The algorithm first checks for sessions with given user names followed by the search for requests for files from the trapfile list and the examination of session agent and IP attributes. By default, sessions receive the user label.

```
function LabelSession( Session )
{
if (session contains request with given login name)
   then return user;
if (session contains request for file from trapfile list)
   then return robot;
if (session agent is contained in the robot agent list)
   then return robot;
if (session IP is contained in the robot IP list)
   then return robot;
if (session IP is contained in the user IP list)
   then return user;
return user;
}
```

Fig. 1. Session labeling heuristics

2.3 Calculation of session attributes

By session labeling a large percentage of robot visits can be detected. The next step is the calculation of session attributes (feature vector). Table 1 presents a summary of the attributes calculated. Some attributes (e.g., AVGREQTIME and STDREQDEV need sessions with at least two requests) have individual requirements and may therefore be missing for corresponding sessions. We included the attributes TOTALPAGES, %IMAGE, %HTML, TOTALTIME, AVGTIME, STDEVTIME, %ERROR, GET, POST, HEAD, OTHER, LENGTH, and %NOREFERRER (referrer="-" in Tan and Kumar (2000)) from Tan and Kumar (2000). The AVGREPEATED attribute is a modification of the "repeated" attribute from Tan and Kumar (2000). We left out %BINARY DOC, %BINARY EXEC, %ASCII, %ZIP, %MULTIMEDIA, and %OTHER because the file types of these attributes played a minor role for the examined websites and we think that they are sufficiently considered within the %HTML and %IMAGE attributes. We excluded the NIGHT attribute because we think that the relevance found in Tan and Kumar (2000) results from well behaving search engine spiders that examine the websites during expected idle times. We do not expect this kind of gentleness from malignant robots and, therefore, left this attribute out. Our experience shows

No.	Name	Description
1	TOTALTIME	session length in seconds
2	LENGTH	number of pageviews
3	TOTALPAGES	total number of requests
4	BYTESSEND	total number of bytes send
5	SITECOVERAGE	$= \frac{min(\text{number of pageviews}, \text{number of requested HTML files})}{\text{examined websites total number of HTML pages}}$
6	%HTML	percentage of HTML files requested
7	%IMAGE	percentage of images requested
8	%NOREFERRER	percentage of requests w. o. referrer
9	MAXREPEATED	maximum number of requests per file
10	AVGREPEATED	average number of requests per file
11*	AVGREQTIME	average time between two requests
12*	AVGTIME	average time between two requests within the same pageview
13*	MINAVGVIEWTIME	minimum average time between two requests within the same pageview
14*	MAXAVGVIEWTIME	maximum average time between two requests within the same pageview
15*	STDREQDEV	deviation of the time between two requests
16*	STDEVTIME	average deviation of the time between two requests within the same pageview
17*	MINSTDEV	minimum deviation of the time between two requests within the same pageview
18*	MAXSTDEV	maximum deviation of the time between two requests within the same pageview
19	%STATUS200	percentage of requests with status code 200 (OK)
20	%STATUS2XX	percentage of requests with status code 2XX (without 200)
21	%STATUS301	percentage of requests with status code 301 (moved permanently)
22	%STATUS302	percentage of requests with status code 3o2 (moved temporarily)
23	%STATUS304	percentage of requests with status code 3o4 (not modified)
24	%ERROR	percentage of requests with all other status codes (server- or client- error)
25*	%AVGHTMLLINKCOV	average percentage of visited HTML links per requested HTML page
26*	%MINHTMLLINKCOV	minimum percentage of visited HTML links per requested HTML page
27*	%MAXHTMLLINKCOV	maximum percentage of visited HTML links per requested HTML page
28*	%AVGDIVLINKCOV	average percentage of visited non-HTML links per requested HTML page
29*	%MINDIVLINKCOV	minimum percentage of visited non-HTML links per requested HTML page
30*	%MAXDIVLINKCOV	maximum percentage of visited non-HTML links per requested HTML page
31	GET	percentage of requests made with the GET method
32	HEAD	percentage of requests made with the HEAD method
33	POST	percentage of requests made with the POST method
34	OTHER	percentage of requests made with other methods

(*=cannot be calculated for every session)

Table 1. Session Attributes. Gray columns correspond to attributes not found in Tan and Kumar (2000,2001).

that modern spiders no longer seem to apply breadth-first search but instead use multiple non-contiguous spider sessions originating from different IPs (cp. the google bots).

The WIDTH and DEPTH parameters were replaced by a set of similar link coverage (LINKCOV) attributes (attributes no. 25-30). The consideration of link coverage parameters calculated for two pages can be difficult if one page contains two linked pages and the other 200. Therefore we added a minimum constraint for the consideration of pages within the calculation of these attributes. If a page contains less links than the minimum constraint, this page is sorted out and not considered for the calculation of link coverage parameters. In doing so, the parameters were calculable for most pages without a too strong influence on important link coverage attributes (especially the %MINDIVLINKCOV and %MINHTMLLINKCOV parameters).

3 Improvement of data quality by RDT

Improvement of data quality is used as generic term for activities as data cleansing, (re)structuring, and calculating derived information. The mass of web data forces the usage of mining tools for such tasks. Our web data preprocessing software RDT aims at supporting the improvement of data quality in connection with web robot detection. During our preprocessing work, we identified the following problems for which we were able to suggest improvements. All of them are addressed by our robot detection tool RDT.

Improvement of acquisition of derived information: The session labeling heuristics relies on the trapfile, robot agent, robot IP, and user IP lists. These lists usually contain many similar entries (trap1.html and trap2. html, Java1.1 and Java1.1.8, crawler10.googlebot.com and crawler11. googlebot.com, 172.22.82.151 and 172.22.82.152). Administration can be highly improved by introducing regular expressions instead of full qualified expressions. Unknown user agents or clumsy selected regular expressions could lead to misclassifications caused by the robot agent or common agent list. This problem has been addressed by a robot detection tool function that alphabetically sorts all agents found in a logfile in one of three lists: unknown agents, robot agents, and common agents. This enables the researcher to quickly overlook the background knowledge classification quality in the area of the session agent field analysis. The robot detection tool RDT helps the user to modify the robot and common agent lists while viewing the classification result. Changes are immediately incorporated in the classification. This user-friendly approach enables the researcher to inspect the analysis results of several thousand different user agents. For convenience, the list of webrobots can be downloaded from the web and imported into the robot detection tool.

Improvement of knowledge about site structure information: Some attributes in the feature vector (e.g. %AVGHTMLLINKCOV, %AVGDIVLINKCOV) rely on information about the site structure. Thus, a site spider was developed as part of our robot detection tool RDT which collects information for the calculation of the set of link coverage parameters.

Improvement of data understanding: Data understanding is important when the information basis is huge and difficult to survey as for web mining. Logfiles are hard to read for humans as they simply log requests successively. It is difficult to see which requests belong to a specific session or pageview. For inspections of the navigation, the set of links contained in one page should be handy available. The robot detection tool RDT incorporates requirements of this kind by offering a site structure explorer that shows all links contained in the underlying web site and calculates site structure statistics (minimum, maximum, average and standard deviation of number of HTML links contained in each page and corresponding parameters for non-HTML links). Requests belonging to the same session are written successively in the output log file. Optionally, sessions are separated by empty lines in the output log. The tool has an interactive mode where it displays every session found together with the contained requests, grouped into pageviews, and the calculated session attributes as session detail view. The tool also offers the possibility to access the lists holding background knowledge for the session labeling heuristics. Another option is that unknown agents may belong to some new kind of robot or browser and that it is worth taking a closer look at such a session. The robot detection tool RDT supports this by the option to display the session detail view for sessions with unknown agents. It is also obviously useful to show session details for those sessions with contradicting heuristics and prediction model results. The robot detection tool RDT enables this by providing a plug-in interface for prediction models. One can easily integrate a generated C score code from data mining tools like the SAS Enterprise Miner into the tool. By using this plug-in interface together with handcrafted decision rules, the tool can be used as flexible preprocessing support for other web mining applications like "filter all sessions with at least 4 pageviews". A session of a client using a non-robot agent but requesting a file from the trapfile list will be detected and presented to the researcher.

4 Robot mining

Prediction models using logistic regression, neural networks, and decision trees were applied for robot mining. Sessions containing only a single request show many missing or constant values in their feature vector (TOTAL-PAGES, LENGTH, SITECOVERAGE, MAXREPEATED, AVGREPEAT-ED, AVGREQTIME, AVGTIME, MINAVGTIME, MAXAVGTIME, STD-REQDEV, STDEVTIME, MINSTDEV, MAXSTDEV), as several attributes require at least two requests for calculation. Therefore, we worked with three different datasets: *all sessions*, *single-request-sessions*, and *2-or-more-requests-sessions*. We did not - like Tan and Kumar (2000) - generate a model for every number of pageviews as we worried about overfitting and too small datasets. The models built from all sessions were used as baseline for the evaluation of models combining single-request- and 2-or-more-requests-situations.

The models were evaluated using standard metrics as misclassification rate, recall and precision. Let S be the set of all sessions, $c : S \to \{0, 1\}$ a map assigning the true class label to each session ($1 =$ robot, $0 =$ user) and $\hat{c} : S \to \{0, 1\}$ a map assigning the predicted class label to each session (for a given prediction model). Then *misclassification rate* is defined as

$$\text{mis} := \frac{|\{s \in S \,|\, c(s) \neq \hat{c}(s)\}|}{|S|},$$

recall as

$$\text{rec} := \frac{|\{s \in S \,|\, c(s) = \hat{c}(s) = 1\}|}{|\{s \in S \,|\, c(s) = 1\}|},$$

and *precision* as

$$\text{prec} := \frac{|\{s \in S \,|\, c(s) = \hat{c}(s) = 1\}|}{|\{s \in S \,|\, \hat{c}(s) = 1\}|}.$$

For different datasets the misclassification rate can reasonably be compared only, if one takes into account its data set specific baseline value. The baseline value is the value that can be achieved by trivial models that always predict the label of the larger class. Let $m \in \{0, 1\}$ be the majority class label, usually the user class label. Then

$$\text{mis}^{\text{base}} := \frac{|\{s \in S \,|\, c(s) = 1 - m\}|}{|S|}.$$

5 Empirical results

For the evaluation of the robot detection tool RDT, we examined a logfile from an educational website (EDU) and another one from a medium sized online shop (SHOP). The EDU logfile had 790142 requests. 2905 different agents could be recognized. 58009 sessions where constructed from the raw data with 28534 identified robot sessions. The single-request-sessions dataset had a volume of 25573 sessions with 26,23% user sessions (which can be a hint that robots use "short" visits and return after session time-out has occurred). The 2-or-more-requests-sessions dataset had a volume of 32436 sessions with 70,19% user sessions. The SHOP logfile contained 1150827 requests from which 52295 sessions could be built. 14068 of these sessions were robot sessions. Correlation analysis showed that our feature vector contained good prediction variables for both logfiles (cp. figure 2). Some attributes were strongly correlated with session labeling for both datasets (%HTML, %IMAGE, %NOREFERRER, AVGREQTIME, %AVGHTMLLINKCOV, %MINHTMLLINKCOV, %MAXHTMLLINKCOV, %AVGDIVLINKCOV, %MINDIVLINKCOV, %MAXDIVLINKCOV) while others (STDREQDEV, %STA-

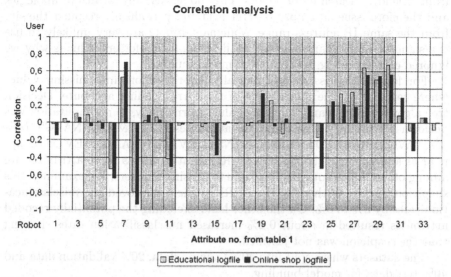

Fig. 2. Correlation analysis. Gray columns correspond to attributes not found in Tan and Kumar (2000,2001).

TUS200, %STATUS2XX, %STATUS304, %ERROR, HEAD) are only essential to one of the two logfiles. For the EDU logfile, the attributes %MAXDIVLINKCOV, %AVGDIVLINKCOV, %MINDIVLINKCOV, %MAXHTMLLINKCOV, %AVGHTMLLINKCOV, %STATUS2XX, and %MINHTMLLINKCOV are very important. Especially the correlations of %MAXDIVLINKCOV with session labeling (stronger than %IMAGE (one of the best attributes from Tan and Kumar (2001))) show that this attribute has to be taken into consideration because typical user sessions should have a high average value for %MAXDIVLINKCOV (as an result of hitting a web page containing only non-HTML links to automatically loaded images). On the other hand, %IMAGE only reaches 100 for user sessions if they download multimedia files linked by external sites without hitting a HTML site. This situation is rare in contrast to robot sessions solely requesting multimedia files because most search indexes have specialized spiders for multimedia content that only examine multimedia files and not download any HTML file (e.g., "FAST-WebCrawler/2.2.10 (Multimedia Search)"). For the SHOP logfile, %IMAGE and %HTML are the strongest attributes followed by the set of link coverage attributes. The correlation of %ERROR, %STATUS200 (OK), and %STATUS304 (not modified) with session labeling shows that user sessions contain primarily requests with the status code "OK" or "not modified".

Very precise models can easily be build using the network part of the IP address or the %NOREFERRER attribute, as most robot traffic originates from "friendly" search index robots. They do not use any stealth technologies and therefore issue an empty referrer field and periodically respider the site from the same IP address range. Malignant robots are very unlikely to use the same IP more than once and easily issue fake referrers. This is why we ignored corresponding attributes for model building.

For logistic regression and neural networks algorithms missing values where replaced by the mean value of the corresponding attribute. Decision tree algorithms can handle missing values intrinsically, so no imputation was performed. Missing values within the attributes AVGTIME, MINAVGTIME, MAXAVGTIME, STDEVTIME, MINSTDEV, and MAXSTDEV could appear as a recoding of the %NOREFERRER attribute as those attributes are among other things not calculable due to missing referrers. We examined this suspicion. Including the %NOREFERRER field improved the misclassification rates by 5% to 8%. On the other hand excluding the potentially recoded attributes resulted in about 0.2% increased misclassification rates showing that the suspicion was not justified.

The datasets where split into 40% training data, 20% validation data and 40% test data for model building.

For the EDU logfile, table 2 shows the baseline misclassification rate together with the mis, rec, and prec metrics calculated for the test datasets of all sessions, the single-request- and the 2-or-more-requests-sessions. For a combination of the best model for the single-request-sessions dataset and the 2-or-more-requests-sessions dataset, we calculated a mis value of 0.0853%. During our research, we identified several typical kinds of robot and user sessions for this website (e.g. survey attendees, single pageview visits originating from search indexes, robot sessions with an extremely low or high number of requested pages). This is a strong hint that navigational patterns do exist and that they can be used as an indicator for distinguishing between user and robot sessions.

Table 3 shows the results for the SHOP logfile. For a combined model, we calculated a mis value of 0.0654%. Again, we identified different typical kinds of user and robot sessions for this website. Additionally, we checked a dataset consisting solely of sessions with at least 3 pageviews. The generated prediction model, a neural network, achieved a mis value of 0.0157%, a rec value of 0.947 and a prec value of 0.954. For 3 or more pageviews, Tan and Kumar (2001) achieved (on a different dataset) precision above 82% and 95% recall, respectively.

6 Conclusions and outlook

The developed robot detection tool RDT enormously speeds up the preprocessing step within the overall web mining task. It's features enable researchers to efficiently produce high quality input data for the robot mining algorithms. The selected feature vector together with the low noise input

No.	Dataset	model	mis^{base}	mis	rec	prec
1	all sessions	logistic regression.	0.4919	0.1196	0.889	0.871
2	all sessions	neural network	0.4919	0.089	0.924	0.897
3	all sessions	decision tree	0.4919	0.0871	0.938	0.891
4	2-or-more-requests-sessions	logistic regression	0.2981	0.0527	0.920	0.908
5	2-or-more-requests-sessions	neural network	0.2981	0.0472	0.927	0.919
6	2-or-more-requests-sessions	decision tree	0.2981	0.0486	0.916	0.924
7	single-request-sessions	logistic regression	0.2623	0.1636	0.940	0.854
8	single-request-sessions	neural network	0.2623	0.1419	0.931	0.883
9	single-request-sessions	decision tree	0.2623	0.1338	0.962	0.871
10	all sessions	combination of 5 & 9	0.4919	0.0853	0.942	0.898

Table 2. Educational logfile: prediction quality

No.	Dataset	model	mis^{base}	mis	rec	prec
1	all sessions	neural network	0.2690	0.0721	0.850	0.880
2	all sessions	decision tree	0.2690	0.0703	0.832	0.901
3	2-or-more-requests-sessions	neural network	0.2013	0.0242	0.948	0.933
4	2-or-more-requests-sessions	decision tree	0.2013	0.0259	0.950	0.924
5	single-request-sessions	neural network	0.4477	0.1945	0.681	0.850
6	single-request-sessions	decision tree	0.4477	0.1743	0.779	0.818
7	all sessions	combination of 3 & 6	0.2690	0.0654	0.902	0.901
8	3 or more pageviews	neural network	0.1592	0.0157	0.947	0.954

Table 3. Online shop logfile: prediction quality

data lead to highly accurate prediction models. As expected, the generated models depend on the examined web site and confirm our decision to support robot mining by web data preprocessing devices as best fitting models have to be generated for every web site.

A methodological shortcoming of all approaches to robot mining so far is the usage of sessions as underlying object structure: first, sessions are built, usually by making use of behavioral parameters as an empirical session time-out, then, in a second step, prediction models for sessions are constructed. As robot sessions may differ considerably in parameters used for session build-ing, e.g., the session timeout, a two stage approach could further improve prediction quality as well as conceptual understanding of the data: at the first stage, a model for predicting crucial session building parameters (as timeout) is learned, then, at the second stage, sessions are built using the dynamically predicted session parameters from the first stage and analyzed by a prediction model for sessions as before. We will address this issue in a forthcoming paper.

A second open problem that robot mining and web usage mining have in common is the adequate handling of dynamically created pages.

References

ALMEIDA, V., RIEDI, R., MENASCÉ, D., MEIRA, W., RIBEIRO, F., and FONSECA, R. (2001): Characterizing and modeling robot workload on e-business sites. *Proc. 2001 ACM Sigmetrics Conference.* http://www-ece.rice.edu/riedi/Publ/RoboSimg01.ps.gz.

ANACONDA partners llc: Anaconda! foundation weather. http://anaconda.net/ap_wxdemo.shtml.

APACHE http server documentation project: Apache http server log files combined log format. http://httpd.apache.org/docs/logs.html\#combined.

ARLITT, M., KRISHNAMURTHY, D., and ROLIA, J. (2001): Characterizing the scalability of a large web-based shopping system. *ACM Transactions on Internet Technology.* http://www.hpl.hp.com/techreports/2001/HPL-2001-110R1.pdf.

BERENDT, B., MOBASHER, B., SPILIOPOULOU, M., and WILTSHIRE, J. (2001): Measuring the accuracy of sessionizers for web usage analysis. *Proceedings of the Web Mining Workshop at the First SIAM International Conference on Data Mining, Chicago.*

BOMHARDT, C.(2002): The robot detection tool. http://www.bomhardt.de/bomhardt/rdt/produkt.html.

CAPTCHA project: Telling humans and computers apart. http://www.captcha.net/.

CATLEDGE, L. and PITKOW, J. (1995): *Characterizing browsing strategies in the World-Wide Web. Computer Networks and ISDN Systems.*

GAUL, W. and SCHMIDT-THIEME, L. (2000): Frequent generalized subsequences - a problem from webmining. In: Gaul, W., Opitz, O., Schader, M. (eds.): *Data Analysis, Scientific Modelling and Practical Application*, Springer, Heidelberg, pp. 429-445.

HENG, C.: Defending your web site / server from the nimbda worm / virus. http://www.thesitewizard.com/news/nimbdaworm.shtml.

IPAOPAO.COM software Inc.: Fast email spider for web. http://software.ipaopao.com/fesweb/.

KOSTER, M. (1994): A standard for robot exclusion. http://www.robotstxt.org/wc/norobots-rfc.html.

MENASCÉ, D., ALMEIDA, V., RIEDI, R., RIBEIRO, F., FONSECA, R., and MEIRA, W. (2000): In search of invariants for e-business workloads. *Proceedings of ACM Conference on Electronic Commerce, Minneapolis, MN.* http://www-ece.rice.edu/riedi/Publ/ec00.ps.gz.

MULLANE, G. (1998): Spambot beware detection. http://www.turnstep.com/Spambot/detection.html.

TAN, P.-N. and KUMAR, V. (2000): Modeling of web robot navigational patterns. *Proc. ACM WebKDD Workshop.*

TAN, P.-N. and KUMAR, V. (2001): Discovery of web robot sessions based on their navigational patterns. http://citeseer.nj.nec.com/443855.html.

THE WEB ROBOTS PAGES. http://www.robotstxt.org/wc/robots.html.

Data Dependent Prior Modeling and Estimation in Contingency Tables: The Order-Restricted RC Model

Giulio D'Epifanio

Dipartimento di Scienze Statistiche,
Universitá di Perugia, Italy
giulio@stat.unipg.it

Abstract. Concerning the problem of estimating structural parameters and smoothing cells in complex contingency tables, we delineate a non standard approach - the "Constrained Fixed Point" - which is pseudo-Bayes (Agresti, 1990, pp. 466) and shares some basic ideas with the Prior Feedback Setup (Casella & Robert, 2002). Applied to a reference data set, it elicits a data-dependent prior which is structured according to the order-restricted log multiplicative model. It might be a practicable alternative to the full maximum likelihood (Ritov & Gilula, 1991) and intensive inferential tools as Gibbs sampling (Brink and Smith, 1996).

1 Introduction

In analyzing questionnaires, scaling of ordinal variables is often requested by cognitive and sociological scientists, for instance in "customer satisfaction" studies. Assuming a pair of quantities, which are continuous and distributed according to a bivariate normal but unobservable over latent dimensions, Goodman (1985, pp. 35-40) showed[1] the discretized distribution to have the structure of the order-restricted log multiplicative model. He interpreted (Goodman, 1991, pp. 1090) row and column parameters - the row and column scores - in term of maximizing the "intrinsic association" parameter.

Under multinomial sampling, for a $R \times C$ table of contingency, Brink *et al.* (1996) considered the following specific version of the order-restricted log multiplicative RC models (RRC):

$$\log \theta_{rs} = \mu + \alpha_r + \beta_s + \phi\, u_r\, v_s, \quad r := 1,..R, s := 1,..,C \qquad (1)$$
$$1 = u_1 \leq u_2 \leq ... \leq u_R = R,\ 1 = v_1 \leq v_2 \leq ... \leq v_C = C.$$

The parameter-scores $u := (u_1, u_2, \ldots, u_R)$, $v := (v_1, v_2, \ldots, v_C)$ allow the possibility of incorporating an overall trend, which reflect the order of the underlying categories, across the table with the association parameter ϕ determining the sign and magnitude. Here, θ_{rs} denotes the usual cell-parameter.

---

[1] He considered a more general setting, in which the marginal distributions are not necessarily normal

The reference data set is reproduced (by Strole, see Agresti, 1990, pp. 289) in table 1.

	high	...	...	...	...	low
well	64(63.635)	57(58.214)	57(57.177)	72(70.332)	36(35.929)	21(22.082)
mild	94(95.434)	94(92.646)	105(105.550)	141(141.074)	97(95.539)	71(72.140)
moderate	58(56.579)	54(53.005)	65(63.673)	77(80.703)	54(56.294)	54(50.541)
impaired	46(45.809)	40(41.569)	60(60.374)	94(92.056)	78(77.634)	71(72.007)

Table 1. Parent's Socioeconomic Status cross-classified with Mental Health Status (in brackets: CFP cell estimates)

In maximizing the likelihood (ML), technical difficulties could arise because parameters functionally depend upon each other (Ritov & Gilula, 1991). The likelihood may not be concave and have several local maxima. Instead, tools as the Gibbs sampling, although very flexible, are computationally very intensive. Moreover, standard non ambiguous stopping rules could be difficult to establish.

Concerning the problem of estimating the structural parameters of RRC model and smoothing the cell parameters, this work would compare a practicable pseudo-Bayes approach (for general references, see Agresti, 1990, pp. 466), over a reference data set against estimates of Gibbs sampling, and delineate developments. The proposed approach - the "Constrained Fixed Point" (CFP) (D'Epifanio, 1999) - shares some basic ideas with Prior Feedback (Casella & Robert, 2002, pp. 203-204). These approaches might be of practical interest (Robert and Hwang, 1996) to perform consistent estimates nearly to ML whenever fast methods were available to calculate posterior means and variances. They could, perhaps, work even when pathological situations occur for the likelihood function (D'Epifanio, 1996). Within the bayesian perspective, the empirical elicited prior might be, perhaps, shared by different people as a type of "standard" prior, to be used then in their specific data context, for benchmarking and comunicating results. For standard bayesian concepts and formulas, implicitly, we will refer to O'Hagan (1994).

2 The methodology

2.1. RRC as a structured prior-belief model. The profile of the cell-parameters is considered as a "virtual" R.V. whose distribution belongs to the parametric class of Dirichlet's distribution. Instead of depicting RRC directly over the cell-parameters (see also Agresti *et al*, 1989 for more references), RRC is viewed as a looser working conjecture which can be depicted over the coordinate space of Dirichlet's priors. Within the class of Dirichlet's distributions, prior distributions can be specified which have expected values satisfying pattern of the model RRC. Our model is structured as follows:

$$X_i \mid \theta \overset{i.i.d.}{\sim} Mult(x; \theta), \ i = 1, \ldots, n, \ (\text{ the measurement model})$$

$$\Theta \mid m, a \sim Dirich(\theta; m, a), \ (\text{"the belief container model"})$$

$$\lambda_{rs} := \log \frac{m_{rs}}{m_{RC}} = \mu + \alpha_r + \beta_s + \gamma_{rs}, \ (\text{"the RRC belief carrier model"})$$

$$\gamma_{rs} := \phi \, u_r \, v_s, \quad \phi > 0 \ (or \ \phi < 0)$$

$$a := w, \ w > 0$$

$$1 = u_1 < u_2 < \ldots < u_R = R, \ 1 = v_1 < v_2 < \ldots < v_C = C.$$

X_i denotes the (vectorized) random response, for a single case from the multinomial $Mult(x; \theta)$, $\theta_{rs} := Pr\{(X_i)_{rs} = 1\}$, for a $R \times C$ table of categories ($R := 4$, $C := 6$). $Dirich(\theta; m, a)$ denotes the Dirichlet's distribution with the (vectorized) expectation $m = E(\Theta; m, a)$ and the scalar hyper-parameter[2] $a > 0$. In this setting, the RRC belief model is viewed (using geometric terminology) as a sub-manifold (see also appendix 4.1) which is regularly embedded within the Dirichlet's model (the "container manifold").

To identify the RRC "belief-carrier" model, we used the (base-line) coordinate system where $\alpha_R = \beta_C = \gamma_{rC} = \gamma_{Rs} = \gamma_{RC} = \gamma_{rC} = 0$, $r := 1, \ldots, R$, $s := 1, \ldots, C$ (so that $\mu = 0$). Subsequent, by normalizing as $\tilde{\phi} := \phi(1 - R)(1 - C)$, we used (see appendix 4.2 for details) transformed scores $\tilde{u}, \tilde{v}$ satisfying the following constraint system: $-1 = \tilde{u}_1 < \tilde{u}_2 < \ldots < \tilde{u}_R = 0$, $-1 = \tilde{v}_1 < \tilde{v}_2 < \ldots < \tilde{v}_C = 0$. By using positive increments, $\delta := (\delta_1, \ldots, \delta_{R-1})$ and $\tau := (\tau_1, \ldots, \tau_{C-1})$, respectively for the row and column scores, the following linear constraints are satisfied: $\delta_1 + \cdots, \delta_{R-1} = 1$, $\tau_1 + \cdots, \tau_{C-1} = 1$. Thus, we used the logistic coordinate: $\tilde{\delta} := (log(\delta_r/\delta_1), \ r := 2, .. R - 1)$ and $\tilde{\tau} := (log(\tau_s/\tau_1), \ s := 2, .., C - 1)$. Therefore, the profile of hyper-parameters $\gamma := (\alpha, \beta, \phi, \tilde{\delta}, \tilde{\tau})$ is a coordinate-point which identifies a specific instance of the RRC belief model.

2.2. The Constrained Fixed Point: an overview.

Over the coordinate space of Dirichlet's distributions, Constrained Fixed Point (CFP) approach uses data to determinate a point-coordinate that elicits a prior which is conformed to the RRC belief model. Operationally, it leads to a "data-dependent prior" (Agresti, 1990, pp. 465-466). Adhering to a version of a principle of "least information", at the light of the actual current data, CFP searches, over the coordinate space of RRC, for that Dirichlet's distribution which would be, the more is possible, insensitive to the Bayesian updating rules if it had actually used as prior[3]. By formally interpreting this principle, we would minimize the "residual from updating":

---

[2]This would measure the strength of prior information; it could be interpreted as the "virtual" number of observation that the prior information would represent (Agresti et al., 1989)

[3]"The less such a prior is updated, the more it already was accounted for by the information added by current data", conditional on the assumed model (D'Epifanio, 1996, 1999). Intuitively, if a coordinate-point γ_0 exists such that, for given w, $\theta_0 = E(\Theta; \gamma_0, w)$ actually satisfies (strictly) RRC (1), then we should expect that $E(\Theta \mid \underline{x}_n; \gamma_0, w) \approx E(\Theta; \gamma_0, w)$, almost surely, for sufficiently large sample size n.

$$\min_{\gamma} \| \, Vec\,(E(\Theta \mid \underline{x}; \gamma, w) - E(\Theta; \gamma, w)\,) \, \| \, .$$

Here, $\underline{x}$ denotes the observed contingency table; $E(\Theta; \gamma, w)$, $Var(\Theta; \gamma, w)$, $E(\Theta \mid \underline{x}; \gamma, w)$ and $Var(\Theta \mid \underline{x}; \gamma, w)$ denote the $(R \times C)$ matrices whose (rs)-th component is, respectively, the expectation, the variance, the updated expectation and the updated variance of the cell (rs)-th. For the sake of simplicity, we considered w here given[4]. As a specific instance (the more general formulation is sketched in appendix 4.3.), we used an euclidean distance, weighted across all the category-cells as follows:

$$\min_{\gamma} \sum_{r,s} \frac{(E(\Theta_{rs} \mid \underline{x}; \gamma, w) - E(\Theta_{rs}; \gamma, w))^2}{\{Var(\Theta_{rs}; \gamma, w) - Var(\Theta_{rs} \mid \underline{x}; \gamma, w)\}}.$$

Assuming that coordinate γ^* exists that $E(\Theta \mid \underline{x}; \gamma^*, w) \approx E(\Theta; \gamma^*, w)$, by using standard formulas, we could see that denominator would be proportional, for any components, to $E(\Theta_{rs} \mid \underline{x}; \gamma^*, w)(1 - E(\Theta_{rs} \mid \underline{x}; \gamma^*, w)$ which is an estimate of the cell-variance. Roughly speaking, denominator might be interpreted as a sample approximation of $Var[E(\Theta_{rs} \mid \underline{x}; \gamma, w)]$, w.r.t. the predictive distribution given (γ, w).

3 Application

Since the Dirichlet's model is conjugate to the binomial, analytic formulas are available which easily and very quickly calculate posterior expectations and variances, at each temporary coordinate-point $\gamma^{(q)}$ of RRC manifold. Subsequent, using iterated geometric projections of weighted variations due to updating, efficient numerical analytic procedures yield sequence $\gamma^{(q)}$, $q := 1, 2, \ldots$ to run over the coordinate space of RRC, until it converges whenever the vector of the "variation due to updating" (see also appendix 4.4) is orthogonal to the sub-manifold RRC. This is a necessary condition in order that the minimum residual from updating is reached.

Asymptotics of unrestricted FP has been considered in other works (D'Epifanio, 1996, 1999; see also Casella & Robert, 2002, pp. 204)

[4]When also w (which determines the "shrinkage" effect) has to be determined by data, a further criterion is necessary which is complementary to that of "least updating". Briefly, we considered the criterion which searches, over the full coordinate space (γ, w), for that prior which - while residual from updating is minimized - assures also an equilibrium between "virtual relative information gain from updating" and "virtual predicted relative cost". Formally, over the coordinate space of the RRC priors, we would, across all the cells, $\{Var(\Theta_{rs}; \gamma, w) - Var(\Theta_{rs} \mid \underline{x}; \gamma, w)\}/Var(\Theta_{rs}; \gamma, w)$ - interpreted as the virtual information gain - meets with $Var(\Theta_{rs} \mid \underline{x}; \gamma, w)/Var(\Theta_{rs}; \gamma, w)$ - the virtual loss. Coordinate-points for which the former is too small would imply the latter is too large. Across all the cells, it yields a non trivial system, whose solutions can have also, in general, a large sample interpretation (D'Epifanio, 1996) which is related to the Fisher's information

Written in S-plus, by starting from preliminary rough values and letting $w := 1$ (the least informative prior), a very fast procedure calculated the scores $u = (1, 2.4759, 2.72145, 4)$, $v = (1, 1.02299, 2.30357, 3.030144, 4.71107, 6)$, in the Brink and Smith parametrization[5], the association $\phi = 0.09833725$ (so that $\exp(\phi) = 1.103335$) and $w = 1659.016$. It calculated $\alpha = (-2.918029, -1.766441, -2.208831)$, $\beta = (-2.437090, -2.492935, -2.150683, -1.756379, -1.910129)$.

Thus, we could check that the column and row scores, and the association parameter nearby meet with estimates of Gibbs sampling, as reported in figure 1.

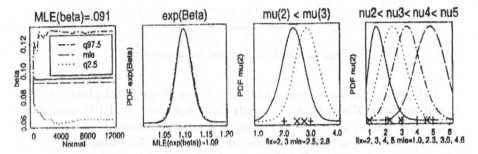

Fig. 1. Results from Gibbs sampling (Brink and Smith, 1996). Here, $Beta := \phi$, $mu := u$, $nu := v$

Let (γ^*, w^*) denote the CFP solution. Conditional on the belief-carrier model RRC, the original table was recovered (see the values within brackets, in table 1) by using the cell estimates $m_{rs}^* := \{E(\Theta; (m, \Sigma)(\gamma^*, w^*))\}_{rs}$. This CFP smoother could be useful when zero counts or missing data occur, for instance, in sparse contingency tables. Of course, the pseudo-empirical Bayes predictor[6] (see O'Hagan, 1994) $E(\Theta_{rs} \mid \underline{x}; \gamma^*, w^*) = A^*(f_{rs} - m_{rs}^*) + m_{rs}^*$ (here, $f_{rs} := \underline{x}_{rs}/n$ denotes the actual observed relative frequency for the cell (r, s), and $A^* := \frac{n}{w^*+n}$ is the shrinking factor) is more accurate than the previous smother. But, by construction from the CFP perspective, their discrepancy would minimized if the prior-belief RRC model had reasonably adhered to the actual data-generating process.

---

[5]In the new parametrization, it calculated the logistic coordinates: $\tilde{\delta} = (0.1435653\ -1.6498580)$ and $\tilde{\tau} = (-4.026379463, -0.006500991, -0.573227125, 0.265533869)$

[6]It should work also if the prior-belief model was non adequate; in fact, automatically, it would combine good characteristics of sample proportion and of model-based estimators (see also Agresti, 1990, pp. 466)

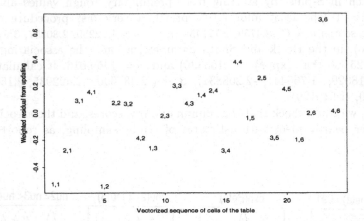

Fig. 2. Weighted residual from updating

Using the "residuals from updating", types of graphical plots could be useful for some diagnostics. To study "discrepancies" of RRC over single cells, for instance, a plot as that of figure 2 would indicate - considering also the high value of w^* - that the belief model RRC was adequate enough, perhaps apart from the cell (3,6) and a slight residual trend due to the rows.

4 Appendix: some detail

4.1 About a differential geometric setting. Let γ denote a profile of identifiable parameters for the RRC belief-model. Recall (O'Hagan,1994) that $(\Sigma)_{rs} := Var(\Theta_{rs}; m, w) = \frac{1}{1+w} \cdot m_{rs}(1 - m_{rs})$. The vector $Vec\,(m, \Sigma)$ describes, by varying the cell parameters m and the scalar w within the proper range, the geometrical container manifold, which depicts the model of Dirichlet's distributions, whose coordinate are provided by parameters $(Vec\,m, w)$. Within this container, the point $(Vec\,m(\gamma), w)$, whose coordinate are the (hyper-)parameters (γ, w), describe the sub-manifold which depicts the RRC belief-model. Thus, the RRC belief-carrier model may be viewed as a specific sub-manifold which is embedded within the model of Dirichlet's distributions.

4.2 About specification of order restriction. By using the transformations $\tilde{u} = (u - R)/(R - 1)$ and $\tilde{v} = (v - C)/(C - 1)$, scores were standardized so that $-1 = \tilde{u}_1 \leq \tilde{u}_2 \leq ... \leq \tilde{u}_R = 0$, $-1 = \tilde{v}_1 \leq \tilde{v}_2 \leq ... \leq \tilde{v}_C = 0$. Thus, we could rewrite: $\gamma_{rs} = \{\phi(1 - R)(1 - C)\}\tilde{u}_r\tilde{v}_s + \phi(1 - R)C\tilde{u}_r + \phi(1 - C)R\tilde{v}_s + \phi RC$. Therefore, recalling that $\mu = 0$ because $\lambda_{RC} = 0$, $\lambda_{rs} = \{\alpha_r + \phi(1 - R)C\tilde{u}_r\} + \{\beta + \phi(1 - C)R\tilde{v}_s\} + \tilde{\phi}\tilde{u}_r\tilde{v}_s = \tilde{\alpha}_r + \tilde{\beta}_s + +\tilde{\phi}\tilde{u}_r\tilde{v}_s$. Thus, RRC may be rewritten as:

$$\lambda_{rs} = \tilde{\alpha}_r + \tilde{\beta}_s + \tilde{\phi}\,\tilde{u}_r\,\tilde{v}_s$$

$-1 = \tilde{u}_1 \leq \tilde{u}_2 \leq \ldots \leq \tilde{u}_R = 0,\ -1 = \tilde{v}_1 \leq \tilde{v}_2 \leq \ldots \leq \tilde{v}_C = 0$, where $\tilde{\phi}_r := \phi(1-R)(1-C)$, $\tilde{\alpha}_r := \alpha_r + \phi(1-R)C\tilde{u}_r$, $\tilde{\beta}_s := \beta_s + \phi(1 - C)R\tilde{v}_r$. Now, by using non negative increments $\delta := (\delta_1, \ldots, \delta_{R-1}) \geq 0$ and $\tau := (\tau_1, \ldots, \tau_{C-1}) \geq 0$, we might re-parametrize the scores as follows: $\tilde{u}_1 = -1, \tilde{u}_2 = -1 + \delta_1, \cdots, \tilde{u}_R = -1 + \delta_1 + \cdots, \delta_{R-1}$; similarly, $\tilde{v}_1 = -1, \tilde{v}_2 = -1 + \tau_1, \cdots, \tau_C = -1 + \tau_1 + \cdots, \tau_{C-1}$. Since $\tilde{u}_R = 0$ we would have $-1 + \delta_1 + \cdots + \delta_{R-1} = 0$, that is the linear constraint $\delta_1 + \cdots + \delta_{R-1} = 1$. Assuming now the increments are strictly positive (by relaxing the equality constraints), this constraint would be automatically fulfilled by using the $(R-2)$ logistic coordinates $\tilde{\delta}$ so that $\delta_r = \exp(\tilde{\delta}_r)/(1 + \sum_{t:=2}^{R-1} \exp(\tilde{\delta}_t))$, $r := 1, \ldots, R-1$. Analogously, we would have $\tau_1 + \cdots, \tau_{C-1} = 1$ and we might consider the $(C-2)$ logistic coordinates $\tilde{\tau}$ so that $\tau_s = \exp(\tilde{\tau}_s)/(1 + \sum_{t:=2}^{C-1} \exp(\tilde{\tau}_t))$, $s := 1, \ldots, C-1$.

4.3 About a more general formulation. Let us consider the following multi-dimensional (column) vector valued operator:

$$(\gamma, w) \longmapsto \mathbf{\Delta}_{\underline{x}}(m, \Sigma)(\gamma, w) := \begin{bmatrix} Vec\,(E(\Theta \mid \underline{x}; (m, \Sigma)(\gamma, w)) - m(\gamma, w)) \\ Vec\,(2\,Var(\Theta \mid \underline{x}; (m, \Sigma)(\gamma, w)) - \Sigma(\gamma, w)) \end{bmatrix}.$$

Varying the coordinate-point $p(\gamma, w)$, the operator $\mathbf{\Delta}_{\underline{x}}(m, \Sigma)(\gamma, w)$ describes a vector field. Recalling notes (3) and (4), the full CFP approach would search for solutions of the following problem:

$$\min_{\gamma, w}\{(\mathbf{\Delta}_{\underline{x}}(\gamma, w))^t \cdot \mathcal{W}^{-1}(\gamma, w) \cdot \mathbf{\Delta}_{\underline{x}}(\gamma, w)\}.$$

Here, $\mathcal{W}(\gamma, w)$ denotes a definite positive weighting matrix. As a specific instance of this general formulation, explicitly, we could consider the following system: $\min_{\gamma, w} \sum_{r,s}(\Delta_{rs})^2(\gamma, w)$, where Δ_{rs} denotes, for the cell (rs)-th, the following weighted vector of variations:

$$\begin{pmatrix} \{Var(\Theta_{rs}) - \mathcal{E}[Var(\Theta_{rs}|\underline{X})]\}^{-1/2} & 0 \\ 0 & Var(\Theta_{rs})^{-1} \end{pmatrix} \begin{bmatrix} E(\Theta_{rs} \mid \underline{x}; \gamma, w) - E(\Theta_{rs}; \gamma, w) \\ 2Var(\Theta_{rs} \mid \underline{x}; \gamma, w) - Var(\Theta_{rs}; \gamma, w) \end{bmatrix}.$$

Here $E\,[.]$ denotes the expectation with respect to the predictive distribution of $\underline{X}$. Recalling again note (4), note here that matching $\{Var(\Theta_{rs}) - Var(\Theta_{rs}|\underline{x})\}/Var(\Theta_{rs})$ (the "relative information gain from updating") with $Var(\Theta_{rs}|\underline{x})/Var(\Theta_{rs})$ (the "virtually predicted relative cost, given the data") would be formally equivalent to match $2Var(\Theta_{rs}|\underline{x}; \gamma, w)$ with $Var(\Theta_{rs}; \gamma, w)$, by weighting each cell with the inverse of its variance $Var(\Theta_{rs})$, across all the cells of the table. The quantity $\{Var(\Theta_{rs}; \gamma, w) - \mathcal{E}[Var(\Theta_{rs}|\underline{X}; \gamma, w)]\}$ may be interpreted as "the expected (over the sample space) predicted information gain, from updating".

4.4 The computational process. Let $\mathbf{P}(\gamma, w) := < \frac{\partial}{\partial(\gamma, w)}, [\frac{\partial}{\partial(\gamma, w)}]^t > ^1$ $\cdot [\frac{\partial}{\partial(\gamma, w)}]$ denote the coordinate projector of the full variation $\mathbf{\Delta}_{\underline{x}}(\gamma, w)$ upon the tangent space of the sub-manifold at $p(\gamma, w)$. Here, $[\frac{\partial}{\partial(\gamma, w)}]$ denotes the basic coordinate (row-)vector system, $< \, . \, >$ the usual inner product. The operator

$$(\gamma, w) \longmapsto \mathbf{P}(\gamma, w)[\mathcal{W}^{-1/2}\mathbf{\Delta}_{\underline{x}}](\gamma, w)$$

is a vector field which yields a vector over the tangent space at coordinate-point (γ, w). This vector field induces a dynamic over the coordinate space, which yields the following iterative process:

$$(\gamma, w)^{(q+1)} = (\gamma, w)^{(q)} + \rho \cdot \mathbf{P}((\gamma, w)^{(q)})[\mathcal{W}^{-1/2}\mathbf{\Delta}_{\underline{x}}](m, \Sigma)((\gamma, w)^{(q)}).$$

Here, ρ denotes the step-length. Due to the non-linearity, ρ should be sufficiently small to assure convergence.

Provided this process converges, the convergence-point would satisfy the orthogonal equation: $\mathbf{P}(\gamma, w)[\mathcal{W}^{-1/2}\mathbf{\Delta}_{\underline{x}}(\gamma, w)] = 0$. The convergence-point would be a CFP solutions, by checking that the process reduces distances progressively.

References

AGRESTI A. (1990): *Categorical Data Analysis*, Wiley, New York

AGRESTI A., CHIANG C. (1989): Model-Based bayesian Methods for Estimating Cell Proportions in Cross-Classification Table having Ordered Categories, *Computational Statistics & Data Analysis*, 7, 245-258

BRINK A.M., SMITH A.F.M. (1996): Bayesian Modelling of the association in Contingency Tables. In: Forcina, Marchetti, Hatzinger, Galmacci (eds): *Proceedings of the 11th International Workshop on Statistical Modelling*,

CASELLA G, ROBERT C.P. (2002): *Monte Carlo Statistical Methods* (third printing), Springer, New York

D'EPIFANIO G. (1996): Notes on A Recursive Procedure for Point Estimation, *Test*, Vol. 5, N. 1, pp.1-24

D'EPIFANIO G. (1999): Properties of a fixed point method, 1999, *Annales de L'ISUP*, Vol. XXXXIII, Fasc. 2-3

GOODMAN L. A. (1985): The 1983 Henry L. Rietz Memorial Lecture, *The Annals of Statistics*. Vol. 13, N.1, pp. 10-69

GOODMAN L. A. (1991): Measures, Model, and Graphical Displays in the Analysis of Cross-Classified Data, *Journal of the American Statistical association*, Vol 86, N. 416, pp. 1085-1111

O'HAGAN A. (1994): *Bayesian Inference*, Kendall's Advanced Theory of Statistics, Vol. 2b, New York: John Wiley & Sons

RITOV Y., GILULA Z. (1991): The Ordered-Restricted RC model for Ordered Contingency Tables: Estimation and Testing of fit. *The Annals of Statistics*, 19, 2090-2101

ROBERT C.P., HWANG G.J.T. (1996): Maximum Likelihood Estimation Under Order Restrictions by the Prior Feedback Method, *Journal of the American Statistical association*, Vol. 91, N. 433, pp.167-172

PLS Typological Regression:
Algorithmic, Classification and Validation Issues[*]

Vincenzo Esposito Vinzi, Carlo N. Lauro, and Silvano Amato

Dipartimento di Matematica e Statistica,
Università di Napoli "Federico II", Italy
{vincenzo.espositovinzi; carlo.lauro; silamato}@unina.it

Abstract. Classification, within a PLS regression framework, is classically meant
in the sense of the SIMCA methodology, i.e. as the assignment of statistical units
to a-priori defined classes. As a matter of fact, PLS components are built with
the double objective of describing the set of explanatory variables while predicting
the set of response variables. Taking into account this objective, a classification
algorithm is developed that allows to build typologies of statistical units whose
different local PLS models have an intrinsic explanatory power higher than the
initial global PLS model. The typology induced by the algorithm may undergo a
non parametric validation procedure based on bootstrap. Finally, the definition of
a compromise model is investigated.

1 Introduction

PLS (Partial Least Squares or Projection to Latent Structures) methods cover
a very broad area of statistical methods, from regression to generalised linear
models, from data analysis to causal and path modelling. This paper aims at
taking into account classification aspects within PLS when a group structure
is pursued. At present, classification in PLS is performed, in the SIMCA (Soft
Independent Modelling of Class Analogy) approach (Wold et al. (1984)), in
order to identify local models for possible groups of statistical units and to
predict a probable class membership for new statistical units.

On the other hand, PLS Discriminant Analysis (PLS-DA, Sjöström et al.
(1986)) is performed in order to sharpen the separation between groups of
statistical units, by hopefully rotating PCA (Principal Components Analysis)
components such that a maximum separation (Barker and Rayens (2003))
among classes is obtained, and to understand which variables carry the class
separating information.

Actually, PLS components are built by trying to find a proper compromise between two purposes: describing the set of explanatory variables and
predicting the response ones. A PLS-based classification should well benefit
from such a property in the direction of building typologies with an intrinsic

---

[*]This paper is financially supported by the EU project ESIS IST-2000-21071.

prediction power. This approach may go further than the classical SIMCA method, that works on the reassignment of units to pre-defined classes, and may be further exploited to identify group structures in PLS Path Modelling.

Namely, this paper proposes a PLS Typological Regression (PLS-T) with the objective to identify, in a PLS regression framework with a real dependence structure between measured variables, a classification of the statistical units in a certain number of classes oriented to a better prediction of the response variable(s). PLS-T shares the same feasibility of PLS regression to data structures showing critical features such as missing data, non–normality, reduced number of units with respect to the number of explanatory variables, a high degree of multi–collinearity. These features explain why, in the following, PLS framework has been preferred to any simultaneous solution based on a singular value decomposition.

The typology is identified by means of a data–driven approach based on cluster analysis and PLS regression. This approach aims at defining a methodology for improving prediction in PLS regression through the identification of a group structure of the statistical units.

In order to assess the stability of the method, the identified classes undergo a bootstrap–based validation procedure (section 4).

In PLS-T, whose algorithm is given in section 3, two groups of variables are assumed to be observed on n statistical units; data are collected in matrices $\mathbf{X} = (\mathbf{x}_1, \ldots, \mathbf{x}_p)$ and $\mathbf{Y} = (\mathbf{y}_1, \ldots, \mathbf{y}_q)$ of n rows and p and q columns (variables) respectively. Furthermore, the existence of a dependence relationship between $\mathbf{X}$ and $\mathbf{Y}$ is assumed, namely:

$$\mathbf{Y} = f(\mathbf{X}) + \mathbf{V} \qquad (1)$$

where $f(\cdot)$ is a linear function and $\mathbf{V}$ is an error matrix. If matrix $\mathbf{X}$ is not well conditioned ($rank(\mathbf{X}) < p$ or multi–collinearity among columns of $\mathbf{X}$ is present) OLS solution leads to unstable estimates. In order to cope with this problem, several solutions exist: Ridge Regression, Principal Components Regression or Partial Least Squares Regression (Wold et al. (1984)) are just few examples. de Jong (1993) shows that PLS outperforms other methods when multi–collinearity is present among $\mathbf{Y}$ columns and/or information in $\mathbf{X}$ relevant to $\mathbf{Y}$ is contained in eigenvectors of $\mathbf{X}$ associated to its lowest eigenvalues.

Actually, PLS searches for two sets of weights, $\mathbf{W} = [\mathbf{w}_1, \mathbf{w}_2, \ldots, \mathbf{w}_m]$ and $\mathbf{Z} = [\mathbf{z}_1, \mathbf{z}_2, \ldots, \mathbf{z}_m]$ for $\mathbf{X}$ and $\mathbf{Y}$ respectively, such that pairwise covariances between components $\mathbf{t}_l = \mathbf{X}\mathbf{w}_l$ and $\mathbf{u}_l = \mathbf{Y}\mathbf{z}_l$ are maximised $\forall l = 1, 2, \ldots, m$. Relation in equation (1) is then exploited by using component matrix $\mathbf{T}$:

$$\mathbf{Y} = \mathbf{TC} + \mathbf{V}_{(m)} \qquad (2)$$

where $\mathbf{T} = \mathbf{XW}$ and $\mathbf{C} = (\mathbf{T'T})^{-1}\mathbf{T'Y}$ is the coefficient matrix from the OLS regression of $\mathbf{Y}$ on $\mathbf{T}$; $\mathbf{V}_{(m)}$ is the error matrix associated to the m-components model. The number of PLS components to retain in the above expression is usually selected by means of cross–validation (e.g. Tenenhaus (1998)).

2 Classification and discrimination with PLS

The SIMCA approach runs, at first, a global PCA or PLS regression (according to the available data structure) on the whole dataset in order to identify G groups of units. Local models are then estimated for each class.

Once the classes have been identified, the prediction of class membership for a new statistical unit is based on its normalised distances from local models by means of:

$$DModX.N_{g,i} = \sqrt{\frac{\frac{\sum_{j=1}^{p} e_{gj,i}^2}{p-m_g}}{\frac{\sum_{i=1}^{n} \sum_{j=1}^{p} e_{gj,i}^2}{(n_g-m_g-1)(p-m_g)}}}$$

where $e_{gj,i}^2$ is the squared residual of the i-th unit on the j-th variable for the g-th PLS local model. The i-th unit is assigned to the g-th model ($g = 1, 2, \ldots, G$) if $DModX.N_i < \sqrt{F_{1-\alpha}(k_1, k_2)}$, where the critical value is chosen according to a Fisher-Snedecor distribution with $k_1 = m_g$ and $k_2 = n - 2$ degrees of freedom (df) and to a significance level α. The assumption that $DModX.N$ follows a Fisher-Snedecor distribution is not completely proved and the df are empirically fixed (see on the matter Eriksson et al. (1999); for an asymptotic distribution of PLS components, Lazraq and Clèroux (2001)).

The SIMCA approach enforces the composition of the classes to be the same as the one initially chosen on the basis of the global model. Furthermore, it computes the distance of each unit from the model with respect to the explanatory variables only and, in order to compute the class membership probabilities, refers to a distribution of this distance whose shape and degrees of freedom are not yet clearly defined and hidden in SIMCA software.

On the other hand, PLS-DA consists in a classical PLS regression where the response variable is a categorical one (replaced by the corresponding set of dummy variables) expressing the class membership of the statistical units. Therefore, PLS-DA does not allow for other response variables than the one needed for defining the classes. As a consequence, all measured variables play an explanatory role with respect to the supervised classification.

In both SIMCA and PLS-DA, the features of PLS regression are not totally exploited as the classification is not optimized with respect to prediction.

3 PLS typological regression: the algorithm

The objective pursued by PLS Typological Regression (PLS-T, firstly presented by Lauro and Esposito Vinzi (2002)) is to identify, in a non symmetrical framework, a classification of the statistical units in G classes oriented to a better prediction of the response variables. Then, on the basis of this classification, a compromise PLS model that is more coherent with the G local models is searched for. The adopted criterion consists in splitting the

PLS global model (considering all statistical units as a single class) into a set of G local models (considering a classification in G classes of the statistical units). The local models shall perform better in terms of distance of the units from the corresponding local models as well as in terms of the explanatory power for the dependent variables.

The PLS-T algorithm consists of the following steps:

1) Perform a PLS global model on all units and retain the significant components.
2) Perform a cluster analysis (e.g. k–means algorithm) for identifying a group structure of the units in G classes based on the PLS components from the global model. As usual in any clusterwise regression method, the choice of the number of classes G is critical and still represents an open issue. In PLS-T, being faithful to the data-driven approach, it is chosen on the basis of a preliminary hierarchical cluster analysis based on the global PLS components. In order to lower the sensitivity of the method to the initial choice, G may be consolidated on the basis of the compromise model discussed in section 3.1.
3) Perform a PLS local model for each of the G previously identified classes.
4) Compute distances of units from local models according to:

$$DModY.N^*_{g,i} = \sqrt{\frac{\frac{\sum_{k=1}^{q}\left[v_{gk,i}^2/Rd(\mathbf{T}^{(g)},\mathbf{y}_k)\right]}{q-m_g}}{\frac{\sum_{i=1}^{n}\sum_{k=1}^{q}\left[v_{gk,i}^2/Rd(\mathbf{T}^{(g)},\mathbf{y}_k)\right]}{(n_g-m_g-1)(q-m_g)}}}$$

that is a normalised distance, where $v_{gk,i}^2$ is the square of the i-th residual on the k-th dependent variable for the g-th PLS model, and $Rd(\mathbf{T}^{(g)},\mathbf{y}_k)$ is the redundancy index for the k-th dependent variable in the PLS model with m_g retained components in $\mathbf{T}^{(g)}$.

$DModY.N^*_{g,i}$ is the normalised distance, with respect to the q response variables $\mathbf{y}_k$'s, of each unit i belonging to the n_g units in the g-th class from the related PLS model with m_g retained components.

The weighting of $DModY.N^*_{g,i}$ attempts to take into account relevant issues for each local model as to the different number of components being retained (m_g), the different number of units being included in each class (n_g) and the different explanation power ($Rd(\mathbf{T}^{(g)},\mathbf{y}_k)$) provided by each local model for each response variable.

5) Reassign each unit to the nearest local model.
6) If there is any change in the composition of the classes implying a modification in the local models, then repeat steps 3 to 5 otherwise go ahead.
7) Describe the obtained classes by means of the characterising explanatory variables by means of the VIP index, defined as:

$$VIP_{m_g j} = \sqrt{\frac{p\sum_{h=1}^{m_g}\left[\sum_{k=1}^{q}R^2\left(\mathbf{y}_{gk},t_h^{(g)}\right)\right]w_{ghj}^2}{\sum_{k=1}^{q}R^2\left(\mathbf{y}_{gk};t_1^{(g)},t_2,\ldots,t_{m_g}^{(g)}\right)}}$$

The interpretation of classical tools, such as the VIP (Variable Importance in the Projection) index inside PLS regression, is shown to be very useful for describing the local models in terms of the characterising explanatory variables for each class. By keeping in mind that the mean of squared VIP's is equal to 1, those explanatory variables showing a VIP greater than 1 are considered to be relevant.

8) Search for a compromise model (see section 3.1), i.e. a model that, with respect to the initial global model, is more coherent with the local ones.

If convergence in step 6 is not attained, either a different number of classes may be selected in step 3 or a class of floating units may be further identified.

3.1 The compromise model

Once local models have been identified and local components $\mathbf{T}_{m_g}^{(g)}$ have been computed, there might be the need to search for a compromise model, that is a global model oriented to local models previously identified in PLS-T. Namely, the compromise model shall have a higher predictive power for the q dependent variables than the global model initially estimated.

Firstly, a common number $\tilde{m}$ of components need to be retained for all local models; $\tilde{m}$ is selected as the maximum number of components retained for the different local models, i.e. $\tilde{m} = \max\{m_1, m_2, \ldots, m_G\}$, so as not to lose relevant information from each class. If one model requires substantially more components than the others, the suspect arises that other classes exist.

Secondly, a new matrix $\tilde{\mathbf{T}}$ is built by stacking the G PLS local score matrices. A PLS Regression of $\mathbf{Y}^*$ (i.e. $\mathbf{Y}$ with the rows being sorted according to the class membership of the units) on $\tilde{\mathbf{T}}$ is performed (Figure 1) in order to yield the compromise model.

Figure 2 provides with a geometrical interpretation of the first two PLS components for the initial global model ($\mathbf{t}_1$ and $\mathbf{t}_2$), the first PLS components for the classes (e.g. $\mathbf{t}_1^{(g_1)}$ and $\mathbf{t}_1^{(g_3)}$) and for the compromise model ($\tilde{\mathbf{t}}_1$).

This procedure leads to the following predictive compromise model for the generic k-th dependent variable for the statistical units in class g:

$$\mathbf{y}_{gk} = \sum_{s=1}^{\tilde{m}} \tilde{c}_{sk} \tilde{\mathbf{t}}_s^{(g)} + residual$$

where $\tilde{c}_{sk}$'s are the coefficients of the compromise model defined similarly to the coefficients in equation (2) for the global model. It is worth noticing that the s-th component compromise score for the i-th unit in the g-th class is $\tilde{t}_{s,i} = \sum_{h=1}^{m_g} \tilde{w}_{sh} t_{h,i}^{(g)}$ where $t_{h,i}^{(g)} = \sum_{j=1}^{p} w_{ghj} x_{j,i}$.

It is now possible to express the prediction of $\mathbf{y}_k$ for the i-th unit, according to the compromise model, in terms of the explanatory variables $\mathbf{x}_j$'s:

$$y_{k,i} = \sum_{s=1}^{\tilde{m}} \tilde{c}_{sk} \left[\sum_{h=1}^{m_g} \tilde{w}_{sh} \left(\sum_{j=1}^{p} w_{ghj} x_{j,i} \right) \right]$$

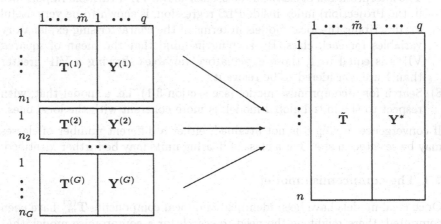

Fig. 1. Construction of the matrices for the search of the compromise model.

The above expression may well be used in order to assign new units with an a-priori unknown class membership to one of the G classes. The following steps need to be performed:

1) Compute the scores $t_{h,new} = \sum_{j=1}^{p} w_{hj} x_{j,new}$ of the new units on the m components in the global model.
2) Project the barycenters of the G classes previously identified by PLS-T on the same m components.
3) In the space spanned by the m components, compute the distance between the new units and the barycenters of the classes.
4) Assign each new unit to the nearest class (local model).
5) Once the class membership is known, compute the predictions for the dependent variables according to the compromise model.
6) Re-assign the new units to the nearest classes according to the scores from the compromise model.
7) Reiterate steps 1) through 6) until convergence.

This procedure further enhances the interest of the compromise model. Coherently with the nature of PLS-T, it aims at a class assignment oriented towards a better prediction.

4 Validation issues

The local models identified by PLS-T may be validated by means of a non parametric procedure (Amato, 2003). A bootstrap–based test is proposed for the coefficients c_{gkh}'s related to the h-th PLS component for the prediction

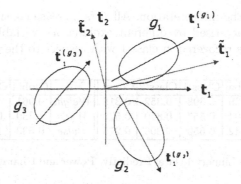

Fig. 2. PLS-T geometrical representation.

of y_k's in the g-th local model. In order to test whether they are significantly different from the global model coefficients c_{kh} in $\mathbf{C}_h$, the following hypotheses are set:

$$\mathrm{H}_0 : \gamma_{kh} - \gamma_{gkh} = 0 \ \text{vs.}\ \mathrm{H}_1 : \gamma_{kh} - \gamma_{gkh} \neq 0 \qquad (3)$$

where γ_{kh}'s and γ_{gkh}'s are the parameters estimated by c_{kh}'s and c_{gkh}'s.

Let $\hat{F}_{(\mathbf{Y},\mathbf{T})}$ be the empirical distribution of the observed dependent variables in $\mathbf{Y}$ and the global model PLS components in $\mathbf{T}$. The validation procedure consists of the following steps:

1) draw B (e.g. greater than 1000) samples (with replication) from $\hat{F}_{(\mathbf{Y},\mathbf{T})}$.
2) for any $b = 1, 2, \ldots, B$, split each resample into G subsets and compute the PLS coefficients c^b_{gkh}'s.
3) compute the differences: $d^b_{gkh} = c_{kh} - c^b_{gkh}$.
4) build the Monte Carlo approximation $\hat{F}_{d(BOOT)}$ of the d^b_{gkh} distribution.

The α-th and the $(1 - \alpha)$-th percentiles of $\hat{F}_{d(BOOT)}$ define the bootstrap decision area for the test in (3) with a nominal 2α significance level.

The procedure may be similarly replicated for any set of coefficients in the local models as well as in the compromise one.

5 An application on Linnerud data and conclusions

The interpretation aspects of PLS-T are shown and discussed by means of an application on the well known Linnerud data (Tenenhaus, 1998) related to 3 physical – explanatory – (*weight, waist, pulse*) and 3 athletic performance – dependent – (*fixed-bar traction, press-ups, jumps*) variables observed on 20 units. Table 1 shows the explanation power, R^2 index, and the characterising variables, VIP index, for each class (G=2) and for the initial global model. The two classes identified by PLS-T clearly improve the goodness of the results as well as the interpretation. All R^2's increase considerably and each class is well characterised by different explanatory variables. For instance, the role of *pulse* is recovered in class 1 with respect to the global model.

R^2	Global	Class 1	Class 2	Comp.	VIP	Global	Class 1	Class 2
Traction	0.220	0.398	0.352	0.316	*Weight*	0.961	0.692	0.604
Press–ups	0.394	0.557	0.810	0.570	*Waist*	1.339	0.754	1.378
Jumps	0.042	0.650	0.206	0.275	*Pulse*	0.533	1.397	0.859

Table 1. PLS-T on Linnerud Data: Predictive Power and Characterising Variables.

Finally, the fifth column of Table 1 shows how the compromise model outperforms the global one in terms of its predictive power. The bootstrap–based procedure proposed in section 4, whose application details are omitted for the sake of brevity, validates the local models.

The proposed PLS Typological Regression has shown to be very useful in searching for a proper group structure of the statistical units. Namely, local PLS models are defined so as to perform better than the single global one in terms of predictive power. Moreover, insights on the explanatory role of specific variables are given. Finally, the identification of a compromise model turns out to be very interesting both in providing an overall picture of the dependence relationships based on the group structure, and in predicting the class membership of new units.

References

AMATO, S. (2003): Validazione non parametrica nella regressione Partial Least Squares. *Tesi di Dottorato*. Università di Napoli "Federico II", Italy.
BARKER, M. and RAYENS, W. (2003): Partial Least Squares paradigm for Discrimination. *Journal of chemometrics 17: 1–8*. United Kingdom.
DE JONG, S. (1993): PLS fits closer than PCR, short communication. *Journal of Chemometrics, 17:166–173*.
ERIKSSON, L., JOHANSSON, E., KETTANEH-WOLD, N. and WOLD, S. (1999): *Multi and Megavariate Data Analysis using Projection Methods*. Umetrics.
LAURO C. and ESPOSITO VINZI, V. (2002): Exploring, Modelling and Classifying with PLS. *Opening lecture at the 26th Annual Conference of the GFKL.* Mannheim, Germany.
LAZRAQ, A. and CLÈROUX, R (2001): The PLS multivariate regression model: testing the significance of successive PLS components. *Journal of Chemometrics. 15:523–536*.
SJÖSTRÖM, M., WOLD, S. and SÖDERSTERÖM, B. (1986): PLS Discriminant Plots. In: *Proceedeings of PARC in Practice*. Elsevier, Noth Holland.
TENENHAUS, M. (1998): *La régression PLS*. Technip. Paris.
WOLD S., ALBANO, C., DUNN, W.J., EDLUND, U., ESBENSEN, K., GELADI, P., HELLBERG, S., JOHANSSON, E., LINDBERG, W., and SJÖSTRÖM, M. (1984): Multivariate Data Analysis in Chemistry. *SIAM Journal of Scientific and Statistical Computing, 5, 735–744*.

Weighted Metric Multidimensional Scaling

Michael Greenacre

Departament d'Economia i Empresa,
Universitat Pompeu Fabra, Barcelona, Espana
michael@upf.es

Abstract. This paper establishes a general framework for metric scaling of any distance measure between individuals based on a rectangular individuals-by-variables data matrix. The method allows visualization of both individuals and variables as well as preserving all the good properties of principal axis methods such as principal components and correspondence analysis, based on the singular-value decomposition, including the decomposition of variance into components along principal axes which provide the numerical diagnostics known as contributions. The idea is inspired from the chi-square distance in correspondence analysis which weights each coordinate by an amount calculated from the margins of the data table. In weighted metric multidimensional scaling (WMDS) we allow these weights to be unknown parameters which are estimated from the data to maximize the fit to the original distances. Once this extra weight-estimation step is accomplished, the procedure follows the classical path in decomposing a matrix and displaying its rows and columns in biplots.

1 Introduction

We are concerned here with methods that transform a rectangular data matrix into a graphical representation of the rows (usually individuals, or subjects) and columns (usually variables, or objects). A typical example of a visualization is the biplot (Gabriel, 1971; Gower & Hand, 1996) in which a distance approximation is achieved with respect to the individuals, while the variables are depicted by arrows defining biplot axes allowing estimation of the original data values.

An example is shown in Figure 1, where data on 12 countries and five variables on different scales are mapped to a biplot where (squared) distances between countries are standardized Euclidean distances of the form:

$$d^2(\mathbf{x}_i, \mathbf{x}_j) = (\mathbf{x}_i - \mathbf{x}_j)' \mathbf{D}_S^{-1} (\mathbf{x}_i - \mathbf{x}_j) = \sum_k (x_{ik} - x_{jk})^2 / s_k \qquad (1)$$

where $\mathbf{x}_i$ and $\mathbf{x}_j$ are the i-th and j-th rows of the matrix and $\mathbf{D}_s$ is the diagonal matrix of standard deviations s_k. The factors $1/s_k$ are standardizing factors which can alternatively be regarded as weights assigned to each variable in the calculation of the distance between countries. In correspondence analysis

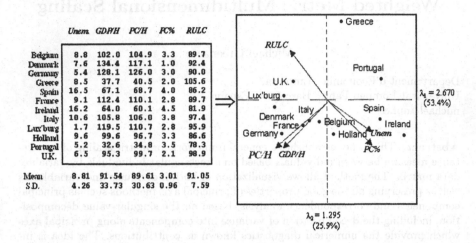

Fig. 1. Data matrix on 12 European community countries in 1990, showing five economic indicators: Unemployment Rate (%), Gross Domestic Product per Head (index), Private Consumption per Head (index), Change in Private Consumption (%) and Real Unit Labour Cost (index). The principal component biplot on standardized data is shown on the right, with vectors indicating biplot axes for each variable.

(CA) of a table of frequencies we have a similar distance function, where the weights for the rows and the columns in the chi-square distance function are proportional to the inverses of the corresponding row and column margins of the table.

In general we can define the weighted Euclidean (squared) distance:

$$d^2(\mathbf{x}_i, \mathbf{x}_j) = (\mathbf{x}_i - \mathbf{x}_j)'\mathbf{D}_w(\mathbf{x}_i - \mathbf{x}_j) = \sum_k w_k(x_{ik} - x_{jk})^2 \qquad (2)$$

where $\mathbf{D}_w$ contains weights w_k, to be determined by a process still to be described.

In several contexts, the practitioner is more interested in distance measures which are non-Euclidean. A good example of this is in ecological studies where the data are species-abundances at different sites where equal area- or volume-sampling has been conducted. In this case, ecologists almost always prefer the Bray-Curtis dissimilarity measure, since it has an immediate and simple interpretation, with values from 0 (exactly the same species composition) to 100 (no species in common at all). The Bray-Curtis index d_{ij} between samples i and j with species abundances denoted by $\{n_{ik}\}$ and $\{n_{jk}\}$ is defined as follows:

$$d_{ij} = 100 \frac{\sum_k |n_{ik} - n_{jk}|}{\sum_k n_{ik} + \sum_k n_{jk}} \qquad (3)$$

Such a dissimilarity measure is simple to understand, but non-Euclidean (see Gower & Legendre, 1986). Often nonmetric MDS is used to analyse these indices (see, for example, Field, Warwick & Clarke, 1982), but our interest here is in metric MDS since there are many relevant spin-offs in the classical metric approach, most importantly the natural biplot framework thanks to the singular value decomposition, as well as the convenient breakdown of variance across principal axes of both the rows and columns which provide useful numerical diagnostics in the interpretation and evaluation of the results. The idea will be to approximate the distances of choice, however they are defined, by a weighted Euclidean distance. The weights estimated in this process will be those that are inherently assigned to the variables by the chosen distance function.

In Section 2 we shall summarize the classical MDS framework with weights. Then in Section 3 we describe how any distance measure between individuals can be approximated by a weighted Euclidean metric. In Section 4 we give some examples of this approach and conclude with a discussion in Section 5.

2 Weighted multidimensional scaling

Our main interest is in weighting the variables in the definition of distances between the individuals, but exactly the same technology allows weighting of the individuals as well to differentiate their effect on determining the eventual solution space. Since the weighting of the individuals serves a different purpose from the weighting of the variables, we shall use the terms *mass* for an individual and *weight* for a variable (in correspondence analysis the term mass is used exactly in the sense used here). Both individual masses and variable weights will be included in our description that follows. This description is essentially that of the geometric definition of correspondence analysis (see Greenacre, 1984, chapter 2), the only difference being that the weights on the variables are unknown, to be determined, and not prescribed.

Suppose that we have a data matrix $\mathbf{Y}$ $(n \times m)$, usually pre-centred with respect to rows or columns or both. Let $\mathbf{D}_r$ $(n \times n)$ and $\mathbf{D}_w$ $(m \times m)$ be diagonal matrices of row (individual) masses and column (variable) weights respectively. With no loss of generality the row masses are presumed to have a sum of 1. The rows of $\mathbf{Y}$ are presumed to be points in an m-dimensional Euclidean space, structured by the inner product and metric defined by the weight matrix $\mathbf{D}_w$. The solution, a low-dimensional subspace which fits the points as closely as possible, is established by weighted least-squares, where each point is weighted by its mass. The following function is thus minimized:

$$In(\mathbf{Y} - \hat{\mathbf{Y}}) = \sum_i r_i (\mathbf{y}_i - \hat{\mathbf{y}}_i)' \mathbf{D}_w (\mathbf{y}_i - \hat{\mathbf{y}}_i) \tag{4}$$

where $\hat{y}_i$, the i-th row of $\hat{Y}$, is the closest low-dimensional approximation of y_i. The function $In(*,*)$ stands for the *inertia*, in this case the inertia of the difference between the original and approximated matrices. The *total inertia*, which is being decomposed or "explained" by the solution, is equal to $I(Y)$. As is well-known (see, for example, Greenacre, 1984, Appendix), the solution can be obtained neatly using the generalized singular value decomposition (GSVD) of the matrix Y. Computationally, using an ordinary SVD algorithm, the steps in finding the solution are to first pre-process the matrix Y by pre- and post-multiplying by the square roots of the weighting matrices, then calculate the SVD and then post-process the solution using the inverse transformation to obtain principal and standard coordinates. The steps are summarized as follows:

$$1 . \; \mathbf{S} = \mathbf{D}_r^{1/2} \mathbf{Y} \mathbf{D}_w^{1/2} \tag{5}$$

$$2 . \; \mathbf{S} = \mathbf{U} \mathbf{D}_\alpha \mathbf{V}' \tag{6}$$

$$3 . \; \text{Principal coordinates of rows: } \mathbf{F} = \mathbf{D}_r^{-1/2} \mathbf{U} \mathbf{D}_\alpha \tag{7}$$

$$4 . \; \text{Standard coordinates of columns: } \mathbf{G} = \mathbf{D}_w^{-1/2} \mathbf{V} \tag{8}$$

The columns (variables) are conventionally depicted by arrows and the rows (individuals) by points. A two-dimensional solution, say, would use the first two columns of $\mathbf{F}$ and $\mathbf{G}$. The total inertia is the sum of squares of the singular values $\alpha_1^2 + \alpha_2^2 + \dots$, the inertia accounted for in two-dimensional solution is the sum of the first two terms $\alpha_1^2 + \alpha_2^2$ while the inertia not accounted for (formula (4)) is the remainder of the sum: $\alpha_3^2 + \alpha_4^2 + \dots$. Apart from this simple decomposition of the variance in the data matrix, there is another benefit of the least-squares approach via the SVD, namely a further breakdown of inertia for each point along each principal axis. Since this decomposition applies to points in principal coordinates, we show it for the row points in Table 1 (a similar decomposition can be shown for column points in principal coordinates by merely scaling the standard coordinates by their respective singular values).

3 Computing the variable weights

We now consider the case when a general distance function is used to measure distance or dissimilarity between individuals, not necessarily a Euclidean-imbeddable distance. Using conventional MDS notation let us suppose that δ_{ij}^2 is the observed dissimilarity between individuals i and j based on their description vectors $\mathbf{x}_i$ and $\mathbf{x}_j$. We use $d_{ij}^2 = d_{ij}^2(\mathbf{w})$ to indicate the weighted Euclidean distance based on (unknown) weights in the vector $\mathbf{w}$. The problem is then to find the weights which give the best fit to the observed dissimilarities, either minimizing fit to distances (least-squares scaling, or LSS) or to squared distances (least-squares squared scaling, or LSSS). As always it is

Principal axes

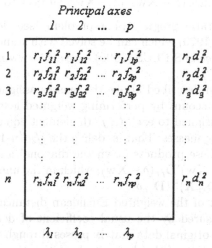

Table 1. Decomposition of inertia of n row points along all p principal axes of the matrix. Each row adds up to the inertia of a point, the mass (r_i) times squared distance (d_i^2) of the point to the centre, while each column adds up to the principal inertia $\lambda_k = \alpha_k^2$ of the corresponding axis. Rows and columns expressed relative to their respective totals constitute the contributions, or numerical diagnostics used to support the interpretation of the solution space.

easier to fit to squared distances, which is the approach we take here. Thus the objective function is:

$$\text{minimize} \sum_i \sum_j (\delta_{ij}^2 - d_{ij}^2(\mathbf{w}))^2 \text{ over all } \mathbf{w} \geq \mathbf{0}$$

that is,

$$\text{minimize} \sum_i \sum_j (\delta_{ij}^2 - \sum_k w_k (x_{ik} - x_{jk})^2)^2 \text{ over all } \mathbf{w} \geq \mathbf{0}.$$

Ignoring for the moment the non-negativity restriction on $\mathbf{w}$, the problem can be solved by least-squares regression without a constant as follows:

- Define $\delta = \text{vec}(\delta_{ij}^2)$ as the $1/2 n(n-1)$ vector of given squared distances, that is the half-triangle of distances strung out as a vector.
- Define $\mathbf{X} = [(x_{ik} - x_{jk})^2]$ as the $1/2 n(n-1) \times m$ matrix of squared differences between the values of a variable, for each pair of individuals.
- Fit the multiple regression model $\delta = \mathbf{X}\mathbf{w} + \mathbf{e}$ which has least-squares solution $\mathbf{w} = (\mathbf{X}'\mathbf{X})^{-1}\delta$.

In our experience it frequently occurs that the weights calculated without constraints turn out to be positive. However, when this is not the case, minimisation has to be performed with constraints:

$$\text{minimize}\,(\delta - \mathbf{Xw})'\,(\delta - \mathbf{Xw}) \text{ subject to } \mathbf{w} \geq 0 \qquad (9)$$

This is a quadratic programming problem (see, for example, Bartels, Golub & Saunders, 1970) which can be solved with standard software, for example function *nlregb* in S-PLUS (1999) - see also www.numerical.rl.ac.uk/qp /qp.html.

In the regression described above the masses assigned to the individuals can be taken into account by performing weighted least-squares regression, with the weights assigned to each (i, j)-th element equal to the product $r_i r_j$ of the corresponding masses. That is, define the $\frac{1}{2}n(n\text{-}1) \times \frac{1}{2}n(n\text{-}1)$ diagonal matrix $\mathbf{D}_{rr}$ with these products down the diagonal and then minimize the quadratic form $(\delta - \mathbf{Xw})'\mathbf{D}_{rr}(\delta - \mathbf{Xw})$, which in the unconstrained case gives solution $\mathbf{w} = (\mathbf{X'D}_{rr}\mathbf{X})^{-1}\mathbf{D}_{rr}\delta$.

The goodness of fit of the weighted Euclidean distances to the original distances can be measured by the usual coefficient of determination R^2. Our visualization of the original data matrix passes through two stages of approximation, first the fitting of the distances by estimating the variable weights, and second the matrix approximation of the GSVD to give the graphical display of the weighted Euclidean distances and the associated biplot vectors for the variables.

4 Application: Bhattacharyya (arc cos) distance

This research was originally inspired by an article in the Catalan statistical journal *Qüestiió* by Vives & Villaroya (1996), who apply *Intrinsic Data Analysis* (Rios, Villaroya & Oller, 1994) to visualize in the form of a biplot a compositional data matrix, specifically the composition in each of the 41 Catalan counties (*comarques*) of eight different professional groups. This analysis is based on the Bhattacharyya distance between counties:

$$d^2(\mathbf{p}_i, \mathbf{p}_j) = arccos(\sum\nolimits_k \sqrt{p_{ik}p_{jk}}) \qquad (10)$$

where the function arc cos is the inverse cosine. The same authors report that their results are almost identical to those of correspondence analysis. Applying weighted MDS to the same data the weights are estimated to be the following for the eight professional groups:

Weights estimated by fitting to Bhattacharyya distances

Pro&Tec	PersDir	ServAdm	Com&Ven	Hot&Alt	Agr&Pes	Indust	ForArm
1.9	4.6	5.7	1.9	2.0	1.6	0.9	41.1

Weights implied by correspondence analysis $(1/c_k)$

Pro&Tec	PersDir	ServAdm	Com&Ven	Hot&Alt	Agr&Pes	Indust	ForArm
9.6	49.4	8.8	8.5	10.0	8.1	2.4	263.0

It is interesting to see that the variable "ForArm" (*forces armades* in Catalan, i.e. armed forces) receives much higher weight than the others, very similar to the situation in CA where it is weighted highly because of very low relative frequency and thus low variance. The arc cos distance inherently weights this variable highly as well even though this is not at all obvious from its definition in (10).

The fit of the weighted Euclidean distances to the arc cos distances is excellent: sum-of-squared distances, SSD = 9.570, with sum-of-squares due to regression, SSR = 9.327 (97.5%) and sum-of-squares due to error, SSE = 0.243 (2.5%).

In Figure 3 we see the *form biplot* of the results. The form biplot scales the rows (counties) in principal coordinates so that we can interpret the inter-row distances, and the columns (professional categories) in standard coordinates. Projecting the rows onto the biplot axes defined by the column vectors will give an approximation to the original percentages in the data matrix. The alternative is to plot the results as a *covariance biplot* where the rows are in standard coordinates and the columns are in principal coordinates, in which case the covariance structure amongst the columns is displayed.

Finally, in Table 2 we have the contributions to inertia that are the spin-off of our approach – we show the contributions for the column points. The columns of Table 1 relative to their sums (the principal inertias, or squared singular values) are given in the columns headed CTR, for each of the two dimensions, often called the *absolute contributions* in correspondence analysis. The rows of Table 1 relative to their sums (the inertias of the column points) are given in the columns headed COR.

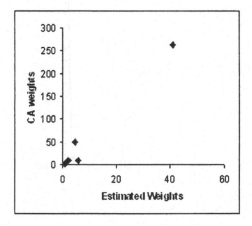

Fig. 2. Comparison of estimated weights to fit optimally to arc cos distances and correspondence analysis weights.

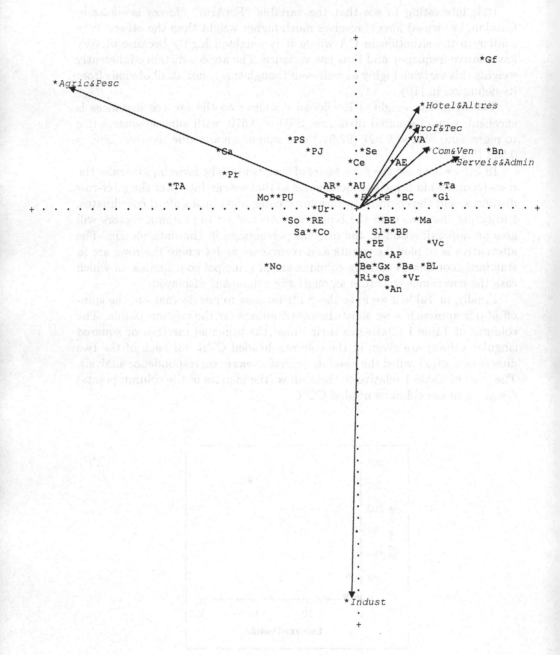

Fig. 3. Form biplot of 41 Catalan counties (in principal coordinates) and 8 professional categories (in standard coordinates)

| | Quality | Principal axes | | | |
| | | 1 | | 2 | |
	QLT	CTR	COR	CTR	COR
Prof&Tec	622	24	304	46	318
PersDir	385	5	308	2	77
Serveis&Admin	832	243	754	46	78
Com&Ven	772	47	604	24	168
Hotel&Altres	608	41	280	89	328
Agric&Pesc	989	636	907	105	82
Indust	998	0	1	676	997
ForArm	148	0	0	8	148

Principal inertias   0.0203   0.0111

(% of total)   (57.1%)   (31.1%)

Table 2. Decomposition of inertia of 8 column points along first two principal axes. The principal inertias (eigenvalues, or squared singular values) are decomposed amongst the points as given in the columns CTR, given in "permills", for example the first axis is determined mostly by points *Agric&Pesc* (63.6%) and *ServAdm* (24.3%). These are the columns of Table 1 relative to their totals. The inertia of a point is decomposed along the principal axes according to the values in the columns COR. These are the rows of Table 1 relative to their totals, and are also squared correlations (angle cosines) of the points with the principal axes. Thus the point *Indust* is mostly explained by the second axis, while *ForArm* is not well explained by either axis and also plays hardly any role in determining the two-dimensional solution, even with the large weight assigned to it. The column QLT refers to quality of display in the plane, and is the sum of the COR columns.

References

BARTELS, R.H., GOLUB, G.H. & SAUNDERS, M.A. (1970): Numerical techniques in mathematical programming. In *Nonlinear Programming* (eds J.B. Rosen, O.L. Mangasarian & K. Ritter), London: Academic Press, pp. 123-176.

FIELD, J.G., CLARKE, K.R. & WARWICK, R.M. (1982): A practical strategy for analysing multispecies distribution patterns. *Marine Ecology Progress Series*, **8**, 37-52.

GABRIEL, K. R. (1971): The biplot-graphic display of matrices with applications to principal component analysis. *Biometrika*, **58**, 453-467.

GOWER, J.C. & LEGENDRE, P. (1986): Metric and Euclidean properties of dissimilarity coefficients. *Journal of Classification*, **3**, 5-48.

GREENACRE, M.J. (1984): *Theory and Applications of Correspondence Analysis*. London: Academic Press.

RIOS, M., VILLAROYA, A. & OLLER, J.M. (1994): Intrinsic data analysis : a method for the simultaneous representation of populations and variables. Research report 160, Department of Statistics, University of Barcelona.

VIVES, S. & VILLAROYA, A. (1996): La combinació de tècniques de geometria diferencial amb anàlisi multivariant clàssica: una aplicació a la caracterització de les comarques catalanes. *Qüestiio*, **20**, 449-482.

S-PLUS (1999). S-PLUS 2000 Guide to Statistics, Volume 1, Mathsoft, Seattle, WA.

An Improved Majorization Algorithm for Robust Procrustes Analysis

Patrick J.F. Groenen[1], Patrizia Giaquinto[2], and Henk A.L. Kiers[3]

[1] Econometric Institute,
Erasmus University, Rotterdam, The Netherlands
groenen@few.eur.nl
[2] Dipartimento di Scienze Statistiche,
Università di Bari, Italy
patrizia_giaquinto@yahoo.it
[3] Department of Psychology,
University of Groningen, The Netherlands
h.a.l.kiers@ppsw.rug.nl

Abstract. In this paper, we focus on algorithms for Robust Procrustes Analysis that are used to rotate a solution of coordinates towards a target solution while controlling outliers. Verboon (1994) and Verboon and Heiser (1992) showed how iterative weighted least-squares can be used to solve the problem. Kiers (1997) improved upon their algorithm by using iterative majorization. In this paper, we propose a new method called "weighted majorization" that improves on the method by Kiers (1997). A simulation study shows that compared to the method by Kiers (1997), the solutions obtained by weighted majorization are in almost all cases of better quality and are obtained significantly faster.

1 Introduction

In exploratory data analysis, quite often situations arise where for the same objects two sets of coordinates are derived that may be approximate rotations of each other. For example, principal components analysis applied to two different samples yields two sets of components that may be rotations of each other. Also, in the area of multidimensional scaling, two dissimilarity matrices of the same objects may yield two configurations where most points are approximate rotations of each other with the exception of a few outlying objects.

For this reason, procedures that aim at detecting such possible similarities in two coordinate matrices are welcome. Procrustes analysis (see Hurley and Cattell (1962)) deals with the problem of fitting a set of points, say matrix $\mathbf{X}$, to a target coordinate matrix $\mathbf{Y}$ by a rotation matrix $\mathbf{T}$, in such a way that $\mathbf{XT}$ resembles $\mathbf{Y}$ as closely as possible.

The starting point in the *ordinary* Procrustes problem is to minimize the badness-of-fit function

$$L_p(\mathbf{T}) = \|\mathbf{Y} - \mathbf{X}\mathbf{T}\|^2 = \sum_{i=1}^{n}\sum_{j=1}^{k}(y_{ij} - \mathbf{x}'_i\mathbf{t}_j) = \sum_{i=1}^{n}\sum_{j=1}^{k}e_{ij}^2, \qquad (1)$$

where $\mathbf{Y}$ and $\mathbf{X}$ are $n \times k$ known coordinate matrices, $\mathbf{T}$ is a $k \times k$ (unknown) rotation matrix and e_{ij} is the residual of the model. Note that by restricting $\mathbf{T}$ to be a rotation matrix, the shape of $\mathbf{X}$ is preserved. This restriction amounts to requiring that $\mathbf{T}$ be orthonormal, that is, $\mathbf{T}\mathbf{T}' = \mathbf{T}'\mathbf{T} = \mathbf{I}$. Green (1952), Cliff (1966), and Schönemann (1966) provided a solution for the rotation matrix $\mathbf{T}$ that minimizes (1).

A disadvantage of least-squares modelling is that outliers may have a large influence on the rotation. To down-weight the effect of large residuals, several proposals exist in the literature, see, for instance, Huber (1964), Beaton and Tukey (1974) and Mosteller and Tukey (1977). In particular, Verboon (1994) proposed a *robust* form of Procrustes analysis, considering the sum of absolute residuals, $L_r(\mathbf{T}) = \sum_{i=1}^{n}\sum_{j=1}^{k}|e_{ij}|$, and solved it by using iterative majorization. For details on iterative majorization, see De Leeuw (1992,1994), Heiser (1995), Borg and Groenen (1997), Kiers (2002). Verboon (1994) also proved that his algorithm is the same as iterated reweighted least-squares, because it requires iteratively minimizing the majorizing function

$$\mu_R(\mathbf{T}, \mathbf{T}^0) = \frac{1}{2}\sum_{i=1}^{n}\sum_{j=1}^{k}\frac{e_{ij}^2}{|e_{ij}^0|} + \frac{1}{2}L_r(\mathbf{T}^0), \qquad (2)$$

where the superscript 0 is used to indicate the estimates from the previous iteration. It is not difficult to see that $\mu_R(\mathbf{T}, \mathbf{T}^0)$ is (up to a constant) a weighted least-squares function in the residual e_{ij} and thus in $\mathbf{T}$. Therefore, it suffices to look at the *weighted* Procrustes problem

$$L_{\text{WProc}}(\mathbf{T}) = \sum_{i=1}^{n}\sum_{j=1}^{k}w_{ij}e_{ij}^2, \qquad (3)$$

with weights $w_{ij} = 1/|e_{ij}^0|$, assuming that $|e_{ij}^0| > 0$. If all the weights w_{ij} are equal, then $L_{\text{WProc}}(\mathbf{T})$ is minimized by the standard least-squares Procrustes Analysis solution. However, when minimizing (3), the weights will generally not all be the same and a nonstandard procedure is needed.

Kiers (1997) discusses an iterative majorization algorithm for weighted Procrustes analysis, which improves upon Verboon (1994). Even though the method by Kiers converges much faster than Verboon's (1994), it can still be quite slow, especially in the case of big differences between the residuals. In this paper, we propose an adaptation of the method by Kiers (1997) called *weighted majorization* and apply it to robust Procrustes analysis. We show that the method by Kiers can be seen as a special case of weighted majorization. Finally, we present a small simulation study on the computational efficiency and quality of the new weighted majorization approach for robust Procrustean analysis.

2 The method by Kiers (1997)

In this section, we discuss the method by Kiers (1997) in some detail and show when this method may become slow.

The weighted least-squares Procrustes loss function in (3) may be written as

$$L_{\mathrm{WProc}}(\mathbf{T}) = \sum_{i=1}^{n} \sum_{j=1}^{k} w_{ij} e_{ij}^2 = \mathbf{e}' \mathbf{D_w} \mathbf{e}, \tag{4}$$

where $\mathbf{e}$ is the nk vector with residuals e_{ij} and $\mathbf{D_w}$ is an $nk \times nk$ diagonal matrix with elements w_{ij} on the diagonal.

The heart of majorization methods consists of a proper majorizing inequality. Let m be the overall maximum value of $\mathbf{W}$, so that $m = \max_{ij} w_{ij}$. Then, Kiers (1997) applies the inequality

$$(\mathbf{e} - \mathbf{e}^0)'(\mathbf{D_w} - m\mathbf{I})(\mathbf{e} - \mathbf{e}^0) \leq 0 \tag{5}$$

which was first used by Heiser (1987) in the context of iterative majorization. This inequality holds because the matrix $\mathbf{D_w} - m\mathbf{I}$ is negative semi-definite. With further expansions and some rearranging we get

$$\mathbf{e}'\mathbf{D_w}\mathbf{e} \leq m\mathbf{e}'\mathbf{e} - 2m\mathbf{e}'[\mathbf{e}^0 - m^{-1}\mathbf{D_w}\mathbf{e}^0] - \mathbf{e}^{0'}\mathbf{D_w}\mathbf{e}^0 + m\mathbf{e}^{0'}\mathbf{e}^0. \tag{6}$$

Define $c_1 = m\mathbf{e}^{0'}\mathbf{e}^0 - \mathbf{e}^{0'}\mathbf{D_w}\mathbf{e}^0$ and $\mathbf{z} = \mathbf{e}^0 - m^{-1}\mathbf{D_w}\mathbf{e}^0$. Now we can write a majorizing inequality for (4) as

$$L_{\mathrm{WProc}}(\mathbf{T}) = \mathbf{e}'\mathbf{D_w}\mathbf{e} \leq m(\mathbf{e} - \mathbf{z})'(\mathbf{e} - \mathbf{z}) - m\mathbf{z}'\mathbf{z} + c_1 = \mu(\mathbf{T}, \mathbf{T}^0). \tag{7}$$

Expression (7) shows the strength of the method by Kiers: the original weighted least-squares problem has been transformed in an unweighted one (since m is a constant) for which an analytical solution is available by the SVD. In addition, the method by Kiers is very general: it is applicable to any *weighted* least-squares model which has for the *unweighted* case an easy least-squares solution or fitting algorithm available. Despite its generality, the method by Kiers can be very slow for particular structures of weights. To see why this is so, we first note that $\mathbf{z}_i$ has elements

$$z_{ij} = e_{ij}^0 - \frac{w_{ij}}{m} e_{ij}^0. \tag{8}$$

Then, we can write

$$(\mathbf{e} - \mathbf{z})'(\mathbf{e} - \mathbf{z}) = \sum_{i=1}^{n} \sum_{j=1}^{k} (e_{ij} - z_{ij})^2$$

$$= \sum_{i=1}^{n} \sum_{j=1}^{k} \left(\left[1 - \frac{w_{ij}}{m} \right] \mathbf{x}_i^{0\prime} \mathbf{t}_j^0 + \frac{w_{ij}}{m} y_{ij} - \mathbf{x}_i' \mathbf{t}_j \right)^2$$

$$= \sum_{i=1}^{n} \sum_{j=1}^{k} (r_{ij} - \mathbf{x}_i' \mathbf{t}_j)^2 = \text{tr } (\mathbf{R} - \mathbf{X}\mathbf{T}')'(\mathbf{R} - \mathbf{X}\mathbf{T}'),$$

where

$$r_{ij} = \left[1 - \frac{w_{ij}}{m} \right] \mathbf{x}_i^{0\prime} \mathbf{t}_j^0 + \frac{w_{ij}}{m} y_{ij}. \tag{9}$$

From (9) we see that $\mathbf{x}_i' \mathbf{t}_j$ is fitted to the convex combination $[1 - w_{ij}/m]\mathbf{x}_i^{0\prime} \mathbf{t}_j^0 + (w_{ij}/m_i)y_{ij}$ for all i, j. Remember that m is the overall largest weight w_{ij} so that $0 \le w_{ij} \le m$ implies $0 \le w_{ij}/m \le 1$. Now, if there is a single weight w_{ij} within the matrix that is much larger than all the other weights, then for those ij we have $w_{ij}/m \ll 1$, so that $\mathbf{x}_i^{0\prime} \mathbf{t}_j^0$ dominates y_{ij}. In other words, when updating the majorizing function $\mu(\mathbf{T}, \mathbf{T}^0)$, $\mathbf{x}_i' \mathbf{t}_j$ is fitted mostly to the previous iteration $\mathbf{x}_i^{0\prime} \mathbf{t}_j^0$ and only to a minor extent to y_{ij}. The consequence is that the more deviant the largest w_{ij} is from the other weights, the slower the algorithm by Kiers (1997) will be.

3 Weighted majorization

The main idea of weighted majorization is to apply the majorization inequality (5) rowwise. The corresponding majorizing inequality can be obtained from (5) by adding a subscript for row i, that is,

$$(\mathbf{e}_i - \mathbf{e}_i^0)'(\mathbf{D}_{\mathbf{w}_i} - m_i \mathbf{I})(\mathbf{e}_i - \mathbf{e}_i^0) \le 0, \tag{10}$$

where $\mathbf{D}_{\mathbf{w}_i}$ is the diagonal matrix of the vector of row weights $\mathbf{w}_i$ with elements w_{ij} and m_i is defined as the maximum row value of $\mathbf{w}_i$. The inequality still holds since $\mathbf{D}_{\mathbf{w}_i} - m_i \mathbf{I}$ is negative semi-definite.

The first consequence of weighted majorization is that instead of a single majorizing function for all the residuals, now we have different majorizing functions for each of the n rows. So, expanding (10) in the same way as (6) and summing over all rows gives

$$L_{\text{WProc}}(\mathbf{T}) = \sum_{i=1}^{n} \mathbf{e}_i{'} \mathbf{D}_{\mathbf{w}_i} \mathbf{e}_i$$

$$\le \sum_{i=1}^{n} m_i \mathbf{e}_i{'} \mathbf{e}_i - 2 \sum_{i=1}^{n} m_i \mathbf{e}_i{'} [\mathbf{e}_i^0 - m_i^{-1} \mathbf{D}_{\mathbf{w}_i} \mathbf{e}_i^0] + \sum_{i=1}^{n} c_{1i}$$

$$= \mu_1(\mathbf{T}, \mathbf{T}^0), \tag{11}$$

with $c_{1i} = m_i e_i^{0'} e_i^0 - e_i^{0'} D_{w_i} e_i^0$. The second consequence is that the elements r_{ij} are constructed differently, and this is just the core of the improvement in our method, as it will be shown in a moment. We need at first some additional notations: we let $c = \sum_{i=1}^n c_i$ and define a matrix Z containing rows $z_i = e_i^0 - m_i^{-1} D_{w_i} e_i^0$. Moreover, we collect the maximum row values m_i in a diagonal matrix D_m, where $m = (m_1, m_2, .., m_n)$. Then we may express $\mu_1(T, T^0)$ as

$$\mu_1(T, T^0) = \sum_i (e_i - z_i)' D_m (e_i - z_i) - \sum_i m_i z_i' z_i + c$$

$$= \text{tr } (E - Z)' D_m (E - Z) - \text{tr } Z' D_m Z + c. \qquad (12)$$

The only important part of (12) is

$$\text{tr } (E - Z)' D_m (E - Z) = \text{tr } (R - XT')' D_m (R - XT') \qquad (13)$$

with

$$r_{ij} = \left[1 - \frac{w_{ij}}{m_i}\right] x_i^{0'} t_j^0 + \frac{w_{ij}}{m_i} y_{ij}. \qquad (14)$$

If there are big differences among the weights, the effect is limited only to the single row to which the large weight belongs, since the term w_{ij}/m_i now depends on the denominator m_i, that is, the largest weight *per row*, while in Kiers (1997) it depends on the *overall* largest weight. Comparing (9) to (14) shows that in the special case of $D_m = mI$ (thus all maximum row weights are the same) weighted majorization coincides with the method by Kiers (1997).

The weighted majorization algorithm will to a large extent fit $x_i' t_j$ to the data y_{ij}, and in those rows with high weights will fit $x_i' t_j$ to the values of the previous iteration. By definition, $w_{ij}/m_i \geq w_{ij}/m$ implying that in weighted majorization $x_i' t_j$ is fitted more to y_{ij} than to $x_i^{0'} t_j^0$ compared to the method by Kiers, so that the method by Kiers is expected to be slower than ours. Another property of weighted majorization is that its majorizing function is always smaller than or equal to the one by Kiers (1997), that is,

$$L_{\text{WProc}}(T) \leq \mu_1(T, T^0) \leq \mu(T, T^0). \qquad (15)$$

The proof can be found in Groenen et al. (2003).

The optimal T in (13) can be found in one step by computing an appropriate singular value decomposition in each iteration. Expanding (13) and taking the constraint $T'T = TT' = I$ into account shows that

$$\text{tr } (R - XT')' D_m (R - XT')$$
$$= \text{tr } R' D_m R + \text{tr } TX' D_m XT' - 2\text{tr } T' X D_m R$$
$$= \text{tr } R' D_m R + \text{tr } X' D_m X - 2\text{tr } T' X D_m R$$
$$= c_2 - 2\text{tr } T' X D_m R.$$

The result in (12) allows us to write

$$L_{\text{WProc}}(\mathbf{T}) \leq c_3 + c_2 - 2\text{tr } \mathbf{T'S} = \mu_1(\mathbf{T}, \mathbf{T}^0), \tag{16}$$

where $\mathbf{S} = \mathbf{XD_mR}$ and $c_3 = c - \text{tr } \mathbf{Z'D_mZ}$. It is easy to realize that minimizing $\mu_1(\mathbf{T}, \mathbf{T}^0)$ over $\mathbf{T}$ is equivalent to maximizing the term tr $\mathbf{T'S}$. According to Ten Berge (1993), the upper bound of tr $\mathbf{T'S}$ is attained at $\mathbf{T} = \mathbf{KL'}$ if one defines the singular value decomposition (SVD) of $\mathbf{S}$ as $\mathbf{S} = \mathbf{K\Lambda L'}$ with $\mathbf{K}$ and $\mathbf{L'}$ orthonormal matrices (that is, $\mathbf{K'K} = \mathbf{L'L} = \mathbf{I}$) and $\mathbf{\Lambda}$ diagonal.

4 Some numerical results

To see how much the proposed method of weighted majorization improves upon the method by Kiers (1997), we set up a small simulation study. The data $\mathbf{X}$ and $\mathbf{Y}$ are generated as follows: $\mathbf{X}$ is drawn from the standard normal distribution, $\mathbf{T}$ was drawn randomly and orthonormal and $\mathbf{Y}$ was obtained as $\mathbf{Y} = \mathbf{XT}$. As we are in the robust context, we also added errors and outliers to $\mathbf{X}$.

In this simulation, we varied the following factors: the size of known matrices $\mathbf{X}$ and $\mathbf{Y}$, n ($n = 20, 40$), k ($k = 2, 4, 8$), the proportion of error $(0, .1, .5, 1)$, and the number of outliers (0%, 10%, 20%), following Verboon and Heiser (1992). In particular, the errors on $\mathbf{X}$ were proportional to the standard deviations of the columns, while outliers were created by choosing randomly p rows of $\mathbf{X}$ and multiplying them by -10. The different combinations yield 72 different data sets. For each data set, we ran the algorithm by Kiers and weighted majorization 100 times, so that a total number of 7200 comparisons were made. In every comparison, we used the same $\mathbf{Y}$, $\mathbf{X}$, and the same initial random $\mathbf{T}$. Both algorithms were stopped whenever difference in $L_{\text{WProc}}(\mathbf{T})$ between two subsequent iterations was smaller than 10^{-8}.

We studied two aspects in our comparison: efficiency and quality of the solution. We define the relative efficiency of the two methods as

$$\text{relative efficiency} = \frac{\text{number of iterations in Kiers (1997)}}{\text{number of iterations in weighted majorization}}$$

Of course, measuring efficiency only makes sense for those runs that stop at the same local minimum. We defined the latter to be the case if both loss function values had at least four decimal places equal. In this way, 377 of the 7200 runs were selected to compute the relative efficiency. On average, weighted majorization was about 14.5 times faster than the method by Kiers. In a single case, both methods used exactly the same number of iterations, in about 4% of the cases, weighted majorization was slower than the method by Kiers, and in the remaining 96% of the runs, weighted majorization was faster than the method by Kiers (up to a factor 131).

It turns out that robust Procrustes analysis suffers from many local minima. Therefore, to study the quality of the solution, we adopted a multistart strategy, consisting of selecting the best solution out of one hundred random starts. Of the 72 different data sets, the weighted majorization approach yielded the lowest local minimum in 98% of the cases and equal loss function values in the other 2%: weighted majorization was never worse than the method by Kiers. The set up of our simulation study produced six data sets with zero error, that necessarily have a minimum with zero loss. Weighted majorization found two zero loss solutions, two cases with a slight nonzero loss (respectively 0.03 and 0.05), and two with strongly nonzero solutions (0.09 and 0.1). The method by Kiers found a strongly nonzero loss in all six cases.

The results seem to indicate that weighted majorization yields superior quality solutions. In cases where the two algorithms reach the same local minimum, weighted majorization is much faster than the method by Kiers.

5 Conclusions

In this paper, we presented a new application of the weighted majorization algorithm to robust Procrustes analysis, and compared it to the one proposed by Kiers (1997). We proved that the method by Kiers is a special case of weighted majorization. The methods coincide if the minimum absolute residual per row is the same for all rows (which hardly happens). Numerical results indicate that our method converges on average 14 times faster to a solution and yields in almost all cases better quality solutions. The weighted majorization method proposed here is not limited to robust Procrustes analysis only. In fact, it can be applied to any decomposition model that minimizes least-squares error with differential weights and that can be solved easily in a diagonal metric $\mathbf{D}$ (see Groenen et al. (2003)).

References

BEATON, A.E. and TUKEY, J.W. (1974): The fitting of power series, meaningful polynomials, illustrated on band-spectroscopic data. *Technometrics, 16, 147–185.*

CLIFF, N. (1966): Orthogonal rotation to congruence. *Psychometrika, 31, 33–42.*

BORG, I. and GROENEN P.J.F. (1997): *Modern multidimensional scaling: Theory and applications.* Springer, New York.

DE LEEUW, J. (1992): Fitting distances by least squares. *Tech.Rep. 130, Interdivisonal Program in Statistics, UCLA, Los Angeles, California.*

DE LEEUW, J. (1994): Block relaxation algorithms in statistics. In: H.-H. Bock and W. Lenski and M. M. Richter (Eds.): *Information systems and data analysis.* Springer, 308-324.

GREEN, B.F. (1952): The orthogonal approximation of an oblique structure in factor analysis. *Psychometrika, 17, 429-440.*

GROENEN P.J.F. and GIAQUINTO, P. and KIERS, H.A.L. (2003): Weighted majorization algorithms for weighted least squares decomposition models. *Tech.Rep. 9, Econometric Institute, Erasmus University, Rotterdam, The Netherlands.*

HEISER, W.J. (1987): Correspondence analysis with least absolute residuals. *Computational Statistics and Data Analysis, 5, 337-356.*

HEISER, W.J. (1995): Convergent computation by iterative majorization: Theory and applications in multidimensional data analysis. In: W. J. Krzanowski (Eds.):*Recent advances in descriptive multivariate analysis.* Oxford University Press, 157-189.

HUBER, P. J. (1964): Robust estimation of a location parameter. *Annals of Mathematical Statistics, 35, 73-101.*

HURLEY, J.R. and CATTELL, R.B. (1962): The Procrustes program: Producing direct rotation to test a hypothesized factor structure. *Behavioral Science, 7, 258-262.*

KIERS, H.A.L. (1997): Weighted least squares fitting using iterative ordinary least squares algorithms. *Psychometrika, 62, 251-266.*

KIERS, H.A.L. (2002): Setting up alternating least squares and iterative majorization algorithms for solving various matrix optimization problems. *Computational Statistics and Data Analysis, 41, 157-170.*

MOSTELLER, F. and TUKEY, J.W. (1977): *Data Analysis and Regression.* Addison-Wesley, Massachusetts.

SCHÖNEMANN, P.H. (1966): A generalized solution of the orthogonal Procrustes problem. *Psychometrika, 31, 1-10.*

TEN BERGE, J.M.F. (1993): *Least squares optimization in multivariate analysis.* DSWO Press, Leiden University, Leiden, The Netherlands.

VERBOON, P. (1994): *A robust approach to nonlinear multivariate analysis.* DSWO Press, Leiden University, Leiden, The Netherlands.

VERBOON, P. and HEISER, W.J. (1992): Resistant orthogonal Procrustes analysis *Journal of Classification, 9, 237-256.*

Generalized Bi-Additive Modelling for Categorical Data

Patrick J.F. Groenen[1] and Alex J. Koning[1]

Econometric Institute,
Erasmus University Rotterdam, The Netherlands
groenen@few.eur.nl, koning@few.eur.nl

Abstract. Generalized linear modelling (GLM) is a versatile statistical technique, which may be viewed as a generalization of well-known techniques such as least squares regression, analysis of variance, loglinear modelling, and logistic regression. In many applications, low-order interaction (such as bivariate interaction) terms are included in the model. However, as the number of categorical variables increases, the total number of low-order interactions also increases dramatically. In this paper, we propose to constrain bivariate interactions by a bi-additive model which allows a simple graphical representation in which each category of every variable is represented by a vector.

1 Introduction

Generalized linear modelling (GLM) is a versatile statistical technique, which may be viewed as a generalization of well-known techniques such as least squares regression, analysis of variance, loglinear modelling, logistic regression (Nelder and Wedderburn (1972); McCullagh and Nelder(1989)). In this paper, we limit ourselves to categorical predictor variables. Then, GLMs may consist of main effects, bivariate, and higher-order interactions. Since higher order interactions are generally difficult to interpret, we consider only bivariate interactions here. Note that as the number of categorical variables m increases, the total number of bivariate interactions increases to $m(m-1)/2$. Let the number of categories for variable j be K_j. Then, the total number of interactions parameters equals $\sum_{j=1}^{m} \sum_{l=j+1}^{m} K_j K_l$. As the number of categories increases, it becomes increasingly more difficult to interpret the estimated interaction parameters because there are so many of them. Our aim here is to provide a simple graphical representation to facilitate the interpretation of all bivariate interactions. To reach this goal, we impose rank restrictions on the bivariate interactions, thus leading to a bi-additive model.

For two categorical variables, van Eeuwijk (1995), De Falguerolles and Francis (1992) and Gabriel (1996) have provided algorithms for a bi-additive model within GLM. Here we propose a bi-additive model for more than two categorical predictors. To some extent, the proposed model can be seen as a generalization of multiple correspondence analysis to GLM.

2 Generalized bi-additive modelling

Let us introduce some notation needed for generalized linear modelling (GLM). Let $\mathbf{y}$ be the dependent vector of n objects that needs to be predicted by m categorical variables. Also, let the categorical variable j be represented by the indicator matrix $\mathbf{G}_j$ with a zero-one variable for each category with $g_{ijk} = 1$ if observation i falls in category k of variable j and $g_{ijk} = 0$ otherwise. Let the number of categories of variable j be denoted by K_j and $\mathbf{g}'_{ij}$ be row i of $\mathbf{G}_j$.

The central idea behind GLM is that the distribution of the dependent variable belongs to a given family of distributions (popular choices are the Normal, Poisson, binomial, gamma, and inverse Gaussian families). This leaves some freedom, which allows the distribution to vary from object to object. Especially, the expectation μ_i of the dependent variable may differ from object to object, and is assumed to depend on the values taken by the predictor variables through the linear predictor η_i (examples are given below). Finally, the inverse of the link function $g(\mu_i) = \eta_i$ relates the linear predictor to μ_i. Some standard link functions are the logarithm, power, logistic, identity, and probit (McCullagh and Nelder(1989)).

A simple linear predictor may be specified by $\eta_i = c + \sum_{j=1}^{m} \mathbf{g}'_{ij}\mathbf{a}_j$, where c is an overall mean and $\mathbf{a}_j$ is a vector of main effect for variable j. However, we are interested in bivariate interactions as well, so that we need the linear predictor

$$\eta_i = c + \sum_{j=1}^{m} \mathbf{g}'_{ij}\mathbf{a}_j + \sum_{j=1}^{m-1} \sum_{l=j+1}^{m} \mathbf{g}'_{ij}\mathbf{B}_{jl}\mathbf{g}_{il},$$

where $\mathbf{B}_{jl}$ is the $K_j \times K_l$ matrix of bivariate interactions between variables j and l. It is easily verified that $\mathbf{g}'_{ij}\mathbf{B}_{jl}\mathbf{g}_{il}$ selects the appropriate row and column element that corresponds to the categories of the variables j and l of object i. Note that summation over $j > l$ or $j < l$ gives the same results, because one can always choose $\mathbf{B}_{jl} = \mathbf{B}'_{lj}$ so that $\mathbf{g}'_{ij}\mathbf{B}_{jl}\mathbf{g}_{il} = \mathbf{g}'_{il}\mathbf{B}_{lj}\mathbf{g}_{ij}$. We can obtain more insight and compact notation by joining the effects of all variables. Let $\mathbf{G}$ be the *super* indicator matrix with all m variables next to each other, that is, $\mathbf{G} = [\mathbf{G}_1, \mathbf{G}_2, \ldots, \mathbf{G}_m]$, $\mathbf{g}'_i$ be row i of $\mathbf{G}$, and $\mathbf{a}$ be the vector of all main effects. Finally, all bivariate interaction effects are joined into the symmetric partitioned block matrix

$$\mathbf{B} = \begin{bmatrix} \mathbf{0} & \mathbf{B}_{12} & \ldots & \mathbf{B}_{1m} \\ \mathbf{B}'_{12} & \mathbf{0} & \ldots & \mathbf{B}_{2m} \\ \vdots & \vdots & \ddots & \vdots \\ \mathbf{B}'_{1m} & \mathbf{B}'_{2m} & \ldots & \mathbf{0} \end{bmatrix}.$$

The diagonal blocks are zero because $j \neq l$. Then, we may write

$$\eta_i = c + \sum_{j=1}^{m} \mathbf{g}'_{ij}\mathbf{a}_j + \sum_{j=1}^{m-1} \sum_{l=j+1}^{m} \mathbf{g}'_{ij}\mathbf{B}_{jl}\mathbf{g}_{il} = c + \mathbf{g}'_i\mathbf{a} + \tfrac{1}{2}\mathbf{g}'_i\mathbf{B}\mathbf{g}_i. \tag{1}$$

The basic idea of this paper is to impose constraints on the interaction terms $\mathbf{B}_{jl}$. The type of constraint that we consider is the one of common rank-reduction, that is, to require that

$$\mathbf{B}_{jl} = \mathbf{Y}_j \mathbf{Y}_l' \qquad (2)$$

with $\mathbf{Y}_j$ a $K_j \times p$ matrix and $\mathbf{Y}_l$ a $K_l \times p$ matrix being of rank not higher than $p > 0$. Such rank constraints are similar to the ones used in multiple correspondence analysis, joint correspondence analysis, or homogeneity analysis. This rank constrained bi-additive model can be expressed as

$$\eta_i = c + \sum_{j=1}^{m} \mathbf{g}_{ij}' \mathbf{a}_j + \sum_{j=1}^{m-1} \sum_{l=j+1}^{m} \mathbf{g}_{ij}' \mathbf{Y}_j \mathbf{Y}_l' \mathbf{g}_{il}. \qquad (3)$$

To avoid that $\mathbf{Y}_j$ also estimates main effects, we impose the restriction that $\mathbf{Y}_j$ has column mean zero. This restriction also implies that $\mathbf{B}_{jl} = \mathbf{Y}_j \mathbf{Y}_l'$ has zero row and column mean, which is a restriction that is usually imposed on bivariate interactions to ensure uniqueness. We shall refer to the matrix $\mathbf{Y}_j$ as the *interaction generating* matrix of variable j, and to the kth column of $\mathbf{Y}_j$ as the kth dimension of interaction generators belonging to the categorical variable j. To fit this model, we have developed a prototype in MatLab that optimizes the likelihood by iterated weighted least squares and iterative majorization.

Note that standard likelihood theory applies to model (3), and hence we may employ the likelihood ratio test to determine the rank p. From this perspective, it is relevant to know the degrees of freedom associated to the rank p model. Observe that the parameters in the rank p model are the constant term c, the main effect vectors $\mathbf{a}_j$ and the elements of the interaction generating matrix $\mathbf{Y}_j$. Hence, the number of parameters in this model equals

$$1 + \sum_{j=1}^{m} K_j + p \sum_{j=1}^{m} K_j.$$

However, we have also imposed several restrictions on these parameters. Each of the m main effect vectors and each of the p dimensions of the m interaction generators should add up to zero. Moreover, the interaction generating matrices $\mathbf{Y}_j$ can be rotated simultaneously by a single orthonormal rotation matrix $\mathbf{T}$ (with $\mathbf{T}'\mathbf{T} = \mathbf{T}\mathbf{T}' = \mathbf{I}$) without affecting $\mathbf{B}_{jl}$ since $\mathbf{B}_{jl} = \mathbf{Y}_j \mathbf{Y}_l' = \mathbf{Y}_j \mathbf{T}\mathbf{T}' \mathbf{Y}_l'$ for all j and l. Therefore, without loss of generality, we impose the restriction that $\sum_j \mathbf{Y}_j$ is orthogonal thereby making the rotation of the $\mathbf{Y}_j$'s unique. This restriction implies fixing $p(p-1)/2$ of the elements of the the $\mathbf{Y}_j$'s. Summarizing, the number of restrictions in the rank p model is equal to

$$m + mp + \frac{p(p-1)}{2}$$

The difference in number of parameters and number of restrictions

$$df_{\text{model}} = \left[1 + \sum_{j=1}^{m} K_j + p \sum_{j=1}^{m} K_j \right] - \left[m + mp + \frac{p(p-1)}{2} \right]$$

$$= 1 + (1+p) \sum_{j=1}^{m} (K_j - 1) - \frac{p(p-1)}{2}.$$

is the degrees of freedom associated to the rank p model. Let n be the number of unique observed combinations of categories. If the data are presented in a contingency table and all cells have a nonzero observation, then n is equal to the number of cells. Now, the residual degrees of freedom df_{res} is obtained by $n - df_{\text{model}}$.

There are several related models in the literature. In the simple case of only two categorical variables, our model is equivalent to the bi-additive models of Van Eeuwijk (1995), De Falguerolles and Francis (1992), and Gabriel (1996). For the case of the identity link and the normal distribution, this model has been discussed by, amongst others, Mandel (1971) and Denis and Gower (1996). For three-way tables, several decomposition models have been proposed, see, for example, Becker and Clogg (1989) and Siciliano and Mooijaart (1997). De Rooij (2001) proposes a decomposition model using squared weighted Euclidean distances for three-way tables. The model proposed in this paper differs from these dimension reduction models in that we allow for more than two or three categorical predictor variables and that it operates on all bivariate interactions simultaneously. In addition, our model does not require that all cells of the m-way table are observed; some or many cells may be empty.

3 Application: lung cancer in China

Lung cancer is one of the leading causes of death in the People's Republic of China. It has been estimated that in the year 2025, the number of new cancer cases in China will reach three million, of which two million are associated with smoking, and the remaining one million attributable to other causes (Peto (1994); Peto, Chen and Boreham (1996)).

A number of epidemiological studies have investigated the association between lung cancer and smoking in China. In Liu (1992), a meta-analysis is presented of eight case-control studies conducted in Beijing, Shanghai, Shenyang, Nanjing, Harbin, Zhengzhou, Taiyuan, and Nanchang. Table 1 cross-classifies a total of 4081 lung cancer cases and 4338 controls according to smoking behaviour and city. In this paragraph, we investigate the relation between smoking and lung cancer in China by applying the generalized bi-additive model introduced in the previous section to the data in Table 1. Note that $m = 3$, $K_1 = 2$, $K_2 = 2$, and $K_3 = 8$, and hence $\sum_{j}^{m} (K_j - 1) = 1 + 1 + 7 = 9$.

Lung cancer	Smoker	City								Total
		Bei-jing	Shang-hai	Shen-yang	Nan-jing	Har-bin	Zeng-zhou	Tai-yuan	Nan-chang	
yes	yes	126	908	913	235	402	182	60	104	2930
yes	no	35	497	336	58	121	72	11	21	1121
no	yes	100	688	747	172	308	156	99	89	2359
no	no	61	807	598	121	215	98	43	36	1979
	Total	322	2900	2594	586	1046	508	213	250	8419

Table 1. Frequencies of occurrence of lung cancer for (non) smokers in eight Chinese cities (taken from Liu (1992), see also Tabel 3.3 in Agresti (1996), p. 60).

Model	Deviance	dfres	p
Main effects	457.1	22	.0000
Bi-additive interaction model, rank 1	35.7	13	.0007
Bi-additive interaction model, rank 2	5.4	5	.3690

Table 2. Summary of fit for different models, using the Poisson family of distributions and the log link function on the data of Table 1.

Table 2 summarizes the fit of three models when using the Poisson family of distributions and a log link function. The main effects model may be regarded as a special case of model (3) with rank $p = 0$. Next, adding a first dimension of bilinear interactions to each variable yields model (3) with rank $p = 1$. Finally, adding a second dimension of bilinear interactions to each variable yields model (3) with rank $p = 2$. Adding further dimensions would lead to models with degrees of freedom exceeding 32, the degrees of freedom of the saturated model; such models are unidentified, and have no statistical use. Note that the three models in Table 2 are nested, and thus may be compared as usual by means of the likelihood ratio test (that is, by relating differences in deviance to the chi-square distribution corresponding to the difference in degrees of freedom). Obviously, the rank 2 model is to be preferred, as it is the only model that fits the data.

Applying the rank 2 bi-additive decomposition model to the Chinese lung cancer-smoking data yields the estimation results listed in Table 3. These results are visualized in Figure 1, where Panel (a) shows the main effects and Panel (b) gives the vectors for the interaction generators $\mathbf{Y}_j$.

Figure 1 may be interpreted as follows. To see the size of the interaction effect, project the vector of one category onto a category of a different variable. For example, Taiyuan is characterized by having more nonsmokers than smokers, when corrected for the main effects of smoking. The reason is the nonsmoking vector projects highly on the vector of Taiyuan. Long vectors lead to longer projections and thus to a stronger interaction effect. Conversely, short vectors have short projections, indicating a small interaction effect. Therefore, the cities Beijing, Harbin, Nanjing, Zengzhou, and Shenyang will only have small interaction effects with the other variables.

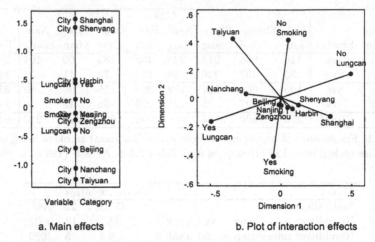

a. Main effects   b. Plot of interaction effects

Fig. 1. Representation of the bi-additive decomposition model of the Chinese lung cancer-smoking data. Panel (a) shows the main effects and Panel (b) the decomposition of the interactions in two dimensions.

In Figure 1, three Chinese cities relatively stand out: Nanchang, Taiyuan and Shanghai. Nanchang was badly battered after the Communist takeover, but reinvented itself as a centre of modern steel and chemical industry (Leffman, Lewis and Atiyah (2000), p. 52). Taiyuan's extensive coal mines were constructed by the Japanese in 1940; serious industrialization began after the Communist takeover and today it is the factories that dominate, relentlessly processing the region's coal and mineral deposits (Leffman, et al. (2000), p.

Variable	Category	Main effects	Interaction generators Dim 1	Dim 2
Overall mean	c	5.005		
Lung cancer	Yes	0.410	-0.494	-0.169
	No	-0.410	0.494	0.169
Smoking	Yes	-0.124	-0.055	-0.413
	No	0.124	0.055	0.413
City	Beijing	-0.727	-0.015	-0.052
	Shanghai	1.557	0.348	-0.133
	Shenyang	1.406	0.124	-0.053
	Nanjing	-0.121	0.004	-0.057
	Harbin	0.472	0.047	-0.071
	Zengzhou	-0.239	0.081	-0.080
	Taiyuan	-1.270	-0.342	0.421
	Nanchang	-1.078	-0.248	0.025

Table 3. Estimation results obtained by applying the rank 2 bi-additive decomposition model to the Chinese lung cancer-smoking data.

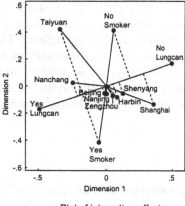 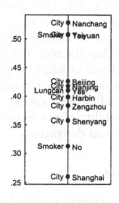

a. Plot of interaction effects   b. Interaction effects conditioned
                                           on having lungcancer

Fig. 2. Interaction terms conditioned on category 'yes' of the variable 'lung cancer'. Panel (a) shows the projections of all other categories on category 'yes' of the variable 'lung cancer' and Panel (b) the values of the interactions.

225). After forty years of stagnation, Shanghai seems certain to recapture its position as East Asia's leading business city, a status it last held before World War II (Leffman, et al. (2000), p. 337).

Recall that Table 1 was compiled by Liu (1992) from the results of eight different case-control studies investigating lung cancer in China. In this respect, the interactions between the variable Lung Cancer on one hand and the variables Smoking and City on the other hand are of primary interest. Thus, to gain insight into the causes of lung cancer in China, we should project each category of the variables Smoking and City onto the category Yes of the variable Lung Cancer, as indicated in Panel (a) of Figure 2. Panel (b) visualizes the interaction values according to the bi-additive interaction model for the categories of Smoking and City conditioned on having lung cancer. As to be expected, smoking is clearly a risk factor for obtaining lung cancer. However, Panel (b) of Figure 2 seems to suggest that there is also an environmental risk factor, as the interaction between the industrial cities of Nanchang and Taiyuan on one hand and the presence of lung cancer on the other hand is much higher than the interaction between the leading business city Shanghai and the presence of lung cancer.

4 Conclusions

We have proposed a new model for representing two-way interactions for a GLM with more than two categorical predictor variables, where we constrain the two-way interactions to have reduced rank. Each category is represented by a vector in a plot. The interaction effect between two categories of different predictor variables is obtained by projecting the vector of one category onto the vector of another. Categories of the same variable should not be compared within the plot, but only by looking at the main effects. The main advantage of the bi-additive interaction model is that interactions between several variables can be visualized in a relatively simple display, even when the total number of categories is large. In future publications we intend to study the stability of the estimated parameters either through the bootstrap or by theoretical derivations.

References

AGRESTI, A. (1996): *An introduction to categorical data analysis*. New York, Wiley.

BECKER, M.P. and CLOGG, C.C. (1989): Analysis of sets of two-way contingency tables using association models. *Journal of the American Statistical Association, 84, 142–151*.

DE FALGUEROLLES, A. and FRANCIS, B. (1992): Algorithmic approaches for fitting bilinear models. In: Y. Dodge and J. Whittaker (Eds.): *Compstat 1992*. Heidelberg, Physica-Verlag, 77–82.

DE ROOIJ, M. (2001): Distance association models for the analysis of repeated transition frequency tables. *Statistica Neerlandica, 55, 157–181*.

DENIS, J.-B. and GOWER, J.C. (1996): Asymptotic confidence regions for biadditive models: Interpreting genotype-environment interactions. *Applied Statistics, 45, 479–493*.

GABRIEL, K. R. (1996): Generalised bilinear regression. *Biometrika, 85, 689-700*.

LEFFMAN, D., LEWIS, S. and ATIYAH, J. (2000): *China*. London, Rough Guides Ltd.

LIU, Z. (1992): Smoking and lung cancer in China. *Internal Journal of Epidemiology, 21, 197-201*.

MANDEL, J. (1971): A new analysis of variance model for non-additive data. *Techometrics, 13, 1–17*.

MCCULLAGH, P. and NELDER, J. A. (1989): *Generalized linear models*. London, Chapman and Hall.

NELDER, J. A. and WEDDERBURN, R. W. M. (1972): Generalized linear models. *Journal of the Royal Statistical Society A, 135, 370-384*.

PETO R (1994): Smoking and death - the past 40 years and the next 40. *British Medical Journal 309, 937–939*.

PETO, R., CHEN, Z. M. and BOREHAM. J. (1996): Tobacco - The growing epidemic in China. *Journal of the American Medical Association, 275, 1683-1684*.

SICILIANO, R. and MOOIJAART, A. (1997): Three-factor association models for three-way contingency tables. *Computational Statistics and Data Analysis, 24, 337–356*.

VAN EEUWIJK, F. A. (1995): Multiplicative interaction in generalized linear models. *Biometrics, 85, 1017-1032*.

Model Selection Procedures in Three-Mode Component Models

Pieter M. Kroonenberg

Department of Education,
Leiden University, Leiden, The Netherlands
kroonenb@fsw.leidenuniv.nl

Abstract. An overview is presented of the various procedures available for model selection in three-mode models, especially the Tucker2 model, the Tucker3 model and the Parafac model. Various procedures will be reviewed such as selecting from a hierarchy, three-mode scree plots, deviance plot, sums of squares partitioning, bootstrap and jackknife procedures.

1 Introduction

Whereas model selection is difficult in any context, in three-mode analysis it is even more complicated due to different models and the lack of a clear stochastic context. Moreover, in the beginning there was the Tucker3 model (Tucker (1966)) for which only the, already difficult, choice of components for each mode had to be made (within-model choice), now also the choice has to be made of the proper model (between-model choice). In many cases, the type of model is dictated by the nature of the data and in other cases one particular class of models is required, but generally which model within a class is the most appropriate is not known. To find a proper model, considerations of parsimony, stability, expected validity in new data sets have to be taken into account. Various tools for evaluating models both for the within-model choice and the between-model choice will be discussed in this paper.

In this paper we will concentrate on component models and their selection. For this class of models, methods are available for selecting models within the class of component models which pay attention to the relative fit of models with different numbers of components and to the fit of different, but comparable models. A second approach to model selection, which is especially useful when the search is narrowed down to a limited number of candidate models is to use resampling to assess the stability of the fit of the models and jackknife procedures to assess the predictive validity. Pioneering work was done by Harshman and DeSarbo (1984) in introducing split-half procedures for the Parafac model and this work was taken up and extended by Kiers and Van Mechelen (2001).

2 Degrees of freedom

Central to model comparison is the concept of degrees of freedom. For modelling three-way interactions in an ANOVA context Gower (1977) proposed to use Mandel (1971)'s idea of simply counting the number of parameters and subtracting them from the number of independent data points to derive at the appropriate degrees of freedom. Weesie and Van Houwelingen (1983) were the first to use this approach to the degrees of freedom when fitting three-mode models. They discussed the degrees of freedom for the Tucker3 model, but the principle can readily be extended to the Tucker2 and Parafac models.

3 Selecting a Tucker model

Timmerman and Kiers (2000) suggested a model-selection procedure, (the *DifFit* procedure), analogous to Cattell's scree plot for two-mode component analysis. In particular, they based the selection on choosing the model with the lowest residual sum of squares (or *deviance sum of squares*), within the class of models with the same sum of numbers of components ($S = P + Q + R$). Their procedure was designed to be equivalent to Cattell's eigenvalue larger than one criterion in two-mode PCA. To visualise the procedure proposed by Timmerman & Kiers, it is proposed to construct a version of Cattell's scree plot, the *Three-mode scree plot*, in which the deviance of each model is plotted versus the sum of numbers of components S. The DifFit is then essentially a way to define the convex hull in the Three-mode scree plot and the models which are taken into consideration are those on the convex hull. The evaluation of the deviance together with the degrees of freedom is an alternative to the Timmerman & Kiers' approach (First used in three-mode analysis by Kroonenberg and Van der Voort (1987).) In this case, the deviance of each model is plotted versus the degrees of freedom *df* (*Deviance plot*). Also in this plot, a convex hull can be drawn to connect favoured models (see e.g. Murakami and Kroonenberg, 2003).

Even though the three-mode scree plot and the deviance plot are designed to assist choosing between Tucker models differing in number of components, it is equally possible to include models from another model classes, such as the appropriate Tucker2 models and Parafac models.

4 Selecting a Parafac model

In theory, selecting a Parafac model is much simpler than a Tucker model because all modes have the same number of components, so that there are only a few models possible; models with more than four components are relatively rare. Because the Parafac model is a model with restrictions, often only model with a limited number of components fit the data. Effectively, one tries to the fit the largest possible Parafac model, in contrast with Tucker models, where one seeks an adequate model for describing the variability. Harshman (1984) gives a whole catalogue of considerations how to search for the maximal Parafac model, amongst others using a type of scree plot and split-half analyses.

Bro (1998, p. 113–122) proposed an approach for selecting the number of Parafac components using the principle of *core consistency* to assess how many Parafac components the data can sustain (see also Bro, 2003). It is assessed how far away the core array derived from the Parafac components is from a superdiagonal core array. The *Degree of superdiagonality* may also be used for the same purpose (see Anderson and Henrion (1999)). It is equal to the sum of squares of the superdiagonal elements divided by the total sum of squares of the core elements. All three measures will be equal to 1 in the superdiagonal case.

5 Selecting from a hierarchy

In two papers Kiers (1988, 1991a) discussed the comparison between several different three-mode component models. He showed explicitly how several three-mode models fit into the hierarchies. The starting point of the hierarchy is that one mode is singled out as the *reference mode*. First, the number of components to adequately describe this mode is determined via a Tucker1 analysis. The fit of this solution is the standard against which the other models are held, and for the other models the extent to which they succeed approaching this fit with far less parameters is evaluated.

6 Model stability and predictive power

In complex models, such as three-mode models, generally no distributional assumptions are or can be made and therefore standard errors cannot be determined. Since the development of high-speed computers, computer-intensive procedures have been developed to find non-parametric estimates of the parameters of arbitrary distributions and their standard errors.

6.1 Bootstrap procedures

The fundamental principle of the bootstrap procedure, that the observed distribution is the best estimate of the population distribution, was established by Efron (1979). Given this principle, sampling from the observed distribution is the best one can do bar sampling from the population distribution. Therefore, in order get an estimate for a population parameter one repeatedly samples with replacement from the observed distribution with equal probability for all data points. For each such sample the value of the estimator for the parameter is calculated and the mean value of the estimates is the best estimate for the population parameter and the standard deviation of the estimates is its standard error. Such an approach can be extremely time consuming especially in three-mode methods where the estimation of the model parameters is already iterative. However, it is the only way to get standard errors for the parameters estimates and it gives at the same time information on the position of the observed results with respect to the sampling distribution. Kiers (submitted) is the most update source on bootstrap procedures for three-mode analysis.

6.2 Jackknife procedures and predictive power

Another concern in model building is the question how the model found will stand up in new samples. Apart from having the data of a similar study, the replication issue has to be solved internally in the data set itself. The basic idea behind this approach, the *jackknife*, is to develop the model on a part of the data and then estimate the values of those data points which were not involved in the estimation. Subsequently, the estimated value is compared to the originally observed value and when across the whole data set such differences are small the parameter estimates are said to have good *predictive power*. The predictive power of a model is generally estimated by the predictive residual error sum of squares ($PRESS$) and it is calculated by comparing the values of all original data points with their estimated values on the basis of models with certain data points left out. Louwerse, Smilde and Kiers (1999) suggested a strategy to minimise the number of models that have to be inspected to find models with sufficiently low $PRESS$ values.

There are several ways to carry out jackknife procedures in three-mode analysis. For instance Riu and Bro (2003) delete a complete level at a time. Their aim was to use the jackknife estimation of standard errors and to search for outliers, but not to assess predictive power of the model at hand. To do so in their case would have been difficult because no reliable and stable estimates can be calculated for the parameters in the component matrix associated with the removed level. A more subtle version of this proposal was put forward by Louwerse et al. (1999), based on Eastment and Krzanowski (1982). They also removed complete slices but developed a sophisticated way to combine the results of leaving each (group of) slices in turn so that the predictive power could be assessed. In that paper it was also proposed to remove each data point in turn (or several of them at the same time) by declaring it to be missing, use the basic missing data Expectation-Maximisation algorithm to estimate the missing data point and compare this estimate with the observed value. In principle, this procedure is what is required, the only drawback is that to leave out single data points is very time consuming for large data sets. A possible compromise, is to leave out a level of an (in principle) stochastic mode, but in order to be able to estimate the associated parameters in the component matrix not all elements of the slice associated with this level are deleted together but only a random half of them. The other half is deleted in the next step, so that all elements of the data array are eliminated once. In this way, there are always data points in a slice to estimate the associated parameter values in the component matrix. The estimation procedure is then the same as in Louwerse et al. (1999) , i.e. via an E-M approach.

7 Conclusion

In this paper we have given an overview of the selection of three-mode models indicating that considerations about the relative goodness-of-fit, the stability, and predictive validity all play a role. Although not emphasized in this brief overview, model comparisons can be made within the same family of models, across different families of models, and at a more detailed level within a particular member of family. In the latter case one can investigate the fit within the model itself to assess whether all parts of the model fit equally well. The fact that we are dealing with three rather than two modes complicates the choice of an adequate model in almost all aspects, and therefore it cannot be stated too emphatically that there goes nothing above the availability of solid substantive theory to guide us in the process of selection.

Acknowledgement

This paper was written while the author was a Fellow at the Netherlands Institute for Advanced Study in the Humanities and Social Sciences (NIAS).

References

ANDERSSON, C.A. and HENRION, R. (1999): A general algorithm for obtaining simple structure of core arrays in N-way PCA with application to fluorometric data. *Computational Statistics and Data Analysis, 31*, 255–278.

BRO, R. (1998): Multi-way analysis in the food industry. Models, algorithms, and applications.. University of Amsterdam, Amsterdam, The Netherlands.

BRO, R. and KIERS, H.A.L. (2003): A new efficient method for determining the number of components in PARAFAC models. *Journal of Chemometrics, 17*, 274–286.

EASTMENT, H.T. and KRZANOWSKI, W.J. (1982): Cross-validatory choice of the number of components from a principal component analysis. *Technometrics, 24*, 73–77.

EFRON, B. (1979): Bootstrap methods: Another look at the jackknife. *Annals of Statistics, 7*, 1–26.

GOWER, J.C. (1977): The analysis of three-way grids. In: P. Slater (Ed.): *Dimensions of intrapersonal space*. Wiley, New York, 163–173.

HARSHMAN, R.A. (1984): "How can I know if it's 'real'?" A catalog of diagnostics for use with three-mode factor analysis and multidimensional scaling. In: H.G. Law, C.W. Snyder Jr, J.A. Hattie and R.P. McDonald (Eds.): *Research methods for multimode data analysis*. Praeger, New York, 566–591.

HARSHMAN, R.A. and DESARBO, W.S. (1984): An application of PARAFAC to a small sample problem, demonstrating preprocessing, orthogonality constraints, and split-half diagnostic techniques. In: H.G. Law, C.W. Snyder Jr, J.A. Hattie and R.P. McDonald (Eds.): *Research methods for multimode data analysis*. Praeger, New York, 602–642.

KIERS, H.A.L. (1988): Comparison of "Anglo-Saxon" and "French" three-mode methods. *Statistique et Analyse des Données, 13*, 14–32.

KIERS, H.A.L. (1991a): Hierarchical relations among three-way methods. *Psychometrika, 56*, 449–470.

KIERS, H.A.L. (2004): Bootstrap confidence intervals for three-way methods. *Journal of Chemometrics, 18*, 22–36.

KIERS, H.A.L. and VAN MECHELEN, I. (2001): Three-way component analysis: Principles and illustrative application. *Psychological Methods, 6*, 84–110.

KROONENBERG, P.M. (1983). *Three-mode principal component analysis. Theory and applications*. DSWO Press, Leiden, The Netherlands [now available as PDF document from: http:\\three-mode.leidenuniv.nl]

KROONENBERG, P.M. and VAN DER VOORT, T.H.A. (1987): Multiplicatieve decompositie van interacties bij oordelen over de werkelijkheidswaarde van televisiefilms [Multiplicative decomposition of interactions for judgements of realism of television films]. *Kwantitatieve Methoden, 8*, 117–144

LOUWERSE, D.J., SMILDE, A.K., and KIERS, H.A.L. (1999): Cross-validation of multiway component models. *Journal of Chemometrics, 13*, 491–510.

MANDEL, J. (1971): A new analysis of variance model for non-additive data. *Technometrics 13*, 1–18.

MURAKAMI, T. and KROONENBERG, P.M. (2003): Individual differences in semantic differential studies and their analysis by three-mode models. *Multivariate Behavioral Research, 38*, 87-96.

RIU, J. and BRO, R. (2003): Jack-knife technique for outlier detection and estimation of standard errors in PARAFAC models., *Chemometrics and Intelligent Laboratory Systems, 65*, 35–69.

TIMMERMAN, M.E. and KIERS, H.A.L. (2000): Three-mode principal components analysis: Choosing the numbers of components and sensitivity to local optima. *British Journal of Mathematical and Statistical Psychology, 53*, 1–16.

TUCKER, L.R. (1966): Some mathematical notes on three-mode factor analysis. *Psychometrika, 31*, 279–311.

WEESIE, J. and VAN HOUWELINGEN, H. (1983): *GEPCAM users' manual: Generalized principal components analysis with missing values*. (Technical report). Institute of Mathematical Statistics, University of Utrecht, Utrecht, The Netherlands

Principal Component Analysis
for Non-Precise Data

Carlo N. Lauro[1] and Francesco Palumbo[2]

[1] Dipartimento di Matematica e Statistica
Universit "Federico II" – Napoli, Italy
clauro@unina.it
[2] Dipartimento di Istituzioni Economiche e Finanziarie
Universit di Macerata – Macerata, Italy
palumbo@unimc.it

Abstract. Many real world phenomena are better represented by non-precise data rather than by single-valued data. In fact, non-precise data represent two sources of variability: the natural phenomena variability and the variability or uncertainty induced by measurement errors or determined by specific experimental conditions. The latter variability source is named *imprecision*. When there are information about the imprecision distribution the *fuzzy* data coding is used to represent the imprecision. However, in many cases imprecise data are natively defined only by the *minimum* and *maximum* values. Technical specifications, stock-market daily prices, survey data are some examples of such kind of data. In these cases, interval data represent a good data coding to take into account the imprecision. This paper aims at describing multiple imprecise data by means of a suitable Principal Component Analysis that is based on specific interval data coding taking into account both sources of variation.

1 Introduction

Generally, in statistical analysis, we handle single-valued variables; however, in many cases, imprecise data represent a variable coding that better preserves the variables information. This paper deals with variables that cannot be measured in a precise way. Therefore, in order to represent the vagueness and uncertainty of the data, we propose to adopt a set-valued coding for the generic variable Y, instead of the classical single-valued one. An interval $[y]$ is a coding able to represent a continuous and uniformly dense set $\mathcal{Y} \subset \mathbb{R}$, under the hypothesis that the distribution of Y is uniform or unknown over the interval. Under these assumptions, any point $\tilde{y} \in \mathcal{Y}$ represents an admissible numerical coding of Y and the interval numerical coding $[y]$ of $\mathcal{Y}$ is given by:

$$[y] = [\min(\mathcal{Y}), \max(\mathcal{Y})] \equiv [\underline{y}, \overline{y}],$$

where $\underline{y}$ and $\overline{y}$ indicate the interval lower bound and upper bound, respectively.

The treatment of interval data is a very fascinating problem in Statistics, it allows to take into account the natural variability of *phenomena* under investigation and the other sources of variability, separately.

This paper proposes a generalization of Principal Component Analysis (PCA) to interval data.

We shortly remind the aim of PCA "...*each point can be considered as a vector in the p dimensional space... The goal of the PCA is to look for the best axis, the best plane or the best subspace to represent the projections of the distances among any generic couple of points with minimum distortion.*" (Lebart et al. 1995). This allows to visualize data as points in reduced subspaces and to analyze the points proximity in terms of their location with respect to the center of gravity. Dealing with interval data, the above definition does not fit anymore and proper definitions and data treatments must be introduced.

It is worth noticing that statistical units described by interval variables are no longer represented by points in $\mathbb{R}^p$ but as segments in $\mathbb{R}$, parallelograms in $\mathbb{R}^2$ and *boxes* in higher dimensional spaces. As a consequence, other aspects than the location can be investigated in the analysis, i.e.: boxes *size* and *shape*.

The example in section (4) describes a situation where data are natively generated as interval-valued and any punctual coding should induce a severe loss of information.

2 Intervals and boxes

Interval data numerical notation adopted in this paper is mainly derived from the *Interval Arithmetic* (IA) notation (Hickey et al. 2001).

The generic interval-valued variable $[X]$ is represented in the following notation:

$$[X] = [\underline{X}, \overline{X}] \qquad \text{with } \underline{X} \leq \overline{X},$$

where $\inf[X] := \underline{X}$ and $\sup[X] := \overline{X}$ indicate the interval *lower bound* and *upper bound*, respectively. The set of all boxes of dimension p is denoted by $\mathbb{IR}^p$ (Kearfott 1996).

A generic row interval vector $[\mathbf{x}] \equiv ([x]_1, \ldots [x]_i, \ldots, [x]_p)$ corresponds to a p-dimensional box and is generally identified with the (nonempty) set of points between its lower and upper bounds, $[\mathbf{x}] = \{\tilde{\mathbf{x}} \in \mathbb{R}^p \mid \underline{x} \leq \tilde{x} \leq \overline{x}\}$, so that a vector $\mathbf{x} \in \mathbb{R}^p$ is *contained* in a box $[\mathbf{x}]$, i.e., $\tilde{x} \in \mathbf{x} \longrightarrow (\underline{x} \leq \tilde{x} \leq \overline{x})$, where $\tilde{x}$ represents a generic (arbitrary) point in a box $\mathbf{x}$. The set of vertices of a box $\mathbf{x}$ represents the polytope $\mathcal{S}$ and corresponds to the 2^p combinations of $\overline{x}$ and $\underline{x}$. Combining all the vertices of $\mathcal{S}$, we define the vertices matrix $\mathbf{z}$, having 2^p rows and p columns, that satisfies the following symmetric relation: $\mathbf{z} \leftrightarrow \mathbf{x}$.

Single valued variables represent a special case of interval variables. An interval of zero width $[\mathbf{x}] = [x, x]$, called *thin* box, is identified with the unique point x it contains.

Interval boxes can also be described in terms of *midpoints* and *radii* (or *ranges*) vectors that are defined as functions of *min* and *max*, as follows:

$$\text{mid}([\mathbf{x}]) \equiv \check{\mathbf{x}} = \frac{1}{2}(\overline{\mathbf{x}} + \underline{\mathbf{x}}),$$

$$\text{rad}([\mathbf{x}]) \equiv \Delta([\mathbf{x}]) = \frac{1}{2}(\overline{\mathbf{x}} - \underline{\mathbf{x}}).$$

We will introduce some very basic definitions of the Interval Arithmetic. They allow to define the mean interval.

The arithmetic operators in the IA framework are defined according to the following basic principle: let $[x]_i$ and $[x]_{i'}$ be two generic bounded intervals in $\mathbb{R}$ and let $x_i \in [x]_i$ and $x_{i'} \in [x]_{i'}$ be two generic values, if $[y] = [x]_i \Diamond [x]_{i'}$ then $x_i \Diamond x_{i'} = y \in [y], \forall (x_i, x_{i'})$, where $\Diamond$ indicates any generic operator.

Sum of $[x]_i$ and $[x]_{i'}$ is defined as:

$$[y] = [x]_i + [x]_{i'} = [(\underline{x_i} + \underline{x_{i'}}), (\overline{x_i} + \overline{x_{i'}})]$$

or equivalently in terms of midpoints and ranges we have

$$\{\check{y}, \Delta([y])\} = \{(\check{x}_i + \check{x}_{i'}), (\Delta([x])_i + \Delta([x])_{i'})\}.$$

The difference between two intervals is defined as $[y] = [x]_i - [x]_{i'} = [(\underline{x_i} - \overline{x_{i'}}), (\overline{x_i} - \underline{x_{i'}})]$. The computation of the product between two intervals corresponds to the min and max values in the set of all possible products between $(\underline{x_i}, \overline{x_i})$ and $(\underline{x_{i'}}, \overline{x_{i'}})$: $[y] = [x]_i * [x]_{i'} = [\underline{y}, \overline{y}]$. Writing the product formula in extended notation we have: $\underline{y} = \min\{(\underline{x_i} * \underline{x_{i'}}), (\underline{x_i} * \overline{x_{i'}}), (\overline{x_i} * \underline{x_{i'}}), (\overline{x_i} * \overline{x_{i'}})\}$ and $\overline{y} = \max\{(\underline{x_i} * \underline{x_{i'}}), (\underline{x_i} * \overline{x_{i'}}), (\overline{x_i} * \underline{x_{i'}}), (\overline{x_i} * \overline{x_{i'}})\}$. The same definition holds for the division of two generic intervals and can be generalized to the case in which one interval is a *tiny* interval.

Taking into account the definitions of sum and product we define the *mean interval* $[\bar{x}]$ as:

$$[\bar{x}] = \frac{1}{n} \sum_{i=1}^{n} [x]_i, \tag{1}$$

where $[x]_i \subseteq \mathbb{R} \ \forall i \in \{1, \ldots, n\}$.

Interval matrices. An *interval matrix* is a $n \times p$ matrix $[\mathbf{X}]$ whose entries $[x]_{ij} = [\underline{x}_{ij}, \overline{x}_{ij}]$ $(i = 1, \ldots, n; j = 1, \ldots, p)$ are intervals and $\tilde{\mathbf{X}} \in [\mathbf{X}]$ is a generic single valued data matrix satisfying the following $\underline{\mathbf{X}} \leq \tilde{\mathbf{X}} \leq \overline{\mathbf{X}}$. The notation for boxes is adapted to interval matrices in the natural component-wise way.

The vertices matrix associated to the generic interval matrix $[\mathbf{X}]$ will be noted as $\mathbf{Z}$ and has $n \times 2^p$ rows and p columns.

As shown in the above definitions, statistical units described by interval variables can be numerically represented in different ways. The choice of the representation affects the global analysis results.

3 Midpoints-Ranges PCA (MR-PCA)

PCA on interval-valued data can be resolved in terms of *ranges*, *midpoints* and *inter-connection* between midpoints and *radii* (Palumbo and Lauro 2003). The basic idea behind this proposal consists in the definition of the variance for interval variables based on the the notion of distance between intervals (Neumaier 1990):

$$d\left([\mathbf{x}]_i, \mathbf{x}_{i'}\right) = d\left([\mathbf{x}]_i, \mathbf{x}_{i'}\right) = |\check{\mathbf{x}}_i - \check{\mathbf{x}}_{i'}| + |\Delta([\mathbf{x}])_i - \Delta([\mathbf{x}])_{i'}| \qquad (2)$$

The quantity

$$\mathrm{var}_{[\cdot]}([\mathbf{x}]) := n^{-1} \sum_i d(\mathbf{x}_i, [\bar{\mathbf{x}}])^2 \qquad (3)$$

represents the variance for interval variables, where $[\bar{\mathbf{x}}]$ indicates the *mean* interval vector obtained by the (1). The generalization of the above definitions to matrices is:

$$Cov([\mathbf{X}]) = \tfrac{1}{n}\check{\mathbf{X}}'\check{\mathbf{X}} + \tfrac{1}{n}\Delta([\mathbf{X}])'\Delta([\mathbf{X}]) + \tfrac{1}{n}\left[\check{\mathbf{X}}'\Delta([\mathbf{X}]) + \Delta([\mathbf{X}])'\check{\mathbf{X}}\right] \qquad (4)$$

The variance decomposition for interval-valued data suggests facing the PCA problem singly; the terms $(\check{\mathbf{X}}'\check{\mathbf{X}})$ and $\Delta([\mathbf{X}])'\Delta([\mathbf{X}])$ are two standard *var-cov* matrices computed on single-valued data. Two independent PCA's could be singly exploited on these two matrices that do not cover the whole variance. We propose a solution that takes into account the residual variance $(|\check{\mathbf{X}}'\Delta([\mathbf{X}])| + |\Delta([\mathbf{X}])'\check{\mathbf{X}}|)$ and, at the same time, allows getting a logical graphical representation of the statistical units as a whole.

Standardization
Moving from (2), we define the *Standard Deviation* for interval-valued variables. Let σ_j^2 be the variance of the generic $[\mathbf{X}]_j$ variable: $\sigma_j = \sqrt{\sigma_j^2}$ is the standard deviation of $[\mathbf{X}]_j$ and the square diagonal $p \times p$ matrix Σ has the generic term σ_j. The standardized interval matrix: $[\mathbf{Y}] = \{\check{\mathbf{X}}\Sigma^{-1}, \Delta([\mathbf{X}])\Sigma^{-1}\}$ assuming $[\mathbf{X}]$ to be centered and divided by $\sqrt{n}$.

Let us denote the correlation matrix by $\mathbf{R}$:

$$\mathbf{R} = \left[(\check{\mathbf{Y}}'\check{\mathbf{Y}}) + \Delta([\mathbf{Y}])'\Delta([\mathbf{Y}]) + |\check{\mathbf{Y}}'\Delta([\mathbf{Y}])| + |\Delta([\mathbf{Y}])'\check{\mathbf{Y}}|\right], \qquad (5)$$

where $(\check{\mathbf{Y}}'\Delta([\mathbf{Y}]))$ and $(\Delta([\mathbf{Y}])'\check{\mathbf{Y}})$ have the same diagonal elements. A noteworthy aspect is given by the decomposition of the total inertia. In fact,

$\mathrm{tr}(\mathbf{R}) = p$ and we observe that the quantity $\mathrm{tr}(\check{\mathbf{Y}}'\check{\mathbf{Y}})$ and the quantity $\mathrm{tr}(\Delta([\mathbf{Z}])'\Delta([\mathbf{Z}]))$ are the partial contributions to the total inertia given by midpoints and ranges, respectively. A residual inertia is given by $2\mathrm{tr}(\check{\mathbf{Y}}'\Delta([\mathbf{Y}]))$.

Midpoints and Ranges analysis

We first consider a partial analysis based on the matrix of centers (or midpoints) values. This is a classical PCA on the interval midpoints whose solutions are given by the following eigensystem:

$$\check{\mathbf{X}}\Sigma^{-1}\mathbf{u}_m^c = \lambda_m^c\mathbf{u}_m^c, \tag{6}$$

where $\mathbf{u}_m^c$ and λ_m^c are defined under the usual orthonormality constraints.

Similarly to the PCA on midpoints, we solve the following eigensystem to get the ranges PCA solutions:

$$\Delta([\mathbf{X}])\Sigma^{-1}\mathbf{u}_m^r = \lambda_m^r\mathbf{u}_m^r, \tag{7}$$

with the same orthonormality constraints on λ_m^c and $\mathbf{u}_m^c$ as in eq. (6) and with $m = [1, \ldots, p]$. Both midpoints and ranges PCA's admit an independent representation. Of course, they have different meanings and outline different aspects. The quantity $\sum_m (\lambda_m^c + \lambda_m^r) \leq p$ but it does not include the whole variability because residual inertia, given by the midpoints-radii interconnection, has not yet been taken into account.

Global analysis and graphical representations

Hereinafter, we propose a reconstruction formula that takes into account the three components of the variance (3). The interval bounds over the Principal Components (PC's) are derived from the midpoints and ranges coordinates, if PC's of ranges are superimposed on the PC's of midpoints. This can be achieved if ranges are rotated proportionally to their connections with midpoints.

There exist several rotation techniques, we verified the properties of many of them. In this paper, as orthogonal congruence rotation criterion, we propose to maximize the congruence coefficient proposed by Tucker between midpoints and *radii*:

$$f(T) = \sum_{l \in [1,p]} \frac{t_l'\Delta([\mathbf{x}])_l'\check{\mathbf{X}}}{(t_l'\Delta([\mathbf{x}])_l'\Delta([\mathbf{x}])_l t)^{1/2}(\check{\mathbf{X}}'\check{\mathbf{X}})^{1/2}}. \tag{8}$$

Verified under several different conditions, this rotation technique ensured best results in most cases. The computation of the rotation matrix $\mathbf{T} = [t_1, \ldots, t_l, \ldots, t_p]$ can be done in several different ways. We choose the one based on the iterative algorithm proposed by (Kiers and Groenen 1996). Let $\psi_\alpha^c - \check{\mathbf{X}}\mathbf{u}_\alpha^c$ be the midpoints coordinates on the αth axis. The interval-described statistical units reconstruction on the same axis is given by the rotated *radii* on $\mathbf{u}_\alpha^r$. In mathematical notation: $\psi^*{}_\alpha^r = \mathbf{T}(\Delta([\mathbf{X}])\mathbf{u}_\alpha^r)$. The interval projection is obtained as:

$$[\psi]_\alpha = [(\psi_\alpha^c - \psi^*{}_\alpha^r), (\psi_\alpha^c + \psi^*{}_\alpha^r)] \tag{9}$$

Like in single-valued PCA, also in interval-valued variables PCA, it is possible to define some indicators that are related to interval contribution.

Measures of explanatory power can be defined with respect to the partial analyses (midpoints and *radii*) as well as with respect to the global analysis. Let us remind that the variability associated to each dimension is expressed by its related eigenvalue.

The proportion of variability associated to the first dimension is given by:

$$In_1 = \frac{\lambda_1^c + \lambda_1^r}{\text{tr}(\Lambda^c + \Lambda^r)}, \tag{10}$$

where λ_1^c and λ_1^r represent the first eigenvalues related to the midpoints and *radii*, respectively. They express a partial information; in fact, there is a residual variability that depends on the *midpoints* and *radii* connection that cannot be explicitly taken into account.

In spite of the role they assume in classical PCA, in MR-PCA the squared cosines have an important role to evaluate the achieved results. Squared cosines, also called *"relative contributions"* represent the amount of the original distances displayed on the factorial plane. From the classical PCA, we define these quantities as the ratio between the vector norms in the Principal Components space and the original norms computed in $\mathbb{R}^p$: $SqCos_i = \sum_{j=1}^p y_{i,j}^2 / \sum_\alpha (\sum_{j=1}^p y_{i,j} u_{j,\alpha})^2$, where $\alpha \in [1, \ldots, p]$ represents the set of eigenvectors with respect to which we intend compute the relative contributes. It is obvious that $0 \leq SqCos \leq 1$, in the case of $\alpha \equiv [1, \ldots, p]$ the $SqCos = 1$.

In the case of interval-data, squared cosines are defined as:

$$SqCos = \frac{\sum_\alpha (\mid \psi^c{}_{i,\alpha} \mid + \mid \psi^*{}^r{}_{i,\alpha} \mid)^2}{\sum_{j=1}^p (\mid \check{y}_{i,j} \mid + \mid \text{rad}([y])_{i,j} \mid)^2}, \tag{11}$$

where $\psi^c{}_{i,\alpha}$ and $\psi^*{}^r{}_{i,\alpha}$ are defined in (9) and are centered variables. Differently from the case of single-valued data, the condition $\alpha \equiv 1, \ldots, p$ does not ensure that $SqCos = 1$. In most cases, we get squared cosines less then one even if we consider the whole set of the eigenvectors $(\mathbf{u}_1, \mathbf{u}_2, \ldots, \mathbf{u}_p)$. Due to the effects of the rotation, it may happen that $SqCos > 1$. In such a case the $SqCos$ reveals that the rectangle associated to the element is oversized with respect to its original size.

The *radii* rotation is obtained in the sense of a *"least squares"* analysis and this rotation does not ensure that the total variance is completely represented by the principal components. A measure of goodness-of-fit allows to evaluate the quality of the representation. We propose to adopt a generalization of the R^2 index obtained as the ratio between the variance defined with respect to the principal components and the variances in the original $\mathbb{R}^p$ space. Variances are determined by the formula in (3).

4 Application: Italian peppers dataset

This section shows the results obtained by the method described in section 3. Data are reported in the table (1) and refer to some characteristics describing eight different species of Italian peppers.

Id	H_2O		Protein		Lipid		Glucide	
Corno di Bue	90.45	93.15	0.67	0.95	0.23	0.30	5.07	7.76
Cuban	90.46	91.55	0.97	1.11	0.24	0.33	6.42	7.65
Cuban Nano	87.89	91.40	0.89	1.25	0.28	0.35	6.80	9.91
Grosso di Nocera	90.91	92.55	0.52	0.80	0.21	0.27	5.98	7.58
Pimiento	89.92	93.43	0.61	1.09	0.23	0.24	5.23	7.94
Quadrato D'Asti	91.31	92.99	0.74	0.90	0.20	0.27	6.64	7.10
Sunnybrook	89.65	92.58	0.85	1.50	0.20	0.28	5.52	8.52
Yolo Wonder	90.80	94.26	0.73	1.30	0.20	0.25	4.39	7.34

Table 1. Italian peppers dataset

Data are natively defined as interval-valued variables, they represent some of the chemio-physical characteristics of eight different species of Italian peppers. This is a good example of data in which we can distinguish two different sources of variability: variability among different species; variation admitted inside one specific breed. Variation associated to each species is represented by the range: difference between the maximum and the minimum value.

The correlation decomposition in the three parts: midpoints, ranges and the congruence between midpoints and ranges is reported in the tables below. Taking into account that the total inertia is equal to p, let we analyze the variance components. The trace of the midpoints correlation matrix is equal to 1.973 and corresponds to 49.32% (1.973/4.000 = 0.4932) of the total variance.

Midpoints variance part (C)			
	H_2O	Protein	Lipid	Glucide
---	---	---	---	---
H_2O	.468	-0.221	-0.468	-0.352
Protein	-0.221	.461	.173	.177
Lipid	-0.468	.173	.612	.341
Glucide	-0.352	.177	.341	.429

The ranges variability is equal to 0.534 and corresponds to 13.35% of the total variability.

Ranges variance part (R)

	H₂O	Protein	Lipid	Glucide
H₂O	.140	.106	-0.063	.008
Protein	.106	.137	-0.042	-0.015
Lipid	-0.063	-0.042	.094	-0.002
Glucide	.008	-0.015	-0.002	.162

The residual part, corresponding to the connection between centers and ranges, is the complement to p. In this case this quantity is equal to $(4 - 1.973 - 0.534) = 1.493$ and corresponds to the 37.32% of the total variance.

Range-midpoints co–variance part (CR)

	H₂O	Protein	Lipid	Glucide
H₂O	0.391	0.339	0.348	0.284
Protein	0.339	0.400	0.042	0.294
Lipid	0.348	0.301	0.292	0.214
Glucide	0.284	0.294	0.214	0.409

The correlation matrix, resulting from the element-wise sum of the partial matrices, can be interpreted as a classical symmetric correlation matrix. It has values equal to one on the main diagonal and values between -1 and 1 otherwise.

Global correlation matrix

	H₂O	Protein	Lipid	Glucide
H₂O	1.000	.225	-0.183	-0.060
Protein	.225	1.000	.432	.457
Lipid	-0.183	.432	1.000	.553
Glucide	-0.060	.456	.553	1.000

The figure (1) shows the midpoints (**a**) and ranges (**b**) variables. Circles indicate the maximum norm that can be represented, determined according to the correlation decomposition. Let us consider the midpoints variables, in the present example the maximum variability is 0.612 (corresponding to the *Lipid* variable); this implies that the maximum variable length is $\sqrt{0.612} = 0.782$. As the two graphics represent a part of the total variance, *radii* are ≤ 1. The interpretation of the graphical results can be done following the usual rules adopted in the case of single-valued data, singly for midpoints and ranges. Figure (2) displays the initial solution (**a**) and the final solution (**b**) obtained after the rotation. In this case the algorithm stopped after 4 iterations. The residual variance resulted to be 0.178 that is equivalent to 4.45% of the total inertia. This little part of residual variance indicates the good result obtained by the analysis. The percentage of inertia associated to the first two principal components is equal to 79.33%. In table (4) we summarized the most important analytical results necessary for a correct interpretation. The first two columns refer to the *SqCos* with respect to the first two factors singly considered. The third one represents the quality of the

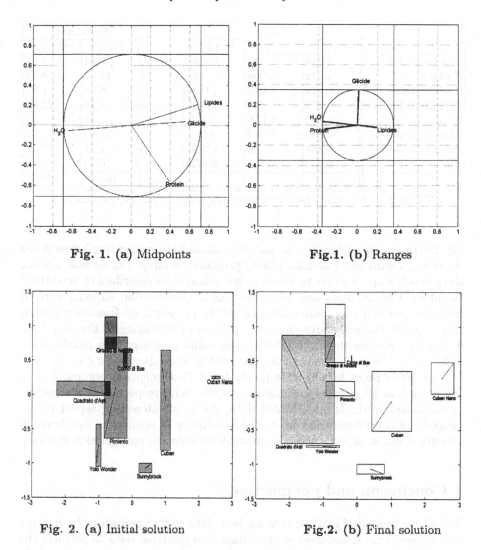

Fig. 1. (a) Midpoints   **Fig.1. (b)** Ranges

Fig. 2. (a) Initial solution   **Fig.2. (b)** Final solution

representation on the factorial plane spanned by the first two factors. Taking into account the *SqCos*, we observe that *Grosso di Nocera* and *Cuban Nano* have the highest values. The segment traced inside each rectangle represents the rotated range and indicate which variables have mainly contributed to the ranges orientation. Referring to *Grosso di Nocera* and *Cuban Nano*, we observe that, with respect to the first factorial plan, their sizes and shapes were characterized by the same variables, but with opposite versus.

Sometimes, the complexity of interval data can generate unclear graphical representations, when the number of statistical units is large, because boxes representation, either in the original $\mathbb{R}^p$ variable space and even more in the $\mathbb{R}^2$ subspaces, can cause a severe overlapping of the statistical units, making

	Cos^2				Abs.Contr.	
	F1	F2	F1+F1		F1%	F1%
Corno di Bue	0.048	0.450	0.498		0.34	7.05
Cuban	0.632	0.068	0.700		12.50	6.33
Cuban Nano	0.979	0.029	1.008		46.09	1.65
Grosso di Nocera	0.358	0.670	1.028		4.25	22.92
Pimiento	0.396	0.019	0.414		5.48	0.25
Quadrato d'Asti	0.646	0.097	0.742		18.69	21.67
Sunnybrook	0.187	0.380	0.567		2.31	27.12
Yolo Wonder	0.704	0.171	0.875		10.34	13.01
				Total	*100.00*	*100.00*

Table 2. *SqCos* and Absolute Contribution for Italian Peppers dataset

any interpretation difficult. Alternatively, instead of representing boxes in the $\mathbb{R}^p$ space, Lauro and Palumbo (2003) proposed to adopt the *parallel axes* as the geometric space where to visualize statistical units described by set-valued variables. Parallel axes can be defined as a visualization support derived from the *parallel coordinates* schema, firstly proposed by Inselberg (1999), who exploits the projective geometry properties consisting in the definition of duality between the $\mathbb{R}^n$ Euclidean space and a system of n parallel axes in $\mathbb{R}^2$. It can be proved that these relationships correspond to a duality *point* $\leftrightarrow$ *line*; each point in $\mathbb{R}^n$ corresponds to (n-1)-segments polygonal line in the projective $\mathbb{R}^2$ parallel coordinates system. With respect to other graphic visualization methods for complex data, the most interesting aspect in the proposal is the relevance given to the possibility of comparing syntheses of statistical units, as well as single variables on different parallel axes systems.

5 Conclusion and perspective

The above presented method is based on a data coding procedure (midpoints and ranges) that transforms interval data into punctual data to perform the treatment and recovers intervals when data are graphically represented. In other words, it is based on the coding process: Interval $\rightarrow$ Punctual $\rightarrow$ Interval. The same approach with a different data coding has been presented by Cazes et al. (1997); they propose a PCA analysis on the vertices matrix $\mathbf{Z}$. On the same vertices data structure, Lauro and Palumbo (2000) introduced a cohesion constraint matrix and a system of vertices weighting. Both approaches represent the boxes on the factorial plan by means of the Maximum Covering Area Rectangles (MCAR) that are obtained as the rectangle recovering all the vertices belonging to the same interval valued statistical unit. The major drawback of these approaches consists in producing oversized MCAR's. On the other hand, the vertices coding assumes an ordinary PCA on the vertices matrix preserving the possibility of using standard interpretation tools.

A direct treatment of interval data should avoid the loss of information due to the coding in the data structure. There are two possible approaches to jointly treat interval data taking into account both midpoints and ranges.

An approach for the direct treatment of interval data was proposed by Giordani and Kiers (2004). They present a model named Principal Components for Fuzzy data (PCAF), where interval data can represent a special case. The advantage of this approach consists in the possibility of treating *fuzzy* numbers, however the formalization of the method substantially corresponds to the vertices approach proposed by Cazes et al. (1997). In fact, they propose an alternate iterative algorithm to minimize the quantity:

$$\Delta^2 = \|\check{\mathbf{X}} - \check{\mathbf{X}}^*\|^2 + \sum_{k=1}^{K} \|(\check{\mathbf{X}} + \mathbf{S}\mathbf{H}_k\Lambda) - (\check{\mathbf{X}}^* + \mathbf{S}^*\mathbf{H}_k\Lambda)\|^2, \qquad (12)$$

where $\check{\mathbf{X}}$ and $\check{\mathbf{X}}^*$ are the matrices of the observed and estimated midpoints, respectively. Matrices $\mathbf{S}$ and $\mathbf{S}^*$ have n rows and p columns and represent the observed and the estimated spread (or ranges), respectively. The matrix $\mathbf{H}$ contains only -1 and 1 values and has no relevance from the point of view of the model and permits to combine all the (min, max) vertices (like in the proposal by Cazes et al.). The matrix Λ is a weight diagonal matrix with generic term λ_j. In case of $\Lambda = \mathbf{I}$, the minimization of the second term in the left hand side of (12) corresponds to the analysis of Cazes et al.. We refer the interested readers to the cited paper for further details about the model estimation procedure. However, it is interesting to notice that results shown in the Giordani and Kiers example are very similar to the ones obtained by Cazes et al., in fact, they were obtained using the same well known (to *intervallers*) Ichino and Yaguchi's oil data set.

A more promising approach is the one based on the Interval Arithmetic principles (Neumaier 1990). IA provides us suitable methods for the direct treatment of the interval variables. As expected, in this context, eigenvalues, eigenvectors, principal components are intervals. This makes the results consistent with the nature of the original data and enriches the data interpretation and visualization, because it preserves the formal aspects of the single-valued PCA. However, it requires high complexity in both numerical and computing aspects.

The eigenanalysis of an interval matrix implies that the matrix should be strictly regular. An interval matrix is said to be regular (Jansson and Rohn 1999) if every matrix $\tilde{\mathbf{X}} \in [\mathbf{X}]$ has full rank and it is said to be *strongly* regular if the following condition holds: $\rho\left(\check{\mathbf{X}}^{-1}|\Delta([\mathbf{X}])\right) < 1$, where $\rho(\cdot)$ indicates the spectral radius. Given a generic square matrix, $\rho(\mathbf{M})$ is defined as:

$$\rho(\mathbf{M}) := \max\{|\lambda| : \lambda \text{ an eigenvalue of } \mathbf{M}\}$$

From a statistical point of view, the regularity property has a remarkable significance. Let us assume that the matrix $[\boldsymbol{\Sigma}] = [\mathbf{X}]'[\mathbf{X}]$ is a $p \times p$ variance-covariance interval matrix; then the covariance midpoints matrix satisfies

$\tilde{\Sigma} = \tilde{X}'\tilde{X}$ and the matrix $\Delta[\Sigma]$ represents the variance and covariance ranges matrix. The regularity condition implies that, for any couple of variables $[x]_j$ and $[x]_{j'}$, with $j, j' = 1, \ldots, p$, the range is lower than the midpoint variability. It is quite intuitive that this condition is very restrictive and the direct application of the interval arithmetic can be exploited only in cases of intervals representing very small data perturbations. In addition, a proposal by Marino and Palumbo (2003) in the interval multiple regression context, based on the optimization/perturbation theory, seems very promising also for Interval PCA. The statistical properties and its interpretability are subjects of actual investigation.

Acknowledgments:

This paper was financially supported by the grant "Metodi statistici e tecniche di visualizzazione grafica per grandi basi di dati" (F.Palumbo, Universit di Macerata, 2002/2003) and by the IST-2000-26341 Vitamin-s European project (C. Lauro, DMS Napoli, 2000/2003).

References

CAZES, P., CHOUAKRIA, A., DIDAY, E. and SCHEKTMAN, Y. (1997): Extension de l'analyse en composantes principales à des données de type intervalle, *Revue de Statistique Appliquée* XIV(3): 5–24.

GIORDANI, P. and KIERS, H. A. L. (2004): Principal component analysis of symmetric fuzzy data, *Computational Statistics and Data Analysis* 45, 519–548.

HICKEY, T., JU, Q. and VAN EMDEN, M. H. (2001): Interval arithmetic: From principles to implementation, *Journal of the ACM* 48(5): 1038–1068.

INSELBERG, A. (1999): Don't panic ... just do it in parallel!, *Comp. Stat.* 14: 53–77.

JANSSON, C. and ROHN, J. (1999): An alghoritm for checking regularity of interval, *SIAM Journal of Matrix Analysis and Applications* 20(3): 756–776.

KEARFOTT, R. B. (1996): *Rigorous Global Search: Continuous Problems*, Kluver, Dordrecht.

KIERS, H. A. L. and GROENEN, P. (1996): A monotonically convergent algorithm for orthogonal congruence rotation, *Psychometrika* 61(2): 375–389.

LAURO, C. N. and PALUMBO, F. (2000): Principal component analysis of interval data: A symbolic data analysis approach, *Comp. Stat.* 15(1): 73–87.

LAURO, C. N. and PALUMBO, F. (2003): Some results and new perspectives in principal component analysis for interval data, *in* 'CLADAG'03 Book of Short Papers', Bologna, pp. 237–244.

LEBART, L., MORINEAU, A. and PIRON, M. (1995): *Statistique exploratorie multidimensionelle*, Dunod, Paris.

MARINO, M. and PALUMBO, F. (2003): Interval arithmetic for the evaluation of imprecise data effects in least squares linear regression, *Stat.Applicata* 14(3): 277-291.

NEUMAIER, A. (1990): *Interval methods for systems of Equations*, Cambridge University Press, Cambridge.

PALUMBO, F. and LAURO, C. N. (2003): A PCA for interval valued data based on midpoints and radii, *in* H. Yanai, A. Okada, K. Shigemasu, Y. Kano and J. Meulman, eds, 'New developments in Psychometrics', Psychometric Society, Springer-Verlag, Tokyo.

A New Version of the Structural Dynamic Model with Unique Latent Scores

Simona Caterina Minotti[1] and Giorgio Vittadini[2]

[1] Dipartimento di Scienze Economiche e Sociali,
Università Cattolica di Piacenza, Italy
simona.minotti@unicatt.it
[2] Dipartimento di Statistica,
Università Milano Bicocca, Italy
giorgio.vittadini@unimib.it

Abstract. The indeterminacy of the Structural Models, i.e. the arbitrariness of latent scores, due to the factorial nature of the measurement models, is, in the dynamic context, more problematic. We propose an alternative formulation of the Structural Dynamic Model, based on the Replicated Common Factor Model (Haagen e Oberhofer, 1999), where latent scores are no more indeterminate.

1 Introduction

It is well known that the causality principle of the Factor Analysis Model (FA) (i.e. to express the indicators as a function of the latent variables) leads to indeterminacy of latent scores (Guttman (1955)), with important consequences on the classificatory validity of the latent variables (Schoenemann and Haagen (1987); Haagen (1991)). The same problem arises in the Structural Equation Models with reflective blocks (SEM) (Vittadini (1989)) and also in the Structural Dynamic Models with latent variables (SDL) (Haagen and Vittadini (1994)), because both use FA as a measurement model. Moreover Haagen and Vittadini (1994) proved that the dynamics increases the indeterminacy. The SDL will be presented in Section 2, while the problem of indeterminacy in SDL will be discussed in Section 3.

It follows that only the introduction of alternative models to the FA as measurement models allows us to definitely overcome indeterminacy. To avoid arbitrariness of common factors, some authors have proposed an estimation procedure which inverts the natural relationship among variables, expressing the latent variables as a linear combination of the indicators. For example, Schoenemann and Steiger (1976) proposed the Regression Component Decomposition method (RCD), successively extended to SEM by Haagen and Vittadini (1991) and applied to some different contexts (Vittadini (1999)). This proposal, however, can not be considered a model, because the solutions can not be interpreted as causes of the indicators. Instead Haagen and Oberhofer (1999) introduced an alternative model to the FA, entitled the Replicated Common Factor Model (RCFM), (successively extended to SEM by Vittadini and Haagen (2002)), which solves the indeterminacy of common factors asymptotically.

Nevertheless, no proposal has been made in the dynamic context, except by Minotti (2002), who introduced a correction of the Kalman filter by means of RCD, providing, at every time interval t, (t=1,...,T), unique values for the latent variables. This new method will be described in Section 3. However, as illustrated previously, the proposal is not a model. Thus, the problem of indeterminacy in the SDL can not be considered definitively overcome.

As an alternative, which overcomes the indeterminacy of latent scores asymptotically, we propose a new version of the SDL based on the RCFM. The extension of the RCFM to the dynamic context will be presented in Section 4. The new model has been applied to an experiment of the Department of Physics, University of Milan. The application will be described in Section 5. Some conclusions will be given in Section 6.

Section 1 is to be attributed to Vittadini, as well as the supervision of the paper; Sections 2-6 were developed by Minotti.

2 The SDL

The SDL, introduced by Otter (1985) as a dynamic generalization of SEM, is the stationary version of the Stochastic Linear State Space Model from Systems Engineering, i.e. it is a linear model with latent variables, where the observations are represented by a single multivariate time series. The SDL consists of a transition equation, which describes the temporal relationships among the latent variables, and a measurement equation, that relates the latent variables to the observed variables:

$$\mathbf{A}_0\boldsymbol{\xi}_t = \mathbf{A}_1\boldsymbol{\xi}_{t-1} + \overline{\mathbf{B}}\mathbf{u}_t + \overline{\mathbf{w}}_t, \qquad \boldsymbol{\xi}_0 \sim N(\boldsymbol{\mu}, \mathbf{V}_{\boldsymbol{\xi}_0}), \qquad t = 1,...,T \qquad (1)$$

$$\mathbf{z}_t = \mathbf{C}\boldsymbol{\xi}_t + \mathbf{D}\mathbf{u}_t + \mathbf{v}_t, \qquad\qquad\qquad\qquad t = 1,...,T \qquad (2)$$

where $\boldsymbol{\xi}_t = [\boldsymbol{\eta}_t, \boldsymbol{\phi}_t]$ are respectively m_1 endogenous and m_2 exogenous latent variables distributed as normal random variables with finite covariance matrix $\boldsymbol{\Sigma}_{\boldsymbol{\xi}_t}$ ($\boldsymbol{\xi}_0 \sim N(\boldsymbol{\mu}, \mathbf{V}_{\boldsymbol{\xi}_0})$); $\overline{\mathbf{w}}_t$ and $\mathbf{v}_t = [\boldsymbol{\epsilon}_t, \boldsymbol{\delta}_t]$ are respectively $m = m_1 + m_2$ and $p = p_1 + p_2$ latent errors, normally distributed and mutually non correlated (for every t), with null expected value and time-invariant covariance matrices $\boldsymbol{\Sigma}_{\overline{\mathbf{w}}}$ and $\boldsymbol{\Sigma}_{\mathbf{V}}$; $\mathbf{u}_t$ is a vector of q deterministic inputs; $\mathbf{A}_0, \mathbf{A}_1, \mathbf{B}, \mathbf{C}$ and $\mathbf{D}$ are time-invariant matrices of respectively $(m \times m)$, $(m \times m)$, $(m \times q)$, $(p \times m)$ and $(p \times q)$ parameters (with invertible $\mathbf{A}_0$); $\mathbf{z}_t = [\mathbf{y}_t, \mathbf{x}_t]$ are p indicators respectively of the $\boldsymbol{\eta}_t$ and the $\boldsymbol{\phi}_t$, with covariance matrix $\boldsymbol{\Sigma}_{\mathbf{z}_t}$.

The reduced form of the SDL is obtained pre-multiplying (1) by $\mathbf{A}_0^{-1}$, i.e.:

$$\boldsymbol{\xi}_t = \mathbf{A}_0^{-1}\mathbf{A}_1\boldsymbol{\xi}_{t-1} + \mathbf{A}_0^{-1}\overline{\mathbf{B}}\mathbf{u}_t + \mathbf{A}_0^{-1}\overline{\mathbf{w}}_t, \qquad\qquad (3)$$

expressed in a compact notation as

$$\boldsymbol{\xi}_t = \mathbf{A}\boldsymbol{\xi}_{t-1} + \mathbf{B}\mathbf{u}_t + \mathbf{w}_t, \qquad\qquad (4)$$

where $\mathbf{w}_t$ is a vector of m latent errors with null expected value and time-invariant covariance matrices $\boldsymbol{\Sigma}_{\mathbf{W}} = \mathbf{A}_0^{-1} \boldsymbol{\Sigma}_{\overline{\mathbf{W}}} (\mathbf{A}_0^{-1})'$.

In the following, the deterministic inputs $\mathbf{u}_t$ will be omitted, which is not an essential restriction, given that they can always be included among the observable variables.

The parameter identifiability of the SDL has been extensively studied by many authors, who proposed some conditions for the local identifiability (Bordignon and Trivellato (1992); Otter (1992)). The estimation of the parameters and the latent scores can be obtained by means of a recursive procedure (as illustrated in Haagen and Vittadini (1994)).

3 The indeterminacy in the SDL and the first solution

Haagen and Vittadini (1994) discussed the indeterminacy of the SDL solution by using the Guttman's result (1955), introduced for the FA. They demonstrated that, if the following equality holds

$$\boldsymbol{\Sigma}_{\mathbf{Z}_t} = \mathbf{C} \boldsymbol{\Sigma}_{\boldsymbol{\xi}_t} \mathbf{C}' + \boldsymbol{\Sigma}_{\mathbf{V}_t}, \tag{5}$$

there exist arbitrary vectors $\boldsymbol{\xi}_t$ which satisfy (2).

These solutions, called "true solutions", have the following structure:

$$\boldsymbol{\xi}_t = \widehat{\boldsymbol{\xi}}_{t|t-1} + \mathbf{K}_t[\mathbf{z}_t - \widehat{\mathbf{z}}_t] + \mathbf{P}_t \boldsymbol{\omega}_t = \widehat{\boldsymbol{\xi}}_{t|t} + \mathbf{P}_t \boldsymbol{\omega}_t, \tag{6}$$

where $\widehat{\boldsymbol{\xi}}_{t|t-1}$ is the efficient predictor for $\boldsymbol{\xi}_t$, based linearly on $\{\mathbf{z}_1, ..., \mathbf{z}_{t-1}\}$, $\widehat{\boldsymbol{\xi}}_{t|t}$ is the Kalman estimator of $\boldsymbol{\xi}_t$, updated on the basis of the last observations $\mathbf{z}_t$, $\mathbf{K}_t = \boldsymbol{\Sigma}_{\widehat{\boldsymbol{\xi}}_{t|t-1}} \mathbf{C}' \boldsymbol{\Sigma}_{\mathbf{Z}_t}^{-1}$ is the Kalman gain, $\widehat{\mathbf{z}}_t = \mathbf{C} \widehat{\boldsymbol{\xi}}_{t|t-1}$ is the forecasting of $\mathbf{z}_t$ by (2), $\mathbf{P}_t = (\mathbf{I} - \mathbf{K}_t \mathbf{C}) \mathbf{F}_t$ with $\mathbf{F}_t \mathbf{F}_t' = \boldsymbol{\Sigma}_{\widehat{\boldsymbol{\xi}}_t}$, $\boldsymbol{\omega}_t$ is an arbitrary vector of m variables and $E[\boldsymbol{\omega}_t] = 0$, $\boldsymbol{\Sigma}_{\boldsymbol{\omega}_t, \mathbf{z}_t} = 0$, $\boldsymbol{\Sigma}_{\boldsymbol{\omega}_t} = \mathbf{I} - \mathbf{C}' \boldsymbol{\Sigma}_{\mathbf{Z}_t}^{-1} \mathbf{C}$. It follows that, as in the static context (FA and SEM), the latent scores obtained by means of the Kalman filter are not unique, due to the arbitrary term $\mathbf{P}_t \boldsymbol{\omega}_t$. Moreover Haagen and Vittadini (1994) demonstrated that in the SDL indeterminacy increases, due to the recursive procedure of Kalman filter, which spreads indeterminacy in time (the indeterminacy of $\widehat{\boldsymbol{\xi}}_t$ influences $\widehat{\boldsymbol{\xi}}_{t+1}$, $\widehat{\boldsymbol{\xi}}_{t+2}$, ...). In addition to this, Minotti (2002) observes that in the dynamic context defining $\widehat{\mathbf{z}}_t$ by (2) makes the situation worse.

As a first attempt of solution, Minotti (2002) proposed a correction of the Kalman filter by means of RCD, described in detail in the following.

Referring to the formulation of Haagen and Vittadini (1991), the RCD provides at each date t the following decomposition of $\mathbf{x}_t$:

$$\mathbf{x}_t = \widetilde{\mathbf{C}}_t \widetilde{\boldsymbol{\phi}}_t + (\mathbf{x}_t - \widetilde{\mathbf{C}}_t \widetilde{\boldsymbol{\phi}}_t), \tag{7}$$

which leads to a definition of the "latent" variables $\widetilde{\boldsymbol{\phi}}_t$, called components, as a linear combination of the observed variables $\mathbf{x}_t$

$$\tilde{\phi}_t = \mathbf{L}'_{\Phi_t} \mathbf{x}_t, \tag{8}$$

where $\mathbf{L}_{\Phi_t} = \Sigma_{\mathbf{X}_t}^{-1} \tilde{\mathbf{C}}_t (\tilde{\mathbf{C}}'_t \Sigma_{\mathbf{X}_t}^{-1} \tilde{\mathbf{C}}_t)^{-1}$ and $\tilde{\mathbf{C}}_t$ can be calculated as a factor loading matrix by means of a factor extraction method (Schoenemann and Steiger (1976)).

By means of an analogous decomposition of $\mathbf{y}_t$, we obtain $\mathbf{L}_{\eta_t}$. The matrix

$$\mathbf{L}_t = \begin{bmatrix} \mathbf{L}_{\eta_t} & 0 \\ 0 & \mathbf{L}_{\phi_t} \end{bmatrix} \tag{9}$$

provided by the RCD is then introduced in the Kalman filter instead of $\mathbf{C}$. Under the assumption that $\mathbf{A}$, $E[\boldsymbol{\xi}_0]$ and $\Sigma_{\boldsymbol{\xi}_0}$ are known, the first step of the Kalman filter at each time t becomes:

$$\overline{\boldsymbol{\xi}}_{t|t-1} = \mathbf{A}\overline{\boldsymbol{\xi}}_{t-1} + \mathbf{w}_t \tag{10}$$

$$\Sigma_{\overline{\boldsymbol{\xi}}_{t|t-1}} = \mathbf{A}\Sigma_{\overline{\boldsymbol{\xi}}_{t-1}}\mathbf{A}' + \Sigma_{\mathbf{W}}, \tag{11}$$

where $\Sigma_{\mathbf{W}}$ is defined in Section 2.

In the second step we update $\overline{\boldsymbol{\xi}}_{t|t-1}$ on the basis of the new observations $\mathbf{z}_t$:

$$\overline{\boldsymbol{\xi}}_t = \overline{\boldsymbol{\xi}}_{t|t-1} + \overline{\mathbf{K}}_t(\mathbf{z}_t - \overline{\mathbf{z}}_t) \tag{12}$$

$$\Sigma_{\overline{\boldsymbol{\xi}}_t} = (\mathbf{I} - \overline{\mathbf{K}}_t \mathbf{L}_t^{-1})\Sigma_{\overline{\boldsymbol{\xi}}_{t|t-1}}, \tag{13}$$

where $\overline{\mathbf{z}}_t = \mathbf{L}_t^{-1}\overline{\boldsymbol{\xi}}_{t|t-1}$, $\overline{\mathbf{K}}_t = \Sigma_{\overline{\boldsymbol{\xi}}_{t|t-1}}(\mathbf{L}'_t)^{-1}\Sigma_{\mathbf{Z}_t}^{-1}$.

The solution $\overline{\boldsymbol{\xi}}_t$ is unique by construction. The indeterminacy of the dynamic solution derives in fact from the arbitrary term $\mathbf{P}_t\boldsymbol{\omega}_t$ in (7), with $\Sigma_{\boldsymbol{\omega}_t} \neq 0$, and the definition of the forecasting $\hat{\mathbf{z}}_t$ in the Kalman filter by model (2), where $\hat{\mathbf{z}}_t = \mathbf{C}\hat{\boldsymbol{\xi}}_{t|t-1}$. In the alternative solution, substituting matrix $\mathbf{C}$ by $\mathbf{L}_t^{-1}$ in the definition of $\hat{\mathbf{z}}_t$, which we indicate by $\overline{\mathbf{z}}_t$, to distinguish the two cases, allows avoiding the arbitrariness of the "latent" scores, due to both the factorial nature of the measurement models and the dynamics, because the Guttman's result (1955) is no longer appropriate. Guttman considers models like (2), in which the indeterminacy of the $\boldsymbol{\xi}_t$ and $\mathbf{v}_t$ results from the impossibility of identifying m+p basis vectors, where only p observable variables are available. The RCD, on the contrary, provides a definition of the latent variables as a linear combination of the observable variables, so that indeterminacy vanishes. Hence, if $E[\boldsymbol{\xi}_0]$ and $\Sigma_{\boldsymbol{\xi}_0}$ are known, the RCD introduced in the recursive procedure of the Kalman filter obtains a unique approximation for "latent" scores.

Otherwise, since $E[\boldsymbol{\xi}_0]$ and $\Sigma_{\boldsymbol{\xi}_0}$ are often not known, we consider at the first step t=1 the estimate $\overline{\boldsymbol{\xi}}_1$ by (9). Following this procedure we eliminate also the indeterminacy which is due to the not unique estimate of $\boldsymbol{\xi}_1$.

However, the new method proposed cannot be considered a model, because the solutions provided cannot be interpreted as causes of the indicators. From here we derive the necessity of the formulation of a proper Structural Dynamic Model with unique latent scores.

4 A new version of the SDL based on RCFM

In analogy with the proposal of Vittadini and Haagen (2002) for the static case, we present an alternative formulation of the SDL, by extending the RCFM of Haagen and Oberhofer (1999), which we will first describe.

The different assumption of the RCFM to the common FA is that every object i, (i=1,...,N), can be observed R-times (i.e. we have repeated observations for every object). Thus we obtain the following model equation:

$$_{(r)}z_i = C\xi_i +_{(r)} v_i, \qquad r = 1, ..., R; i = 1, ..., N \qquad (14)$$

where the r-th repetition is denoted with the index r, $_{(r)}z_i$ is a $p \times 1$ vector of observable variables, C is a $p \times m$ matrix of factor loadings, ξ_i is a $m \times 1$ vector of common factors and does not depend on r, $_{(r)}v_i$ is a $p \times 1$ vector of specific factors.

Moreover, further assumptions are:

$$p > m, \qquad (15)$$

$$rank(C) = m, \qquad (16)$$

$$E[\xi] = 0; E[_{(r)}v] = 0, \qquad r = 1, ..., R \qquad (17)$$

$$\Sigma_\xi = I, \qquad (18)$$

$$\Sigma_{\xi_{(r)}v} = 0, \qquad r = 1, ..., R \qquad (19)$$

$$\Sigma_{(r)v_{(s)}v} = \delta_{rs}D, D = diag(d_1, ..., d_p), \qquad r, s = 1, ..., R \qquad (20)$$

with $d_j > 0, j = 1, ..., p$.

By writing equation (14) in a compact notation, we get the RCFM:

$$_Rz =_R C\xi +_R v, \qquad (21)$$

where $_Rz = (_{(1)}z', ...,_{(R)} z')'$ $(pR \times 1)$, $_RC = (C', ..., C')'$ $(pR \times m)$, $\xi = (\xi_1, ..., \xi_m)'$ $(m \times 1)$, $_Rv = (_{(1)}v', ...,_{(R)} v')'$ $(pR \times 1)$.

Equation (21) represents a Common Factor Model with pR observable variables and m common factors; the number of parameters is fixed.

Haagen and Oberhofer (1999) demonstrated that, for given C and D, the indeterminacy vanishes as $R \to \infty$, so that RCFM solves the indeterminacy of common factors asymptotically. In fact Haagen and Oberhofer (1999) demonstrated that in the RCFM

$$_R\widehat{\xi} =_R C'\Sigma_{_Rz}^{-1} _Rz, \qquad (22)$$

e.g. the regression estimator of factor scores, can always be written as:

$$_R\widehat{\xi} = C'(CC' + \frac{1}{R}D)^{-1}\overline{z}, \qquad (23)$$

with $\overline{z} = \frac{1}{R}\sum_{r=1}^R {}_{(r)} z$, and converges to ξ in quadratic mean as $R \to \infty$.

Moreover they demonstrated that the covariance matrix of the arbitrary part

ω_t, i.e. the arbitrariness $\Sigma_{\omega_t} \to 0$ as $R \to \infty$.

Assuming that at every time interval t, (t=1,...T), each object i, (i=1...,N), can be observed R-times on vector z_t, we reformulate the SDL through the RCFM as follows (with no distributional assumptions):

$$\xi_t = A\xi_{t-1} + w_t \qquad\qquad t = 1,...,T \qquad (24)$$

$$_Rz_t = _R C\xi_t + _R v_t, \qquad\qquad t = 1,...,T \qquad (25)$$

with $\xi_t = [\eta_t, \phi_t]$ $(m \times 1)$, A $(m \times m)$, w_t $(m \times 1)$, $_Rz_t = [_{(1)}z'_t, ...,_{(R)} z'_t]'$ $(pR \times 1)$, $_RC = (C', ..., C')'$ $(pR \times m)$, $_Rv_t = (_{(1)}v'_t, ...,_{(R)} v'_t)'$ $(pR \times 1)$, $\xi_t = (\xi_{t1}, ..., \xi_{tm})'$ $(m \times 1)$.

At time t=1 we propose estimating ξ_1 by means of (22). At time t, (t=2,...,T), supposing that A and $_RC$ are known, ξ_t is estimated by means of the Kalman filter, which in the first step becomes:

$$\widehat{\xi}_{t|t-1} = A\widehat{\xi}_{t-1} + w_t \qquad (26)$$

$$\Sigma_{\widehat{\xi}_{t|t-1}} = A\Sigma_{\widehat{\xi}_{t-1}} A' + \Sigma_W. \qquad (27)$$

In the second step $\widehat{\xi}_{t|t-1}$ is updated on the basis of the new observations $_Rz_t$:

$$\widehat{\xi}_t = \widehat{\xi}_{t|t-1} + _R K_t(_Rz_t - _R \widehat{z}_t) \qquad (28)$$

$$\Sigma_{\widehat{\xi}_t} = (I - _RK_{t R}C)\Sigma_{\widehat{\xi}_{t|t-1}}, \qquad (29)$$

where $_R\widehat{z}_t = _R C\widehat{\xi}_{t|t-1}$ and $_RK_t = \Sigma_{\widehat{\xi}_{t|t-1} R}C'\Sigma^{-1}_{_Rz_t}$ of dimension $(m \times pR)$.

As $R \to \infty$ the solution $\widehat{\xi}_1$ is unique and satisfies the fundamental hypothesis of the FA indicated in (19), as we demonstrate in the following.

In fact, with reference to model (21) we have:

$$_RC = _R z_1\xi'_1(\xi'_1\xi_1)^{-1} = _R z_1\xi'_1. \qquad (30)$$

Then, under the hypothesis that $R \to \infty$ and substituting ξ_1 by the (22) and $_RC$ by the (30), equation (21) can be rewritten as:

$$_Rz_1 = _R C\xi_1 + _R v_1 =$$

$$= _R C_RC' \sum_{_Rz_1}^{-1} _Rz_{1 R}z_1 + (_Rz_1 - _R C_RC' \sum_{_Rz_1}^{-1} _Rz_{1 R}z_1) =$$

$$= _R z_1\xi'_1\xi_1 _Rz'_1 \sum_{_Rz_1}^{-1} _Rz_1 + (_Rz_1 - _Rz_1\xi'_1\xi_1 _Rz'_1 \sum_{_Rz_1}^{-1} _Rz_1) =$$

$$= _R z_1P_{\xi_1} P_{z_1} + (_Rz_1 - _R z_1P_{\xi_1} P_{z_1}) =$$

$$= _R z_1P_{\xi_1} + (_Rz_1 - _R z_1P_{\xi_1}) =$$

$$= _R z_1P_{\xi_1} + _R z_1Q_{\xi_1}, \qquad (31)$$

where P_{ξ_1} is the projector onto the space spanned by ξ_1 and $Q_{\xi_1} = I - P_{\xi_1}$. Consequently, as $R \to \infty$, both causes of indeterminacy of the SDL, indicated in Section 3, vanish and the estimates for the latent variables, provided by the Kalman filter, become unique.

By the end, it should be noted that the (15) and the (16) are also fundamental hypotheses of the FA, while the replicability of the observations and the (20) are the basis for the RCFM. The (17) and the (18) are instead not essential; the model proposed can be surely extended to a more general case.

We conclude that, by using the new formulation of the SDL expressed in the (22)-(23) and under the assumption to consider at the first step $t = 1$ the estimator $\widehat{\xi}_1$ defined by (22), the indeterminacy of the SDL is definitely overcome.

5 The application

The application regards an experiment of the Department of Physics, University of Milan. The goal of the experiment is the measurement of the system temperature of a radiometer for microwaves astronomy. Different level of system temperature are observed at different times due to the effect of different operating temperature. At each time t the experiment is repeated 2,000 times at the same conditions, i.e. the observed variable, which measures the "true" variable with white noise, is collected 2,000 times.

In order to obtain, at each time t, unique values for the "true" measure underlying the observations, the model proposed in (24) and (25) is applied. The application corresponds to the theoretical issues of the model proposed. In fact, first of all we have, at the same time t, several replications (under equal conditions) of the same observed variable. Therefore, the assumptions inherent to the replicability of observations are respected. Secondly, the measurement model (25) is a model with errors in variables, (i.e. a particular case of the FA), with replicated observations. By the end, the (24) represents the relation between the measure of interest at time t and the same measure at time t-1. For sake of simplicity, we have supposed that passing from time t to t-1 occurs with a constant change of temperature, i.e. the "true" measure at time t differs from the "true" measure at time t-1 of a constant, which represents the change of temperature between time t and t-1.

6 Conclusions

The model proposed, which provides unique latent scores in a dynamic context, seems to be a reasonable alternative to the SDL, because it not only represents a statistical model, but it definitely overcomes the latent score indeterminacy.

The question is whether the consideration $R \to \infty$ is realistic. The main interesting issue is that the result of Haagen and Oberhofer (1999) is not only valid for $R \to \infty$, but also for finite R, if R increases. Simulation studies to verify the empirical validity of the RCFM show that the estimates converge for R=50 (Taufer, 1992).

The applicability of this model to real problems is surely limited by the assumption that the vectors of latent variables do not depend on replications. A field of application always compatible with the assumption is the case of physical experiments, where it is not difficult to produce a large number of replications.

References

BORDIGNON, S. and TRIVELLATO, U. (1992): Errori nelle variabili e variabili latenti in modelli strutturali stocastici: un quadro di riferimento. *Statistica*, *LII, 3, 325–345.*

GUTTMAN, L. (1955): The determinacy of factor score matrices with implications for five other basic problems of common factor theory. *British Journal of the Mathematical and Statistical Psychology, 8, II, 65–81.*

HAAGEN, K. (1991): Necessary and sufficient conditions for vanishing the arbitrariness in a common-factor model. *The Statistician, 40, 401–408.*

HAAGEN, K. and OBERHOFER, W. (1999): The replicated common factor-analysis model. *Metron, LVII, 3-4, 35–45.*

HAAGEN, K. and VITTADINI, G. (1991): Regression component decomposition in structural analysis. *Communications in Statistics - Theory and Method, 20, 4, 1153–1161.*

HAAGEN, K. and VITTADINI, G. (1994): Sul problema dell'osservabilità nei modelli strutturali dinamici. In: *Atti XXXVII Riun. Scient. SIS (Sessioni Specializzate).* Sanremo, 247–258.

MINOTTI, S.C. (2002): Some Structural Dynamic Models Overcoming Latent Score Indeterminacy. In: *Atti XLI Riun. Scient. SIS (Sessioni Spontanee).* Cleup, Padova, 423–426.

OTTER, P.W. (1985): Dynamic Feature Space Modelling, Filtering and Self-Tuning Control of Stochastic Systems: A Systems Approach with Economic and Social Applications. In: M. Beckmann and W. Krelle (Eds.): *Lecture Notes in Economics and Mathematical Systems, Vol.246.* Springer, Berlin.

OTTER, P.W. (1992): Dynamic models with latent variables from a system theoretic perspective: theory and applications. *Statistica, LII, 3, 347–363.*

SCHOENEMANN, P.H. and STEIGER, J. (1976): Regression Component Analysis. *British Journal of Mathematical and Statistical Psychology, 29, 175–189.*

SCHOENEMANN, P.H. and HAAGEN, K. (1987): On the use of Factor Scores for Prediction. *Biometrical Journal, 29, 7, 835–847.*

TAUFER, E. (1992): Studio sulla validità empirica di un modello di analisi fattoriale con osservazioni ripetute. *Quaderni di Statistica e Matematica applicata alle Scienze Economico-Sociali, XIV, 1-2, 127–140.*

VITTADINI, G. (1989): Indeterminacy Problems in the Lisrel Model. *Multivariate Behavioral Research, 24, 4, 397–414.*

VITTADINI, G. (1999): Analysis of Qualitative Variables in Structural Models with Unique Solutions. In: M. Vichi and O. Opitz (Eds.): *Classification and Data Analysis: Theory and Application.* Springer, Berlin, 203–210.

VITTADINI, G. and HAAGEN, K. (2002): A Causal Model with Latent Variables and Unique Solutions. In: *Atti XLI Riun. Scient. SIS (Sessioni Specializzate).* Cleup, Padova, 211–220.

Some Issues About the Use of Experts

Paola Monari and Patrizia Agati

Dipartimento di Scienze Statistiche,
Università di Bologna, Italy
paola.monari@unibo.it, patrizia.agati@unibo.it

Abstract. In condition of uncertainty regarding a random phenomenon, particularly in decision making and risk analysis, valuable information may be provided by "experts" in terms of subjective probability distributions for a random variable. In this paper, some ideas about this topic are discussed.

1 Introduction

In the course of the last forty years, numerous algorithms — axiomatic procedures, as well as Bayesian models — have been proposed to solve the 'expert problem': typically, to aggregate the individual functions from experts in a combined probability distribution (for a critical review up to the nineties, see Clemen and Winkler (1999)).

However, the most recent studies on this topic have only marginally approached the problem within the framework of multivariate statistical analysis. The attention of researchers has been principally oriented towards the estimation of unknown quantities (risks or events) and has conceptually followed the guidelines of classical statistical inference, based on distribution models and likelihood functions.

The development of experimental and social research, where these methods can find useful applications, has however highlighted certain contradictions, above all when we wish to combine heterogeneous information coming from different sources characterized by different degrees of reliability. Since all sources of information (research centers, experts, privileged witnesses) produce data (generally estimates of unknown parameters) or models (generally probability distributions) related to one or more variables, combining heterogeneous information introduces at least three kinds of problems intrinsic to multivariate analysis:

- the calibration of individual information by an aggregator (or expert) called to evaluate its degree of reliability and interdependence;
- the formulation of a combined model which represents the synthesis of models and/or parameters produced by each source of information;
- the measure of spread in the density data set due to discrepancies between the different sources of information and the combined distribution.

The formulation of an unifying model in the context of the combining of information from experts can find some strong analogies with the Conjoint Analysis, from which it can adopt some interesting technical solutions (Allenby et al. (1995)). Moreover, the two approaches could reciprocally exchange useful investigative tools. The Combining of Information, as well as the Conjoint Analysis, is carried out at an individual level for each subject. In order to predict preferences or other responses, at the disaggregate level individual response has to be performed separately and predictive accuracy calculated for each subject. Only afterwards, can the individual results be combined to describe an overall model (Hair et al. (1998)). In this context, calibration is essential for determining corrections with respect to the aggregator's scale. In the presence of multivariate information (or measurements) the aggregator must develop a system of summated scales, for which several variables are joined in a composite measure to represent an estimation of the unknown quantities. The calibration techniques become tools for assessing reliability and incorporating scales referred to different experts in the aggregator's combined curve.

The aim of this work is to explore the meaning of some concepts, criteria and results about the subject, point out some remarks and submit them to the discussion. The substance of the considerations presented in the following sections of the paper is independent at all of the procedure chosen for aggregating information from the experts. Not so examples and graphs, which need an algorithm for calculation: the reference, here, is the Bayesian combining model proposed by Morris (1977), where the calibration function — which encapsulates the investigator's state of knowledge with regard to each expert's probability assessment ability and the degree of reciprocal correlation among the experts — is specified by using a fiducial procedure (Monari and Agati (2001)).]

2 About the meaning of the combined distribution

"The [...] combined probability distribution — Clemen and Winkler (1999) write — can ideally be viewed as representing a summary of the current state of expert opinion regarding the uncertainty of interest".

The question is: *what* kind of *summary* should we expect from a combining algorithm? The summary curve must, in a way, 're-draw' the individual components (and so reflect each opinion) or must 'pass among' the experts' judgments (and so be a compromise between them)? Certainly, the answer to this question can depend, to some extent, on the purposes and the context of the expert consulting. But on this answer it depend what we may expect from an aggregation algorithm: so, let us reason about a simple example, at least to clarify the alternative.

Two experts are perceived as unbiased and equally informative by the consultant: let us suppose both experts' densities for the uncertain quantity are Normal, with equal variances but locations such that the overlapping area is very small. In a situation such as this, "it might seem more reasonable to have a bimodal posterior distribution reflecting the two experts' opinions [than a compromise distribution, which puts almost all of the probability density in a region that neither of the individual experts thought likely at all]" (Clemen and Winkler (1999)).

However, let us think of the n experts' distribution as n informative points in a geometric space: is the real aim of a synthesis line to pass through each single point, or rather to interpolate the scatter of points? So, even in a border-line example like the 'two-experts problem', it can not be denied that a density which re-draws the experts' curves adds little or nothing to what is already in the curves themselves: it is the synthesis — a sufficient synthesis, which does not involve the loss of relevant information — that reflects the 'tendency line' of the phenomenon and so enables the *information* provided by the experts to become *knowledge* for the consultant.

Indeed, it is so for any problem regarding *statistical* sets. And, by looking at the question in such a light, the distribution synthesizing n density functions plays, in a sense, the same role as a mean with respect to n observations. It is no coincidence that the first synthesis algorithm — the linear opinion pool, proposed by Laplace (*Théorie analytique des probabilités*, 1812) — results in a distribution which averages the (weighed) individual components[1].

3 Measuring the spread in a 'density-data set'?

When a subject performs a modelized aggregation process, the synthesis curve usually results from the various interacting of several parameters: some assessed by the experts, others by the consultant. So it can happen that deeply different density-data sets yield a same synthesis curve: and — it is worth underlining — this is an eventuality whatever the model chosen for combining may be.

Let us consider — by way of an example only — the following two situations, where two experts, Q_1 and Q_2, consulted about a random quantity $\theta \in \Theta$, provide Normal densities $g_1(\cdot)$, $g_2(\cdot)$ characterized as follows:

- locations $m_1 = 1.6$, $m_2 = 1.4$; variances $v_1 \equiv v_2 = 1.57$ (situation "A");
- locations $m_1 = 3.1$, $m_2 = -0.1$; variances $v_1 \equiv v_2 = 2.70$ (situation "B").

Now, the difference between the two situations is clear: the locations assessed by the experts are very close in "A", whereas they are rather distant in "B"; besides, the variances are higher in "B" than in "A" (Fig. 1). But if, in both situations, a Bayesian-fiducial model (Morris (1977); Monari and Agati (2001)) is adopted for combining the two densities and the experts

---

[1]And, as concerns the puzzling 'two-experts problem', if this was the real situation it would be advisable to consult at least a third expert.

are assumed as unbiased and equally informative[2] (with a linear correlation coefficient $r = 0.3$), the resulting combined curves $h_A(\theta)$ and $h_B(\theta)$ turn out to be nearly coincident, with the same arithmetic mean and the same variance: in particular, if the consultant's prior is hypothesized as Uniform, the arithmetic mean is 1.5 and the variance 1.525.

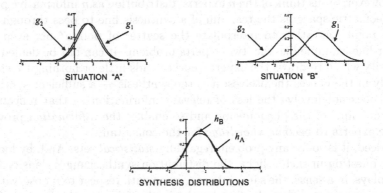

Fig. 1. Different density-data sets can yield a same synthesis curve.

The synthesis distribution is the same in both situations, but its 'representativeness' towards the individual components is different: and measuring the 'representative strength' of the obtained final density can be not less relevant than constructing the density itself. So, the information which a combined distribution carries about a random phenomenon could be reasonably and usefully integrated by a measure of the 'density-data set' spread, which gauges how 'distant' the experts' densities are, on average, from the synthesis density. In general terms, let us denote with:

- $g_i(\theta)$ and $h(\theta)$, respectively, the density function from expert Q_i, for $i = 1, 2, ..., n$, and the combined density function;
- $KL(g_i : h) := \int_\Theta g_i(\theta) \cdot \ln[g_i(\theta)/h(\theta)]\, d\theta$ the Kullback-Leibler divergence (Kullback and Leibler (1951)) of $g_i(\cdot)$ with respect to $h(\cdot)$;
- $J(g_i, h)$ the Jeffreys distance (Jeffreys (1946)) between $g_i(\cdot)$ and $h(\cdot)$, which can be written as,

$$J(g_i, h) := \int_\Theta [g_i(\theta) - h(\theta)] \cdot \ln[g_i(\theta)/h(\theta)]\, d\theta =$$
$$= KL(g_i : h) + KL(h : g_i) \tag{1}$$

[2]So the calibration parameters assessed by the consultant are the same for both experts. In the case in point, by adopting the notation used in Monari and Agati (2001), the following positions have been fixed: $t_1 \equiv t_2 = 0.5$, $s_1 \equiv s_2 = 2$.

The quantity expressed by (1) is the symmetric version of the Kullback-Leibler divergence, so that it can be read just as a measure of *distance* between the curve provided by expert Q_i and the curve resulting from the aggregation process: it is, in a sense, the analogue of the absolute deviation of a data point from the median of a data set. So, a natural way to measure the dispersion of the $g_i(\cdot)$s set could be to compute the distance $J(g_i, h)$ for each function $g_i(\cdot)$ and then average these (non-negative) values, i.e.

$$\bar{J} := \frac{1}{n} \sum_{i=1}^{n} J(g_i, h) \tag{2}$$

The expression (2) — substantially, an analogue of an average absolute deviation from the median — turns out to be zero when each $g_i(\theta)$ coincides with $h(\theta)$, and take values higher the more distant the experts densities are from the synthesis curve: it measures how far each density $g_i(\cdot)$ would be from the combined curve if all the n densities were equally distant from it.

In situations "A" and "B", $\bar{J} = 0.044$ and $\bar{J} = 1.747$ are obtained respectively. To give an operational meaning and intuitive interpretation to these quantities, it can help to know that a value $J = J_0$ measures the Jeffreys distance between $N(0, 1)$ and $N(\mu, 1)$ where $\mu = \sqrt{J_0}$: so, the value $\bar{J} = 0.044$ reflects the distance between two Normal densities, both having standard deviation 1 but locations, respectively, 0 and 0.20 ($= \sqrt{0.044}$); instead, the value $\bar{J} = 1.747$ corresponds to the distance between $N(0, 1)$ and $N(1.32, 1)$.

Now, the measure (2), gauging the spread of the $g_i(\cdot)$s set with respect to a 'mean' density $h(\cdot)$, highlights a particular aspect of the expert consulting: it captures, in a sense, the link between the input (the experts' curves) and the output (the combined curve) of the aggregation process, thus constituting a natural complement of the final function $h(\cdot)$. A different but not less important aspect of the expert consulting can be pointed out by a quantity which, leaving aside the reference to the combined density (and, consequently, to any calibration parameter the consultant may introduce in the model), describes the density-data set *before* the aggregation is performed.

To this end, let us consider the *overlapping area* A_{il} between two densities, $g_i(\theta)$ and $g_l(\theta)$: it is the geometric expression of the "transvariation area" (Gini and Livada (1955)) and may be calculated as,

$$A_{il} = \int_{\Theta} \Psi(\theta) \, d\theta \qquad \text{where} \ \ \Psi(\theta) = min(g_i(\theta), g_l(\theta)) \tag{3}$$

Measure (3) ranges from 0 (when the two curves do not overlap) to 1 (when they are perfectly coincident). If such a measure is computed for each of the $n(n-1)/2$ pairs of densities (g_i, g_l) where $i \neq l$, the experts' curves set can be described in terms of *average transvariation area* $\bar{A}$ and *standard deviation* $\varrho(A)$, that is,

$$\bar{A} = \frac{1}{n(n-1)/2} \sum_{i \neq l} A_{il} \tag{4}$$

$$s(A) = \left[\frac{1}{n(n-1)/2} \sum_{i \neq l} (A_{il} - \bar{A})^2 \right]^{1/2} \tag{5}$$

The value of (4) measures how much overlap there would be between any two experts' densities if the curves of all the pairs were equally overlapped[3]. In particular, $\bar{A} = 0$ if and only if $A_{il} = 0$ for each pair (g_i, g_l); it is $\bar{A} = 1$ if and only if $A_{il} = 1$ for each pair (g_i, g_l), i.e. if and only if the experts' curves are all coincident. As far as $s(A)$ is concerned, its meaning is, neither more nor less, that of a measure of spread: in the case in point, it gauges how different the transvariation areas A_{il} are from the average $\bar{A}$.

Figure 2 highlights the relevance of $s(A)$ by comparing two situations, (a) and (b), both characterized by four Normal densities $g_i(\theta)$ provided by as many experts: for each of the two situations, the averages m_i and the standard deviations s_i are presented in Table 1. In both the cases, the average overlapping area gives $\bar{A} = 0.406$: it is the standard deviation that allows us to distinguish between the former $(s(A) = 0.144)$ and the latter $(s(A) = 0.420)$[4].

	Situation (a):				Situation(b):			
	$g_1(\theta)$	$g_2(\theta)$	$g_3(\theta)$	$g_4(\theta)$	$g_1(\theta)$	$g_2(\theta)$	$g_3(\theta)$	$g_4(\theta)$
m_i	-2	-1	+1	+2	-2	-2	+2	+2
s_i	2	1	1	2	1.25	1.25	1.25	1.25

Table 1. Situations (a) and (b): averages and standard deviations of four Normal densities.

4 About the combined effect of some aggregation parameters on the synthesis distribution spread

A (positive) dependence among experts, which is reflected in the tendency to report distributions characterized by a large transvariation area, is the rule rather than the exception in empirical studies: it arises from factors such as common training, shared experience and information, similar assumptions

---

[3]It is just worth noting that the average $\bar{A}$ of the areas A_{il} does not coincide, in general, with the overlapping area $A_{12...n}$ of the n curves considered all together.

[4]More generally, when the averages $\bar{A}$ don't coincide, the different variability of two or more sets of overlapping areas can be measured by the variation coefficient $VC(A) = s(A)/\bar{A}$

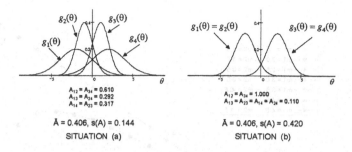

Fig. 2. Description of the situations (a) and (b) in terms of average overlapping area $\bar{A}$ and standard deviation $s(A)$.

and analysis techniques. A negative dependence, due (for example) to opposite training, is less frequent, but not impossible: in such a case, the experts will be inclined to give densities characterized by a small transvariation. Now, if two experts — who are perceived as equally informative by the consultant — submit identical distributions, it is reasonable to expect that, all the other things being equal, the provided information is more redundant the stronger the perceived positive dependence between the experts: coherently, the synthesis distribution should be more spread the more the dependence is strong. The Bayesian-fiducial algorithm shows such a behavior. But is the behavior of the spread always so, even when the locations of the curves do not coincide?

The graph in Figure 3 shows, for (seven) different pairs of experts' locations m_1 and m_2 — particularly, for distances $d = |m_1 - m_2| = 0, 1, ..., 6$ —, how the variance of the synthesis distribution changes as the linear correlation coefficient r between the two experts' performances moves from -0.9 to $+0.9$.[5] The combined density has been obtained by using the Bayesian-fiducial procedure and admitting that: a) both experts were unbiased and equally informative (therefore both have been calibrated with equal "weights"); b) their densities were Normal with equal variances ($v_1 \equiv v_2 = 1$); c) the consultant's prior was Uniform. Briefly, it is worth noting that:

- as r moves away from -0.9 and approaches $+0.9$, the spread always increases when $d = 0$ only. When $d > 0$, the spread increases, reaches its maximum for some value $r_M < +0.9$ (which is smaller the greater the distance d between the two locations), and then decreases: substantially, a (relatively) high positive correlation can lead to an increase of concentration of the synthesis curve when compared with a situation of absent or weak dependence. So, the non-coincidence of the experts' judgments has the effect of down-regulating the increase of the spread caused by

---

[5]To be more precise, in the Bayesian-fiducial model r measures the dependence among the experts in terms of linear correlation between log-odds transforms of the experts' performance indicators (Monari and Agati (2001)).

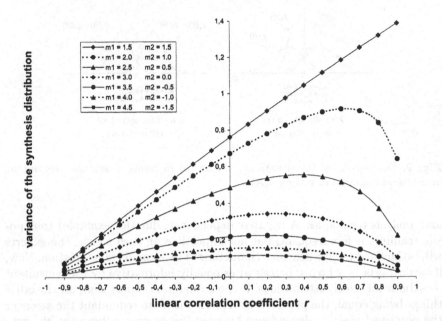

Fig. 3. Effect of changes in the degree of linear correlation between two experts on the spread of the synthesis distribution, for various distances between the individual locations. The two experts are perceived by the consultant as unbiased and equally informative.

an increase of the (positive) correlation between the experts: this effect is stronger the greater the distance between the locations of the curves. It is reasonable, indeed, that a serious discrepancy of opinions is 'more informative' when it comes from experts which have a very similar background, a common knowledge, and use the same analysis techniques, that when it arises from experts judged as independent or weakly dependent;
- also the changes in the spread as r moves away from -0.9 and approaches $+0.9$ are smaller the greater d: that is, the spread of the synthesis curve is more indifferent to changes in r the greater the discrepancy between experts' judgments;
- the correlation degree r being equal, the spread is smaller the greater the distance d: i.e., a synthesis distribution resulting from non-coinciding curves, all the other things being equal, is less spread than a synthesis of coinciding judgments. Actually, it is the heterogeneity between the experts' judgments, rather than the homogeneity, to yield a more concentrated curve.

5 About the behavior of some information measures in a sequential expert consulting

When, in a sequential consulting process, an investigator uses selecting and stopping rules which are founded on some synthetic measure of information (Agati (2004)), it may be useful to know how two traditional measures behave at the various stages of the procedure: in particular, the Kullback-Leibler divergence of the synthesis curve at stage k with respect to the synthesis at stage zero (and at the previous stage), and the Fisher observed information (i.e., a second-order estimate of the spherical curvature) at the maximum of the synthesis function.

To this end, let us consider the following border-line example: four experts, who are perceived as unbiased, equally informative and independent by the consultant, submit absolutely identical (also for the locations) distributions. Each expert gives the same information: the curvature of the synthesis function catches this aspect of the consulting and so increases, at each stage, in the same measure (Fig. 4): at the fourth stage, it is four times as much as it was at the first stage. The 'informative value' of the four experts, yet, is not always the same for the investigator: once he has consulted the first one, the judgments of the others are nothing but confirmations; the Kullback-Leibler divergence (Fig. 5), reflecting the situation from this point of view, is a concave function of the consulting stage.

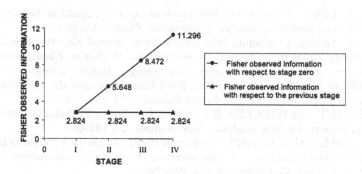

Fig. 4. The behavior of the Fisher observed information at the various stages of a sequential consulting.

6 Concluding remarks

The paper submits to the discussion some considerations about the topic of the expert use. In particular, the role of the combined density is investigated,

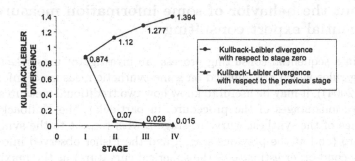

Fig. 5. The behavior of the Kullback-Leibler divergence at the various stages of a sequential consulting.

also in order to define the sort of output we expect from an aggregation algorithm; the suitability of measuring the density-data set spread is underlined and some measures are proposed; the effects of the various interacting of correlation and distance between experts' locations are analyzed and, finally, the behavior of two traditional information measures at the various stages of a sequential consulting process is shown.

References

AGATI, P. (2001): *La sintesi di informazioni esperte. Aspetti metodologici e applicativi in ambito decisionale e scientifico.* Clueb, Bologna.

AGATI, P. (2004): Combining Information from Several Experts: Selecting and Stopping Rules in Sequential Consulting. In: *Studies in Classification, Data Analysis and Knowledge Organization.* Springer, Berlin (in press).

ALLENBY et al. (1995): Incorporating Prior Knowledge into the Analysis of Conjoint Studies. *Journal of Marketing Research, 32,* 152–162.

CLEMEN, R.T. and WINKLER, R.L. (1999): Combining Probability Distributions from Experts in Risk Analysis. *Risk analysis, 19,* 187–203.

GINI, C. and LIVADA, G. (1955): Nuovi contributi alla teoria della transvariazione. In: G. Ottaviani (Eds.): *Transvariazione. Memorie di metodologia statistica,* vol. II, Libreria Goliardica, Roma, 254–280.

HAIR, J.F. et al. (1998): Conjoint Analysis. In: *Multivariate Data Analysis,* 5th edition, Prentice-Hall International, 556–599.

JEFFREYS, H. (1946): An Invariant Form for the Prior Probability in Estimation Problems. *Proceedings of the Royal Society A, 186,* 453–461.

KULLBACK, S. and LEIBLER R.A. (1951): On Information and Sufficiency. *Annals of Mathematical Statistics, 22,* 79–86.

MONARI, P. and AGATI, P. (2001): Fiducial Inference in Combining Expert Judgements. *Statistical Methods and Applications. Journal of the Italian Statistical Society, 10,* 81–97.

MORRIS, P. A. (1977): Combining Expert Judgments: a Bayesian Approach. *Management Science, 23,* 679–693.

Nonparametric Methods in Survey Sampling

Giorgio E. Montanari[1] and M. Giovanna Ranalli[2]

[1] Dipartimento di Scienze Statistiche,
Università degli Studi di Perugia, Italy
giorgio@stat.unipg.it
[2] Dipartimento di Scienze Statistiche,
Università degli Studi di Perugia, Italy
giovanna@stat.unipg.it

Abstract. Nonparametric techniques have only recently been employed in the estimation procedure of finite population parameters in a model-assisted framework. When complete auxiliary information is available, the use of more flexible methods to predict the value taken by the survey variable in non sampled units allows building more efficient estimators. Here we consider a general class of nonparametric regression estimators of a finite population mean. Four different nonparametric techniques that can handle multivariate auxiliary information are employed, their properties stated and their performance compared by means of a simulation study.

1 Introduction

Availability of auxiliary information to estimate parameters of interest of a survey variable has become fairly common: census data, administrative registers, remote sensing data and previous surveys provide a wide and growing range of variables eligible to be employed to increase the precision of the estimation procedure. A simple way to incorporate known finite population means (or totals) of auxiliary variables is through generalized regression estimation (Särndal et al. (1992)). This method has been proposed within a model-assisted approach to inference. By model-assisted is meant that a working model ξ describing the relationship between the auxiliary variables and the survey variable is assumed. Then estimators are sought to have desirable properties like asymptotic design unbiasedness and design consistency over repeated sampling from the finite population, irrespective of whether the working model is correctly specified or not, and to be particularly efficient if the model holds true.

Generalized regression estimation implies rather simple statistical models for the underlying relationship between the survey and the auxiliary variables: essentially a linear regression model. The efficiency of the procedure relies on a good prediction of the values taken by the survey variable in non sampled units. As a consequence, introduction of more general models and flexible techniques to obtain the above predictions seems of great interest in particular when auxiliary information is available for each unit of the population.

The first attempt to consider more general working models through a nonparametric class of models for ξ is within the model-based approach to inference. In particular, kernel smoothing is adopted by Kuo (1988) in order to obtain estimators of the distribution function and the total of a survey variable using a single auxiliary variable. Dorfman (1993), Chambers et al. (1993) and Dorfman and Hall (1993) study and extend these techniques to allow models to be correctly specified for a larger class of regression functions.

Breidt and Opsomer (2000) first consider nonparametric models for ξ within a model-assisted framework and obtain a local polynomial regression estimator as a generalization of the ordinary generalized regression estimator. Such a technique is not easily extendable to multivariate auxiliary information. The problem of the *curse of dimensionality* makes kernel methods and local polynomials inefficient in more than, say, two dimensions. Further attempts to handle multivariate auxiliary information make use of Recursive Covering in a model-based perspective as in Di Ciaccio and Montanari (2001). Within a model-assisted framework, Generalized Additive Models have been employed to this end by Opsomer et al. (2001); Breidt et al. (2003) have recently proposed the use of penalized splines, while Montanari and Ranalli (2003) consider Neural Networks in the more general context of model calibration. Introduction of nonparametric methods has shown to supply good improvements in the prediction of the value of the variable of interest in non sampled units. This feature increases the efficiency of the resulting estimators when compared with the classical parametric ones, in particular when the underlying functional relationship is rather complex. In this paper we employ different nonparametric methods to estimate the regression function of the survey variable; predicted values are then used to obtain regression-type estimators within a model-assisted framework. A multivariate scenario is handled by means of Neural Networks (NN), Recursive Covering with the algorithm DART (Friedman (1996)), Multivariate Adaptive Regression Splines (MARS; Friedman (1991)) and Generalized Additive Models (GAM; Hastie and Tibshirani (1990)). The theoretical properties of the various estimators are stated and their performance explored through a simulation study.

2 Nonparametric regression estimators and their properties

Consider a finite population $\mathcal{U} = \{1, \ldots, N\}$. For each unit in the population the value of a vector $\boldsymbol{x}$ of Q auxiliary variables is available, for example from census data, administrative registers, remote sensing or previous surveys; hence, the row vector $\boldsymbol{x}_i = (x_{1i}, \ldots, x_{qi}, \ldots, x_{Qi})$ is known $\forall i \in \mathcal{U}$. A sample s of elements is drawn from $\mathcal{U}$ according to a without replacement probabilistic sampling plan with inclusion probabilities π_i and π_{ij}, $\forall i, j \in \mathcal{U}$. Let $\delta_i = 1$ when $i \in s$ and $\delta_i = 0$ otherwise; then we have that $E(\delta_i) = \pi_i$, where expectation is taken with respect to the sampling design. Let n be the size of the sample. The survey variable y is observed for each unit in the sample, hence y_i is known $\forall i \in s$. The goal is to estimate the population mean of the survey variable, i.e. $\bar{Y} = N^{-1} \sum_{i \in \mathcal{U}} y_i$.

The generalized regression estimator of the population mean,

$$\hat{\bar{Y}}_R = N^{-1} \sum_{i \in \mathcal{U}} x_i \hat{\beta} + N^{-1} \sum_{i \in s} (y_i - x_i \hat{\beta})/\pi_i, \tag{1}$$

is derived under a linear regression model for ξ, i.e. $E_\xi(y_i) = x_i \beta$, where the last expectation is taken with respect to the model; estimates of β are sought to account for the sampling plan. Prediction for the values of y on the non sampled units is given by $x_i \hat{\beta}$, where $\hat{\beta} = (\sum_{i \in s} x_i' x_i / \pi_i)^{-1} \sum_{i \in s} x_i' y_i / \pi_i$. This estimator is asymptotically design unbiased and consistent for $\bar{Y}$ under mild assumptions (see e.g. Särndal et al. (1992)). Apart from its simplicity, estimator (1) has gained great popularity since only population means of the auxiliary variables have to be known to effectively calculate it. This is a less restrictive condition than that of complete auxiliary information required for any nonparametric regression estimators we will consider next. Therefore, a larger amount of information is needed for a more complex modelling of the data. Breidt and Opsomer (2000) propose a model-assisted nonparametric regression estimator based on local polynomial smoothing. A nonparametric superpopulation model is assumed for which $E_\xi(y_i) = m(x_i)$, where $m(\cdot)$ is a smooth function of a single auxiliary variable x. A local polynomial kernel estimator of degree p is employed to obtain predictions of y for non sampled units. Let $K_h(u) = h^{-1} K(u/h)$, where K denotes a continuous kernel function and h is the bandwidth. Then, a sample based design consistent prediction for the unknown $m(x_i)$ is given by $\hat{m}_i = e_i'(X'_{si} W_{si} X_{si})^{-1} X'_{si} W_{si} y_s$, where $e_1 = (1, 0, \dots, 0)'$ is a column vector of length $p+1$, $y_s = (y_1, \dots, y_n)'$, $W_{si} = \text{diag}\{\pi_j^{-1} K_h(x_j - x_i)\}_{j \in s}$ and $X_{si} = \{1, (x_j - x_i), \cdots, (x_j - x_i)^p\}_{j \in s}$. Then, the local polynomial regression estimator for the population mean is obtained from (1) replacing $x_i \hat{\beta}$ with $\hat{m}_i$, i.e.

$$\hat{\bar{Y}}_{LP} = N^{-1} \sum_{i \in \mathcal{U}} \hat{m}_i + N^{-1} \sum_{i \in s} (y_i - \hat{m}_i)/\pi_i. \tag{2}$$

Estimator (2) has been proved to be asymptotically design unbiased and consistent for $\bar{Y}$ and has shown good gains in efficiency with respect to the classical generalized regression estimator (Breidt and Opsomer (2000)). However, as noted in the introduction, the problem of the sparseness of the regressors' values in the design space makes this estimator inefficient when even a few auxiliary variables are considered. To overcome this limitation we now consider different nonparametric techniques introduced in literature and known to handle multivariate settings and explore their relative behavior in a finite population inference setting.

Following Breidt and Opsomer approach, we assume a general model ξ, while allowing for multivariate auxiliary information. That is we consider ξ such that $E_\xi(y_i) = f(x_i)$, where $f(\cdot)$ is a continuous function of the argument. Then, a general class of nonparametric regression estimators is defined to be

$$\hat{\bar{Y}}_* = N^{-1} \sum_{i \in \mathcal{U}} \hat{f}_*(x_i) + N^{-1} \sum_{i \in s} (y_i - \hat{f}_*(x_i))/\pi_i, \tag{3}$$

where the predictions $\hat{f}_*(x_i)$ can be obtained by means of a nonparametric technique. Generally speaking, any nonparametric technique can be adopted. Here, we consider four methodologies and compare the performance of the resulting estimators in different settings. As previously introduced, we consider NN, DART, MARS and GAM. Notation works as follow: neural networks provide predictions $\hat{f}_{NN}(x_i)$, DART $\hat{f}_{DART}(x_i)$ and so forth. Resulting estimators of the mean will be denoted as $\hat{\bar{Y}}_{NN}$, $\hat{\bar{Y}}_{DART}$ and similarly for the other nonparametric techniques. In what follows, it is useful to introduce the following class of difference estimators

$$\tilde{\bar{Y}}_* = N^{-1} \sum_{i \in \mathcal{U}} \hat{f}_*(x_i) + N^{-1} \sum_{i \in s} (y_i - \hat{f}_*(x_i))/\pi_i, \tag{4}$$

where $\tilde{f}_*(x_i)$ is the nonparametric prediction obtained if all the population values for y were available (population prediction).

To assess the design properties of the class of estimators in (3), we will use the traditional finite population asymptotic framework (see e.g. Isaki and Fuller (1982)) in which both the population $\mathcal{U}$ and the sampling design $p(s)$ are embedded into a sequence of such populations and designs indexed by ν, $\{\mathcal{U}_\nu, p_\nu(\cdot)\}$, with $\nu \to \infty$. Both the size of the population, N_ν, and of the sample, n_ν, go to infinity as $\nu \to \infty$. Subscript will be dropped for ease of notation. To prove our results, we make the following technical assumptions.

A1. The population and the sample based predictions are such that

$$N^{-1} \sum_{i \in \mathcal{U}} (\hat{f}_*(x_i) - \tilde{f}_*(x_i))(1 - \delta_i/\pi_i) = o_p(n^{-1/2}). \tag{5}$$

A2. The sampling plan is such that the class of difference estimators in (4) satisfies a central limit theorem, $\sqrt{n}(\tilde{\bar{Y}}_* - \bar{Y}) \xrightarrow{\mathcal{L}} \mathcal{N}(0, V(\tilde{\bar{Y}}_*))$, where

$$V(\tilde{\bar{Y}}_*) = N^{-2} \sum_{i,j \in \mathcal{U}} (\pi_{ij} - \pi_i \pi_j)(y_i - \tilde{f}_*(x_i))(y_j - \tilde{f}_*(x_j))/\pi_i \pi_j. \tag{6}$$

Assumption A1 ensures that both the population and the sample based predictions have a regular asymptotic behavior and that their difference decreases with ν. This assumption depends on the distribution of the x_i, as well as on the complexity parameters each nonparametric method depends on. A1 suggests that a consistent way of getting sample based predictions is to account for the sampling plan. Montanari and Ranalli (2003) include the inclusion probabilities in the minimization procedure that provides predictions $\hat{f}_{NN}(x_i)$ and show conditions under which the quantity in (5) is $O_p(n^{-1})$ for NN. Opsomer et al. (2001) argue that A1 is satisfied for GAM under conditions similar to those in Bredit and Opsomer (2000) if additive local polynomials are considered. Detailed conditions for MARS and DART have not been assessed. A reasonable approach, however, seems to calculate predictions by a weighted MARS or DART procedure with weights given by the normalized inverse value of the inclusion probabilities, i.e. rescaled sampling weights in order to sum up to one. Not accounting for the sampling plan would provide predictions whose limit in design probability differs form the population predictions considered above. This would not affect the consistency of the estimator if $\tilde{f}_*(x_i)$ is properly redefined, while, as it will become clear in what follows, different limiting population predictions may affect its efficiency. A central limit theorem as required in A2 can be established for a difference estimator, as well as for the Horvitz-Thompson estimator, for commonly used fixed sample size designs in reasonably behaved finite populations. For example in simple random sampling without replacement this would hold if $y_1, y_2, \ldots, y_{N_\nu}$ were observations from i.i.d. variates with finite $(2 + \ell)$-th moment, for some $\ell > 0$. Conditions for simple random sampling as well as for other common sampling schemes are given in Thompson (1997; chapter 3).

In summary, feasibility of the class of estimators (3) involves the behavior of the population under consideration as well as the nonparametric technique adopted. From a strictly practical point of view, conditions A1 and A2 imply some basic regularity requirements: highly skewed populations and the presence of extreme outliers might harm the accuracy of the mentioned nonparametric techniques in general and in inference for finite populations as a particular case. The following theorem shows that the class of nonparametric regression estimators in (3) is design consistent and shares the asymptotic distribution of the difference estimator in (4).

Theorem 1. Under assumptions A1-A2, the class of nonparametric regression estimators $\hat{\bar{Y}}_*$ is design $\sqrt{n}$-consistent for $\bar{Y}$ in the sense that $\hat{\bar{Y}}_* - \bar{Y} = O_p(n^{-1/2})$, and has the following asymptotic distribution:

$$(\hat{\bar{Y}}_* - \bar{Y})/\sqrt{V(\tilde{\bar{Y}}_*)} \xrightarrow{\mathcal{L}} \mathcal{N}(0,1)$$

with $V(\tilde{\bar{Y}}_*)$ given in equation (6).

Proof. Design consistency follows from rewriting $\hat{\bar{Y}}_*$ as

$$\hat{\bar{Y}}_* - \bar{Y} = \tilde{\bar{Y}}_* - \bar{Y} + N^{-1} \sum_{i \in \mathcal{U}} (\hat{f}_*(x_i) - \tilde{f}_*(x_i))(1 - \delta_i/\pi_i)$$

$$= \tilde{\bar{Y}}_* - \bar{Y} + o_p(n^{-1/2})$$

by A1 and by noting that the leading term is $\tilde{\bar{Y}}_* - \bar{Y} = O_p(n^{-1/2})$ by A2. Convergence in distribution then follows from convergence in probability.

3 Simulation study

The simulation has been conducted in order to compare the behavior of the various estimators in a multivariate setting. Regression functions have been generated as

$$f(x) = a \left(b_0 + \sum_{q=1}^{Q} b_q x_q \right) + \sum_{q \leq q'} c_{qq'} (x_q - \bar{x}_q)(x_{q'} - \bar{x}_{q'}), \quad (7)$$

where the number of auxiliary variables Q has been set equal to 3 and

- each auxiliary variable x_q, for $q = 1, 2, 3$ has been generated from a Beta distribution with parameters g_q and h_q drawn from a uniform distribution in the interval $[1; 10]$;
- a, b_0, b_q $(q = 1, 2, 3)$ and $c_{qq'}$ $(q, q' = 1, 2, 3)$ are randomly drawn from uniform distributions in the intervals $[0; 4]$, $[-5; 5]$, $[-5; 5]$ and $[-50; 50]$, respectively.

Two hundreds finite populations of size $N = 1000$ were generated by first drawing the values of a, b_0, b_q, $c_{qq'}$, g_q, h_q, for all q and q'. Secondly, conditionally on the latter, we extracted 1000 values for the auxiliary variables and rescaled the values of the systematic component obtained from equation (7) in order to have a constant variance equal to 8 for all populations. Moreover, the value of $c_{qq'}$ for $q \neq q'$ in (7) was appropriately rescaled to have populations with no interactions (I=0, i.e. an additive model), with interactions contributing for one third to the variance of the systematic component (I=1) and interactions contributing for two thirds (I=2). This setting allowed to generate models with different levels of nonlinearity, with or without first order interactions and with different levels of asymmetry for the auxiliary variables. Finally, we added i.i.d. $N(0; 2)$ errors to the rescaled values of the systematic component $f(x)$: this implied that the signal to noise ratio took value 4:1, thereby ensuring that the signal would explain 80% of the total variability of y. The value of the determination index R^2 for a linear regression of y on x_1, x_2 and x_3 had been calculated for each generated population.

For each population, 1000 simple random samples without replacement of size $n = 100$ were extracted and the following estimators calculated (note that since the sampling plan is self-weighting, predictions can be simply calculated on the sample data):

- $\bar{y}$, the sample mean, i.e. the Horvitz-Thompson unbiased estimator;
- $\hat{Y}_R$, with β estimated by ordinary least-squares;
- $\hat{Y}_{NN}$, with predictions obtained by means of the splus function nnet() and by setting the number of units in the hidden layer and the weight decay parameter as follows: (3,0.05), (6,0.15), (12,0.15), (6,0.2), (12,0.2); the weight decay parameter is analogous to ridge regression introduced for linear models as a solution to collinearity. Larger values of it tend to favor approximations corresponding to small values of the parameters of the net and therefore shrink the weights towards zero to avoid overfitting.
- $\hat{Y}_{GAM}$, with predictions obtained through an additive splines model by means of the splus function gam(). The number of degrees of freedom for the splines have been set equal to the values: 2, 3, 4, 5;
- $\hat{Y}_{DART}$, with predictions computed by means of the AVE procedure (Friedman (1996)) with the default trimming factor and with the minimum number of units in the terminal region and the approximating strategy in the terminal region (l=linear and c= constant) set as follows: (10,l), (15,l), (20,l), (5,c);

- $\hat{Y}_{MARS}$, with predictions computed by means of MARS 3.6, the original collection of Fortran subroutines developed by J.H. Friedman. The maximum interaction level has been fixed to 1 and with the following values of the number of basis functions: 5, 10, 15, 20.

4 Main results and conclusions

The performance of an estimator is evaluated by the scaled mean squared error defined to be $Smse(\hat{Y}_*) = \widehat{mse}(\hat{Y}_*)/[0.2\,\widehat{mse}(\bar{y})]$, where $\widehat{mse}(\hat{Y}_*)$ is the Monte Carlo design mean squared error and the 0.2 coefficient is implied by the signal to noise ratio employed in generating the population values. In this way we compare the mean squared error of an estimator with that of an estimator that perfectly captures the behavior of the signal, and whose left variation is only due to the irreducible error of the noise. Hence, the smaller the value taken by $Smse$ is, the more efficient the estimator. The values of $Smse$ for each estimator reported in Table 1 are averaged over populations with R^2 belonging to selected intervals and different level of interactions (I=0,1,2); each mean is coupled with the coefficient of variation of the averaged values. Biases of estimators are all negligible and not reported. As expected, the effi-

R^2 range		0-0.27		0.27-0.53		0.53-0.80		0-0.27		0.27-0.53		0-0.27	
Interaction		I=0		I=0		I=0		I=1		I=1		I=2	
Estimator		Smse	CV%	Smse	CV%	Smse	CV%	Smse	CV%	Smse	CV%	Smse	CV%
$\bar{y}$		5.00	2.5	5.01	2.6	4.98	2.6	5.02	4.7	4.90	4.1	4.95	3.6
$\hat{Y}_R$		4.62	8.1	3.11	14.2	1.75	25.5	4.46	13.1	3.11	12.1	4.50	11.5
$\hat{Y}_{NN}$	(3, 0.05)	1.72	15.0	1.55	9.9	1.41	8.8	1.63	8.4	1.60	7.5	1.66	7.4
	(6, 0.15)	1.84	23.6	1.54	10.6	1.30	12.1	1.68	7.9	1.57	8.7	1.72	8.7
	(12,0.15)	1.83	23.5	1.54	10.5	1.30	11.9	1.66	7.9	1.57	9.0	1.71	8.9
	(6, 0.20)	1.86	24.9	1.54	11.3	1.29	13.2	1.68	7.9	1.56	9.0	1.74	9.1
	(12,0.20)	1.85	24.7	1.53	11.2	1.29	13.0	1.67	8.0	1.56	8.7	1.72	9.0
$\hat{Y}_{GAM}$	2	1.63	6.9			1.15	10.7	2.88	6.9	2.65	6.4	4.13	4.9
	3	1.19	7.7	1.17	7.4	1.09	7.6	2.73	6.5	2.70	6.4	4.26	5.2
	4	1.15	8.0	1.16	7.6	1.10	7.2	2.81	6.7	2.82	6.8	4.46	5.8
	5	1.17	8.2	1.18	7.7	1.13	7.0	2.92	6.9	2.97	7.2	4.68	6.4
$\hat{Y}_{DART}$	(10, 1)	2.69	35.8	2.13	21.0	1.79	28.3	2.26	14.0	2.07	15.5	2.16	14.8
	(15, 1)	1.89	15.1	1.72	9.3	1.62	8.9	1.83	7.4	1.79	6.3	1.89	6.4
	(20, 1)	1.74	16.1	1.54	10.3	1.37	10.0	1.71	8.8	1.62	8.1	1.79	8.1
	(5, c)	1.76	17.9	1.52	11.2	1.31	10.8	1.74	10.4	1.64	8.2	1.85	9.4
$\hat{Y}_{MARS}$	5	1.78	29.5	1.56	16.6	1.28	14.7	2.37	13.2	2.34	11.6	3.23	17.0
	10	1.41	10.8	1.38	8.3	1.24	10.5	1.77	11.2	1.68	10.3	1.97	16.0
	15	1.50	11.5	1.42	8.0	1.30	11.2	1.71	9.8	1.63	9.9	1.71	12.7
	20	1.58	11.6	1.50	7.1	1.35	10.4	1.72	7.9	1.66	9.0	1.66	10.8

Table 1. Averages and coefficients of variation of scaled mean squared errors of the estimators for intervals of R^2 and proportions of first order interactions.

ciency of the generalized regression estimator is highly related to the value of R^2 in the population. GAM estimators are always the most efficient when an additive model has been employed to generate the population; in fact, values of $Smse$ are stable and close to one in all cases except when the degrees of freedom are too few for non linear relationships. On the other hand, GAM's performance is extremely poor when interaction terms are used to generate the population values. Therefore, when interactions are suspected another nonparametric method should be used.

The efficiency of the other nonparametric estimators does not seem to be as affected by the presence of interactions. The performances of NN and MARS are quite similar, while DART is less stable when there are too few units for a local linear fit. The little impact of the choice of the number of hidden units for NN once a weight decay penalty is employed is noticeable. Therefore, when careful model selection cannot be conducted, NN can be recommended, since this penalization procedure provides more stable predictions over different values of the tuning parameters.

References

BREIDT, F.J. and OPSOMER, J.D. (2000): Local polynomial regression estimators in survey sampling, *The Annals of Statistics*, 28, 1026–1053.

BREIDT, F.J., CLAEKENS, G. and OPSOMER, J.D. (2003): Model-assisted estimation for complex surveys using penalized splines. Manuscript.

CHAMBERS, R.L., DORFMAN, A.H. and WEHRLY, T.E. (1993): Bias robust estimation in finite populations using nonparametric calibration, *Journal of the American Statistical Association*, 88, 268–277.

DI CIACCIO, A. and MONTANARI, G.E. (2001): A nonparametric regression estimator of a finite population mean. In: *Book of Short Papers*. CLADAG 2001, Palermo, 173–176.

DORFMAN, A.H. (1992): Non-parametric regression for estimating totals in finite populations. In: *Proceedings of the Section on Survey Research Methods, American Statistical Association*. Alexandria, VA, 622–625.

DORFMAN, A.H. and HALL, P. (1993): Estimators of the finite population distribution function using nonparametric regression, *The Annals of Statistics*, 21, 1452–1475.

ISAKI, C. T. and FULLER, W. A. (1982): Survey design under the regression superpopulation model, *Journal of the American Stat. Association*, 77 , 89–96.

FRIEDMAN, J.H. (1991): Multivariate adaptive regression splines (with discussion), *The Annals of Statistics*, 19, 1–141.

FRIEDMAN, J.H. (1996): DART/HYESS User Guide, Technical Report, Dept. of Statistics, Stanford University, available at http://www-stat.stanford.edu/~jhf.

HASTIE, T.J and TIBSHIRANI, R.J. (1990): *Generalized Additive Models*. Chapman & Hall, London.

KUO, L. (1988): Classical and prediction approaches to estimating distribution functions from survey data. In: *Proceedings of the Section on Survey Research Methods, American Statistical Association*. Alexandria, VA, 280–285.

MONTANARI, G.E. and RANALLI, M.G. (2003): Nonparametric model calibration estimation in survey sampling. Manuscript.

OPSOMER, J.D., MOISEN, G.G. and KIM, J.Y. (2001): Model-assisted estimation of forest resources with generalized additive models. In: *Proceedings of the Section on Survey Research Methods, American Stat. Assoc.*. Alexandria, VA.

SÄRNDAL, C.E., SWENSSON, B. and WRETMAN, J. (1992): *Model Assisted Survey Sampling*. Springer-Verlag, New York.

THOMPSON, M.E. (1997): *Theory of Sample Surveys*. Chapman & Hall, London.

A Different Approach for the Analysis of Web Access Logs

Gabriella Schoier[1] and Giuseppe Melfi[2]

[1] Dipartimento di Scienze Economiche e Statistiche,
Università di Trieste, Italy
gabriella.schoier@econ.units.it
[2] Groupe de Statistique
Université de Neuchâtel
giuseppe.melfi@unine.ch

Abstract. The development of Internet-based business has pointed out the importance of the personalisation and optimisation of Web sites. For this purpose the study of users behaviours are of great importance. In this paper we present a solution to the problem of identification of dense clusters in the analysis of Web Access Logs. We consider a modification of an algorithm recently proposed in social network analysis. This approach is illustrated by analysing a log-file of a web portal.

1 Introduction

The analysis of usage behaviour on the Web has acquired an always greater importance in the development of Web strategies, mainly in the field of e-commerce. Web personalisation can be defined as any action whose aim is to optimise the profitability of a site both from the owner and from the user viewpoint. Personalisation based on Web Usage Mining or Web Log Mining has several advantages comparing with more traditional techniques: the type of input is not a subjective description of the users, since log-files contain detailed information about the usage of a Web site. Web Usage Mining has been developed in order to extract interesting patterns in Web access logs (Srivastava et. al. (2000); Mobasher et al. (2002)).

Many statistical packages nowadays contain useful tools for handling web data. In this paper we illustrate a new approach. The data consist of a set of units (the I.P. addresses) on which one relational variable is measured. This forms a network, i.e., a set of units and relation(s) defined over it (see Wasserman et al. (1994)). The huge increase in the amount of data available on Internet has outstripped our capacity to meaningfully analyse such networks and run into significant computational barriers in large networks.

Some help in the analysis may derive by two classical social network theories. First the small-world literature has shown that there is a high degree of local clustering in the networks (see e.g. Kochenet al. (1989)); this suggests that an approach for studying the structure of large networks would involve first the identification of local clusters and then the analysis of the relations within and between clusters. Second, literature on peer influence shows that, based on an endogenous influence process, close units tend to converge on similar attitudes (see e.g. Friedkin (1998)) and thus clusters in a small-word network should be similar along multiple dimensions.

In this paper we present a solution to the problem of identification of dense clusters in the analysis of Web access logs, by considering a modification of an algorithm proposed by Moody (2001) in the field of social network analysis. The principal advantage regards the possibility of handling a huge amount of data in a short time; in fact, in order to build up the groups only influence variables, which represent the position of the units, are considered. This results in a reduced and more flexible structure on which different techniques such as blockmodeling (see Schoier (2002)) may be used. The advantage of blockmodeling is that a differentiated structure for the degree of similarity within and between cluster is allowed.

2 Identifying dense clusters in large networks

We illustrate our approach on the basis of the log-files of the Web site www.girotondo.com, a non dynamical portal for children comprising seven different sections containing 362 jhtml pages are. The period of observation is from the 29th November 2000 to the 18th January 2001.

```
                                  ...
212.75.0.22–[08/Jan/2001:10:14:39+0100]GET / HTTP/1.1
212.75.0.22–[08/Jan/2001:10:14:41+0100]GET /picts/index_03.gif HTTP/1.1 304
212.75.0.22–[08/Jan/2001:10:14:41+0100]GET /picts/index_02.gif HTTP/1.1 304
212.75.0.22–[08/Jan/2001:10:14:41+0100]GET /picts/index_01.gif HTTP/1.1 304
212.75.0.22–[08/Jan/2001:10:14:41+0100]GET /picts/index_04.gif HTTP/1.1 304
213.136.136.60–[08/Jan/2001:22:50:01+0100] GET /favolando/11_00/picts/09.swf HTTP/1.0
209.55.1.99–[08/Jan/2001:22:50:01+0100] GET /picts/index_31.gif HTTP/1.0
                                  ...
```

Table 1. Example of a log-file

The original file contained 300'000 records, each of which corresponds to a line in the log-file. Records of log-files containing auxiliary information (e.g. .gif, .jpeg. files) are ignored. This first cleaning produces a file as in Table 2.

We then proceed with a re-codification of the Web pages by associating, according to their alphabetical order, the URLs with numbers 1 to 362 for easier handling.

Then we consider only the pages which have been visited by at least 5 I.P. addresses. This reduces our analysis over 117 pages. Furthermore we consider two fields in the original log-file: the I.P. address and the code corresponding

...
130.93.25.19 20/DEC/2000:10:19:44+0100 "GET/mappa/01.jhtml HTTP/1.0"   2472
235.58.54.78 20/DEC/2000:10:19:41+0100 "GET/news/archivio.jhtml HTTP/1.0" 115
267.12.83.56 20/DEC/2000:10:19:40+0100 "GET/news/01/01/01.jhtml HTTP/1.0" 793
241.27.83.61 20/DEC/2000:10:19:37+0100 "GET/favolando/01.jhtml HTTP/1.0"   88
...

Table 2. The first cleaning of a log-file

...
/links/12_00/02.jhtml   257
/links/12_00/022.jhtml   258
/mappa/01.jhtml   259
/news/01.jhtml   260
/news/02.jhtml   261
/news/archivio.jhtml   262
/news/form.jhtml   263
...

Table 3. Part of the index file

to the visited page. Each I.P. address corresponds to at least one viewed page. After a further preprocessing phase, a file of 1000 I.P. addresses with the relative set of viewed pages has been considered.

This allows to build up a matrix X of dimension 1000×117 where the lines represent the I.P. addresses and each column represent one of the 117 pages selected for the aim. The coefficient is 1 if the page has been viewed by the I.P. address, 0 otherwise. According to the social network theory (see Wasserman, (1994)) this corresponds to a 2-mode matrix. The next step is to produce a 1-mode matrix on the basis of a suitable relation between I.P. addresses.

We consider the following relation: the I.P. addresses v_i and v_j are in relation if they have visited at least 35 pages in common. The number defining the relation (in our case 35) must be a number that discriminates nodes that have a relation from nodes that have not a relation. In particular it must be not too small and not too large: 35 appear as a suitable value. The set of nodes together with the above relation can be interpreted as a network that can be represented as a finite graph $G(V, E)$ where V represents the set of nodes (in our case the I.P. addresses) and E the set of pairs of adjacent nodes: v_i is in relation to v_j if and only if $(v_i, v_j) \in E$. In other words, elements of E are edges with adjacent nodes at their extremities.

The set of all nodes adjacent to node v_i is called its neighbourhood. A path in the network is defined as an alternating sequence of distinct nodes and edges which begin and end with nodes and in which each edge is incident with its preceding and following nodes. The node v_i can reach the node v_j if there is a path in the graph starting with v_i and ending with v_j. The length of a path from v_i to v_j is given by the number of edges in the path. The distance between v_i and v_j is the minimal lenght of a path from v_i to v_j. A network is connected if there is a path between all pairs of nodes. When the ties are concentrated within subgraphs (a subgraph is a graph whose nodes and edges form a subset of the nodes and edges of a given graph G) the network is clustered.

The level of clustering depends on the uniformity of the ties distributed throughout the network. In order to efficiently analyse a large network, as is our case, it is suitable first to individuate local clusters and then to analyse the internal structures of the clusters and relations between them.

Given the adjacency 2-mode matrix X and the relation defined above, we may produce a 1-mode matrix $\tilde{X}$ of dimension 1000×1000 where lines and columns represent I.P. addresses and the coefficient $\tilde{x}_{ij}$ for $i, j = 1, \ldots, 1000$ is the number of pages which have been viewed by both I.P. addresses v_i and v_j.

This matrix can be transformed into a binary matrix X^* representing an adjacency matrix, by setting

$$x_{ij}^* = \begin{cases} 1 \text{ if } \tilde{x}_{ij} \geq 35 \\ 0 \text{ otherwise} \end{cases} \qquad i, j = 1, \ldots, 1000.$$

The 1-mode matrix X^* (I.P. addresses $\times$ I.P. addresses) can be obtained via the program UCINET (Borgatti et al. (1999)). Of course the diagonal coefficients are 1, but this information is not of interest and will be ignored.

	138.222.202.11	151.15.169.130	151.2.15.154	151.20.111.0	......
138.222.202.11	1	0	1	1	...
151.15.169.130	0	1	0	0	...
151.2.15.154	1	0	1	1	...
151.20.111.0	1	0	1	1	...
....	...	...	...	...	...

Table 4. Adjacency matrix

At this point we introduce a matrix Y, called influence matrix, of dimension $N \times m$ where N is the number of I.P. addresses (in our case $N = 1000$), and m represents the number of components describing the reciprocal influences. A reasonable assumption is to set $m = 3$. This corresponds to assume that each user associated to an I.P. address may be influenced by the behaviour of three other users, identified by their I.P. addresses.

In order to build the matrix Y we use a modified version of the *Recursive Neighbourhood Mean* (RNM) algorithm , proposed by Moody (2001). Our algorithm has been implemented in SAS. The *Modified Recursive Neighbourhood Mean* (MRNM) algorithm consists in the computation of a suitable weightted mean by iteration, and generalises the RNM algorithm. This can be described as follows:

1. We assign to each I.P. address of the network, corresponding to a line of the influence matrix Y, a random number issued from a uniform distribu-

tion in $(0, 1)$ for each of the m coefficents of the line. We obtain a matrix $Y^{(0)}$ ($N \times m$) made of random numbers.

2. The matrix $Y^{(t+1)}$ is defined by

$$Y_{ik}^{(t+1)} = \frac{\sum_{j \in L_i} Y_{jk}^{(t)} \tilde{x}_{ij}}{\sum_{j \in L_i} \tilde{x}_{ij}} \qquad k = 1, \ldots, m, \qquad i = 1, \ldots, N,$$

where L_i is the subset of $1, \ldots, N$ corresponding to the I.P. adresses which are in relation with the address v_i, and $\tilde{x}_{ij}$ is the number of pages viewed by both v_i and v_j.

3. Repeat n times Step 2.

Remark 1. For $\tilde{x}_{ij} \equiv 1$, the algorithm corresponds to the classical RNM algorithm.

This procedure requires as input the list of adjacences, that is, the pairs of nodes v_i, v_j such that $x_{ij}^* = 1$.

In an ideal situation $Y = \lim_{n \to \infty} Y^{(n)}$. However $n = 7$ suffices to get a stable matrix.

I.P.	$Y_{\cdot 1}$	$Y_{\cdot 2}$	$Y_{\cdot 3}$	cluster
138.222.202.11	0.4881	0.4255	0.5359	1
151.15.169.130	0.4882	0.4259	0.5358	3
151.2.15.154	0.4881	0.4255	0.5359	1
...	......	......	......	......

Table 5. Summary of MRNM procedure

In Table 5 are reported the three columns of the matrix Y and the results of the Ward's minimum variances cluster analysis, carried out on the basis of the three components of Y. In such a way we obtain a clear clustering that reveals a structure of three groups as one can see from Figure 1.

The first cluster, which contains most of elements, is made up by the I.P. addresses which have a high frequency of relations, the second one, up on the left, is identified by I.P. addresses which have not many relations while the third one by I.P. addresses which have few relations. The two isolated I.P. addresses are referred to those that have no relation with other I.P. addresses.

3 Conclusions

In this paper we have presented a solution to the problem of identification of dense clusters in the analysis of Web access logs, by considering a modification of an algorithm known from social network analysis. Following the cluster analysis eventually block-modelling techniques can be applied. In doing so

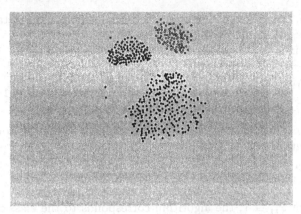

Fig. 1. Clustering according to MRNM algorithm

we have obtained an useful tool to study and profile customers in terms of their browsing behaviour and personal information. This allows us to build up useful business intelligence for the improvement of Web sites and the development of systems when data sets are large or even huge.

References

BATAGELJ, V. and MRAVR, A. (2002): *PAJEK: Program for large Network Analysis. http://vlado.fmf.uni-lj.si/pub/networks/pajek/*

BORGATTI, S.P., EVERETT, M.G and FREEMAN L. C. (1999): *Ucinet for Windows Software for Social Network Analysis, Harvard: Analytic Technologies.http://www.analytictech.com/.*

FRIEDKIN, N. and JOHNSEN, E. C. (1998): Social position in influence networks, *Social Networks, 19, 122–143.*

KOCHEN, M. (1989) : The small World. *Ablex Publishing Corporation*, Norwood, New York.

MOBASHER, B., DAI, H., LUO, T., SUNG Y. and ZHU, J. (2002): Integrating Web Usage and Content Mining for more Effective Personalization. *http://www.maya.cs.depaul.edu/ mobasher/personalization*

MOODY, J. (2001) : Peer influence groups: identifying dense clusters in large networks , *Social Networks, 23, 261–283.*

SCHOIER, G. (2002): Blockmodeling Techniques for Web Mining. In W. Haerdle and B. Roenz, *Proceedings of Compstat 2002*, Springer & Verlag, Heidelberg, 10–14 .

SRIVASTAVA, J., COLLEY, R., DESHPAND, M. and TON P. (2000): Web Usage Mining: Discovery and Applications of Usage Patterns from Web Data, *http://www.maya.cs.depaul.edu/ mobasher/personalization* .

WASSERMAN, S. and FAUST, K. (1994): *Social Network Analysis: Methods and Applications*, Cambridge University Press, New York.

Blending Statistics and Graphics in Visual Data Mining

Antony Unwin

Department of Computer-Oriented Statistics and Data Analysis
University of Augsburg, Germany
antony.unwin@math.uni-augsburg.de

Abstract. Graphics are a good means for exploring and presenting data and for evaluating models. Statistical models are valuable for testing ideas and for estimating relationships between variables. The two complementary approaches need to be integrated more strongly, especially in the analysis of large data sets.

1 Introduction

Graphical displays of data are good for suggesting ideas, for highlighting features and for identifying structure. They are also useful for judging results of models, mainly by providing tools for exploring residuals effectively. They are not appropriate for testing theories. A scatterplot may imply a linear relationship between two variables, but the correlation coefficient measures the strength of the relationship. This example illustrates the complementary strengths and weaknesses of the two approaches: graphics are more general (the scatterplot might show a non-linear relationship or some outliers, both of which would lead to a low value of r) but less specific (what exactly is the association we see?). It is always possible to think of graphics which can be used to check model results; it is not always easy to find an appropriate model for assessing ideas arising from a graphic display.

Take the example of a scatterplot. Suppose there appears to be a distinctive group of outliers, how should this be tested? The group may be distinctive because it is far away from the rest of the data or it may be distinctive because it forms a special pattern different from the rest of the data (e.g. data parallel to the main body of data, separate, though quite close). Perhaps linking to other displays will suggest an explanation for the group of data. How that should then be tested is not necessarily obvious, especially in a large data set, where many different variables may be considered to see if they can explain the observed features.

Figure 1 shows a set of plots from the well-known bank data set (Roberts 1979). The scatterplot shows current salary against age for employees. The employees involved in security have been selected in the barchart of jobs. From the bar chart of gender we can see that they are all male, while the scatterplot shows that they are older and lower-paid. Interestingly, we can also see that they are paid pretty much the same irrespective of age and that one appears to earn less than the others.

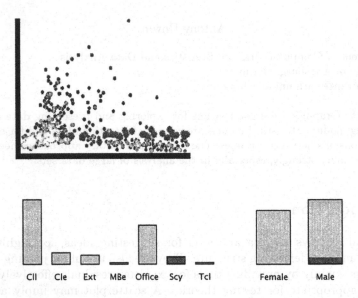

Fig. 1. A scatterplot of current salary v. age and barcharts of job category and gender with the security staff selected

Although the difference is slight, the point stands out because of the lack of variability in the salaries of the other security staff. Graphically the obvious thing to do next is to zoom in on the area of interest. Figure 2 shows the new scatterplot view (with unselected points drawn smaller to improve discrimination) and we can see that there are perhaps two levels of salary and the one clear outlier.

Testing these conclusions statistically would not be entirely straightforward and we might also ask if it would be appropriate. Perhaps more background information would be useful, such as whether there are really two levels of employment. In this example we could argue that the results are conclusive and also consistent with what we might expect for security guards, so there is no particular need for testing. But if the results were not so clear-cut and if we had insufficient additional information to validate the conclusions, then it would be more difficult to decide how to proceed.

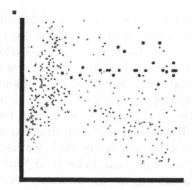

Fig. 2. A magnification of the selected points in the scatterplot of Figure 1

2 Combining graphics and models

There are many situations where graphics and models fit together. If we were interested in the gender distribution by age in the bank data set, then we could estimate a smoothed rate by age and plot it with bootstrapped confidence intervals. We could compare the smooth with a model in which the rate was constant.

If we were interested in the gender distribution by job category, we could use a spine plot with females highlighted for our graphic display and a chi-square test of independence of the two variables for a statistical test. This kind of example shows again the complementary strengths of the two approaches. The graphic may suggest different gender rates, but without test significance we should be careful not to draw firm conclusions. On the other hand, if the test is highly significant, we would want to know why, and we can see that readily from the graphic.

Graphics are often rightly criticised for being open to subjective interpretation, which is why it is important to confirm any conclusions drawn with statistical modelling. Models are criticised more for whether the assumptions on which they are based may be deemed to hold or not. The validity of the chi-square distribution for the test statistic used in comparing two categorical classifications is a typical case. When there are many categories in one variable, it is quite likely that at least one has low frequency and correspondingly low expected values under the independence model. A graphics display can show if this is a problem and clarify what needs to be done about it perhaps aggregating related groups or comparing only groups above a certain size.

3 Looking at a larger data set

Of course, the bank data set is rather small (only 474 cases and 9 variables). Any analytic approach should do well. Looking at the kind of data set we come across in Data Mining is substantially more difficult. Take the Needham Lifestyle Survey data set (available from the website www.bowlingalone.com) discussed in Robert Putnamss book Bowling Alone (Putnam 2000). 3000 to 3500 different Americans were interviewed in each year over 20 years providing a data set with a total of 85000 individuals and almost 400 questions.

Amongst other things respondents were asked on a scale of 1 to 6 whether they disagreed (1) or agreed (6) with the statement I would do better than average in a fist fight. Responses were doubtless influenced by age and by gender, but possibly by other factors as well, for instance marital status, social standing and the interview year. In his book Putnam considers average responses by US State, assuming, not unreasonably, that age and gender need not be controlled for.

Building statistical models in large data sets may be strongly affected by patterns of missings amongst the variables. With surveys over a number of years this is particularly relevant. Assumptions of missing at random should be made with care. A good example is the Fistfight question itself. We can see from linking missings to a barchart of year that the question was not asked in the first year (1975), which accounts for over 80% of the missings on that variable. The other few hundred are spread fairly randomly over the other years.

Linking barcharts of possible factors of interest here (fistfight, age, gender, year, state, churchgoing, marital status and number of children at home) turns out to be very informative. Clearly the State question was not asked in the years 1980-1984 and age was not asked in 1980. Marital status is also a more recent question (in the early years of the study only married people were asked, so the question was not necessary), and was first asked in 1981. Interestingly, it has only been asked regularly since 1991. To get a better picture of the multivariate pattern of missings we can first use missing value plots and then fluctuation diagrams. Figure 3 displays individual bars for each variable (sex and year are not included as they are never missing) with the proportion missing represented by the white section to the right. It is clear that if the number of children at home is missing so is marital status (almost always). We should not assume that there are no missings in the churchgoing and fistfight questions when the number of children at home is missing. It is possible that with such a large data set the resolution of the screen will not be good enough to display a small proportion of highlighted cases. In fact querying the display reveals that there are 124 highlighted out of 1502 missings for churchgoing and 142 highlighted out of 4175 missings for fistfight.

A more complete picture of the multivariate pattern of missings can be achieved with fluctuation diagrams showing the numbers of cases missing simultaneously on sets of variables. Figure 4 shows the patterns for five of the variables in Figure 3 (Marital status has been ignored because it is missing so often). When all rectangles are drawn with area proportional to size, the cell for which all cases are non-missing on the five variables dominates. To

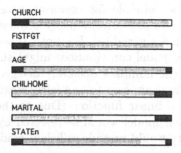

Fig. 3. A missing value plot for six variables with the missings for the variable number of children at home selected

assess the combinations with smaller counts we have to zoom in. Censored zooming involves limiting the maximum size of a rectangle and drawing the boundary of any limited rectangle in red. In the software MANET (Hofmann (2000)) censored zooming can be performed interactively so that comparisons at different levels of resolution can be made. Fluctuation diagrams are complicated displays and need interactive querying and linking for effective use. The left-hand diagram in Figure 4 shows that there are distinct patterns of missings. The right-hand diagram permits a more detailed comparison (the first two cells in the top row have red boundaries).

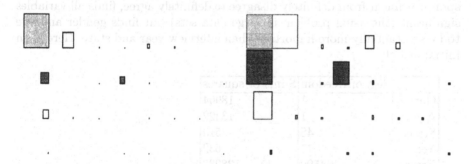

Fig. 4. Fluctuation diagrams for five variables. In the diagram on the left a rectangle with area proportional to count is drawn for each of the possible 32 combinations of missing/non-missing. On the right censored zooming has been used to better compare the patterns. The same selection applies as in Fig 3

Patterns of missing in large surveys are an important issue, especially when comparing models. For instance, a model including the above variables and marital status would perforce be based on far fewer cases than a model without marital status.

Graphics can also be valuable for exploring possible model structures. In a survey data set there are usually many ordered categorical variables and hardly any continuous variables. For both types it is useful to see if linear, single parameter model contributions might suffice. Figure 5 shows a spineplot of year with the numbers definitely disagreeing with the fistfight question highlighted. There appears to be a fairly steady decline, which could indeed be modelled as a linear function. (Due to the size of the data set, the hypothesis of a linear model would be rejected by a test. Even smallish deviations from linearity would provide sufficient evidence to reject.)

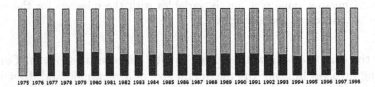

1975 1976 1977 1978 1979 1980 1981 1982 1983 1984 1985 1986 1987 1988 1989 1990 1991 1992 1993 1994 1995 1996 1997 1998

Fig. 5. A spineplot of year with those definitely disagreeing with the fistfight statement selected

4 Modelling a larger data set

A simple linear model in the explanatory variables, which also treats the response as linear from definitely disagree to definitely agree, finds all variables significant (the usual problem in large data sets) but finds gender and age to be substantially more important than interview year and state. Here is an initial model:

	deg. of freedom	Sums of squares
Gender	1	18964
Age	1	13422
State	48	513
Year	17	632
Error	64599	138238
Total	64566	171769

Males are on average one point more aggressive than females and respondents' aggressiveness declined by about one point for every 35 years. Even in this simple model some 20,000 cases are excluded because of missing values, mostly due to the State variable. However, State was the factor of most interest in the book, so it has to stay in.

Displaying and assessing the full results of such models is tricky. Even displaying three of the five variables involved in this model simultaneously is problematic. Figure 6 shows a mosaic plot of age (aggregated into subgroups) and gender with the response definitely disagree highlighted.

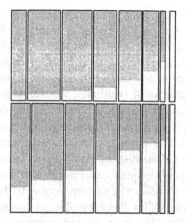

Fig. 6. A mosaic plot of age groups by increasing age with males above, females below and the people who responded definitely disagree to the fistfight question highlighted

The differences between males and females and a strong increase with age are clearly visible, but the detailed breakdown of the responses including all 6 answers is not given and the state and interview year effects are also not included. Despite the significance of the individual coefficients the overall model criteria are not particularly good. R^2 is only 19.5%. A histogram of predicted values in Fig 7 is very revealing. Hardly any 1's are predicted (the most frequent choice in the data) and no 5's or 6's.

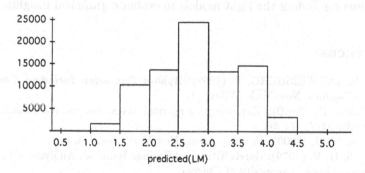

Fig. 7. Predicted values from the initial model.

Graphics can be used in other ways to evaluate the quality of individual models, both through a variety of residual plots or through a range of diagnostic plots. Such displays are well-known and need no further discussion here (although the use of smoothers to assess the local fit of a model, as suggested in Cook and Weisberg (1999), deserves to be more widely used). But in applications like the Bowling Alone study it is not the evaluation of individual models which is of most importance, it is the choice of an acceptable model amongst many. Not only can a large number of models reasonably be investigated (only a few of the several hundred variables have been referred to here), but modern computing power makes this a feasible option. We need ways of comparing models, not just on a single criterion such as AIC or BIC, but in terms of the patterns of residuals, the variables included and the estimated coefficients. Global criteria are valuable for determining a subset of best models, but are not so helpful in discriminating between models within such a subset. Two kinds of graphics would be advantageous, for global and for local analyses. The global display could be a scatterplot of all models on two critical measures (say deviance and degrees of freedom) to aid in defining a best subset and to offer interactive access to both other criteria and to the individual models. (The TwoKey plot for association rules (Unwin et al (2001)) illustrates the idea in a related context.) The local displays for examining smaller groups of neighbouring models might be based on parallel coordinates as proposed in Unwin et al (2003).

5 Further work

Large data sets require a different analytic approach than classical small data sets. Large numbers of cases make many results significant even though differences are small and large numbers of variables make it easy to find some significant result somewhere. Graphics can assist in sifting through the results and in interpreting them, but there is much work to be done in displaying effectively many variables simultaneously. On the modelling side we need more ideas on finding the right models to evaluate graphical insights.

References

COOK, R. D., WEISBERG, S. (1999): *Applied Regression Including Computing and Graphics*. New York, Wiley.

HOFMANN, H. (2000): Exploring categorical data: interactive mosaic plots. *Metrika 51(1): 11-26*.

PUTNAM, R. D. (2000): *Bowling Alone*. New York, Touchstone.

ROBERTS, H. V. (1979): Harris Trust and Savings Bank: an Analysis of Employee Compensation, University of Chicago.

UNWIN, A. R. (1999): Requirements for interactive graphics software for exploratory data analysis. *Computational Statistics, 14, 7-22*.

UNWIN, A. R., HOFMANN, H., BERNT, K. (2001): The TwoKey Plot for Multiple Association Rules Control. In: L. De Raedt and A. Siebes (Eds.) *PKDD*. Freiburg, Springer: 472-483.

UNWIN, A. R., VOLINSKY, C., WINKLER S. (2003): Parallel Coordinates for Exploratory Modelling Analysis. *Computational Statistics & Data Analysis 43(4): 553-564*.

Confidence Regions in Multivariate Calibration: A Proposal

Diego Zappa[1] and Silvia Salini[2]

[1] Istituto di Statistica,
Università Cattolica del Sacro Cuore, Italy
diego.zappa@unicatt.it
[2] Dipartimento di Economia Politica e Aziendale,
Università di Milano, Italy
silvia.salini@unimi.it

Abstract. Most of the papers on calibration are based on either classic or bayesian parametric context. In addition to the typical problems of the parametric approach (choice of the distribution for the measurement errors, choice of the model that links the sets of variables, etc.), a relevant problem in calibration is the construction of confidence region for the unknown levels of the explanatory variables. In this paper we propose a semiparametric approach, based on simplicial depth, to test the hypothesis of linearity of the link function and then how to find calibration depth confidence regions.

1 Introduction

Statistical calibration, broadly used in chemistry, engineering, biometrics and potentially useful in several practical applications, deals with the inference on the unknown values of explanatory variables given a vector of response variables. This is generally done using a model identified through a preliminary calibration experiment (general references on calibration are Brown (1993), Sundberg (1999)).

In Section [3] 2 we describe the multivariate calibration problem and in particular the difficulties in the construction of confidence regions in a parametric context; in Section 3, using a semi parametric approach, it is proposed a new methodology based on simplicial depth, able to overcome some problems of the parametric approach.

---

[3]The contents of this paper have been shared by both Authors. In particular Section 2 is due to S.Salini and Section 3 is due to D.Zappa.

2 Multivariate Calibration: the parametric approach

In univariate calibration the properties of the classical and the inverse estimators are known. Most of these results may be extended also to the multivariate context where the main and relevant problem is the construction of multivariate confidence regions (Salini 2003, II).

Following Brown (1993), we consider two steps.

1) *The calibration step.* We run an experiment of n observations on q response variables $Y_1, Y_2, ..., Y_q$ and p explanatory variables $X_1, X_2, ..., X_p$ in order to identify the transfer function that links the two sets of variables. Suppose that the transfer function is a linear model. Let E be a matrix of random variables (r.v.s) to represent the measurement errors. Then the calibration model is:

$$Y_1 = 1\alpha^T + \mathbf{X}\mathbf{B} + E_1 \tag{1}$$

where is $1(n \times 1)$ the unit vector, $\mathbf{B}(p \times q)$ and $\alpha(q \times 1)$ a matrix and a vector of parameters respectively.

2) *The prediction step.* Analogously to the previous step, suppose that a matrix $Y_2(m \times q)$ of response variables is available, the prediction model is

$$Y_2 = 1\alpha^T + 1\xi^T\mathbf{B} + E_2 \tag{2}$$

where we are interested on the unknown values $\xi(p \times 1)$ of $\mathbf{X}$.

Let E_{1i} and E_{2j} be the i-th and the j-th column of E_1 and E_2, respectively. It will be assumed that $E(E_{1i}) = E(E_{2j}) = \mathbf{0}$, $E(E_{1i}E_{1i}^T) = E(E_{2j}E_{2j}^T) = \mathbf{\Gamma}$, $E_{1i}, E_{2j} \sim N(\mathbf{0}, \mathbf{\Gamma})$, and that the errors E_{2j} are not correlated with E_{1i}.

To find the confidence region for ξ, the most favorable situation is when $p=q$. Supposing that the variables $\mathbf{X}$ are standardized, it may be shown that

$$\left(\hat{\alpha} + \hat{\mathbf{B}}^T\xi\right) \sim N\left(\alpha + \mathbf{B}^T\xi, \mathbf{\Gamma}\left(\frac{1}{n} + \xi^T(\mathbf{X}^T\mathbf{X})^{-1}\xi\right)\right) \tag{3}$$

where $\left(\hat{\alpha}, \hat{\mathbf{B}}\right)$ are the maximum likelihood estimators of $(\alpha, \mathbf{B})$.

As the log-likelihood function of the mean sample vector $\bar{\mathbf{y}}_2$, conditional to ξ is:

$$l(\bar{\mathbf{y}}_2|\xi) \propto \left(\bar{\mathbf{y}}_2 - \alpha - \mathbf{B}^T\xi\right)^T \mathbf{\Gamma}^{-1} \left(\bar{\mathbf{y}}_2 - \alpha - \mathbf{B}^T\xi\right) m,$$

replacing $\alpha, \mathbf{B}, \mathbf{\Gamma}$ by their maximum likelihood estimate $\hat{\alpha}, \hat{\mathbf{B}}, \mathbf{S}$ respectively, we have the maximum likelihood estimator for ξ as :

$$\hat{\xi}_C = \left(\hat{\mathbf{B}}\mathbf{S}_1^{-1}\hat{\mathbf{B}}^T\right)^{-1} \hat{\mathbf{B}}\mathbf{S}_1^{-1}(\bar{\mathbf{y}}_2 - \alpha) \tag{4}$$

where $\mathbf{S}_1 = \left(\mathbf{Y}_1 - \mathbf{X}\hat{\mathbf{B}}\right)^T \left(\mathbf{Y}_1 - \mathbf{X}\hat{\mathbf{B}}\right)$. To find a confidence region for ξ, using (3) and (4), the $100(1-\gamma)\%$ prediction ellipsoid for the unknown levels ξ is the volume

$$\xi : T^2 = \left(\overline{y}_2 - \widehat{\alpha} - \widehat{B}^T\xi\right)^T S^{-1} \left(\overline{y}_2 - \widehat{\alpha} - \widehat{B}^T\xi\right) \leq c\left(\xi\right) K \qquad (5)$$

where $K = \frac{q}{\nu}F_{1-\gamma,q,\nu}$ and $F_{1-\gamma,q,\nu}$ is the upper $100(1 - \gamma)\%$ point of the standard F distribution on q and ν degrees of freedom, $c\left(\xi\right) = \frac{1}{m} + \frac{1}{n} + \xi^T(X^TX)^{-1}\xi$ and $S\,(q \times q)$ is the *pooled* matrix of S_1 and S_2. It may be shown that the volume (5) is convex only when the matrix $C = \widehat{B}\widehat{S}^{-1}\widehat{B}^T - K(X^TX)^{-1}$ is positive definite and even so it may collapse to a point, the estimate (4).

When $q > p$, the ML estimator is a function of (4) and of a quantity that depends on an inconsistency diagnostic statistic. It may be shown that the left part of (5) may be decomposed in

$$T^2 = \left(\widehat{\xi}_C - \xi\right)^T \widehat{B}S_1^{-1}\widehat{B}^T \left(\widehat{\xi}_C - \xi\right) + $$
$$+ \left(\overline{y}_2 - \widehat{\alpha} - \widehat{B}^T\xi\right)^T S^{-1} \left(\overline{y}_2 - \widehat{\alpha} - \widehat{B}^T\xi\right) = V + R \qquad (6)$$

where R is a measure of the consistency of $\overline{y}_2$ to estimate ξ, while V may be used to find confidence region for ξ. Note that $R = 0$ when $p = q$, because $\widehat{\xi}_C$ is the solution of the system of equations $\overline{y}_2 = \widehat{\alpha} + \widehat{B}\widehat{\xi}_C$.

Williams conjectured that Q and R have approximate F distribution as follows

$$\frac{n - p - q}{p}Q_\gamma \sim c\left(\xi\right) F_{p,n-p-q} \qquad \frac{n - p - q}{q - p}R_\gamma \sim c\left(\xi\right) F_{q-p,n-p-q}$$

and then the statistical significance of R may be tested. The confidence region (5) may have an anomalous behavior with respect to R (Brown 1993, pag. 89): the width of the region increases as R decreases and decreases as R increases. Alternative techniques to find a calibrating confidence region are based on profile likelihood. The resulting regions have the desirable property to be expanded as R increases and to be reduced as R decreases. Unfortunately even in this case, we may obtain boundless confidence regions. Some very recent parametric proposals are due to Bellio (2002) and Mathew and Sharma (2002). In these papers accurate confidence regions are reported and in the latter the problem of finding joint confidence regions is treated only when the response and the explanatory variables have the same dimensions, or when the explanatory variable is one-dimensional. Another recent proposal is based on Kalman filter theory. Under certain hypothesis on the error measurement correlation matrix (Salini (2003)) Kalman filter may be used to upgrade the statistical information relative to the classical estimator so that it can be dynamically adjusted to give an update posterior estimate.

3 A proposal: semiparametric depth calibration regions

Most of the statistics reported in the previous paragraph have distributional properties mainly based on the assumption of multinormality. The problems connected to this assumption (or more generally to any parametric assumption) are well known and additionally in multivariate calibration it has been shown that the problem of finding an empty calibration confidence region may exists. Some of these problems may be overcome by a nonparametric approach. Our proposal will exploit the results of the data depth method proposed by Liu and Singh (1993). References and some applications of data depth may be found e.g. in Zappa (2002). For the sake of readability of the rest of the paper some preliminaries, comments and description of notation are needed.

Generally speaking a depth function, $D(\cdot, \cdot)$, is an application $D(\cdot, \cdot)$: $\mathbb{R}^k \times \mathcal{F} \to \mathbb{R}^1$, where $\mathcal{F}$ is a class of distributions on the Borel sets of $\mathbb{R}^k$. In a recent paper of Zuo and Serfling (2000) the basic properties that $D(\cdot, \cdot)$ should possess are reported. Among them probably the most relevant property is that $D(\cdot, \cdot)$ should be affine invariant, that is, for any non singular matrix $\mathbf{A}$ and any constant vector $\mathbf{b}$, $D(\mathbf{Ax} + \mathbf{b}; F_{\mathbf{Ax}+\mathbf{b}}) = D(\mathbf{x}, F_{\mathbf{x}})$.

There are several notions of depth functions. We will focus on the simplicial depth. Let $\{z_1, \ldots, z_n\} \subset \Xi_z \in \mathbb{R}^k$ a sample of n k-dimensional observations, with $n > k$. $S[z_{i_1}, \ldots, z_{i_{k+1}}]$ will stand for the simplex with vertices $\{z_{i_1}, \ldots, z_{i_{k+1}}\}$ for any i set of $k + 1$ different points taken from n. Then, for any point z in $\mathbb{R}^k$, the sample simplicial depth at z, $SD(z)$, is defined as the number of simplexes that include z. In particular the relative rank, $r_{G_n}(z^*)$, of a new observation z^* with respect to the empirical distribution G_z that is

$$r_{G_{z_n}}(z^*) = \#\{z_i | SD(z_i) \leq SD(z^*) \text{ , for } i = 1, \ldots, n\}/(n + 1), \qquad (7)$$

is a measure of how much outlying z^* is with respect to the data cloud Ξ_z. A relevant property of the simplicial depth is given by theorem 6.2 of Liu and Singh (1993) that will be used in the following . Synthetically, consider two samples, $\mathbf{X} = \{x_1, x_2, \ldots, x_n\}$ from distribution G and $\mathbf{Y} = \{y_1, y_2, \ldots, y_m\}$ from distribution F. Let $Q(G_{X_n}, F_{Y_m}) = \frac{1}{m} \sum_{j=1}^{m} r_{G_{Xn}}(y_j)$ where $r_{G_{Xn}}(y_j)$ is the proportion of x_i's having, with respect to the distribution G, $SD_G(x_i) \leq SD_G(y_i)$ and let $Q(G_{X_n}, G) = E[Q(G_{X_n}, F_{Y_m})|\mathbf{X}]$. Then

$$\sqrt{m}[Q(G_{X_n}, F_{Y_m}) - Q(G_{X_n}, G)] \overset{L}{\to} N\left(0, \frac{1}{12}\right) \quad \text{as } n \to \infty, \ m \to \infty$$

Some additional notation, that will be used in the rest of the paper, must be presented. For every set $A_z \subseteq \Xi_z$, it will be defined by convex hull the intersection of all the possible convex subsets of Ξ_z containing A_z. Let $\{A_{z_1}^*, A_{z_2}^*, \ldots, A_{z_w}^*\}$ a set of subsets of Ξ_z such that $A_{z_1}^* \supset A_{z_2}^* \supset \ldots \supset A_{z_w}^*$. $co(A_z^*)$ will be the convex polytope connecting the vertices of the convex hull containing A_z^* such that $\forall z \subset A_z^*$

$$\exists \, S[z_{i_1}, \ldots, z_{i_{k+1}}] \subseteq A_z^* : z = \sum_{j=1}^{k+1} \lambda_j z_{i_j} \quad \text{with} \quad \sum_{j=1}^{k+1} \lambda_j = 1, 0 \leq \lambda_j \leq 1$$

and $\mathcal{A}_z = \{A_{z_1}, A_{z_2}, ..., A_{z_w}\}$ will be the collection of sets of Ξ_z such that $co(A^*_{z_i}) = A_{z_i}$ for $i = 1, 2, ..., w$ with $A_{z_i} \cap A_{z_j} = \emptyset$ and $\cup^w_{i=1} A_{z_i} \subseteq \Xi_z$.

The most popular approach to multivariate calibration passes through two steps: 1) the application of data reduction techniques in order to reduce the complexity of the problem; 2) the implementation of parametric or non-parametric extrapolation methods to find a functional relationship between the set of variables. Criticism to this approach is mostly focused on the loss of information that the implementation of these techniques implies and on the assumption of linearity. These are the main two reasons that support the following proposal where: 1) all the information included in the set of variables will be used and 2) a preliminary test is run in order to verify if the hypothesis of linear relationship between the set of variables is true. The counterpart of this approach is the relevant computational effort needed. At present no sufficiently powerful (fast and reliable) software has been prepared and most of the available algorithms (alike the ours) have been programmed for research reasons or may be operatively used when the dimension of the dataset is not too large [4].

Consider an asymmetric relationship between two sets of multivariate variables, Y, X. For the sake of graphical representability we will focus on the case $p = q$. In the following we will give some details on the extension to the case $p \neq q$. Suppose that $\{\Omega_Y, \mathcal{B}_Y, G_{Y|X,\theta}, \Theta\}$ is the parametric probabilistic space of Y, where $\theta \in \Theta$ is a parameter vector (or matrix of parameters). Suppose that a transfer function $g : \Omega_X \to \Omega_Y$ exists and that measurement errors mask the true g. We will approximate g by a function $f(X, \theta, E)$ where E is a matrix of r.v.s.. As most of the calibrating models are supposed to be linear (see §2), then it turns out to be relevant to study the 'degree of linearity' of f or more extensively its (at least locally) 'degree of invertibility'.

Let us first define what functional f we consider and then how to test if f is linear. Consider the following symbolic transformation

$$\mathcal{A}_X = \{A_{X_1}, ..., A_{X_w}\} \underbrace{\to \{A^*_{Y_1}, ..., A^*_{Y_w}\}}_{f} \overset{co(A^*_Y)}{\to} \{A_{Y_1}, ..., A_{Y_w}\} = \mathcal{A}_Y \quad (8)$$

where for each convex polytope $A_{X_i} \in \mathcal{A}_X, i = 1, 2, ..., w$, we take the set $A^*_{Y_i}$ with elements in Y matching the vertices of A_{X_i} and then we consider the polytope $co(A^*_{Y_i}) = A_{Y_i}$. If $co^{-1}(A_Y)$ exists then $\mathcal{A}_X \overset{f}{\to} \mathcal{A}_X$ is a 1:1 application. If the points left after the $(w-1)$th polytope are less then $q+1$, they will be considered as a unique set simply transferred through f to the corresponding data in Y.

If f is linear and in the not statistical case where the r.v. E does not exists, we will obtain a result similar to the one given in Fig.1b where $\mathbf{B}$ is a matrix of known coefficients. If we introduce the disturbance $E \sim N_2(0, \sigma^2 I)$,

---

[4]We ourself have implemented a software to draw the $co(\cdot)$ function and to simulate the overall proposal (see. Zappa and Salini (2003)).

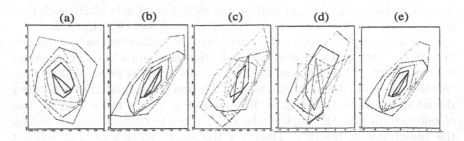

Fig. 1. Convex hulls of *(a)* $\mathbf{X}$; *(b)* $\mathbf{Y} = \mathbf{XB}$; *(c)* $\mathbf{Y} = \mathbf{XB} + \mathbf{E}_1$ where $\mathbf{E}_1$ comes from $E_1 \sim N(0, \frac{1}{16}\mathbf{I})$; *(d)* $\mathbf{Y} = \mathbf{XB} + \mathbf{E}_2$ where $\mathbf{E}_2$ comes from $E_1 \sim N(0, \frac{1}{16}\mathbf{I})$; *(e)* $\hat{\mathbf{Y}} = \mathbf{X}\hat{\mathbf{B}}$ using case (b) and the least squares estimate for $\mathbf{B}$

from Fig 1c,1d it emerges that (8) will reproduce with a good approximation the true $\mathcal{A}_Y$ only when the contribution of the r.v.s is small that is when the explanatory variables are well identified and only errors likely due to measurement errors give low contribution to distortion. This is the typical calibration problem where the calibrating sample is generally accurately chosen.

To test if f is at least locally linear, making use of Liu's Q statistics and recalling that it has the properties to be invariant if f is affine, proceed as follows. For each element $A_{X_i} \in \mathcal{A}_X$, using (8) compute the sets A_{Y_i}, $A_{Y_i}^*$. Then compute

$$Q(G_{X_n}^*, A_{X_i}) = \frac{1}{m_{X_i}} \sum_{j=1}^{m_{X_i}} r_{G_{X_{n_i}}^*}(x_j) \qquad Q(G_{Y_n}^*, A_{Y_i}) = \frac{1}{m_{Y_i}} \sum_{j=1}^{m_{Y_i}} r_{G_{Y_{n_i}}^*}(y_j)$$

where $m_{X_i}(m_{Y_i})$ is the number of elements in $A_{X_i}(A_{Y_i})$, n_i is the number of samples in $\mathbf{X}(\mathbf{Y})$ after having peeled off the set $A_{X_i}(A_{Y_i}^*)$, and $G_{X_n}^*(G_{Y_n}^*)$ is the empirical distribution of $X(Y)$ without the set $A_{X_i}(A_{Y_i}^*)$. Suppose that the paired samples in $\{\mathbf{X}, \mathbf{Y}\}$ are independent. We wish to compare $Q(G_{Y_n}^*, A_{Y_i})$ with $Q(G_{X_n}^*, A_{X_i})$ (which has the role of conditioning value). Using theorem 6.2 of Liu and Singh (1993) we may state the following result:

$$\sum_{i=1}^{w} [Q(G_{Y_n}^*, A_{Y_i}) - Q(G_{X_n}^*, A_{X_i})] \overset{n_i \to \infty}{\sim} N\left(c, \frac{1}{12} \sum_{i=1}^{w} \frac{1}{m_{Y_i}}\right) \qquad (9)$$

The proof of (9) is resides in the sum of independent normal variables. For small samples the distribution in (9) should be premultiplied by the ratio (m_{Y_i}/m_{X_i}): this is needed because the set A_{Y_i} may not have the same cardinality of the corresponding A_{X_i}. As the dataset increases, under H_0, this ratio is almost 1.

Then the test on linearity may be formulated as:

$$\begin{cases} H_0 : c = 0 & \text{then } f \text{ is a linear application} \\ H_1 : c \neq 0 & \text{then } f \text{ is not a linear application} \end{cases}$$

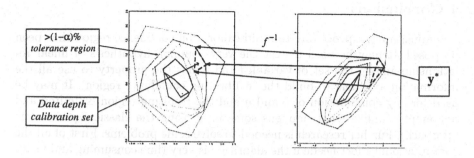

Fig. 2. Data depth calibration set. (At the left: $co(\mathbf{X})$; at the right $co(\hat{\mathbf{Y}} = \mathbf{X}\hat{\mathbf{B}})$)

Note that the above procedure may be implemented for any combination of p, q. Some problems may exist only for $p < q$. A_{X_i} must have at least $q + 1$ vertices otherwise we cannot build a convex set in Ω_Y. A conservative solution is to search for $q - p$ additional points, possibly internal to the region defined by the convex hull of A_{X_i}, such that volume of the corresponding hull A_{Y_i} is the largest. The results of a simulation based on 500 replications of (9) under the hypothesis of existence of linearity is reported in Zappa and Salini (2003). It has been noticed that the convergence of (9) to a normal distribution is matched even when n is as small as 10.

If the non parametric procedure is tested to be appropriate, then a standard parametric calibrating model may be implemented. In Fig.2 how to find a "data depth calibration set" is illustrated.

The procedure is:

1) Compute $\hat{\mathbf{Y}} = \mathbf{X}\hat{\mathbf{B}}$ and apply (8).
2) Consider a new observation $\mathbf{y}^*$: find the smallest simplex (with $q + 1$ vertices) in Ω_Y that contains $\mathbf{y}^*$.
3) Through f^{-1} find the corresponding simplex in Ω_X: this will be called the *data depth calibration set*.
4) Find in Ω_X the convex hull that contains a pre-chosen $(1 - \alpha)\%$ of points. It will be interpreted as the fiducial region for the depth calibration set. Translating this region so that the depth calibration set is at the centre will result in the fiducial region for ξ: alike the fiducial approach on the construction of confidence region, we are $(1 - \alpha)\%$ sure of being right in this particular case, regarding the observations as fixed and setting up regions based on some belief in the values of the parameters that have generated those observations. This is the typical calibration context where a calibration experiment is run under well controlled conditions.

To find the calibrating depth region when $q < p$, use the vertices of the calibration depth region plus additional, possibly internal, $p - q$ points such that the simplex in Ω_X is the smallest.

4 Conclusions

A semiparametric procedure to build calibration confidence regions has been proposed. It may be used to test the very common hypothesis of linear relationship among the set of variables and it has the property to use all the information available to build the 'calibrating confidence region'. It may be used for any combination of p and q and the resulting region is limited and not empty (unlike what happens sometimes using the classical parametric approach). Further research is needed to solve some problems. First of all the computational effort needed: the algorithm is very time consuming and faster procedure must be implemented. A general form must be defined for the H_1 (the aim is to measure the power of the test) and it must be shown if the family of f to be tested in H_0 include only the linear model or other locally linear models. If the convex hull are each inside the others, it means that the link f is invertible: to what family does the link function belong to? Finally it must be measured up to what degree the random error disturbs the identification of the (supposed true) linear link and some simulations must be run to compare the classical and our new approach. A prospective can be the use of non parametric approach also in the estimation problem: either classical smoothing techniques, artificial neural networks or Kalman filter theory can be useful in presence of complexity and non normal error distributions.

References

BELLIO, R. (2002): Likelihood Methods for Controlled Calibration. *In printing in Scandinavian Journal of Statistics.*.

BROWN, P. J. (1993): *Measurement, Regression and Calibration*, Oxford University Press, Oxford.

LIU, R., SINGH K. (1993): A Quality index based on Data Depth and Multivariate Rank Tests. *Journal of the American Statistical Association, 88, 252-260.*

MATHEW T., SHARMA M. K. (2002): Joint confidence regions in the multivariate calibration problem. *Journal of Statistical planning and Inference, 100, 427-441.*

SALINI S. (2003): *Taratura Statistica Multivariata*, Doctoral Thesis in Statistics - XV ciclo, Universit degli Studi di Milano - Bicocca.

SUNDBERG, R. (1999): Multivariate calibration - direct and indirect regression methodology (with discussion). *Scandinavian Journal of Statistics, 26, 161-207.*

ZAPPA D. (2002): A Nonparametric Capability Index for Multivariate Processes. *Studi in Onore di Angelo Zanella, Vita e Pensiero, 709-726.*

ZAPPA D., SALINI S. (2003): Some notes on Confidence Regions in Multivariate Calibration. *Istituto di Statistica, Universita' Cattolica del Sacro Cuore, SEP. 118*

ZUO Y., SERFLING R. (2000): General notions of statistical depth function. *The Annals of Statistics, 28, 2, 461-482.*

Applied Multivariate Statistics

Nonparametric Analysis of Air Pollution Indices Compositions

Francesca Bruno, Daniela Cocchi, and Meri Raggi

Dipartimento di Scienze Statistiche
Università di Bologna, Italy
{bruno, cocchi, raggi}@stat.unibo.it

Abstract. Synthetic indices are useful tools used to summarize multivariate information by means of a single value. In the environmental framework these indices are frequently proposed both for measuring pollution and for measuring the associated risks. The drawback of using synthetic indices is, however, that some important information about their components is lost. In this paper we propose to save and interpret these components by transforming them into compositional data. The interpretation of compositions is performed conditionally on the meteorology. In particular, much attention is directed towards explaining the absence of specific pollutants in the index determination.

1 Introduction

Synthetic indices for summarizing complex phenomena are relatively popular tools that permit synthetic information and comparisons in space and time. Decision makers need synthetic evaluations of the situations to be monitored, rather than masses of data. The adoption of a synthetic index pays however an informative cost, since the specific contribution of its different components is lost. This drawback is particularly upsetting for decision makers themselves, who would need going back to the index components at the moment when special policies ought to be undertaken. Synthetic air quality indices are a typical example of this duality. They are becoming a common tool for monitoring air quality, but suffer from the difficulty of having hidden their determinants.

Synthetic evaluations of air pollution in a city, obtained by means of air quality indices as synthetic measures (Ott and Hunt, 1976; Bruno and Cocchi, 2002), can be constructed by successively selecting the maximum (or another percentile) of an ordered set of values. Since a percentile isolates a single value of a distribution, each index value is due to the contribution of only one pollutant. For each value of the index it is possible to go back to the pollutant which gave rise to the index value. For a set of air quality indices it is possible to count the number of times that each pollutant determines the daily value. The framework for further analyses is therefore the one of compositional data.

In this work we propose a method for recovering and interpreting the information about the pollutant which give rise to the synthetic value of the index. It consists of analyzing the compositional data derived from a set of air quality indices with special reference to:
- quantifying the influence of meteorological variables on pollutant compositions;
- overcoming the problem of zero values in compositional data.

Section 2 describes a class of air quality indices and illustrates the idea of saving the information about the components by using compositional data theory. An introduction to compositional data is given in Section 3, with particular attention to the methods for dealing with zero values. A case of study is proposed in Section 4 where the air pollution in the city of Bologna is analyzed, where the usual techniques for compositional data cannot be directly used because of the presence of many zero values. A nonparametric analysis aiming at detecting the meteorological conditions under which each pollutant produces the index value is performed in Section 5. Some concluding remarks are included in Section 6.

2 The air quality index structure

In this paper the synthetic quality index for air pollution suggested in Bruno and Cocchi (2002) is analyzed. The aim of a synthetic air quality index varies from monitoring the performance of a single site to monitoring the behavior of a set of similar sites, or of an extended metropolitan area. When a set of sites is available, the data at disposal refer to three dimensions to be reduced: time, space and type of pollutant. The temporal dimension is removed first, since the pollution data are collected hourly, but daily values are the most popular syntheses for measuring air quality. The aggregating functions to use are suggested by national laws (e.g. for Italy the D.M. Ambiente 15/4/1994 and the D.M. Ambiente 16/5/1996 state the following time aggregations: daily mean for sulphure dioxide and total suspended particulate and daily maxima for nitrogen dioxide, carbon monoxide and ozone). The second step is the aggregation over one of the two remaining dimensions: for the scope of this paper, choosing one of the two possible directions for aggregation is sufficient. In what follows we aggregate according to the spatial dimension, obtaining the maximum values between monitoring sites for each pollutant. Given the choice above, the remaining step consists of aggregating between pollutants. Before obtaining the final index value a further data transformation is required, consisting in the application of a standardization function. This is mainly required by the differences in measurement scale and in severity on health effects. A continuous scale is used, and the standardizing transformation can be based on the segmented linear function proposed by Ott and Hunt (1976):

$$f(Y) = \frac{b_{c+1} - b_c}{a_{(c+1)i} - a_{ci}}(Y - a_{ci}) + b_c \quad \text{for } c = 1, ..., C; \; \forall i = 1, ..., N \quad (1)$$

where Y denotes the concentration value obtained by former aggregations, a_{ci} represents the threshold that define the different classes of air quality for each pollutant in the different units of measure and b_c represents the standardized threshold. The threshold a_{ci} is settled exogenously according to expert evaluations.

The index value is finally obtained as the maximum between the standardized pollution syntheses:

$$I1_{M(M)} = \max_i f\{\max_k [q_h(X_{ikh})]\} \quad (2)$$

where k, i and h index respectively the sites, the pollutants and the time occurrences within the predefined time interval. Function q_h permits to aggregate pollutant i over time. Function f represents the "standardizing function".

The daily air quality index depends on the concentration of just one pollutant and the choice of maxima as aggregation functions aims at highlighting severe episodes.

2.1 Obtaining compositional data from daily air quality indices

The values of the daily index of air pollution $I1_{M(M)}$ represent the severity of air pollution in a city, by means of the choice of maxima instead of other aggregating functions as percentiles or means. The advantage of this index is that, with a single value, it is able to represent a complex and multivariate scenario, and can be used to compare different situations in space or in time. Unfortunately, it has the drawback of loosing information about the determination of the value index, which are needed to better understand the pollution phenomena.

As a tool for recovering and interpreting the information about the pollutants that gave rise to each synthetic value, we introduce the variable "monthly pollutant composition", i.e. the number of days per month in which a pollutant determines the air quality index. This new variable will be analyzed in the next sections.

3 Compositional data

In this section we summarize the basics concepts of compositional data analysis and sketch the problem of zero values in compositions.

Compositional data are vectors of proportions describing the relative contribution of each of N categories to the whole. Recent theoretical developments in the field of the statistical analysis of compositional data revealed a broad field of applications, among which environmental applications (Billheimer et al., 2001).

Let $\mathbf{y} = (\mathbf{y}_1, ..., \mathbf{y}_i, ..., \mathbf{y}_N)'$ denote a N-part composition, where $\mathbf{y}_i$ represents a n dimensional vector of i-th constituent proportions, $\mathbf{y}_i = (y_{i1}, ..., y_{ij}, ..., y_{in})'$. The elements of $\mathbf{y}$ satisfy the two following constraints:

$$y_{ij} \geq 0, \text{ for all } i = 1, ..., N; \; j = 1, ..., n; \text{ and } \sum_{i=1}^{N} y_{ij} = 1 \text{ for each } j = 1, ..., n.$$

In this case, standard multivariate statistical techniques cannot be applied, since the presence of unit-sum constraints leads to a covariance matrix with at least one negative value in each row (Aitchison, 1986). A transformation of each $\mathbf{y}_i$ is thus suggested to avoid this problem. In order to achieve a new support defined in the $N - 1$ dimension, a link function $K(\cdot)$ is proposed: $z_{ij} = K(y_{ij}/y_{Nj})$, with $i = 1, ..., N - 1$, $j = 1, ..., n$, where y_{Nj} is the benchmark composition for each observation $j = 1, ..., n$. By means of the ratio y_{ij}/y_{Nj}, the dimensionality of the component space is preserved. Function $K(\cdot)$ is chosen to ensure that the resultant vector has real components. Aitchison (1982, 1986) first proposed a log-transformation for $K(\cdot)$, but logarithmic transformations are undefined when zeroes exist in the data.

3.1 The problem of zeroes in compositional data analysis

In statistical literature, two explanations for the occurrence of zero values are given. These can be "rounding" or "essential" zeroes. Rounding zeroes derive from problems in the measurement process, whereas essential zeroes are due to the occurrence of zero values in the underlying data generating process (see Fry et al., 1996). In order to overcome the problem of treating essential zeroes, Rayens and Srinivasan (1991) suggested a Box-Cox transformation. Box-Cox transformed data usually follow a nearly multivariate normal distribution and can be treated using standard techniques.

4 The investigation of air quality index composition

Air pollution and meteorology data are regularly collected in urban areas. The proposal of this paper is checked by means of data collected in the Bologna area (years 1995-2001). The pollutants considered are: carbon monoxide (CO), nitrogen dioxide (NO_2), ozone (O_3), total suspended particulate (TSP) and sulphure dioxide (SO_2). Many monitoring stations are present in the city: 7 monitoring sites have been operating until 1997 and 6 are present since 1998.

The meteorological variables measured at Bologna airport are: temperature (daily maxima, minima and average), humidity (daily maxima, minima and average), pressure, wind speed, wind direction, rainfall. Their corresponding monthly syntheses have been computed for further analyses. By means of an additional variable, the year of measurement, we have taken into consideration the structural change in the monitoring network.

4.1 The emergence of an exceess of essential zeroes

Each monthly composition of the index, *i.e.* the contribution of one or more pollutants, may be null: some components are indeed essential zeroes, as shown in Table 1, where NO_2 never appears as an essential zero. On the contrary, in the computation of these compositions SO_2 never contributes to the determination of the air quality index. For this reason we will not take into consideration this pollutant in the following analyses.

CO=0	TSP=0	O_3=0	NO_2=0	Occurrence
×				37
×	×			15
×		×		16
		×		16
				84

Table 1. Essential zeroes in monthly air quality index

Compositions of monthly air quality indices have been obtained, where a large amount of essential zeroes occur, specially for some pollutants. This high occurrences of zero values is typical of air pollution, where some pollutants can be prevailing in determining the values of the indices. In this case, Box-Cox transformations do not solve the problem of non normality and the maximum likelihood estimates of the transforming parameter (Bruno et al., 2003) lead to data that are not normally distributed.

In a situation of structural exceedance of essential zeroes, attention moves towards explaining the conditions under which essential zero values occur. The solution proposed for identifying conditions for essential zeroes relies on nonparametric techniques.

5 A nonparametric approach for identifying essential zeros

In this section the problem of essential zeroes is faced by means of nonparametric techniques, proposing CART regression trees (Breiman et al., 1993) as a tool to characterize essential zeroes with respect to the main environmental features.

A CART regression tree is built through a process known as binary recursive partitioning. This is an iterative process which splits data into partitions, and then splits them up further on each of the branches. The algorithm breaks up the data, using every possible binary split performed by every explanatory variable. It chooses the split that minimizes the sum of the squared deviations from the mean in the separate parts. The process continues until each node reaches a specified minimum node size and becomes a terminal node. To obtain the right sized tree a pruning step based on 1-SE rule is performed (Breiman et al., 1993).

Our goal is to explain responses on a continuous dependent variable (monthly pollutant composition) and to quantify the influence of meteorological variables on the pollutant compositions. A regression tree was built for each pollutant composition.

In Figure 1 the regression tree for ozone monthly composition is reported.

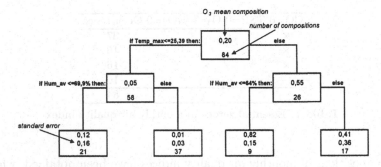

Fig. 1. Regression tree for ozone monthly composition.

In this Figure, O_3 monthly compositions constitute the dependent variable. Monthly maximum temperature is the first splitting variable: when it is less than about 25°C, then O_3 composition is predicted as very close to zero. The successive split is determined by choosing monthly average humidity as the discriminant variable. When this variable assumes a value higher than 70 per cent of humidity, ozone monthly compositions have a mean value very close to zero. This terminal node contains 37 cases. In Table 1, 32 ozone values out of the 84 were identified as essential zeroes: the tree standard error rate, estimated by cross-validation, is about 0.006.

Figure 2 reports the regression tree where TSP monthly composition is the dependent variable. In this tree, monthly average temperature is selected as the first splitting variable. Four essential zeroes are detected when monthly average temperature is higher than 17°C and humidity is less than 61 per cent. Other 12 cases belong to a terminal node characterized by monthly average humidity higher than 61 per cent and pressure higher than 1014 hPa. In this case the tree standard error rate, estimated by cross-validation, is about 0.004.

In Table 1, 68 months report essential zeroes for CO composition. The regression tree for CO is able to isolate these zero values mainly according to meteorology. We describe the structure of this tree without reporting it

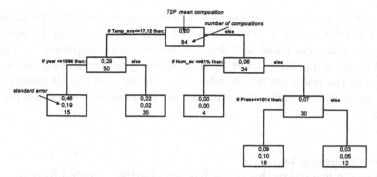

Fig. 2. Regression tree for total suspended particulate monthly composition.

graphically. The first split is due to average temperature: in correspondence of an average temperature higher than 15°C, 38 essential zero values occur. For the remaining 46 compositions, the following split is due to the reference year. If the year of reference is successive to 1998, 18 essential zero values are recognized as essential zero. Indeed, 1998 has been the year of monitoring sites relocation. Other important splits are due to wind conditions: average wind speed greater than 2 m/s and wind direction less than 217° (*i.e.* coming from the west direction) segregate further 9 essential zero values. When the wind direction is greater than 217° the very special average wind speed between 2 m/s and 2.2 m/s occur we observe further 5 essential zeroes. The tree standard error rate estimated by cross-validation is less than 0.0003.

The NO$_2$ monthly composition never assumes essential zero values, and its regression tree can be interpreted essentially with respect to low values. The summary of the tree description, which is not reported, states that NO$_2$ monthly composition has its lowest values when the temperature is higher than 29°C and the monthly average humidity is lower than 65 per cent. The tree standard error rate is about 0.007.

6 Conclusions

In this paper, we face the problem of integrating meteorological information within air quality index evaluations. Aggregations by time, space and pollutants are needed to obtain a synthetic index, but they suffer from loosing information about the most influent pollutants and the relationship between pollutants and meteorology. For this reason, we construct new variables as compositional data. Unfortunately, the common compositional techniques cannot be applied due to a strong presence of essential zero values. Our proposal is to use nonparametric techniques as regression trees for quantifying the influence of meteorology on air quality indices composition. The high overall dependence of pollutant compositions on temperature and humidity is highlighted: essential zeroes of TSP and CO compositions mainly depend on these meteorological characteristics. These results confirm the knowledge about the relationship between air pollution and meteorology. In particular, ozone essential zero cases are characterized by low temperatures and high humidity, meaning that, under these meteorological conditions, ozone never features as the pollutant which determines the value of the air quality index. NO_2 composition is high when temperature assumes low values and humidity is high.

Acknowledgements

The research leading to this paper has been partially funded by a 2002 grant (Sector 13: Economics and Statistics, Project n.7, protocol n. 2002134337 01 for Research Project of National Interest by MIUR). We thank Carlo Trivisano for the helpful discussion about the organization of this work.

References

AITCHISON, J. (1982): The statistical analysis of compositional data (with discussion). *Journal of the Royal Statistical Society, Series B, 44, 139-177.*

AITCHISON, J. (1986): *The Statistical Analysis of Compositional Data.* Chapman and Hall, New York.

BILLHEIMER, D., GUTTORP, P. and FAGAN, W.F. (2001): Statistical Interpretation for Species Composition. *Journal of the American Statistical Association, 96, 1205-1214.*

BREIMAN, L., FRIEDMAN, J.H., OLSHEN, R.A. and STONE J.C. (1993): *Classification and regression trees.* Chapman and Hall, Boca Raton.

BRUNO, F. and COCCHI, D. (2002): A unified strategy for building simple air quality indices. *Environmetrics, 13, 243-261.*

BRUNO, F., COCCHI, D. and RAGGI, M. (2003): Compositional analysis of air pollutant data. In: Book of short paper, *CLADAG 2003.* Bologna, 83-86.

D.M. Ambiente (15/4/1994): Norme tecniche in materia di livelli e di stati di attenzione e di allarme per gli inquinanti atmosferici nelle aree urbane. In Italian.

D.M. Ambiente (16/05/1996): Attivazione di un sistema di sorveglianza di inquinamento da ozono. In Italian.

FRY, J.M., FRY, T.R.L. and McLAREN, K.R. (1996): Compositional data analysis and zeros in micro data. Centre of Policy Studies. *General Paper No. G-120.*

OTT, W.R. and HUNT, W.F. (1976): A quantitative evaluation of the pollutant standards index. *Journal of the Air Pollution Control Association, 26, 1051-1054.*

RAYENS, W.S. and SRINIVASAN, C. (1991): Box-Cox transformations in the analysis of compositional data. *Journal of Chemometrics, 5, 227-239.*

VAR Models for Spatio-temporal Structures: An Application to Environmental Data

Aldo Lamberti, Alessia Naccarato

ISTAT - Roma, Italy
aldo.lamberti@istat.it, naccarat@istat.it

Abstract. In this work we propose the use of Vector Autoregressive Models (ST-VAR) and Generalized Vector Autoregressive Models (ST-GVAR) for spatio-temporal data in which relations among different sites of a monitoring network are not exclusively dependent on the distance among them but take also into account intensity and direction that a phenomenon measured on the whole network has on a single site of the network. We present an application of these models using data of fifteen italian meteorological locations of Mediterranean Basin.

1 Introduction

Since there are in nature phenomena whose spatial diffusion is not exclusively dependent on the distance among different sites of the monitoring network, in this work we propose the use of VAR models for spatio-temporal data which take into account intensity and direction that a phenomenon measured on the whole network has on a single site. This means that relations among observed sites are not necessarily symmetric and/or bi-directional. The models proposed are suitable for the analysis of environmental data and, particularly, for meteorological phenomena. In this paper we present an application of the models proposed using data of solar radiation and sunshine duration, where with solar radiation we mean *solar energy measured in a certain time instant by the instrument* and with sunshine duration we mean *time interval during which there is not cloudiness.*
There are two different kind of interest in the study of solar radiation. The first one is related to environmental problems. In fact the level of solar radiation is strictly connected with the presence of pollutants which, beside worsen the quality of the air we breathe, cause the rarefaction of the ozone reducing the ability of the stratosphere to hold the UV-C waves, the most dangerous for human health. Hence monitoring the level of solar radiation is important for checking a possible increase of this level in time due to many different phenomena that have to be kept under control.
The second kind of interest is from a statistical point of view. The level of solar radiation measured in a certain time instant on a single site, depends on the behaviour of those nearby as a function of cloud amount (Law of Angstrom). Streams and humidity rate cause the movement of clouds and then the intensity of solar radiation measured in a given site. For this reason

we need suitable models to understand and predict solar radiation and, in general terms, for all the phenomena whose spatial diffusion is not exclusively dependent on the distance among sites.

The proposed models explain solar radiation at time t, in a given site, as a linear function of past observations in the same site, of past and simultaneous observations of the remaining sites and of the simultaneous observations of the pure exogenous component sunshine duration. Since the models proposed need that the observed sites define a climatic area, in the application we used spatio-temporal data of fifteen meteorological sites - as reported in Section 3 - which satisfy the condition required. The paper is organised as follow: in Section 2 we write the models proposed, in Section 3 we describe the data used, in Section 4 we give some empirical results and in Section 5 some conclusions and future works.

2 The models

The two models proposed distinguish in accordance with the use of the simultaneous spatial component (Naccarato, 2001). The first one, called ST-VAR(K), does not include the simultaneous spatial component and, with reference to a spatial network with S sites, is defined as:

$$y_t = \alpha_t + A_1 y_{t-1} + A_2 y_{t-2} + \ldots + A_K y_{t-K} + u_t \tag{1}$$

$$E(u_t) = 0, E(u_t u_t') = \Sigma_u = \sigma^2 I_S, E(u_{t_1}, u_{t_2}) = 0, \forall t = 1, \ldots, T, \forall t_1 \neq t_2$$

where y_t is the vector of the observations in the S sites at time t, u_t is the error vector and $A_1, \ldots, A_K$ are the coefficient matrices, non-symmetric, in which the diagonal elements are the time autoregressive effects of the model while the extra-diagonal elements are the spatio-temporal autoregressive effects (e.g. $_k a_{ij}, k = 1, \ldots K$, is the effect that the phenomenon collected at time $t - k$ on site i has on the phenomenon collected on site j at time t). Using matrix notation we can write the model ST-VAR(K) as:

$$vec\left(Y^T\right) = \left(I_S \otimes Z^T\right) vec\left(B^T\right) + vec\left(U^T\right) \tag{2}$$

with $\Sigma_{vec(U^T)} = (\Sigma_u \otimes I_T)$ and $\Sigma_u = \sigma^2 I_s$.

The second model, called ST-GVAR(K), includes simultaneous spatial effect and is defined as:

$$y_t = \alpha + W_0 y_t + A_1 y_{t-1} + A_2 y_{t-2+\ldots+A_K y_{t-K} u_t} \tag{3}$$

where W_0 is a matrix in which the diagonal elements are zero and the extra-diagonal elements represent the simultaneous spatial effect among sites. Using matrix notation we can write the model ST-GVAR(K) as:

$$vec\left(Y^T\right) = \left(I_S \otimes Z^T\right) vec\left(A_0^{-1} B\right)^T + \left(A_0^{-1} \otimes I_T\right) vec U^T \tag{4}$$

with error covariance matrix given by $(\Omega \otimes I_T)$, where $\Omega = A_0^{-1} \Sigma_u \left(A_0^{-1}\right)^T$. In the case of ST-GVAR(K) model the OLS estimates are not consistent because of spatial correlation among errors in different sites at the same time. For this reason, under the assumption that the process is normally distributed, we will use ML estimates. Even if ST-VAR(K) and ST-GVAR(K) models do not impose neither bi-directional nor symmetric relations among each pair of sites, they require a high number of parameters to be estimated. If the phenomenon has a spatial structure which is repeated in time, we can formalize a constrained model which takes into account this structure. In this way it is possible to reduce the number of unknown parameters. The constrained ST-VAR(K) model is:

$$vec\left(Y^T\right) = \left(I_S \otimes Z^T\right) R \, \Psi + vec\left(U^T\right) \tag{5}$$

where $vec\left(B^T\right) = R \, \Psi^T$, R is a $[S(SK+1), M]$ matrix of known coefficient, with rank $r(R) = M$ and Ψ is a $[M, 1]$ vector of unknown and unconstrained parameters with $M < S(SK+1)$.

To obtain the analytic form of the ML estimates for the model ST-GVAR(K) in the form (4), we need to define the following vectors:

$$\eta = vec\left\{\left[A_0^{-1}(\alpha, A_1, \ldots, A_K)\right]^T\right\}$$

Hence model (4) becomes:

$$vec\left(Y^T\right) = \left(I_S \otimes Z^T\right) \eta + \left(A_0^{-1} \otimes I_T\right) vecU^T \tag{6}$$

If the constrains are of the form $\beta = R\Psi + r$ it can be shown that the ML constrained estimator of Ψ is:

$$\begin{aligned}
\hat{\Psi} = &\left[R^T H^T \left(\Omega^{-1} \otimes ZZ^T\right) HR\right]^{-1} R^T H \left(\Omega^{-1} \otimes Z^T\right) vecY^T \\
&- \left[R^T H^T \left(\Omega^{-1} \otimes ZZ^T\right) HR\right]^{-1} R^T H^T \left(\Omega^{-1} \otimes ZZ^T\right) Hr
\end{aligned} \tag{7}$$

with $H = \partial\eta\backslash\partial\beta^T$, $\eta = vec\left\{\left[A_0^{-1}(\alpha, A_1, \ldots, A_K)\right]^T\right\}$.

3 Description of the data

The data used in our application are daily spatio-temporal series of solar radiation and sunshine duration concerning the fifteen italian meteorological sites of Mediterranean Basin - Pisa San Giusto (01), Elba (02), Pianosa (03), Vigna di Valle (04), Roma Ciampino (05), Ponza (06), Napoli Capo di Chino (07), Capo Palinuro (08), Messina (09), Ustica (10), Trapani Birgi (11), Pantelleria (12), Cagliari Elmas (13), Capo Bella Vista (14), Olbia Costa Smeralda (15) - during the period 1 january 1991 - 31 december 1998. Considering sunshine duration as variable the sites, whose behaviour is homogeneous with respect to this variable, have been chosen using cluster analysis and in particular the non-hierarchical algorithm of K-means fixing five groups. The method has been applied to the data collected in 1991 on 50 meteorological sites in Italy; the stability of the partitions during the years has been verified applying the algorithm to the data for every year of the series. Moreover, the fifteen sites obtained are under the influence of streams coming from the English Channel and the Gulf of Gascony which determine the main movements of the clouds - in the North-South direction - on the Tyrrhenian sea. For these reasons the fifteen sites define a climatic area.

First of all, we carried out the analysis of global and partial autocorrelations of solar radiation series in each site to underline a possible non-stationarity in mean of the phenomenon. For all the series considered, the estimated global autocorrelation function goes to zero very slowly and in a straight way; the partial autocorrelation is in practice one at lag 1 and almost zero elsewhere and the estimated inverse autocorrelation goes to $-\frac{1}{2}$ at lag 1. In the ST-VAR(K) model the non-stationarity in mean is eliminated transforming the variable using first order differentiation and the differentiated series showed an autoregressive scheme of second order (AR(2)) for all the sites. Spatio-temporal effects for lags greater than two were also taken into account but their inclusion in the models was not significant. Including in the model simultaneous spatial effect - using hence ST-GVAR(K) model (6) - the data do not show non-stationarity in mean probably due to the fact that simultaneous spatial effect underline the long term trend effect. In this case we used the original series and the model ST-GVAR(2).

4 Results

As noted before, the main problem on the use of models proposed is the high number of parameters to be estimated.

A_1	01	02	03	04	05	06	07	08	09	10	11	12	13	14	15
01	0.56	-0.14	0.39	0.74	0.71	0.29									
02	0.22	0.61		0.48	0.57	0.71	0.32	0.17							0.41
03		0.53	0.36		0.29	0.19	0.06	0.21	0.34					0.37	
04				0.49	0.69	0.27	0.74	0.69	-0.14	0.38					
05					0.73	0.64	0.81	0.58	0.33	0.47					
06						0.51	0.18	0.67	0.48	0.57	0.67				
07							0.36	0.83	0.67	0.48	0.58				
08								0.58	0.52		0.23				
09									0.63	0.31	0.28				
10										0.44	0.69	0.54			
11											0.27	0.78			
12											0.47	0.21			
13						0.12			0.25	0.70	0.75	0.69	0.39		
14					0.51			0.39	0.42	0.82	-0.29	0.48	0.19	0.41	
15				0.17	0.22	-0.33	-0.18			0.36	0.30			0.57	0.87

Table 1a

A_2	01	02	03	04	05	06	07	08	09	10	11	12	13	14	15
01	0.03		0.39	0.74		0.29	0.14								
02		0.13		0.23	0.19	0.71	0.32	0.17							
03		0.53	0.07			0.19	0.06	0.21	0.07						
04				0.38		0.27	0.74	0.69	-0.32		0.01				
05					0.05	0.11	0.81	0.58	0.33	0.47					
06				0.14		0.23	0.21	0.67	0.48	0.29					
07						0.09	0.83	0.67	0.48	0.45	0.03				
08							0.12	0.52	0.10	0.23					
09								0.20	0.31	0.28					
10										0.28	0.19	0.15			
11										0.07	0.08	0.78			
12											0.09	0.11			
13										0.70	0.75	0.69	0.07		
14					0.02				0.42	0.82	0.27	0.33	0.19	0.21	
15						0.08	0.11			0.36	0.30			0.57	0.34

Table 1b

In our application, besides the parameters relative to the spatio-temporal effects, we had to consider even those of the pure exogenous component sunshine duration. To reduce the number of these parameters, we used a priori information about meteorological features of the climatic area. In particular, the fifteen sites are under continuous and predominant influence of the streams coming from the English Channel and the Gulf of Gascony, which cause the movements of clouds in the same directions for two or three days; hence we assumed that the spatio-temporal effect of the phenomenon is constant in the same period. This is equivalent to suppose that the extra-diagonal elements of the matrix A_2 are the same as those of the matrix A_1. To verify this hypothesis of constancy in time of the spatial relations we used the Likelihood Ratio Test and on the basis of the results of this test, we put all the constrains of constancy in time of the spatial relations among the sites. In Table 1a and 1b we show the estimated coefficient matrices for ST-VAR(2) wrote as

$$y_t = \alpha + C_0 x_t + \sum_{k=1}^{2} A_k y_{t-k} + u_t$$

where C_0 is the coefficient matrix of the exogenous variable.

In matrix A_2 we reported in bold the parameters which remain constant between lag 1 and lag 2. As we can see the number of parameters to be estimated is reduced and the model fit well the data ($R^2 = 0.77$). To take into account the effect that the phenomenon measured on the whole network at time t has on a single site at the same time, we considered also the simultaneous observations of solar radiation. Hence we used the model ST-GVAR(2) in the form

$$y_t = \alpha + C_0 x_t + W_0 y_t + \sum_{k=1}^{2} A_k y_{t-k} + u_t$$

where the original series are not differentiated supposing that the simultaneous observations could underline the long term trend effect. The results of the Likelihood Ratio Test underlined that, if it is still possible to consider valid the hypothesis of constancy of the relations from lag 1 to lag 2, it is not convenient to constrain to this hypothesis the simultaneous coefficients. In Table 2a, 2b and 2c we show the estimated coefficient matrices obtained maximazing the log-likelihood function.

A_0	01	02	03	04	05	06	07	08	09	10	11	12	13	14	15
01	1	0.54	0.82	0.59	0.69	0.23									0.33
02	0.74	1	0.81	0.48	0.71	0.56	0.31	0.46						0.18	0.64
03	0.52	0.63	1	0.14	0.33	0.49	0.28	0.14						0.39	0.53
04	0.84	0.79	0.72	1	0.61	0.54	0.70			0.15				0.44	0.41
05	0.33	0.25	0.49	0.65	1	0.69	0.74	0.21	0.41	0.12				0.38	0.12
06				0.18	0.42	1	0.53	0.86	0.74	0.59					
07						0.89	1	0.81	0.52	0.62					
08								1	0.79						
09								0.83	1		0.73				
10										1	0.64	0.58			
11										0.75	1	0.59			
12											0.48	1			
13											0.71	0.75	1		
14							0.11	0.46	0.42	0.54	0.58	0.22		1	
15				0.25	0.36	0.78	0.65				0.69	0.52			1

Table 2a

A_1	01	02	03	04	05	06	07	08	09	10	11	12	13	14	15
01	0.28	0.12	0.31	0.57	0.67	0.11	0.25								
02	0.18	0.31		0.32	0.43	0.38	0.19	0.11							0.28
03	0.23	0.26	0.44			0.16	0.12	0.09	0.10					0.13	
04				0.13		0.23	0.61	0.52	-0.32	0.27	0.09				
05					0.81	0.29	0.66	0.56	0.29	0.31	0.11				
06						0.63	0.33	0.73	0.41	0.64	0.37				
07							0.29	0.59	0.61	0.72	0.62				
08								0.52	0.34		0.19				
09									0.65		0.23				
10											0.32	0.47	0.36		
11											0.15	0.48			
12											0.41	0.18			
13								0.13	0.11	0.55	0.68	0.64	0.27		
14						0.58		0.22	0.25	0.79	-0.27	0.37	0.29	0.23	
15				0.31	0.33	-0.24	-0.15				0.28	0.23		0.68	0.73

Table 2b

A_2	01	02	03	04	05	06	07	08	09	10	11	12	13	14	15
01	0.09			0.57	0.67	0.09	0.14								
02		0.14		0.39	0.43	0.38	0.19	0.11							
03	0.23	0.26	0.31			0.02	0.12	0.09	0.10						
04				0.02		0.23	0.61	0.52	-0.32	0.27	0.05	0.02			
05					0.12	0.29	0.66	0.56	0.29	0.31	0.07	0.06			
06					0.08	0.41	0.33	0.73	0.41	0.32					
07							0.07	0.59	0.61	0.51	0.58				
08							0.11	0.34	0.06	0.19					
09								0.35	0.05	0.23					
10										0.18	0.47	0.36			
11										0.01	0.06	0.48			
12											0.01	0.21			
13										0.55	0.68	0.64	0.14		
14					0.58		0.22	0.25	0.63	0.25	0.37	0.29	0.08		
15				0.31	0.33	0.09				0.28	0.23			0.47	0.52

Table 2c

Again (Table 2a) in matrix A_2 we reported in bold numbers the parameters which remain constant between lag 1 and lag 2. Also in this case the number of parameters to be estimated is reduced and the fitting to the data is improved ($R^2 = 0.85$). It must be noted that at lag 2 there are spatial effect among farer sites that were not at lag 1 as those among sites $4 - 5$ and sites $11 - 12$ as shown in matrix A_2.

5 Conclusions

In this work we presented two models - ST-VAR(K) and ST-GVAR(K) that are very flexible and appropriate to understand the directional effects in the analysis of meteorological phenomena. However, to use this models we need a priori knowledge on the spatio-temporal structure of the phenomenon under study. To face this problem, in our application we used the results of the cluster analysis as well as information about the movements of the clouds on the target area and their constancy over time. It is worth to note that the estimated spatio-temporal coefficients of the two models are in accordance with the main movements of clouds in the Mediterranean Basin. In particular they capture the effects of the main movements of clouds in the NW - SE direction as those from Tuscany Archipelago and Sardinia to the south of Italy. This fact is evident looking at the matrices of spatio-temporal coefficients where, after ordering the meteorological sites from the north to the south, we can see that almost all the under-diagonal elements are zero. Moreover, the models proposed point out that the spatial effects may change as a function of the temporal lag considered; as noted in our application, it is not possible to hold the constancy constrain for the relations among all the sites and, in particular, using generalized model we can see that at lag 2 there are spatial effects among farther sites. As future works, we are trying to generalize the models proposed to make them independent from a priori knowledge of the spatio-temporal structure of the phenomenon under study. This could be done defining classes of models for different spatio-temporal structures through partial spatio-temporal autocorrelation functions. Moreover, it would be possible to consider many different climatic areas simultaneously in order to analyze relations among them.. This would imply putting different types of constrains in the models and hence building mixed coefficient matrices.

References

DEUTSCH S.J., PFEIFER P.E. (1980): Three Stage Iterative Procedure for Space-Time Modeling. *Technometrics, vol.22, n 1.*

DEUTSCH S.J., PFEIFER P.E. (1981): Space-Time ARMA Modeling With Contemporaneously Correlated Innovations. *Technometrics, vol.23, n 4.*

LUTKEPOL H. (1991): *Introduction to Multiple Time Series Analysis.* Springer-Verlag, Berlin.

MAGNUS J.R., NEUDECKER H. (1998): *Matrix Differential Calculus with Applications in Statistics and Econometrics.* J. Wiley & Sons.

NACCARATO A. (2001): Uno studio sulla diffusione di fenomeni meteorologici mediante particolari modelli spazio-temporali, *Working Paper n 22, Dipartimento di Economia, Universit degli Studi Roma Tre.*

TERZI S. (1995): Maximum Likelihood Estimation of a Generalised STAR (p; lp) Model. *Journal of The Italian Statistical Society, vol.4, n3.*

Analysis of Spatial Covariance Structure for Environmental Data

Aldo Lamberti[1] and Eugenia Nissi[2]

[1] ISTAT - Roma, Italy
aldo.lamberti@istat.it
[2] Dipartimento di Metodi Quantitativi e Teoria Economica
Università G. d'Annunzio Chieti, Italy
nissi@dmqte.unich.it

Abstract. Formulation and evaluation of environmental policy depend upon a general class of latent variable models known as multivariate receptor models. Estimation of the number of pollution sources, the source composition profiles and the source contributions are the main interests in multivariate receptor modelling. Different approaches have been proposed in the literature when the number of sources is unknown (explorative factorial analysis) and when the number and type of sources are known (regression models). In this paper we propose a flexible approach on the use of multivariate receptor models that takes into account the extra variability due to the spatial dependence shown by the data. The method proposed is applied to Lombardia air pollution data.

1 Introduction

Interest around the identification of main pollution sources and their compositions needed to implement air pollution control programs has increased in the past decade. Observing the quantity of various pollutants emitted from all potential sources is virtually impossible. For this reason multivariate receptor models are used to analyze concentrations of airborne gases or particles measured over time in order to gain insight about the unobserved pollution sources. When the number and the composition of the sources are unknown, factor analytic approaches have been employed in order to identify pollution sources. As in the factor analysis models the choice of the number of sources (factors) to be used in receptor models is pivotal. The number of sources is often chosen using ad- hoc methods suggested in the literature. Park, Henry and Spiegelman (1999) provide a review with discussion of several of these methods. Once a model with k sources has been fitted, interest often lies in describing the composition of each pollution source and the amount of pollution emitted from each of them. To make sound decisions from the data, it is necessary to make statistical inference about the fitted model; however statistical tools for such data have not received much attention in the literature. Pollution data collected over time and/or space often exhibit dependence which needs to be accounted for in the procedures for inference on model parameters. In this paper we present a flexible approach to multivariate receptor models that take into account the spatial dependence exhibited by the data and we show the usefulness of the procedure using air pollution data from Lombardia area.The paper is organized as follow: in Section 2 we restate the model from a statistical point of view, Section 3 contains the methodological issues related to spatial covariance estimation, in Section 4 we present an application of the proposed model to air pollution data and in Section 5 some concluding remarks and some possible future developments.

2 The model

The basic multivariate receptor model used in the literature can be written as follow:

$$\mathbf{y}_t = \Lambda \mathbf{f}_t + \mathbf{e}_t \qquad t = 1, \ldots, M \tag{1}$$

where $\mathbf{y}_t$ is a p vector of concentrations of ambient particles observed at time t, Λ is a $p \times k$ matrix of non-negative source compositions (source profile matrix) and $\mathbf{f}_t$ is a k-vector of non-negative pollution source contributions. Two different approaches have been used in the literature. When the number and nature of the pollution sources are known (this means that Λ is known), the pollution source contributions can be estimated using regression or measurement error models. Instead when all or some of the elements of the matrix Λ are not known, it is possible to estimate the pollution source contributions using linear factor analysis models. The use of factor analytic techniques requires additional assumptions on the model. The unknown number of sources (factors) k, is the first obstacle because Λ and $\mathbf{f}$ depend on k in the model (1). Secondly, the parameters in model (1) are not uniquely defined, even under the assumption that k is known. This means that there are other parameterizations that produce the same data. This is called nonidentifiability in latent variable models and additional restrictions on the parameters are required to remove it. Park et al. (2001) discussed a wide range of identifiability conditions for multivariate receptor models when the number of sources k is assumed to be known. In a receptor modeling feasibility study Javitz, Watson, Guertin and Muller (1988) expressed the need for future development of a physically meaningful hybrid model which could be used with only partial source composition information and pointed out the importance of estimates of uncertainties associated with the model which are necessary for inference. The use of a flexible latent variable model allows the researcher to incorporate physical constrains, past data or other subject matter knowledge in the model and guarantees valid model fits using only limited information about the relationship between the observed ambient species and the pollution sources. The main difference between multivariate receptor models used in the literature and linear factor analysis models is that the observations in a pollution data set are rarely if ever independent. Multivariate receptor models, in fact, are used to model data that exhibit temporal and/or spatial dependence. Several potential hazards arise when factor analysis ignores dependence structure, most of them related to invalidity of inferential techniques. In this paper we make the assumption of temporal stationarity because of the lack of auxiliary variables such as meteorological ones and hence we focus on spatial dependence.

3 Spatial covariance estimation

We need some additional notation in order to formulate the general problem of spatial covariance estimation for multivariate space-time data. Let

$$\mathbf{Y} = \{\mathbf{Y}(\mathbf{s},\mathbf{t}), \mathbf{s} \in \Re^2, \mathbf{t} \in \Re_+\} \tag{2}$$

be a multivariate spatio-temporal process with

$$\mathbf{Y}(\mathbf{s},\mathbf{t}) = (\mathbf{Y}^1(\mathbf{s},\mathbf{t}), ..., \mathbf{Y}^q(\mathbf{s},\mathbf{t}))^T \tag{3}$$

We assume that $\mathbf{Y}$ can be observed at a collection of sites $\mathbf{S} = (\mathbf{s}_1,..., \mathbf{s}_n)$ and for a collection of times $\mathbf{T} = (\mathbf{t}_1,..., \mathbf{t}_M)$ and write $\mathbf{y}_i$ for an observed realization of $\mathbf{Y}$. If $\mathbf{Y}$ is temporally ergodic we can define the $q \times q$ matrix valued spatial covariance function of $\mathbf{Y}$ as

$$\mathbf{R}_Y(\mathbf{s},\mathbf{u}) = [Cov(Y^i(\mathbf{s},\mathbf{t}), Y^j(\mathbf{u},\mathbf{t})]_{1 \le i,j \le q} \tag{4}$$

and we can estimate spatial covariance between pairs of monitored sites by averaging over time. With spatial trend estimated by site means , a spatial covariance matrix $\mathbf{\Gamma}$ can be estimated as:

$$\mathbf{\Gamma} = \frac{1}{M} \sum_{i=1}^{M} (\mathbf{y}_i - \bar{\mathbf{y}})(\mathbf{y}_i - \bar{\mathbf{y}})^T \tag{5}$$

where $\bar{\mathbf{y}}$ is the spatial mean vector. Given an estimate of $\mathbf{\Gamma}$, it is important in many spatial modelling problem to estimate valid (non-negative definite) covariance function for $\mathbf{Y}$ based on the information in $\mathbf{\Gamma}$. Following the method suggested by Nott and Dunsmuir (1998), one way to achieve this goal is by reproducing $\mathbf{\Gamma}$ at monitored sites and then describing conditional behaviour given monitoring sites values by a stationary process or collection of a stationary processes. To describe the idea of Nott and Dunsmuir, we need some more notation. Let $\{W(\mathbf{s}); \mathbf{s} \in \Re^d\}$ be a multivariate zero mean, stationary Gaussian process with q components,

$$W(\mathbf{s}) = (W^1(\mathbf{s}) ..., W^q(\mathbf{s}))^T \tag{6}$$

with covariance function R(h). Let W denote the vector

$$\mathbf{W} = (W^1(\mathbf{s}_1), ..., W^1(\mathbf{s}_n), W^q(\mathbf{s}1), ..., W^q(\mathbf{s}_n))^T \tag{7}$$

and write $\mathbf{C}$ for the covariance matrix of $\mathbf{W}$. Also write the $nq \times q$ cross-covariance matrix between $\mathbf{W}$ and as W (s) as

$$\mathbf{c(s)} = (\mathrm{Cov}(W^1(\mathbf{s}_1), W^1(\mathbf{s}), ..., \mathrm{Cov}(W^q(\mathbf{s}_1), ..., W^q(\mathbf{s}),) \tag{8}$$

If we observe values of the process at the monitored sites , $\mathbf{W=w}$ say, then for an arbitrary collection of sites we can write down the joint distribution of W at these sites.These are the finite dimensional distributions of a random field which describes the conditional behaviour of $W(.)$ given $\mathbf{W=w}$, and such a random field has a representation:

$$\mathbf{c(s)}^T \mathbf{C}^{-1} \mathbf{w} + \delta(\mathbf{s}) \tag{9}$$

where $\delta((\mathbf{s})$ is a zero mean Gaussian process with covariance function:

$$R_\delta(\mathbf{s}, \mathbf{u}) = R(\mathbf{u} - \mathbf{s}) - \mathbf{c(s)}^T \mathbf{C}^{-1} \mathbf{c(u)} \tag{10}$$

To obtain a valid non-negative definite covariance function, which reproduces the empirical spatial covariance matrix Γ at the monitored sites, is to replace w in the above representation by a random vector $\mathbf{W}^*$ which has zero mean and covariance matrix Γ independent of $\delta(\mathbf{s})$. Intuitively we are constructing a process with covariance matrix Γ at the monitored sites but with the conditional distribution given values at monitored sites the same as those of the stationary random field $W(\mathbf{s})$. It must be noted that the covariance function of $W(\mathbf{s})$ is not the model used for the unconditional covariance but is part of a construction to obtain valid, non-negative definite non -stationary spatial covariance function model for $\mathbf{Y}$:

$$\mathrm{Cov}(Y(\mathbf{s}, \mathbf{t}), Y(\mathbf{u}, \mathbf{t})) = R(\mathbf{u} - \mathbf{s}) - \mathbf{c(s)}^T \mathbf{C}^{-1}(\Gamma - \mathbf{C})\mathbf{C}^{-1}\mathbf{c(u)} \tag{11}$$

This covariance function reproduces Γ (that is, evaluating (10) at $(\mathbf{s}, \mathbf{u})$) = (s_i, s_j) gives Γ_{ij})) since $\mathbf{c}(s_i)$ is simply the i-th column of $\mathbf{C}$. Hence one simple way of constructing a non -negative definite estimate of spatial covariance is to fit a stationary model to Γ and to then compute (10) with $R(\mathbf{u}, \mathbf{s})$, $\mathbf{C}$, $\mathbf{c(s)}$ and $\mathbf{c(u)}$ evaluated according to the fitted stationary process.

4 A case study of air pollution

We apply the model to air pollution data in the Milano- Bergamo districts. In particular we consider the daily observation of CO, NOX, NO2 and SO2 obtained from 23 monitoring sites for two months, june and december 2000,

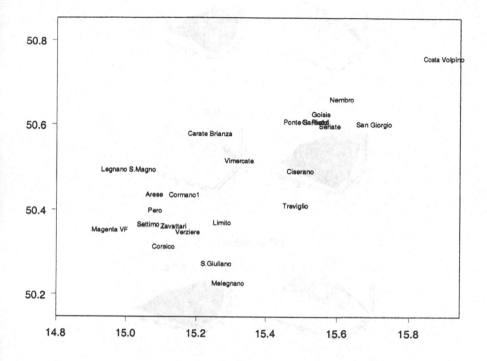

Fig. 1. Monitoring sites

(Figure 1). We consider as reference days the 1st of june and the 15th of december and the plots of the original data are shown in Figure 2.

First of all analyzing the time series of pollutants for each sites, we verified the temporal stationarity of the data. After data reconstruction and spatial trend analysis we estimate the spatial covariance matrix using the above proposed method. For the analysis we assume only limited information on the source profile matrix **Λ** that yields an identified model. From past studies we know that there are three major pollution sources for this type of data: vehicle exhaust, industrial emissions and non-industrial emissions, so we applied the model with k=3 sources (factors) for each variable. As we can see in Table 1 the analysis carried out with k=3 sources is quite satisfying, with cumulative variance explained ranging from 81.5 % (NOX) to 96.5 % (SO2) for the 1st of june and 97,5 %(NO2) to 98,5 % (NOX) for the 15th of december.

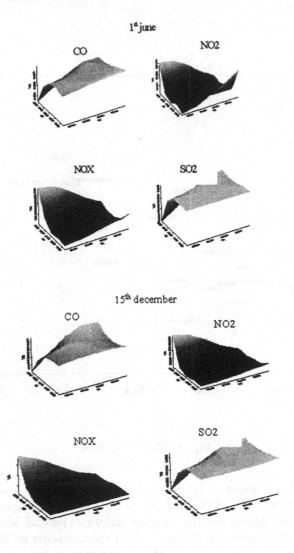

Fig. 2. Plot of the original data

Then, we can say that the model with k=3 sources is appropriate to describe the data we used for the analysis and this is in accordance with past information about this kind of data. Carrying out the analysis without taking into account the dependence exhibited by the data could be very misleading.

	1 giugno			15 dicembre		
	Factor1	Factor2	Factor3	Factor1	Factor2	Factor3
NO	0.4953621	0.9214263	0.9478569	0.5071043	0.9690619	0.9791124
CO	0.4629952	0.8399392	0.8976428	0.5061407	0.9632459	0.9752146
NOX	0.3848596	0.7121577	0.8150148	0.5079809	0.9793872	0.9859020
SO2	0.5028432	0.9478037	0.9650166	0.5071043	0.9690619	0.9791124

Table 1. Importance of factor - Cumulative Variance

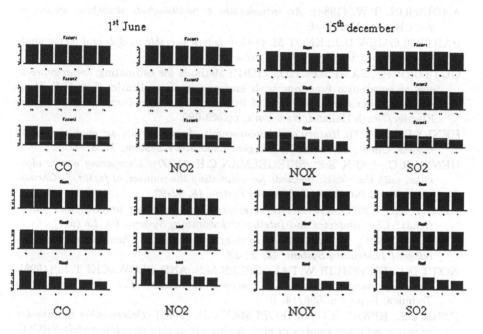

Fig. 3. Plot of factors for each variable

5 Conclusions

Identification of major pollution sources and their contributions can be assessed by a class of latent variable models known as multivariate receptor models. Air quality data exhibit temporal and/or spatial dependence that is often ignored at the expense of valid inference. In this paper we incorporate dependence structure shown by the data estimating a non-stationary spatial covariance matrix for multivariate space-time data where a given spatial covariance matrix is reproduced at a collection of monitored sites and conditional behaviour, given monitored site values, is described by a stationary process. In this way it is possible to fit a multivariate receptor model that is uniquely identified and the model parameter estimates have meaningful interpretation. A possible extension for future works is to introduce meteorological variables in the model that play an important role in the explanation of the air pollution. Moreover it would be interesting to compare the results obtained using other methods for the estimation of the spatial covariance matrix.

References

ANDERSON, T.W. (1984): *An introduction to multivariate statistical analysis& John Wiley , New York.*

BARTHOLOMEW D.J., KNOT M. (1999): *Latent variable models and factor analysis & Oxford University Press, New York.*

GUTTORP P. , SAMPSON P.D.: (1994): Methods for estimating heterogeneous spatial covariance functions with environmental applications",in G.P. Patil and C.R. Rao eds. Handbook of Statistics XII: : *Environmental Statistics*, Elsevier/North Holland, New York, pp.663-690

HENRY R.C. (1997): *History and fundamentals of multivariate air quality receptor models.* Chemometrics and Intelligent Laboratory System, 37, 37-42.

HENRY R.C., PARK E.S., SPIEGELMAN C.H. (1999): *Comparing a new algorithm with the classic methods for estimating the number of factors" ,Chemometrics and Intelligent Laboratory System 48, 91-97.*

HENRY R.C. (2002):*Multivariate receptor models: current practice and future trends" Chemometrics and Intelligent Laboratory System, 60, 43-48.*

HOPKE L. (1991): *An introduction to receptor modelling" Chemometrics and Intelligent Laboratory System, 10, 21-43.*

NOTT D.J., DUNSMUIR W.T.M. , SPEER M.S. AND GLOWACKI T.J.: (1998): *Non-Stationary Multivariate Covariance Estimation For Monitoring Data* Technical Report n. S98/14.

PARK E.S., HENRY R.C., SPIEGELMAN C.H. (1999): *Determining the number of major pollution sources in multivariate air quality receptor models* NRCSE, TSR No.43 .

PARK E.S. GUTTORP P., HENRY R.C. (2000): *Multivariate receptor modelling for temporal correlated data by using MCMC* NRCSE, TRS No. 34 .

PARK E.S., HENRY R.C., SPIEGELMAN C.H. (2000): *Estimating the number of factors to include in a high-dimensional multivariate bilinear model* Communications in Statistics, B 29, 723-746 .

PARK E.S., OH M.S., GUTTORP P. (2002): *Multivariate receptor models and model uncertainty* Chemometrics and Intelligent Laboratory System, 60, 49-67.

SAMPSON P.D., GUTTORP P. (1992): *Nonparametric estimation of nonstationary spatial covariance structure* JASA, 87, 108-119.

Bayesian Clustering of Gene Expression Dynamics: An Application

Sara Lodi[1], Paola Sebastiani[2], Daniela Cocchi[3], and Marco Ramoni[4]

[1] Dipartimento di Scienze Statistiche,
Università di Bologna, Italy
saralodi@yahoo.com
[2] Department of Biostatistics,
Boston University, MA
sebas@bu.edu
[3] Dipartimento di Scienze Statistiche,
Università di Bologna, Italy
cocchi@stat.unibo.it
[4] Children Hospital Informatics Program,
Harvard Medical School, MA
marco_ramoni@harvard.edu

Abstract. This paper describes an application of Caged (Cluster Analysis of Gene Expression Dynamics) to a data set of gene expression temporal profiles from Saccaromicys Cerevisiae. The goal of the analysis is to identify groups of genes with similar temporal patterns of expression during the cell cycle. We show that Caged groups gene expression temporal profiles into meaningful clusters and identifies genes with a putative role in the cell cycle.

1 Introduction

Several applications of genome-wide clustering methods focus on the temporal profiling of gene expression patterns measured in temporal experiments. Temporal profiling offers the possibility of observing the cellular mechanisms in action and tries to break down the genome into sets of genes involved in the same or related processes. However, standard clustering methods, such as the hierarchical clustering method of Eisen et al. (1998) or the self organizing maps (Tamayo et al.,1999), analyse the data generated from these experiments under the assumption that the observations for each gene are independent and identically distributed (iid). Gene expression data collected from temporal experiments are the realizations of a time series, where each observation may depend on prior ones (Box and Jenkins,1976; West and Harrison, 1977). However, standard similarity measures currently used for clustering gene expression data, such as correlation or Euclidean distance, are invariant with respect to the order of observations: if the temporal order of a pair of series is permuted, their correlation or Euclidean distance will not change.

A second critical problem of clustering approaches to gene expression data is the arbitrary nature of the partitioning process. This operation is often done by visual inspection, by searching for groups of genes with similar expression patterns. Permutation tests are sometimes used to validate the partitions found by this procedure (Eisen et al. 1998), and a bootstrap-based validation technique is presented in Kerr and Churchill (2001). The gap statistic of Tibshirani et al. (2001) is also used to find the optimal number of groups in the data.

CAGED (Cluster Analysis of Gene Expression Dynamics) is a model based, Bayesian clustering procedure developed by Ramoni et al. (2002) to cluster gene expression profiles measured with microarrays in temporal experiments. Contrary to popular clustering methods, CAGED takes into account explicitly the fact that expression profiles in temporal experiments may be serially correlated and uses a model-based, Bayesian procedure to identify the best grouping of the gene expression data in an automated way. An important property of CAGED is that it automatically identifies the number of clusters and partitions the gene expression time series in different groups on the basis of the principled measure of the posterior probability of the clustering model. In this way, CAGED allows the investigator to assess whether the experimental data convey enough evidence to support the conclusion that the pattern of a set of genes is significantly different from the pattern of another set of genes. This feature is particularly important because decades of cognitive science research have shown that the human eye tends to overfit observations by selectively discounting variance and "seeing" patterns in randomness (Kahneman et al. 1982). By contrast, a recognized advantage of a Bayesian approach to model selection is the ability to automatically constrain model complexity and to provide appropriate measures of uncertainty.

We apply CAGED to cluster a data set of gene expression temporal profiles from Saccaromicys Cerevisiae. The goal of the analysis is to detect those genes whose transcript levels vary periodically within the cell cycle. Cell cycle is a very complex ordered set of events that consists of several phases culminating in cell growth and division into daughter cells (*mitosis*). During this period, the cell is constantly synthesizing RNA, producing protein and growing in size. In the *G1* phase, the cell increases in size, produces RNA and synthesizes proteins. The next step is the synthesis phase S in which DNA replication occurs. This phase is followed by the *G2* phase in which the cell continues to grow and to produce new proteins, and by the mitosis (*M* phase). Many genes are involved in DNA synthesis, budding and cytokinesis that occur only once per cell cycle. In addition, many of these genes are also involved in controlling the cell cycle itself. For this reason, the expression levels of the genes that have a regulatory role in cell cycles are expected to show periodical behaviors across time and to present at least one peak during the phase in which they are activated. The data were originally analyzed by Spellman et al., (1988), using Fourier models, and the authors identified several clusters by visual inspections. We show that Caged finds automatically clusters of gene expression temporal profiles that exhibit periodic behavior.

The next section gives a brief description of the model based clustering procedure that is implemented in CAGED. Section 3 provides details of the analysis and conclusions and suggestions for further work are in Section 4.

2 Caged

The clustering method implemented in CAGED is based on a different concept of similarity for time series: two time series are similar when they are generated by the same stochastic process. Therefore, the components of CAGED are a model describing the dynamics of gene expression temporal profiles, a metric to decide when two gene expression temporal profiles are generated by the same stochastic process, and a search procedure to efficiently explore the space of possible clustering models.

CAGED models gene expression temporal profiles by autoregressive equations (West and Harrison, 1977). Let $S_j = \{x_{j1}, \ldots, x_{jt}, \ldots, x_{jn}\}$ denote a stationary time series. An autoregressive model of order p, say $AR(p)$, for the time series can be described in matrix form as $x_j = X_j \beta_j + \epsilon_j$, where x_j is the vector $(x_{j(p+1)}, \ldots, x_{jn})^T$, X_j is the $(n - p) \times (p + 1)$ regression matrix whose tth row is $(1, x_{j(t-1)}, \ldots, x_{j(t-p)})$ for $t > p$, β_j is the vector of autoregressive coefficients and ϵ_j the vector of uncorrelated errors that are assumed normally distributed with expected value $E(\epsilon_{jt}) = 0$ and precision τ_j, for any time point t. Given the data, the model parameters can be estimated using standard Bayesian procedures, and details are in Ramoni et al. (2002).

To select the set of clusters, CAGED uses a novel model-based Bayesian clustering procedure. A set of clusters $C_1, \ldots, C_c$, each consisting of m_k time series, is represented as a model M_c. The time series assigned to each cluster are treated as independent realizations of the dynamic process represented by the cluster, which is described by an autoregressive equation. The posterior probability of the model M_c is computed by Bayes theorem as $P(M_c|y) \propto P(M_c) f(x|M_c)$ where $P(M_c)$ is the prior probability of M_c and $f(x|M_c)$ is the marginal likelihood. Assuming independent uniform prior distributions on the model parameters and a symmetric Dirichlet distribution on the cluster probability p_k, the marginal likelihood of each cluster model M_c can be easily computed in closed form by solving the integral: $f(x|M_c) = \int f(x|\theta_c) f(\theta_c) d\theta_c$. In this equation, θ_c is the vector of parameters that describe the likelihood function, conditional on a clustering model M_c, and $f(\theta_c)$ is the prior density. In this way, each clustering model has an explicit probabilistic score and the model with maximum score can be found. In practice, we assume that each clustering model has the same prior probability so that the marginal likelihood $f(x|M_c)$ is the scoring metric of the clustering model M_c.

As the number of clustering models grows exponentially with the number of time series, CAGED uses an agglomerative search strategy, which iteratively merges time series into clusters. The procedure starts by assuming that each of the m gene expression time series is generated by a different process. Thus, the initial model M_m consists of m clusters, one for each time series, with score $f(x|M_m)$. The next step is the computation of the marginal likelihood of the $m(m-1)$ models in which two of the m profiles are merged into one cluster, so that each of these models consists of $m-1$ clusters. The model M_{m-1} with maximal marginal likelihood is chosen and the merging is rejected if $f(x|M_m) \geq f(x|M_{m-1})$ and the procedure stops. If $f(x|M_m) < f(x|M_{m-1})$ the merging is accepted, a cluster C_k merging the two time series is created, and the procedure is repeated on the new set of $m-1$ time series that consist of the remaining $m-2$ time series and the cluster profile. Although the agglomerative strategy makes the search process feasible, the computational effort can be extremely demanding when the number of time series is large. To further reduce this effort, we use a heuristic strategy based on a measure of similarity between time series.

The intuition behind this strategy is that the merging of two similar time series has better chances of increasing the marginal likelihood. The heuristic search starts by computing the $m(m-1)$ pair-wise similarity measures of the time series and selects the model M_{m-1} in which the two closest time series are merged into one cluster. If the merging increases the marginal likelihood, the two time series are merged into a single cluster, a profile of this cluster is computed by averaging the two observed time series, and the procedure is repeated on the new set of $m-1$ time series. If this merging is rejected, the procedure is repeated on the two time series with second highest similarity until an acceptable merging is found. If no acceptable merging is found, the procedure stops. Note that the clustering procedure is actually performed on the posterior probability of the model and the similarity measure is only used to increase the speed of the search process and to limit the risk of falling into local maxima. Similarity measures implemented in CAGED are Euclidean distance, correlation and cross correlation. Empirical evaluations have shown that the accuracy loss of this heuristics is limited (Sebastiani and Ramoni, 2001; Sebastiani et al., 2003). Compared to other clustering methods such as hierarchical clustering or self organizing maps, CAGED identifies the set of clusters with maximum posterior probability without requiring any prior input about the number of clusters and avoids the risk of overfitting.

Standard statistical diagnostics are used as independent assessment measures of the cluster model found by the heuristic search. Once the procedure terminates, the coefficients β_k of the AR(p) model associated with each cluster C_k are estimated by Bayesian Least Squares, while $\hat{\sigma}_k^2 = RSS_k/(n_k - p)$ is the estimate of the within-cluster variance and RSS_k is the within cluster residual sum of squares. The parameter estimates can be used to compute the fitted values $\hat{x}_{ik}$, for the series in each cluster, from which we compute the residuals $x_{ik} - \hat{x}_{ik}$. If AR(p) models provide an accurate approximation of the processes generating the time series, the standardized residuals should behave like a random sample from a standard normal distribution. A normal proba-

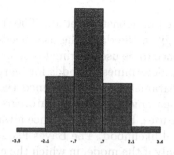

Fig. 1. Histogram of the standardized residuals for the time series assigned to Cluster 1.

bility plot, or the residual histogram per cluster, can be used to assess normality. Departures from normality cast doubt on the autoregressive assumption, so that some data transformation, such as a logarithmic transformation, may be needed. Plots of the fitted values versus the observed values and of the fitted values versus the standardized residuals in each cluster provide further diagnostics. To choose the best autoregressive order, we repeat the clustering for different autoregressive orders, $p = 0, 1, \ldots, w$ for some preset w, and compute a goodness-of-fit score defined as $s = cq + \sum n_k \log(n_k - q) - \sum n_k \log(\text{RSS}_k)$, where c is the number of clusters, n_k the total number of time points in cluster C_k. We introduced this score in Ramoni et al. (2002) to generalize the well known AIC goodness-of-fit criterion of Akaike (1973) to a set of autoregressive models. We choose the autoregressive order that maximizes the goodness of fit score.

3 Application

3.1 Materials

The data we analyze are expression levels of genes from the budding yeast Saccaromyces Cerevisiae that were collected on spotted cDNA microarrays. Data were drawn from time courses during the cell cycle after synchronization by alpha factor arrest in 18 time points. The original data set is available at http://genome-www.stanford.edu/Saccharomyces and consists of expression profiles of 6178 genes. About 1500 expression profiles had missing data and, because the shortness of time series would make traditional imputation methods not very reliable, those gene expression profiles were disregarded. To reduce the noise, we excluded those time series in which the ratio between the minimum and maximum expression level did not exceed 2. This filter is justified by the fact that significant biological events are characterized by at least a 2-fold change, see Sebastiani et al., (2003) for a discussion and further references. With this filter we selected 1574 temporal profiles.

3.2 Methods

We analyzed the data set with CAGED. The software is freely available and can be downloaded from http://www.genomethods.org/caged. Details about the software are described in Sebastiani et al., (2003). For selecting the most probable cluster model given the data, the user needs to specify the autoregressive order, the distance to be used during the heuristic search, a threshold on the Bayes factor that determines the odds for merging similar time series, and some prior hyper-parameters. We performed the analysis several times varying both the hyper-parameters and the autoregressive order. Among the available similarity measures, Euclidean distance always lead to cluster models with greater marginal likelihood. The Bayes Factor was set to 10 so that an aggregation occurs only if the model in which the clusters are merged is 10 times more probable than the model in which they are separated. This choice is recommended in Kass and Raftery (1995) to force the model selection toward significant dependencies. We also run some sensitivity analysis to prior settings that lead to set the prior precision to 10. Once the parameters were chosen, the last step was the choice of the autoregressive order by comparing the goodness of fit of clustering models induced by different autoregressive orders. The model that best fitted the data was an autoregressive model of order 2. Therefore, the method found a temporal dependency in the data: each observation of a gene expression time series depends on its two immediate predecessors. This model fits the data better than the autoregressive model of order 0, in which observations are assumed to be marginally independent. Goodness of fit statistics confirm that autoregressive models of order 2 provide a good fit. As an example, Figure 1 shows the standardized residuals for the cluster of time series in Figure 2 (Cluster 1 in the top-left panel). The symmetry confirms that the model assumptions are reasonable.

3.3 Results

CAGED merged the 1574 genes time series into 13 distinct clusters and by querying the GeneOntology database (http://www.geneontology.org/), genes assigned to each cluster were annotated by their biological processes. Five of the thirteen clusters have periodical profiles, while four of the clusters have at least one spike of expression during the cell cycle, and two clusters group genes that are systematically upregulated or downregulated during the cell cycle. Two clusters group genes that do not appear to have cell-cycle related change of expression. Among the clusters found by the algorithm, particularly noteworthily are four clusters in which either a periodical trend is detected (Cluster 1 and 2 in Figure 2) or only one spike is detected (Cluster 3 and 4 in Figure 2). All genes belonging to these clusters are strongly cell cycle regulated. Cluster 1 contains 18 genes that spike at 7 and 70 minutes, so that one can conjecture that they are coregulated during the M/G1 transition of the cell cycle. Peak expressions occur in early G1 phase that consists of growth and preparation of chromosomes for replication. Most of the genes are involved in cell wall, which is laid out during the division of the cell. Five of the 18 genes have unknown functions, and the fact that they are merged into a cluster of genes involved with cell wall suggests that they may have the same function. Cluster 2 contains 66 genes that are characterized by two

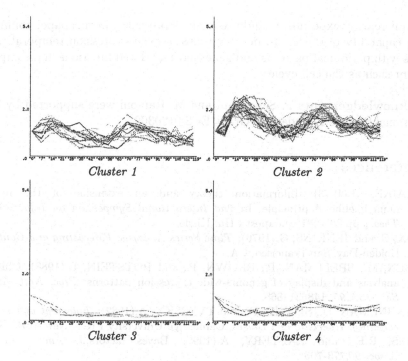

Fig. 2. Plot of the gene expression profiles assigned to significant clusters by CAGED.

spikes at time 21 minutes and 77 minutes and, because of the time shift, the conjecture is that these genes are involved in the S/G2 phase. A large proportion of these genes have DNA replication and repair functions, thus confirming the conjecture that the cluster groups genes involved in the S/G2 phase. The third cluster contains four genes that are systematically down regulated during the cell cycle. All genes have a role in cell fusion. The six genes assigned to Cluster 4 are down regulated during the first hour and then spike at about 70 minutes. The functions of the genes assigned to this clusters have already been associated with the cell cycle, and include cell fusion, cell cycle arrest, and completion of separation.

4 Conclusions

Several applications of genome-wide clustering methods focus on the temporal profiling of gene expression. The intuition behind this analytical approach is that genes showing a similar expression profile over time are acting together, because they belong to the same, or similar, functional categories. The novelty and strength of the clustering algorithm implemented in CAGED is that it takes into account the dynamic nature of gene expression data in temporal microarray experiments and the analysis presented in this paper confirms the capability of CAGED to detect groups of gene expression temporal profiles with periodical patterns and genes having related functions in a complex event such as the cell cycle.

Acknowledgements P. Sebastiani and M. Ramoni were supported by the National Science Foundation: Grant ECS-0120309.

References

AKAIKE, H.(1973): Information theory and an extension of the maximum likelihood principle. In *2nd International Symposium on Information Theory*,pp.267-281 Budapest , Hu. Kiado.

BOX, G. and JENKINS, G.(1976): *Time Series Analysis: Forecasting and Control*, Holden-Day, San Francisco, CA.

EISEN, M., SPELLMAN, P., BROWN, P., and BOTSTEIN, D.(1988): Cluster analysis and display of genome-wide expression patterns. *Proc. Natl. Acad. Sci. USA,95*, 1486314868.

KANHNEMAN, D., SLOVIC, P., and TVERSKY, A.(1982): *Judgment under Uncertainty: Hueristic and Biases*, Cambridge University Press, New York, NY.

KASS, R.E., and RAFTERY, A.(1995): Bayes factors.*J. Amer. Statist. Assoc.,90*,773-795

KERR, M.K., and CHURCHILL, G.A.(2001): Bootstrapping cluster analysis: Assessing the reliability of conclusions from microarray experiments. *Proc. Natl. Acad. Sci. USA,98*, 8961-8965.

RAMONI, M., SEBASTIANI, P., and KOHANE, I.(2002): Cluster analysis of gene expression dynamics. *Proc. Natl. Acad. Sci. USA,99(14)*, 9121-6.

SEBASTIANI, P., GUSSONI, E., KOHANE, I., and RAMONI, M. (2003): Statistical challenges in functional genomics (with discussion). *Statist. Sci.,18*, 33-70.

SEBASTIANI, P., and RAMONI, M. (2001): Common trends in european school populations. *Res. Offic. Statist.,4(1)*, 169-183.

SEBASTIANI, P., RAMONI, M., and KOHANE, I.S.(2003): Bayesian model-based clustering of gene expression dynamics.In *The Analysis of Microarray Data: Methods and Software,pp.409-427*. Springer, New York, NY.

SPELLMAN, P.T., SHERLOCK, G., ZHANG, M.Q., IYER, V.R., ANDERS, K., EISEN, M.B., BROWN, P.O., BOTSTEIN, D., and FUTCHER, B.(1998): Comprehensive identification of cell cycle-regulated genes of the yeast Saccharomyces cerevisiae by microarray hybridization. *Molec. Biol. Cell,9*, 3273-3297.

TAMAYO, P., SLONIM, D., MESIROV, J., ZHU, Q., KITAREEWAN, S., DMITROVSKY, E., LANDER, E.S., and GOLUB, T.R.(1999): Interpreting patterns of gene expression with self-organizing maps: Methods and application to hematopoietic differentiation. *Proc. Natl. Acad. Sci. USA,96*, 29072912.

TIBSHIRANI, R., WALTHER, G., and HASTIE., T. (2001): Estimating the number of clusters in a dataset via the Gap statistic. *J. Roy. Statist. Soc. B,63*, 411-423.

WEST, M. and HARRISON, J.(1997): *Bayesian Forecasting and Dynamic Models*. Springer, New York, NY.

A Hierarchical Mixture Model
for Gene Expression Data

Luisa Scaccia[1] and Francesco Bartolucci[2]

[1] Dipartimento di Scienze Statistiche,
Università degli Studi di Perugia, Italy
luisa@stat.unipg.it

[2] Istituto di Scienze Economiche,
Università di Urbino "Carlo Bo", Italy
Francesco.Bartolucci@uniurb.it

Abstract. We illustrate the use of a mixture of multivariate Normal distributions for clustering genes on the basis of Microarray data. We follow a hierarchical Bayesian approach and estimate the parameters of the mixture using Markov chain Monte Carlo (MCMC) techniques. The number of components (groups) is chosen on the basis of the Bayes factor, numerically evaluated using the Chib and Jelaizkov (2001) method. We also show how the proposed approach can be easily applied in recovering missing observations, which generally affect Microarray data sets. An application of the approach for clustering yeast genes according to their temporal profiles is illustrated.

1 Introduction

Microarray experiments consist in recording the expression levels of thousands of genes under a wide set of experimental conditions. The expression of a gene is defined as its transcript abundance, i.e. the frequency with which the gene is copied to induce, for example, the synthesis of a certain protein. One of the main aims of researchers is clustering genes according to similarities between their expression levels across conditions. A wide range of statistical methods (see Yeung et al. (2001) for a review) have been proposed for this purpose. Standard partitioning or hierarchical clustering algorithms have been successfully applied by a variety of authors (see, for instance, Spellman et al. (1998) and Tavazoie et al. (1999)) in order to identify interesting gene groups and characteristic expression patterns. However, the heuristic basis of these algorithms is generally considered unsatisfactory.

Microarray data are affected by several sources of error and often contain missing values. Outcomes of standard clustering algorithms can be very sensitive to anomalous observations and the way missing ones are imputed. A second generation of studies (see, for example, Brown et al. (2000) and Hastie et al. (2000)) sought further progress through more sophisticated and ad-hoc clustering strategies, employing resampling schemes, topology-constrained and/or supervised versions of partitioning algorithms, and "fuzzy" versions of partitioning algorithms that can perform particularly well in the absence of clear-cut "natural" clusters. Recently, an increasing interest has been devoted to the model-based approach in which the data are assumed to be generated from a finite mixture (Fraley and Raftery (1998)). The main advantage is represented by straightforward criteria for choosing the number of components (groups) and imputing missing observations.

In this paper we show how Bayesian hierarchical mixture models may be effectively used to cluster genes. As in Yeung et al. (2001), we assume that the components of the mixture have multivariate Normal distribution with possibly different shape, location and dimension. An important issue is the choice of the number of components. We use the Bayes factor (Kass and Raftery (1995)), numerically computed through the Chib and Jelaizkov (2001) approach, as a selection criterion. We also outline how our approach may be used to recover missing data, which are frequent in Microarray datasets. Details on the model are given in Section 2. In Section 3, we describe the Bayesian estimation of the parameters, while in Section 4 we illustrate the model selection problem. Finally, in Section 5, we present an application of the proposed approach to the analysis of a Microarray study performed to identify groups of yeast genes involved in the cell cycle regulation.

2 The model

Let S be the number of experimental conditions and $\mathbf{x} = \left(x_1 \cdots x_S\right)'$ be the vector of the corresponding expression levels for a gene. We assume that the distribution of such a vector is a mixture of Normal distributions, that is

$$\mathbf{x} \sim \sum_{k=1}^{K} \pi_k N(\boldsymbol{\mu}_k, \boldsymbol{\Sigma}_k)$$

where K is the number of components of the mixture, $\boldsymbol{\mu}_k$ is the mean of the k-th component, $\boldsymbol{\Sigma}_k$ its variance-covariance matrix and π_k its weight. In a Bayesian context, we also assume that:

- the number of components K is a priori unknown and uniformly distributed in the interval $[1; K_{\max}]$, where $K_{\max}$ is a suitable integer;
- the vector $\boldsymbol{\pi} = \left(\pi_1 \cdots \pi_K\right)'$ has Dirichlet distribution with parameters $\beta_1, \ldots, \beta_K$;
- the $\boldsymbol{\mu}_k$'s are independent and have Normal distribution $N(\boldsymbol{\nu}, \boldsymbol{\Omega})$;
- the $\boldsymbol{\Sigma}_k$'s are independent and have inverse Wishart distribution $IW(\boldsymbol{\Xi}, \upsilon)$ where $\boldsymbol{\Xi}$ is an $S \times S$ symmetric, positive definite scale matrix, and υ is a precision parameter;
- $\boldsymbol{\nu}, \boldsymbol{\Omega}, \boldsymbol{\Xi}$ and υ have noninformative improper prior (Jeffreys (1939)) with density $f(\boldsymbol{\nu}) = 1$, $f(\boldsymbol{\Omega}) = 1$, $f(\boldsymbol{\Xi}) = 1$ and $f(\upsilon) = 1$, $\forall \, \boldsymbol{\nu}, \boldsymbol{\Omega}, \boldsymbol{\Xi}$ and υ.

This setting gives rise to the hierarchical model presented in Figure 1, where $\boldsymbol{\mu}$ and $\boldsymbol{\Sigma}$ denote, respectively, $\boldsymbol{\mu}_1, \ldots, \boldsymbol{\mu}_K$ and $\boldsymbol{\Sigma}_1, \ldots, \boldsymbol{\Sigma}_K$. We follow the

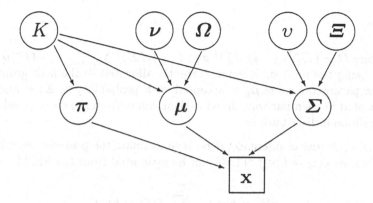

Fig. 1. Directed acyclic graph for the hierarchical mixture model.

usual convention that square boxes represent fixed or observed quantities and circles represent unknowns.

3 Bayesian estimation

3.1 Bayesian estimation without missing data

Let $\mathbf{X}$ be the $n \times S$ data matrix, where n is the number of genes. The complexity of the mixture model presented here requires MCMC methods to approximate the joint posterior distribution of the parameters. For computational reason, we introduce the latent allocation variables $\mathbf{z} = (z_1 \cdots z_n)$, where z_i indicates the component to which the i-th gene belongs; note that $p(z_i = k) = \pi_k$ a priori. Conditionally on $\mathbf{z}$, the observations $\mathbf{x}_i$'s are independent with conditional distribution $N(\boldsymbol{\mu}_{z_i}, \boldsymbol{\Sigma}_{z_i})$, given $\mathbf{z}, \boldsymbol{\mu}, \boldsymbol{\Sigma}$.

For a fixed number K of components, the sampler we consider performs the following operations for a suitable number of times, T, after allowing for a burn-in period:

- update ν, Ω, Ξ and υ, in turn, through separate Metropolis-Hastings steps. For example, to update ν we draw ν^* from an appropriate proposal distribution $q(\nu^*|\nu)$ and accept it as the new value of the parameter vector with probability

$$\alpha(\nu, \nu^*) = \min\left\{1, \frac{p(\mu|\nu^*, \Omega)q(\nu|\nu^*)}{p(\mu|\nu, \Omega)q(\nu^*|\nu)}\right\}.$$

  Ω, Ξ and υ are updated in a similar way.
- update $\boldsymbol{\mu}, \boldsymbol{\Sigma}, \boldsymbol{\pi}$ and $\mathbf{z}$, in turn, through separate Gibbs steps. For example, to update $\boldsymbol{\mu}$, we draw, independently for each k, a new value $\boldsymbol{\mu}_k^*$ from the full conditional distribution of $\boldsymbol{\mu}_k$ given all the other parameters:

$$\mu_k | \cdots \sim N\left(\tilde{\nu}, \tilde{\Omega}\right),$$

where $\tilde{\Omega} = (\Sigma_k^{-1} n_k + \Omega^{-1})^{-1}$ and $\tilde{\nu} = \tilde{\Omega}(\Sigma_k^{-1} \sum_{i:z_i=k} \mathbf{x}_i + \Omega^{-1}\nu)$, with n_k being the number of genes currently allocated to the k-th group. The new parameter value μ_k^* is accepted with probability 1. Σ, π and $\mathbf{z}$ are updated in a similar way, drawing their values from the corresponding full conditional distributions.

The main purpose of inference, here, is to estimate the posterior membership probabilities $p(z_i = k|\mathbf{x}_i)$. These can be estimated from the MCMC output as

$$\hat{p}(z_i = k|\mathbf{x}_i) = \sum_{t=1}^{T} \delta(z_i^{(t)} = k)/T$$

where $z_i^{(t)}$ is the value of z_i at sweep t and $\delta(\cdot)$ denotes the indicator function. Membership probabilities provide a *soft* or *fuzzy* partition in which genes may not be univocally assigned to one component. However, it is possible to derive a standard (hard) partition by assigning each gene to the component which maximizes the membership probability. By averaging over the sweeps, we can also obtain estimates of the parameters of the model. For instance, the means of the clusters can be estimated as $\hat{\mu}_k = \sum_{t=1}^{T} \mu_k^{(t)}/T$.

3.2 Bayesian estimation with missing data

In missing data problems, both the parameters and the missing values are unknown. Since their joint posterior distribution is typically intractable, we can simulate from it iteratively, through the data augmentation (DA) algorithm: we sample from the distribution of the missing values, conditional on the current value of the parameters, and then we sample from the distribution of the parameters, conditional on the value imputed to the missing observations. Let us split $\mathbf{x}_i$ into two subvectors, $\mathbf{x}_i^o$ and $\mathbf{x}_i^u$, which refer, respectively, to the observed and unobserved expression levels for gene i. Let also $\mathbf{X}_o$ and $\mathbf{X}_u$ denote, respectively, the observed and unobserved expression levels for all the n genes. The DA algorithm consists in iterating the following steps:

I-step (imputation step): given the current values $\mathbf{z}^{(t)}, \mu^{(t)}, \Sigma^{(t)}$ of the parameters, draw a new value $\mathbf{X}_u^{(t+1)}$ for the missing observations from its conditional predictive distribution $p(\mathbf{X}_u|\mathbf{X}_o, \mathbf{z}^{(t)}, \mu^{(t)}, \Sigma^{(t)})$. This is straightforward since, for each i, $\mathbf{x}_i^u$ can be drawn independently from a $N(\mu_{z_i}, \Sigma_{z_i})$, conditioned on $\mathbf{x}_i^o$.

P-step (posterior step): given $\mathbf{X}_u^{(t+1)}$, draw $\mathbf{z}^{(t+1)}$, $\mu^{(t+1)}$ and $\Sigma^{(t+1)}$ from their complete data posterior $p(\mathbf{z}, \mu, \Sigma|\mathbf{X}_o, \mathbf{X}_u^{(t+1)})$ as within the sampler described in Section 3.1.

As before, estimates of the missing data, as well as of the parameters of the model, can be obtained by averaging over the sweeps of the algorithm (Tanner and Wong (1987)), e.g.:

$$\hat{\mathbf{X}}_u = \frac{1}{T} \sum_{t=1}^{T} \mathbf{X}_u^{(t)}.$$

4 Model selection

To select the number of components we make use of the *Bayes factor* (BF). Denote by M_K the mixture model at issue when K components are used and by $p(K)$ its prior probability. The BF between two models, say M_K and M_L, is defined as

$$B_{LK} = \frac{p(\mathbf{X}|L)}{p(\mathbf{X}|K)} \qquad \text{or, equivalently,} \qquad B_{LK} = \frac{p(L|\mathbf{X})}{p(K|\mathbf{X})} \Big/ \frac{p(L)}{p(K)}$$

where $p(\mathbf{X}|K)$ and $p(K|\mathbf{X})$ are, respectively, the *marginal likelihood* and posterior probability of model M_K (Kass and Raftery (1995)). The larger is B_{LK}, the greater is the evidence provided by the data in favor of M_L.

Direct computation of the BF is almost always infeasible and different algorithms have been proposed to estimate it. For example, the well-known Reversible Jump (RJ) algorithm (Green (1995)), which draws samples from the joint posterior distribution of the number of components and model parameters, allows to estimate $p(K|\mathbf{X})$ as the proportion of times the algorithm visited model M_K. However, when dealing with so many observations as in a typical Microarray study, RJ is expected to perform badly as the posterior distribution of the parameters is likely to be very peaked and this makes it hard to jump from one model to another. Therefore, we follow the approach of Chib and Jelaizkov (2001). They show that the marginal likelihood of each model can be obtained as the product of the likelihood and the prior distribution of the parameters, divided by the posterior distribution and this holds for all parameter values, i.e.:

$$p(\mathbf{X}|K) = \frac{p(\mathbf{X}, \boldsymbol{\theta}_K|K)}{p(\boldsymbol{\theta}_K|\mathbf{X}, K)} \qquad \forall \boldsymbol{\theta}_K \in \boldsymbol{\Theta}_K$$

where $\boldsymbol{\theta}_K$ is a short hand notation for the parameters $\mathbf{z}, \boldsymbol{\mu}, \boldsymbol{\Sigma}$ under the model with K components. So, by substituting an estimate to $p(\boldsymbol{\theta}_K|\mathbf{X}, K)$ for a suitable chosen $\boldsymbol{\theta}_K$, say $\bar{\boldsymbol{\theta}}_K$, we can estimate the marginal likelihood of M_K, $p(\mathbf{X}|K)$ and so the BF. Chib and Jelaizkov (2001) showed that a suitable estimate of $p(\bar{\boldsymbol{\theta}}_K|\mathbf{X}, K)$ may be obtained on the basis of the Metropolis-Hastings output for sampling $\boldsymbol{\theta}_K$ from its posterior distribution under model M_K; such an algorithm uses as acceptance probability for moving from $\boldsymbol{\theta}_K$ to a proposed $\boldsymbol{\theta}_K^*$

$$\alpha(\boldsymbol{\theta}_K, \boldsymbol{\theta}_K^*) = \min\left\{1, \frac{p(\mathbf{X}, \boldsymbol{\theta}_K^*|K)q(\boldsymbol{\theta}_K|\boldsymbol{\theta}_K^*)}{p(\mathbf{X}, \boldsymbol{\theta}_K|K)q(\boldsymbol{\theta}_K^*|\boldsymbol{\theta}_K)}\right\},$$

where $q(\boldsymbol{\theta}_K^*|\boldsymbol{\theta}_K)$ is the proposal distribution from which $\boldsymbol{\theta}_K^*$ is drawn. In fact, we have

$$
\begin{aligned}
p(\bar{\boldsymbol{\theta}}_K|\mathbf{X}, K) &= \frac{\int_{\boldsymbol{\Theta}_K} \alpha(\boldsymbol{\theta}_K, \bar{\boldsymbol{\theta}}_K)q(\bar{\boldsymbol{\theta}}_K|\boldsymbol{\theta}_K)p(\boldsymbol{\theta}_K|\mathbf{X}, K)d\boldsymbol{\theta}_K}{\int_{\boldsymbol{\Theta}_K} \alpha(\bar{\boldsymbol{\theta}}_K, \boldsymbol{\theta}_K)q(\boldsymbol{\theta}_K|\bar{\boldsymbol{\theta}}_K)d\boldsymbol{\theta}_K} \\
&= \frac{\mathrm{E}\{\alpha(\boldsymbol{\theta}_K, \bar{\boldsymbol{\theta}}_K)q(\bar{\boldsymbol{\theta}}_K|\boldsymbol{\theta}_K)\}}{\mathrm{E}\{\alpha(\bar{\boldsymbol{\theta}}_K, \boldsymbol{\theta}_K)\}}
\end{aligned}
$$

that, consequently, may be estimated through

$$\hat{p}(\bar{\boldsymbol{\theta}}_K|\mathbf{X}, K) = \frac{\sum_{t=1}^{N_1} \alpha(\boldsymbol{\theta}_K^{(t1)}, \bar{\boldsymbol{\theta}}_K)q(\bar{\boldsymbol{\theta}}_K|\boldsymbol{\theta}_K^{(t1)})/N_1}{\sum_{t=1}^{N_2} \alpha(\bar{\boldsymbol{\theta}}_K, \boldsymbol{\theta}_K^{(t2)})/N_2},$$

where $\boldsymbol{\theta}_K^{(11)}, \ldots, \boldsymbol{\theta}_K^{(N_1, 1)}$ is a sample from $p(\boldsymbol{\theta}_K|\mathbf{X}, K)$ and $\boldsymbol{\theta}_K^{(12)}, \ldots, \boldsymbol{\theta}_K^{(N_2, 2)}$ is a sample from $q(\boldsymbol{\theta}_K|\bar{\boldsymbol{\theta}}_K, K)$.

Chib and Jelaizkov (2001) also suggested to split the parameters into blocks, which are updated separately (as illustrated in Section 3.1), to increase the estimator efficiency. The point $\bar{\boldsymbol{\theta}}_K$ in practice is chosen as a point of high posterior density, generally the posterior mean of $\boldsymbol{\theta}_K$, in order to maximize the accuracy of the approximation.

5 Application

We show an application of the proposed approach to a real Microarray experiment on a yeast genome (the *Saccharomyces cerevisiae*), aimed at identifying groups of genes involved in the cell cycle and, therefore, characterized by periodic fluctuations in their expression levels. Data refer to $n = 696$ genes observed at $S = 12$ consecutive times during the cell division cycle. A full description of the experiment, carried out by Spellman et al. (1998), and complete data sets are available at http://cellcycle-www.stanford.edu.

The results reported here correspond to 50,000 sweeps of the MCMC algorithm described in Section 3, including a burn-in of 5,000 sweeps. The algorithm seems to mix well over the parameter space and the burn-in seems to be more than adequate to achieve stationarity. This can be seen, for example, in Figure 1(a), which shows the traces of π against the number of sweeps (for sake of clarity, data are plotted every 10 sweeps), for the model with $K = 3$ components.

The estimated marginal loglikelihood is plotted in Figure 1(b) against different values of K. It is immediately evident that the model with $K = 3$ components is favored. The BF of this model against the second most favored model, the one with 4 components, is $B_{3,4} = 98716$, implying an

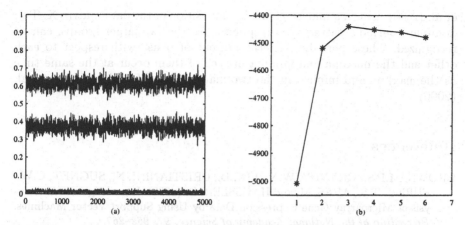

Fig. 2. (a) Traces of π against the number of sweeps for the model with three components and (b) marginal loglikelihood for models with up to six components.

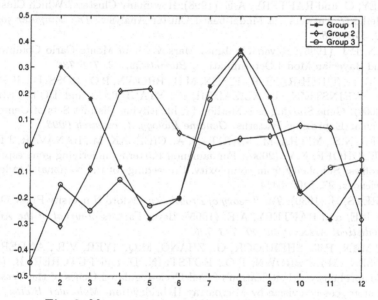

Fig. 3. Mean expression profiles for the three groups.

overwhelming evidence in favor of the model with $K = 3$, compared to any other model.

The estimated weights we obtained for the 3 groups of genes are respectively $\pi = (0.012, 0.373, 0.615)'$, resulting in a large group including approximately 428 genes, an intermediate group with 244 genes and a residual one made of just 8 genes.

Figure 3 shows the estimated mean expression profiles for the three groups of genes. The results we found are in accordance with those obtained by Holter et al. (2000) using a standard value decomposition of the data matrix X. Two dominant periodic patterns, corresponding to the two larger groups, can be recognized. These periodic patterns are out of phase with respect to each other and the maxima and minima in each of them occur at the same time as the maxima and minima in the two main patterns found by Holter et al. (2000).

References

BROWN, M.P.S., GRUNDY, W.N., LIN, D., CRISTIANINI, N., SUGNET, C.W., FUREY, T.S., ARES, M. and HAUSSLER, D. (2000): Knowledge-Based Analysis of Microarray Gene Expression Data by Using Support Vector Machines. *Proceeding of the National Academy of Science, 97, 262–267.*

CHIB, S. and JELIAZKOV, I. (2001): Marginal Likelihood from the Metropolis-Hastings Output. *Journal of the American Statistical Association, 96, 270–281.*

FRALEY, C. and RAFTERY, A.E. (1998): How many Clusters? Which Clustering Method? Answers via Model-based Cluster Analysis. *The computer journal, 41, 570–588.*

GREEN, P.J. (1995): Reversible Jump Markov Chain Monte Carlo Computation and Bayesian Model Determination. *Biometrika, 82, 711–732.*

HASTIE, T., TIBSHIRANI, R., EISEN, M.B., BROWN, P.O., ROSS, D., SCHERF, U., WEINSTEIN, J., ALIZADEH, A., STAUDT, L. and BOTSTEIN, D. (2000): Gene Shaving as a Method for Identifying Distinct Sets of Genes with Similar Expression Patterns. *Genome Biology, 1, research 0003.*

HOLTER, N.S., MITRA, M., MARITAN, A., CIEPLAK, M., BANAVAR, J.R. and FEDOROFF, N.V. (2000): Fundamental Patterns underlying gene espression profiles: Simplicity from complexity. Proceedings of the National Academy of Sciences, 97, 8409–8414.

JEFFREYS, H. (1939): *The Theory of Probability.* Oxford University Press, Oxford.

KASS, R.E. and RAFTERY, A.E. (1995): Bayes Factors. *Journal of the America Statistical Association, 90, 773–795.*

SPELLMAN, P.T., SHERLOCK, G., ZHANG, M.Q., IYER, V.R., ANDERS, K., EISEN, M.B., BROWN, P.O., BOTSTEIN, D. and FUTCHER, B. (1998): Comprehensive Identification of Cell Cycle-regulated Genes of the Yeast Saccharomyces cerevisiae by Microarray Hybridization. *Molecular Biology of the Cell, 9, 3273–3297.*

TANNER, M.A. and WONG, W.H. (1987): The Calculation of Posterior Distributions by Data Augmentation. *Journal of the America Statistical Association, 82, 528–540.*

TAVAZOIE, S., HUGHES, J.D., CAMPBELL, M.J., CHO, R.J. and CHURCH, G.M. (1999): Systematic Determination of Genetic Network Architecture. *Nature Genetics, 22, 281–285.*

YEUNG, K.Y., FRALEY, C., MEURUA, A., RAFTERY, A.E. and RUZZO, W.L. (2001): Model-based Clustering and Data Transformation for Gene Expression Data. *Bioinformatics, 17, 977–987.*

Sequence Analysis of BHPS Life Course Data[*]

Arnstein Aassve[1], Francesco C. Billari[2], and Raffaella Piccarreta[3]

[1] ISER, University of Essex, Colchester, UK
aaassve@essex.ac.uk
[2] Istituto di Metodi Quantitativi and IGIER
Università Bocconi, Milano, Italy
francesco.billari@uni-bocconi.it
[3] Istituto di Metodi Quantitativi
Università Bocconi, Milano, Italy
raffaella.piccarreta@uni-bocconi.it

Abstract. We apply a methodology for clustering data from the British Household Panel Survey (BHPS) on employment and family trajectories of women. We represent life courses as sequences on a monthly time scale and we apply optimal matching analysis to compute dissimilarities between individuals. We then use standard clustering algorithms to identify distinctive groups. As the interpretation and presentation of cluster analysis of life-course data is an important and still unresolved issue, we elaborate on possible approaches for how to best illustrate the composition of groups. Our results are interpreted in light of the socio-demographic literature.

1 Introduction

In this paper we apply methods for clustering individual life courses. The central idea is to develop a method with which we can identify clusters of individuals who follow similar life-course trajectories, in terms of family and employment, during early adulthood. To do this we use data from the British Household Panel Survey on women born 1960 to 1968. The main rationale for our strategy is that these pathways are the outcome of 1) complex planning and strategies made by individuals and their families as a means to best combine family and working life, and 2) unforeseen life-course contingencies or events that shape lives with long-lasting effects (see i.e. Siegers et al., 1991). It is thus important to be able to study complex life-course trajectories as they actually occur, and to obtain ideal-types of trajectories that can be meaningfully interpreted and analysed. This is of course one of the main challenges in life-course research, which up to now has remained largely unsolved, and has lead many to adopt qualitative approaches as an alternative to the quantitative tradition. (see i.e. Dex, 1991).

---

[*]The authors have equally contributed to this work. However, A. Aassve and F.C. Billari drafted Section 1, R. Piccarreta drafted Section 2, F.C. Billari and R. Piccarreta drafted Section 3

Using a sequence-type representation together with sequence analysis is the main methodological contender in the study of complex trajectories of the life course (see Abbott, 1995). In this paper, we follow women over the age span 13-30, excluding cases with missing information. For each woman we build, on a monthly time scale, a sequence-type representation of three life course domains: employment, co-resident partnership, , and childbearing. We analyse data on 578 women, each of them with 204 time points. In particular, employment (**W**) and partnership status (**U**) for each month are represented in a dichotomous manner, while for fertility, according to the number of children, each woman has 4 possible states (from 0 to 3 children and over). The states in the sequences are obtained by combining the categories of the involved domains. For example, **U** means in a certain period a woman has a partner (does not employment and has no children), **WU** means a woman is employed and has a partner and **1WU** means a woman is employed, has a partner and has one child. The employment and partnership status can change in either direction at any time, while for fertility, once a number of children is reached, women cannot reverse to a lower number of children. All life course combinations yield a total number of 16 states.

State	0	U	W	WU	1	1U	1W	1WU	2	2U	2W	2WU	3	3U	3W	3WU
No. children	0	0	0	0	1	1	1	1	2	2	2	2	3+	3+	3+	3+
Employment	N	N	Y	Y	N	N	Y	Y	N	N	Y	Y	N	N	Y	Y
Union	N	Y	N	Y	N	Y	N	Y	N	Y	N	Y	N	Y	N	Y

Table 1. Life course states possible during each month.

2 Clustering sequences

Frequencies of specific sequences will in general be very low. As a result they cannot be described by simple descriptive statistics. The main issues addressed in this paper are 1) how can one best obtain clusters of life course sequences and 2) how can one represent the obtained clusters in a meaningful way. As far as 1) is concerned, the application of standard (hierarchical) algorithms necessitate the definition of a distance (dissimilarity) matrix. In the Social Sciences *Optimal Matching Analysis* (OMA) has become a widely accepted criterion to measure dissimilarity between sequences (Abbott, 1995). The basic idea of OMA is to measure the dissimilarity between two sequences by properly quantifying the effort needed to transform one sequence into another. In the most elementary approach, a set composed of three basic operations to transform sequences is used, $O = \{\iota, \delta, \sigma\}$, where:

insertion (ι): one state is inserted into the sequence;
deletion (δ): one state is deleted from the sequence;
substitution (σ): one state is replaced by another one.

To each elementary operation ω_i, $\omega_i \in O$, $i=1,\ldots,k$, a specific cost can be assigned, $c(\omega_i)$. Suppose that k basic operations have to be performed to transform one sequence into another one. Then, the cost of applying a series of k elementary operations can be computed as:

$$c(\omega_1, \omega_2, \ldots, \omega_k) = \sum_{i=1}^{k} c(\omega_i)$$

The distance between two sequences can thus be defined as the minimum cost of transforming one sequence into the other one. This means that the computed distance takes into account the entire sequences.

The assignment of costs (i.e. substitution costs) to transform one life status into the other one is challenging. We adopt a data-driven approach, using substitution costs that are inversely proportional to transition frequencies. We compute OMA distances using TDA (Rohwer and Pötter, 2002). On the basis of the distance matrix defined with OMA, we apply different clustering algorithms to our data (single linkage, complete linkage, centroid, ward, median). Here we choose the solution provided by Ward's algorithm, since the other algorithms tend to separate few clusters having very high sizes from small, residual clusters. Using standard criteria (analysis of R^2, pseudo F and pseudo T statistics), we choose the 9-clusters partition (for a detailed description of the criteria to choose a cluster solution, the interested reader can refer to Jobson, 1992).

The main remaining problem is how to meaningfully characterize clusters. This is particularly important because states are qualitative variables and their order in time is fundamental. A first possibility is to synthesize clusters with *modal* vectors: thus, for each period t, we consider the most frequent state (in the cluster). Since the number of states is very high, to better represent the modal vectors (as well as the sequences themselves) we introduce the notion of *state-permanence* sequences (in the following s/p—sequences). The *state*-sequence is the sequence of the *states* "visited" by an individual (note that the ordering of the visits is important since some states can be visited more than once). The *permanence*-sequence is the sequence of the length of the periods an individual "remained" in each of the visited states. For example, the s/p-sequence of the sequence **W-W-WU-WU-W-W** is $\mathbf{W_2}$-**WU$_2$-W$_2$**. Using the s/p-representation for the modal vectors, we have a first characterization of the clusters.

Unfortunately, modal vectors are not necessarily observed sequences; occasionally it may happen that they are inconsistent. For example, the modal vector for the 8th cluster (cfr. Table 2) is 0_{41}-$\mathbf{W_{32}}$-$2U_{11}$-$3U_1$-$2U_1$-$3U_2$-$2U_7$-$3U_{109}$ and is not consistent since it is not possible to observe the s-sequence $2U$-$3U$-$2U$. In fact we have assumed the number of children can only increase.

This suggests that clusters should be synthesized by referring to "typical" sequences, not being "artificial". One possibility is to consider for each cluster its *medoid* (see e.g. Kauffman and Rousseeuw, 1990). This is the individual (sequence) which is less distant from all the other individuals in the cluster. The analysis of the *s/p-sequences* of the medoids permits a consistent characterization of the clusters. Moreover, it is possible to get a measure of the dispersion of sequences around the medoid (calculating the minimum, the maximum, the average distance). One can also measure the proportion of dissimilarity explained by each medoid by calculating the ratio between the average distance from the medoid and the total distance between sequences in a cluster. Notice that this is not possible when considering the modal vectors, since one cannot calculate the OMA distance between an observed sequence and an artificial one. Modal vectors and medoids are reported in Table 2.

As we can see from Table 2, for some clusters the synthesis provided by the medoid is satisfactory (low – mean and maximum – distances from the medoid) whereas for others the dispersion around the medoid is high. To analyze clusters in more detail, we define the *mean-s/p-sequences*. Given an *s*-sequence, say $s_1, \ldots, s_h$, common to n_h cases, we attach the *p-sequence* $m_1, \ldots, m_h$, m_i being the average of $(p_{i1}, \ldots, p_{inh})$. For each cluster we can evaluate the mean period of permanence in a certain state (for a given *s*-sequence). By analyzing medoids and *mean-s/p-sequences*, we noticed the following.

Some clusters are characterized by short *s*-sequences. In these situations, the *s*-sequence of the medoid frequently coincides with the modal *s*-sequence. Moreover the *p*-sequence of the medoid is very similar to the *mean-p*-sequence of the modal *s*-sequence. Thus, the medoid adequately represents the cluster. Nevertheless, we do find other *s*-sequences with high frequency, which are different from the medoid. To better represent a cluster (even in case when the medoid is a good synthesis) it may be sensible to evidence these sequences. At this aim, we choose a cut-off point, and individuate "representative" sequences within a given cluster, i.e. *s-sequences* characterized by a frequency higher than the cut-off (in this preliminary analysis the cut-off was set equal to 0.1).

A major difficulty is encountered when analyzing more heterogeneous clusters. For instance, some clusters are constituted by very long *s*-sequences. Individuals in these clusters tend to experiment many states (often different), and the medoid provides an unsatisfactory synthesis of sequences in the cluster. In these heterogeneous clusters, the problem lies in that the frequencies are very low (and generally well below the cut-off). Consequently there are no representative sequences. We notice that in these clusters the *s*-sequences are similar for the first states, but from a certain period onwards each individual follows a different path, thus being characterized by "peculiar" states (for higher periods). In order to individuate "common" paths in more heterogeneous clusters we "prune" long *s*-sequences to evaluate whether there are at least common "initial paths", i.e. short *s*-(sub)-sequences (regarding the first

Size: 50   Mean: 37.45   Max: 75.89   %: 31%   Mo: O_{61}-W_1-O_1-W_{141} Me: O_{63}-W_{141}
Size: 100   Mean: 93.02   Max: 234.57   %: 28%   Mo: O_{114}-W_{44}-WU_{46} Me: O_{116}-W_{39}-WU_{49}
Size: 56 : Mean: 54.79   Max: 119.52   %: 30%   Mo: O_{55}-W_{40}-WU_{109} Me: O_{63}-W_{40}-WU_{101}
Size: 107   Mean: 76.40   Max: 205.82   %: 28%   Mo: O_{45}-W_{101}-WU_3-W_1-WU_{54} Me: O_{46}-W_{106}-WU_{52}
Size: 88   Mean: 119.00   Max: 232.86   %: 26%   Mo: O_{53}-W_{53}-WU_{50}-$1WU_{48}$ Me: O_{63}-W_{56}-WU_{54}-$1WU_7$-$1U_{24}$
Size: 62   Mean: 145.12   Max: 338.97   %: 26%   Mo: O_{49}-W_{39}-$1U_{10}$-$2U_{106}$ Me: O_{45}-W_{12}-O_2-W_{19}-WU_{21}-$1WU_6$-$1U_{21}$-$2U_{68}$-$3U_{10}$
Size: 62   Mean: 109.83   Max: 185.64   %: 25%   Mo: O_{47}-W_{52}-WU_{14}-$1WU_2$- WU_3-$1U_1$-WU_1-$1U_2$-$1WU_5$-$2WU_{77}$ Me: O_{46}-W_{58}-WU_{26}-$1WU_6$-$1U_8$-$2U_1$-$2WU_{16}$-$2U_9$-$2WU_{34}$
Size: 29   Mean: 99.07   Max: 183.5   %: 22%   Mo: O_{41}-W_{32}-$2U_{11}$-$3U_1$-$2U_1$-$3U_2$-$2U_7$-$3U_{109}$ Me: O_{42}-W_{10}-$1W_4$-$1WU_4$- $1U_6$-$2U_2$-$2WU_6$-$2U_{17}$-$3U_{113}$
Size: 24   Mean: 153.57   Max: 265.27   %: 21%   Mo: O_{52}-W_{33}-O_4-WU_1- 1_{55}-$1W_1$-1_{58} Me: O_{59}-W_{48}-WU_{11}-$1W_5$- 1_{71}-$1W_6$-$2W_4$

Table 2. Modal vectors and medoids for the clusters[a].

[a] Size is the number of sequences in the cluster, Mean and Max are the mean and the maximum distance between sequences in the cluster and the medoid. % is the proportion of the total dissimilarity within the cluster accounted from the medoid.

states visited). To do this, we consider the longer sequences and remove last states, substituting them by a residual state "R". As an example, consider the two s-sequences (s_1, s_2, s_3, s_4) and (s_1, s_2, s_3, s_5), both characterized by a low frequency. If we remove the last states in the sequences we obtain an s-sequence (s_1, s_2, s_3, R), characterized by a higher frequency. In this way, we obtain shorter sequences characterized by higher frequencies, which are useful for description. We thus define an algorithm, which "prunes" an s−sequence if it has a frequency lower than the cut-off. The algorithm starts by considering longer sequences (i.e. long s-sequences), which are pruned and aggregated until the resulting s-sequence is characterized by a frequency higher than the cut-off (as a further step in research we are interested in evaluating how to avoid the necessity to specify the cut-off). The algorithm ends when all the s-sequences have frequency higher than the cut-off. In this way, we find the characteristic sub(or initial)-s—sequences in a cluster.

Proceeding in this way, we obtain a description both for clusters where representative sequences are present, and for more heterogeneous clusters in which pruning is necessary. The most frequent *mean-s/p*-sequences can be represented graphically in a "tree structure". For each cluster a tree is obtained. The nodes represent the states visited implying that each branch represents an *s-sequence*. The arrow connecting two (consecutive) states s_1 and s_2 (in a certain s-sequence) have length proportional to m_1 the average time of permanence in state s_1 before experimenting state s_2. Due to space limitation we only report the trees describing clusters 1, 4 and 7. If the sequences have been pruned due to low frequency a final "R" node is reported.

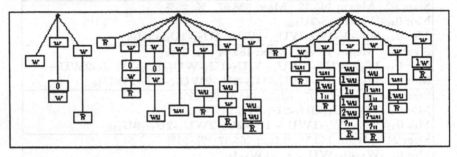

Fig. 1. Tree representation of mean-s/p-sequences for clusters 1, 4, and 7.

3 An interpretation and discussion of results

We now focus on the interpretation of our results. We interpret the results in terms of observed orientations towards employment (or "career" in general) and family, keeping in mind "preference theory" as elaborated by Hakim (for a concise illustration of preference theory see Hakim 2002; 2003). According to Hakim, women tend to hold enduring orientations towards three distinct directions: mostly working life (about 20% of all women), mostly family life (about 20% of all women), combining employment and family (about 60% of all women). Hakim thus maintains that the majority of women in Western societies lie in the group that would prefer to combine employment and family. Of course Hakim's typology is on preferences, while we analyse actual behaviour. Let us look at our results in detail.

As we have earlier noticed, characterising clusters is one of the most difficult tasks in the analysis of life courses based on a sequence-type representation. For this interpretation, we mainly refer to: 1) the medoid of each cluster, together with the average and maximum distance (according to OMA) to individuals of the same cluster; and 2) the representation of each cluster described in the past section.

Cluster 1 contains 8.7% of all women. Its medoid woman spends 63 months in the initial state, and subsequently 141 months working without interruption, without any family formation event. The cluster is the most compact both in terms of average OMA distance to the medoid (37.45) and of distance to the farthest member of the cluster (75.89). In this cluster we can see life courses of women who did not continue towards higher education (the medoid starts working just after age 18) and who do not combine employment and family at least in their twenties. This is also a general feature of women in the cluster since all of them spend most of their early adulthood without any family event. *Focus on employment* is the main feature of this group, which clearly falls, in terms of observed behaviour, in the employment-oriented group of Hakim.

Cluster 2 contains 17.3% of all women. This group is characterised by a late entry into the labour market, possibly due to long permanence in education. The medoid woman, has the highest age at entering the labour marked (about 23) for instance, subsequently starts working and works only for 39 months, and then starts a partnership which lasts until age 30. The average OMA distance from the medoid is 93.02 and the maximum distance is 234.57, indicating that there is a noteworthy level of heterogeneity within the cluster. In fact, d*elayed entry into the labour market* is the only clear commonality of this group, which cannot be clearly classified in terms of employment versus family orientation (although a higher share of women focuses on employment).

Cluster 3 contains 9.7% of all women. The life-course trajectory of the medoid of this cluster is similar in terms of types of events to the medoid of cluster 2, but there is a large difference in age at entry into the labour market: here the medoid enters around age 18. The earlier entry in the labour market translates family events to an earlier age, and in general the period spent as working and without an own family is relatively short. The average OMA distance from the medoid is 54.80 and the maximum distance is 119.52, which indicates a relatively low heterogeneity within the cluster. *Family formation without fertility* seems to be the main characteristic of this group. This is a group for which we seem to observe the combination of employment and family.

Cluster 4 contains 18.5% of all women, and is the most numerous. This cluster, when we look at the medoid woman, is characterised by an early entry into the labour market (before age 17), a long presence inside it without partnership formation, and no significant presence of childbearing. The average OMA distance is 76.40 and the maximum distance from the medoid is 205.82. Looking at the more detailed description of the cluster, the general pattern is the length of the period spent before starting a family. *Early entry into the labour market and delayed family formation* are the main signs of this group.

The observed trajectories are consistent with a mostly employment-oriented strategy.

Fertility events start appearing as a prominent feature in cluster 5, which represents 15.2% of all women. Here the medoid woman has a particularly interesting life course path. She enters the labour market around age 18, she works without interruptions for more than 4 years, and starting a partnership she combines employment and partnership for more than 4 years (up to about age 27). Then she has a child and 7 months after the birth of the child she leaves the labour market. At age 30, 2 and a half years after the birth of her first child she is still out of the labour market. So this is a typical pattern of exit from the labour market during the first years of a child. The OMA distance from the medoid is 119.00 and the maximum distance is 232.86 indicating a relatively high heterogeneity within the cluster. *Family formation and mixed work-family strategies* are the main features of this group. The combination of employment and family for women in this cluster is a complex one with the possibility of leaving a job after the transition to motherhood. This would also be consistent with family orientation.

Cluster 6 represents 10.7% of all women. The average OMA distance here is 145.11, and the maximum distance is 338.97, indicating a high heterogeneity within the cluster. Life courses are typically complex: if we look at the medoid woman, she enters early the labour market (before age 17), she starts working but then interrupts work probably due to unemployment for 2 months, before re-entering employment. After 19 months she starts a partnership, and after 21 months she gives birth to a child. She then leaves the labour market (6 months after the birth of the first child) and subsequently gives birth to 2 other children without re-entering the labour market. *Short labour market attachment before family formation* is the main feature of cluster 6. In terms of Hakim's categorisation, this group contains trajectories that appear as family-oriented.

Cluster 7 also represents 10.7% of all women. The medoid woman here enters the labour market before age 17, she then has about 5 years of continuous employment and starts a partnership. After 2 years she gives birth to a child and subsequently she leaves the labour market and gives birth to a second child. After the birth of the second child she re-enters the labour market and starts a new employment career marked by a relatively long interruption (9 months). The average OMA distance from the medoid is 109.83, the maximum distance is 185.64. The main feature here is *propensity to high fertility with discontinuous labour market attachment*. This is a mainly family-oriented group although with repeated job spells.

Cluster 8 represents a smaller subset of women, 5.0%, but refers to particularly complex pathways, as seen from the medoid. The medoid woman starts employment at age 16 and a half, she is then employed for 10 months ad has a child without living with a partner (she thus gives birth being a single mother). However, 4 months after the birth she starts a partnership, and after 4 months she leaves the labour market, within 6 months she gives birth

to a second child, and after 2 months again working, she does not employment and gives birth to a third child without re-entering the labour market.
The average OMA distance from the medoid is 99.07, the maximum distance
is 183.5, which indicates a medium level of heterogeneity within the cluster. However, single motherhood is not the only major feature of this group,
where family orientation seems more a consequence of life-course contingencies rather than the outcome of deliberate planning.

Cluster 9 represents 4.2% of all women. The medoid woman starts employment at about age 19 and subsequently starts a partnership. The partnership
is however dissolved at the birth of a child. The woman then leaves employment for 6 years, after which she starts a new partnership; 6 months after she
gives birth to a second child. The cluster is heterogeneous and the medoid
is the least representative of all medoids, given that the average OMA distance from the medoid is 153.57 and the maximum distance is 265.27. We
can see *family instability* as the main feature of this cluster. As most women
remain attached to the labour market, we could classify this cluster within
the employment-oriented typology of Hakim.

To interpret our data, we referred to "preference theory" as elaborated by
Hakim. Complementary to Hakim's approach, our analytical strategy allows
us to analyse employment and family behaviour (strategies of combination
implying different entries and exits from a job, instead of simultaneous combination for instance arise from our analysis) in a dynamic fashion rather
than static orientation. For this reason, our categories are more complex
than the three-group categorisation by Hakim, who however recognises the
possible existence of sub-groups in her groups. In our future research, we aim
at studying the determinants of life course pathways, together with their consequences. Sequence analysis and the representations we introduced in this
paper are adequate tools for such endeavour.

References

ABBOTT, A. (1995): Sequence Analysis: New Methods for Old Ideas, *Annual Review of Sociology, 21, 93–113.*

DEX, S. (Ed.) (1991): *Life and Employment History Analyses: Qualitative and
Quantitative Developments*, Routledge, London.

HAKIM, C. (2002): Lifestyle Preferences as Determinants of Women's Differentiated Labor Market Careers, *Employment and Occupations, 29, 4, 428–459.*

HAKIM, C. (2003): A New Approach to Explaining Fertility Patterns: Preference
Theory, *Population and Development Review, 29, 3, 349–374.*

JOBSON, J. D. (1992): *Applied multivariate data analysis*, Vol. II: *Categorical and
multivariate methods*, Springer-Verlag, New York.

SIEGERS J.J., DE JONG-GIERVELD, J. and VAN IMHOFF, E. (Eds.) (1991):
Female Labour Market Behaviour and Fertility: A Rational-Choice Approach,
Springer-Verlag, Berlin/Heidelberg/ New York.

KAUFFMAN L., and ROUSSEEUW, P.J. (1990): *Finding Groups in Data*, Wiley
& Sons, New York.

Robust Multivariate Methods for the Analysis of the University Performance

Matilde Bini

Dipartimento di Statistica "G. Parenti"
Università di Firenze, Italy
bini@ds.unifi.it

Abstract. One of the most important problems among the methodological issues discussed in cluster analysis is the identification of the correct number of clusters and the correct allocation of units to their natural clusters. In this paper we use the forward search algorithm, recently proposed by Atkinson, Riani and Cerioli (2004) to scrutinize in a robust and efficient way the output of k-means clustering algorithm. The method is applied to a data set containing efficiency and effectiveness indicators, collected by the National University Evaluation Committee (NUEC), used to evaluate the performance of Italian universities.

1 Introduction

The forward search is a powerful general method for detecting multiple masked outliers and for determining their effect on models fitted to data. The aim of this study is to show how the forward search algorithm can be used to validate the output of a cluster analysis algorithm. The suggested approach enables us to scrutinize in a robust and efficient way the degree of belonging of each unit to its appropriate cluster and the degree of overlapping among the different groups which have been found. As an illustration of the suggested approach, we tackle the problem of the performance university measurement. The data set considered in the analysis includes indicators, which derive from data of the past census survey conducted by NUEC in 2000, concerning 50 public universities of the academic year 1998-99. The variables have been actually defined using the information that each university usually has to collect for the National Statistical System and for the Ministry of Education and Research, and they have been proposed in 1998 by National University Evaluation Committee (NUEC) (ex Observatory for the Evaluation of University System until 1998) as a minimum set of indicators to perform efficiency evaluation of the universities activities (see details in Biggeri and Bini, 2001). Among the large number of the proposed indicators (29), in order to show how the new method works, we have selected only few of them.

After the presentation, in section 2, of the data set used and the results of the classical cluster analyses, here conventionally named *"traditional"*, the application of the forward search and the comments of the results obtained are illustrated in section 3. Finally, the last section is devoted to some concluding remarks.

2 The data set and the traditional cluster analysis

Starting from March 2000, the NUEC yearly conducts census surveys with the co-operation of all the 73 Italian universities, to implement a statistical information system useful to monitor the university organization and carry out the requested evaluations. The information collected concern many aspects of the educational service (for the detailed list of variables and the data set, see the web site www.cnvsu.it). On the basis of this information, it is possible to compute a set of indicators (29) for the measurement and the evaluation of the performance of single units which produce this service. The set can be arranged in four classes (Ewell, 1999): **Outcome (output) indicators**, that should inform about the final results and the degree of quality of the teaching and research activities; **Resources indicators**, i.e. indicators of resources as funds, staff, etc. available; **Contextual indicators**, i.e. indicators of the context where the university is working, of the socio-economic environment; **Process indicators**, that should inform about the organization, facilities and results of the teaching and research processes.

To implement the present study on clustering the Italian universities in homogeneous groups of units, the data of the survey conducted in 2000 are used. They include a set of 50 public universities obtained by the exclusion of the private universities, since they did not received the most part of the ordinary resources from the MIUR, and of the universities established less than 6 years ago, because they do not have information available. Considering the number of elementary units and the objective of this study, only the following indicators have been considered: graduation rate within institutional time (X_1) (outcome indicator); faculty/students ratio (X_2), research funds (X_3) and administrative staff per faculty (X_4) (resources indicators); private research grants per single member of faculty (X_5) and expenditure for technical staff per "traditional funds" (X_6) (process indicators).

The *"traditional"* clustering techniques, usually, do not assure that units are allocated to the appropriate clusters, and this can lead to the problem of the incorrect assignment of policies to units belonging to "wrong" groups that causes with no doubt side effects and iniquity among interventions. The forward search applied to this algorithm can be used to solve this problem. Before to perform the cluster analysis, the inspection of the scatter plot matrix of the data shows that the distribution of some variables is highly skewed and that maybe some outliers are present in the data. We therefore proceed to estimate the values of the Box-Cox (1964) transformation parameters using the robust procedure described in Riani and Atkinson (2001) (for details

Groups	X_1	X_2	X_3	X_4	X_5	X_6
G_1	$0,3500$	$0,1309$	$0,5938$	$0,6304$	$0,2787$	$-0,3780$
G_2	$-0,8829$	$-0,8775$	$-0,2352$	$-0,4380$	$-0,5938$	$-0,3867$
G_3	$0,5806$	$0,8375$	$-0,4459$	$-0,2600$	$0,3386$	$0,8919$

Table 1. Centroids of groups from k-means algorithm

concerning the transformation parameters which have been found, see Riani and Bini, 2002).

Given that the data appropriately transformed satisfy the multivariate normality assumption, the cluster analysis have been performed using the transformed data. We started according to classical approach using first the hierarchical and then the non-hierarchical methods. Several hierarchical cluster analyses (Krzanowski and Marriott, 1995) are performed on data set, using different distances (Euclidean and Mahalanobis) and different linkages (single, complete and average). A reasonable clustering in terms of number of groups and degree of homogeneity among units in each group could be the one having 3 groups of units obtained with Euclidean distances and average linkages. Starting from this result, the study continues with the non-hierarchical k-means algorithm, using Euclidean distances and a starting number of groups equal to three. The method yields three clusters (G1, G2, G3), each one having respectively size of 18, 17, 15 units, and with specific characteristics, as it is outlined by the centroids of groups reported in Table 1: G1 contains universities with high resources performance; into G2 there are universities with low resources and process performance; universities included in G3 have high global performance. Some graphical representations given in Figure 1, that plot units against the first three principal components as axes, allow us a further useful identification of the characteristics of groups, and also enable us to identify the degree of possible overlapping among groups. The components correspond to the 68% of the total variance. In particular, their proportions are respectively equal to 30%, 19.6% and 18.4%.

The degree of overlapping of the different clusters can be highlighted by plotting robust bivariate contours (Zani, Riani and Corbellini, 1998; Rousseeuw, Ruts and Tukey, 1999), containing the 50% of the data for each group which have been found (see Figure 1). They clearly show that the central parts for the 3 groups are separated in the space of the first two principal components, but overlap considerably in the space of the second and third principal components.

As concerns the interpretation of these plots, the correlation histograms suggest that the first component is positively correlated with all variables. This means that it can be interpreted as a global performance indicator. Regarding the second principal component, the universities with high scores in this dimension are those which have high rates of research funds, administrative personnel, expenditure for technical staff, and a lower rate of graduation,

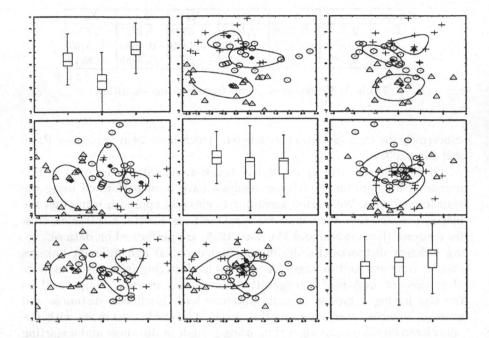

Fig. 1. Position of the units in the space of the first 3 principal components with univariate boxplots (main diagonal) and bivariate contours containing 50% of the data for each group. The black diamond denotes the position of the robust centroid for each group

but bad performance in terms of private grants (X_5 having negative sign). High values for the third principal component identify universities with very bad profile as concerns the research and private funds (X_3 and X_5 have negative sign) and quite high values of graduation rate and faculty/student ratio.

3 Robust validation of cluster analysis output through the forward search

In most statistical analyses, it occurs that single or groups of observations may affect inappropriately the results obtained using statistical methods. Robust procedures clearly reveal this problem and they solve it by downweighting or even discarding the influential units from the bulk of data. Very recently, a powerful general procedure based on the *forward search* through the data, as alternative approach to the traditional ones used to detect outliers, has been proposed by Atkinson and Riani (2000) for generalized linear models, and by Atkinson, Riani and Cerioli (2004) for multivariate methods. It is able to identify observations, referred as *outliers*, which are different to the majority of the data, and to determine their effects on inference made about the model or on results from statistical methods. They may be a few units or they may well form a large part of the data and indicate unsuspected structure which is often impossible to be detected from a method applied to all the data. The feature of this new approach is that at each stage of the forward search it is fundamental to use information such as parameters and plots of Mahalanobis distances to guide to a suitable model.

In the present paper we apply this algorithm (fs) to cluster analysis, but to identify possible clusters (named tentative clusters) in the preliminary analysis, we perform the k-means algorithm as alternative method to the one adopted by the mentioned authors, and that we briefly summarize as follows: "In the preliminary analysis the data can be explored using scatter plots combined with forward plots of Mahalanobis distances of the units in order to find some tentative clusters. Groups of units are tentatively detected by looking at the behaviour of Mahalanobis distances at seemingly interesting points in the forward search. These often correspond to apparent separations in forward plots of distances, or of peaks in plots such as that of maximum distances of units within the subset..." (see details in chapters 2 and 7 of Atkinson, Riani and Cerioli book).

Hence, our starting point is the output which comes from a k-means cluster analysis using Euclidean distances. As a result we obtained three clusters of sizes 18, 17 and 15. We numbered the units arbitrarily within the groups. Questions of interest include whether the clusters are well separated and whether the units are correctly clustered. In the confirmatory stage of a cluster analysis we used the forward search with a few units in one of the tentative clusters. Let there be m units in the subset. We take as our next subset the units with the m+1 smallest distances. The process continues until all n units are included. During this process we monitor the distances of units of interest. If the units are correctly and strongly clustered, all units in a cluster will have distances that follow similar trajectories to each other. These trajectories will be markedly different from those of units in other clusters. Figure 2 is a plot of the distances for the 17 units of Group 2 from a search that starts by fitting some of the units in Group 2.

We see that unit 20, which is the last to join the group, is far from the other units in Group 2 until it affects the estimated Mahalanobis distances by being used to estimate the parameters. Unit 28 steadily diverges from the group as the search progresses and units from other clusters are included in the subset used for estimation. We can also look at forward plots of distances for units in all groups. Figure 3 plots distances for all units for the search shown in Figure 2. The central three panels, for units in Group 2, separate out, by unit number, the 17 traces of distances we saw one on top of another in Figure 2. In the first panel of the row unit 20 stands out as different, as does, to a lesser extent, unit 28 in the second panel. Otherwise the units seem to have similar traces of their distances, which are generally rather different from those in the top row for units in Group 1. All units in Group 1 seem to

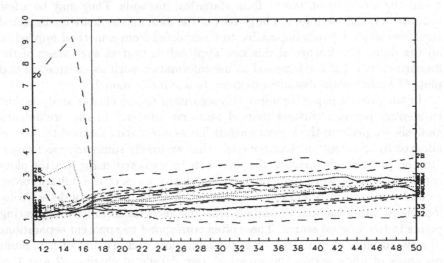

Fig. 2. Monitoring of Mahalanobis distances for the 17 units classified in group 2 by the k-means algorithm

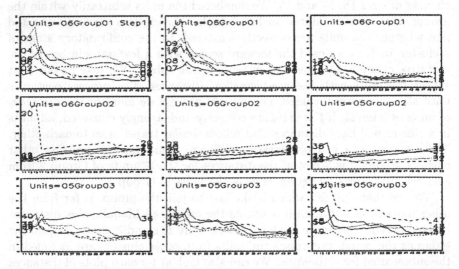

Fig. 3. Forward plot of Mahalanobis distances divided into the 3 groups produced by the k-means algorithm. Each row refers to a group

have a peak around m = 16 and decline thereafter. Unit 20 looks as if it might belong to this group, although its trace increases at the end. The traces in the last row, for units in Group 3, are again somewhat different, particularly

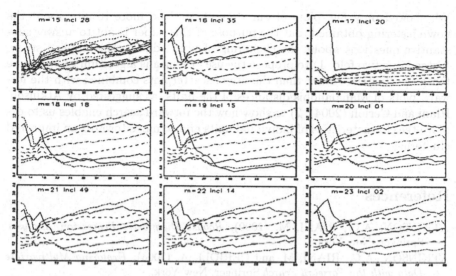

Fig. 4. Mahalanobis distances plots from m=15 for individual units from a search starting in group 2. The plotted percentage points are at 2.5%, 12.5%, 25%, 50% and the symmetrical upper points of the empirical distribution

in the second panel, where they decline steadily. We can repeat these plots for searches starting in Group 1 and in Group 3 and so get a clearer idea of which units have distances that vary together and so form a natural cluster. We would indeed present these plots, but instead, we close with Figure 4 which shows the trajectories for individual units during the search, starting with units in Group 2. The first panel of Figure 4 shows the distances for the first 15 units to join. These are used to form a reference distribution. In the second panel of the first row we show the distance for unit 35 which joins when m = 16 against a background of the reference distribution. It has a sharp peak at m = 15, just before it joins, which however is as nothing compared to the peak for unit 20, which we have already discussed. The three units in the central row of panels all come from our tentative cluster 1 and all do behave similarly; they have broad peaks around m = 15 and then have distances that decrease markedly. The bottom row shows units 49, 14 and 2, which join as m increases from 21 to 23. These traces are very similar to those in the second row, except that the distances do not decrease to such an extent later in the search. This analysis shows that Group 2 seems to be a coherent cluster, apart from units 20 and 28. However, Figure 4 confirms the impression from some panels of Figure 3 that the current separation between Groups 1 and 3 is not satisfactory.

4 Concluding remarks

We showed only few plots of our example and no more results about the new clustering obtained, but the purpose of this paper is not to answer substantive questions about the clustering of units, due to this applied study. Instead it is two fold: 1) to propose the use of k-means algorithm to find some tentative clusters, rather than the use of scatterplots combined with the forward plots of Mahalanobis distances of the units, as suggested by Atkinson, Riani and Cerioli (2004); 2) to show how the forward search enables us to explore the characteristics of individual units and so move towards an improved clustering.

References

ATKINSON, A.C., RIANI, M. (2000): *Robust Diagnostic Regression Analysis.* Springer, New York.

ATKINSON, A.C., RIANI, M. and CERIOLI, A. (2004): *Exploring Multivariate Data with the Forward Search.*Springer, New York.

BIGGERI, L., BINI, M. (2001): Evaluation at university and state level in Italy: need for a system of evaluation and indicators. *Tertiary Education and Management, 7, 149-162.*

BOX, G.E.P., COX, D.R. (1964): An analysis of transformations (with discussion).*Journal of the Royal Statistical Society, Series B, 26, 211-246.*

EWELL, P.T. (1999): Linking performance measures to resource allocation: exploring unmapped terrain. *Quality in Higher Education, 5(3), 191-208.*

KRZANOWSKI, W.J. and MARRIOTT, F.H.C. (1995): *Kendall's Library of Statistics 2: Multivariate Analysis, Part 2.* London:Edward Arnold.

RIANI, M., ATKINSON, A.C. (2001): A Unified Approach to Outliers, Influence, and Transformations in Discriminant Analysis. *Journal of Computational and Graphical Statistics, Vol. 10, 513-544.*

RIANI, M., BINI, M. (2002): Robust and Efficient Dimension Reduction. *Atti della XLI Riunione Scientifica della Società Italiana di Statistica, 295-306.* Milano, 5-7 Giugno 2002.

ROUSSEEUW, P.J., RUTS, I. and TUKEY, J.W. (1999): The bagplot: A Bivariate Boxplot. *The American Statistician, Volume 53, Number 4, 382-387.*

YORKE, M. (1998): Performance Indicators Relating to Student Development: Can They be Trusted?. *Quality in Higher Education, 4(1), 45-61.*

ZANI, S., RIANI, M. and CORBELLINI, A. (1998): Robust Bivariate Boxplots and Multiple Outlier Detection, *Computational Statistics and Data Analysis, Vol. 28, 257-270.*

Some Insights into the Evolution of 1990s' Standard Italian Using Text Mining Techniques and Automatic Categorization[*]

Sergio Bolasco[1] and Alessio Canzonetti[2]

[1] Dipartimento di SGLSSAR,
Università di Roma "La Sapienza", Italy
sergio.bolasco@uniroma1.it
[2] Dipartimento di SGLSSAR,
Università di Roma "La Sapienza", Italy
alessiocanzonetti@tiscali.it

Abstract. Text Mining (TM) is a competitive statistical technology to extract relevant information from huge textual unstructured databases (document warehousing). In this paper, from an immense linguistic archive such as that coming of 10 years of daily "La Repubblica", we describe several examples on the language productivity and the changes of language in the Nineties, with a particular attention of the use evolution of declining of verb mood, tense and person.

1 Introduction

Undoubtedly, the texts collected over a period of ten years from the daily press are particularly significant in relation to language usage and language change in the given period of time. They also constitute a concrete example of a huge document warehouse (over 22 million records a year), available for each newspaper, that can be explored for various reasons, such as search for facts, events and personalities[1]. Among possible Text Mining (TM) applications for the "La Repubblica" warehouse (Bolasco et al. (2002)), is also that of extracting overall information of linguistic type on the behaviour of some classes of words (Balbi et al. (2002)), as well as that of proceeding with statistical measurements that may be used as references in the study of other shorter texts, and compared with them (press reviews). Generally speaking, so far there have not been, for the Italian language, systematic statistics on the frequency of lexical units according to the variation of linguistic kinds

---

[*]The present research was funded by MIUR 2002 - C26A022374. The paper is a combined job of the two authors: paragraphs 1, 3.2, 4 were written by S. Bolasco, and paragraphs 2, 3.1, 3.3 were written by A. Canzonetti.

[1]For example, RCS Ltd. collects all articles that appeared in the last 15 years in daily newspapers (Corriere della Sera, Il Sole 24ore, ...) and manages the databases using text mining techniques in Information Extraction operations.

(formal/informal, written/spoken), with the exception of a few comparisons between some frequency dictionary (LIF e LIP: Giordano, Voghera 2002). Nor are data on the different probability of linguistic elements according to the variation of field (legal, economic, medical lexicon) available. Text Mining approach (Sullivan (2001)) may render these measurements much easier, accessible to all and standardised.

Every text has its own "mark", a sort of DNA determined in the first place by the author, but also by the content (subject), the context of communication, medium used, as well as receiver. These sets of information, defined in the Taltac software as text *imprinting* (Bolasco, in Mazzara (2002)), constitute real and appropriate features that, once measured, can be very useful not only to identify in a univocal way the text itself, but above all to compare it with others. Today, the incredible increase in the availability of linguistic resources (dictionaries, grammars etc.) and computer-assisted tools to use them (parsers and categorisers such as taggers, grammatical and/or semantic lemmatisers), make it possible to reconstruct this "molecular text structure"[2].

In practice, text profiling identifies different word distribution according to parts of speech, number of letters, morphological characteristics, as well as the incidence of the various class of words (abstract nouns, adjectives with positive (constructive) / negative (destructive) elements, cfr. DellaRatta (2003)) in order to reveal the syntactic structure of sentences, punctuation or other complexity elements of the discourse.

In this paper we would like to describe first of all the chosen procedure to manage the "La Repubblica" document warehouse, then some basic statistics on classes of words to show the latter's robustness as well as some time-related trends. Subsequently some statistics will be compared with other kinds of language, in order to show the structural differentiation value and propose some initial quantitative references for further discussion.

It is necessary to specify that the present job does not aim to arrive at an absolute measurement of some characteristics of the texts, but to define a methodology of comparison and appraisal of the similar ones.

2 The procedure to build up the "La Repubblica" database

In order to reconstruct the "vocabulary" of a daily over an extended period of time (ten years), the pre-processing and normalisation phase (a fundamental prerequisite of any TM operation) is crucial for good results. The extraction of articles from the CdRom archives of "La Repubblica" required special operations that can be summarised as follows.

As every year of a daily generates a text file of approximately 140Mbytes,

---

[2]Using Taltac software (Bolasco (2002)) it is possible to extract the *imprinting* by a single query.

it was difficult to process in acceptable time only one file of over 1.4 Giga-bytes. Therefore, the first phase was dedicated to the separate extraction of each year's vocabulary (by the Lexico2 software) and to the creation of one database (by using Microsoft Access) of the 10 vocabularies[3], having previ-ously selected words with initial small and capital letters[4]. The second phase consisted in the grammatical tagging of small letters words with Taltac, gen-erating two sub-databases, one of recognised grammatical forms and one of un-recognised forms (broken or misspelled words, proper names with small letters etc.). In the third phase, with the aid of Text Mining techniques, based mostly on queries of morphological kind, over 20,000 words correctly spelled or resulting from linguistic productivity of proper names (derivations such as: *ex-andreottiano, ipercraxismo*, etc.) were identified. In this way, a final matrix of the kind of *forms per year*, which juxtaposes the vocabularies of the set of 291,649 recognised words in the years 1990-1999, was formed. This huge database (called Rep90), other than containing approximately 3 million cells of occurrences of every word per year, collects other informations useful to define the *imprinting* of the language of the press and to study some lexical evolutions of the Nineties. Every query on such material produces thousands of examples in terms of variety of inflected forms and, for the words with very low occurrences, also to tens or hundred of extracted inflected forms.

3 Insights into the evolution of 1990s' Italian language

3.1 Vocabulary growth

The first considerations regard the process of growth of the vocabulary, which can be measured by comparing the collected vocabularies year by year with Rep90 (Table 1). Despite the great dimensions of the texts, in ten years the vocabulary doubles the words (from 143,000 to 291,000 different inflected forms), with an progressive annual growth rate[5] that has decreased from 22% in 1991 to 3% in 1999. Even after the extraction of 230 million occur-rences, we are far from exhausting the vocabulary (Figure 1) and there is no stability in terms of quantity of different words. In this perspective, the inci-dence of neologisms or forms that disappeared in the decade provides some

---

[3]On this regard, in October 2003, this restriction was overcome, thanks to the increasing calculating capacity of the available computers. In fact, it is now possibile to reproduce the same database by processing the whole corpus as a single file of 1,4 Gigabytes.

[4]By this way we have separated proper names of persons, toponyms, companies and other entities and stored them in another database.

[5]The rate (column "% Increases" in Table 1) corresponds to the ratio of the absolute increment (column "Increases" on the same table) and the amount of different words (column "Cumulative Sum of Different Words") referring to the previous year.

interesting points (see Bolasco and Canzonetti (2003)).

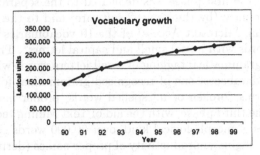

Fig. 1. Vocabulary growth curve.

Year	Cumulative sum of Different Words	Increase	% Increases
1990	143,609		
1991	175,610	32,001	22.3
1992	199,796	24,186	13.8
1993	218,004	18,208	9.1
1994	235,022	17,018	7.8
1995	249,547	14,525	6.2
1996	263,655	14,108	5.7
1997	274,214	10,559	4.0
1998	283,281	9,067	3.3
1999	291,649	8,368	3.0

Table 1. Vocabulary growth data

3.2 Stable Trends

3.2.1 Length of words

The average length of words is an index of the complexity of the language, according to the well-known Zipf's laws (Chiari (2002), pp. 69-77). This property has a stable distribution throughout the ten years. Observing the distribution of the different inflected forms (V) in Figure 2a, we can see how 10 letters words constitute the modal value of the Italian language.

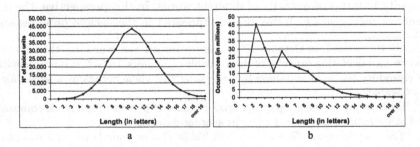

Fig. 2. Distribution of different inflected forms and occurrences by length (in letters).

With reference to the distribution of the occurrences (N), we can observe a bimodal trend (Figure 2b). The minimum length of 4 letters is due to the specific distribution of articulate prepositions, which in Italian have the following statistical distribution:

Lunghezza	V	N
3 letters	22	13 millions
4 letters	13	3 millions
5 letters	40	8 millions

Table 2. Distribution of articulate prepositions

The distributive anomaly is due to the fact that syllables made up of 3+2 letters (i.e.: del+la/e/o, dal+la/e/o, nel+la/e/o, but also ne+gli, su+gli etc.) prevail on those of type 2+2 (al+la/e/o). This result is very stable even in short texts.

The average length, in terms of arithmetic mean, is absolutely stable in the period (that referring to V - equal to 10.3 - reveals the richness of the "La Repubblica" lexicon, independently from the number of the occurrences of the words; that relative to the amount of words (N) - equal to 5 - records the average value typical of the usage of that language). To the contrary, the variation of these average values from a corpus to the other points out the complexity of the text which can be inferred by comparing different kinds of language according to the decreasing complexity (formal, written, standard, spoken), as shown by the mean values in Table 3.

3.2.2 Profile of the grammatical categories
More complex is the data related to parts of speech, as the results mentioned earlier on are related to the grammatical tagging free context done (that is to say list-based), which can only classify non-ambiguous inflected forms. This determines statistics that cannot be compared with others coming from entirely lemmatised texts[6]. To the contrary, it has the advantage of speed of calculation and of standard measurements. Therefore, the comparison between the amounts presented here and those coming from other works would not be possible due to the different methods used to calculate them. In our case, the rate of ambiguity of the words from Rep90 in the decade is stable and equal to 20.2% of the vocabulary (V) and to 56.2% of occurrences (N)[7]. Without counting the ambiguous forms, the incidence of the main parts of the discourse (nouns, verbs, adjectives and adverbs) turns out to be extremely

---

[6]Moerover this comparisons are very difficult without homogenous criteria in the lemmatization process.

[7]The latter reduces to 34.9% by forcing the category of about thirty terms having very high frequency, like *di, e, a, in* etc., ambiguous only in a theoretical way, as in fact more than 99% of their occurrences belong to only one category, for example the preposition in the case of the form *di*.

steady in the decade, considering as average values for the period under consideration those highlighted in bold in Table 3. The same table indicates the values found in other lexicons[8]. The trend in the variation between lexicons is illustrated in Paragraph 4.

	Political language		Rep90		Standard language		Spoken lexicon	
	a		b		c		d	
	V	N	V	N	V	N	V	N
Average lenght	9.0	5.2	**10.3**	**5.0**	8.5	5.0	8.3	4.3
Nouns	29.9	33.6	**24.7**	**32.5**	32.3	30.3	35.8	32.2
Verbs	47.1	18.9	**55.9**	**23.7**	48.3	27.9	45.3	30.0
Adjectives	18.0	8.5	**15.1**	**5.5**	15.3	5.7	11.8	13.8
Adverbs	4.2	2.9	**1.6**	**3.3**	2.9	4.0	2.9	5.2

Table 3. Comparison between average length of words and main parts of speech in different lexicons (political language, press, standard language, spoken language)[9]

3.3 Evolutive Trends

Verb tenses
Other classes of lexical units in Rep90 are not steady throughout the decade. In verbs, for example, tense, mood and person present significant evolutions. Among verbal tenses, the present tense prevails (77%), as one could easily predict in newspaper articles, and increases by one percentage; the past tense (16%) decreases by 0.6%, whereas the future tense (6%) decreases by only 0.3%. Seen in relative terms, the future tense decreases by 5.4% and the past tense by 3.5%, whereas the present tense increases by 1.2%: considering that the volumes of Rep90 are so vast, these variations are definitely relevant.
In order to analyse these trends we used the IT index[10] (cfr. Bolasco, Canzonetti (2003)) which allows to find which kinds of words have determined the aforesaid trends. The calculation of the IT index on the

---

[8]The amount shown belong to homogeneous measurements carried out on the four corpus taking in account only not ambiguous inflected forms.

[9]*Source*: political (formal): *TPG*, Bolasco (1996); standard language: *Polif*, Bolasco e Morrone (1998); spoken lexicon: *LIP*, De Mauro (1993).

[10]$IT_1 = IT_0(Occ_1 - Occ_n/Occ_1 + Occ_n)$
where:

$$IT_0 = \frac{\Pi_{j=1}^n [(Scarto\_norm_j)(Scarto\_norm_{j-1})] - 1}{2}$$

Scarto_norm$_j$ is the difference between observed occurrence in the j-th period and mean occurrence, standardized regarding the absolute value; Occ_1 is the normalized observed occurrence in the first period; Occ_n is the normalized observed occurrence in the last period; n is the number of the years of the whole considered period.

verbal forms of the present tense revealed an increase in verbs of common usage and of generic meaning in the ten years, vis a vis a decrease in verbs relating to formal language and having a more precise meaning (for instance: *smettere-finire/cessare, diventare/divenire, arrivare/giungere, dire/affermare-dichiarare*). This indicates that one of the reasons for the increase in the usage of the present tense, may lie in a simplification of language.

The modes

The analysis of the verb modes seems to confirm this hypothesis. In fact, the indicative mode is, as it is expected, the most widely used (62.8%). It is surprising, though, that this is the only mode that increases in the decade under consideration (1.9% in relative terms), whereas other modes decrease, with variations comprised in a range which goes from the -8.2% of the participle to the -2.4% of the conjunctive[11].

It is possible to summarize the above trends in tenses and modes in a graphic which illustrates a factorial analysis of the correspondences in the data deriving from the *imprinting*. In Figure 3a the first factor characterizes quite clearly the time and it is possible to notice how the indicative and the present tense are typical of the last years, while the participle characterizes the beginning of the period.

The verb persons and personal pronouns

On analyzing verb subjects and personal pronouns, we can notice some interesting changes (Figures 3b and 4).

Among verb subjects, the first person, singular and plural, records a growth in relative terms (42.5% singular, 15.2% plural). Moreover, it is possible to notice how the first singular is "overcoming" the first plural (cfr. Figure 4a). The use of the second singular person is increasing too (34%). The third person, the most used, is instead decreasing, but the third singular person shows a decrease rate that is lower than the plural person (respectively -0.8% and -9.1%).

Among pronouns (Figure 4b), the use of the first person is still increasing, as it is also the case with the second person, although its use in absolute terms is very low.

This seems to suggest that direct speech is now the preferred form, probably because journalists tend to present interviews or quotations in their articles. Figure 3b confirms these results, as it shows in detail the positions assumed by the verb persons (in the corresponding pronouns and verb forms) on the first factorial plan. This shows the increasing use of singular pronouns in recent years as compared to the corresponding usages of plural pronouns.

---

[11]It is curious to notice that the conjuntive is the mode with the lower decline rate. However, it is easy to assume that the descendent dynamics has been more evident in previous periods.

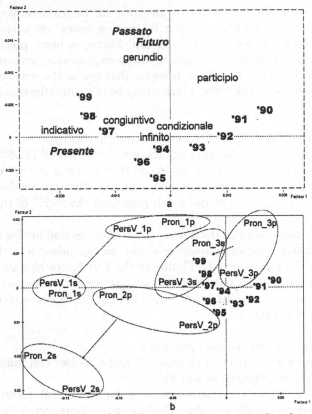

Fig. 3. Verb tenses and modes (a) and personal pronouns and verb persons (b) on the first factorial plain

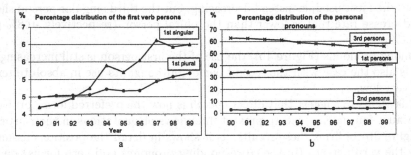

Fig. 4. Evolution of verb persons and personal pronouns

The complex forms

The analysis of the morphologic structure of words reveals an increase in the usage of complex forms: verb enclitics, derivations/alterations and forms constituted by prefix+stem+suffix (respectively 10.5%, 11.8% and 22.2% in relative terms). This occurs despite the simple inflected forms (seen as entries of the "basic language" in a dictionary), that show a slightly decrease through-out the 10 years under examination, however meaningful in absolute terms since such forms constantly represent over 99% of the occurrences. Along with syntactic simplification, there is a tendency to "agglutinate" some words as if they were one. This is shown by the average word length in Rep90, which is considerably higher in comparison with other lexicons (Table 3) which can be explained with the characteristics of press lexicon, which is particularly synthetic due to the quick impact it is meant to have on the readers.

4 Avenues for further research

In the light of these results, it is possible to notice how, in the Nineties, there is tendency to use a simpler and more straightforward lexicon (present tense, indicative mode, first and second person) and to use complex forms. This transformation is due to a need for synthesis that does not compromise communication and understanding in so much as we deal with written concepts. The examples presented here show only a number of properties that constitute the *imprinting* of a text. Their robustness in terms of frequency stability, within the limits of the measurement of unambiguous inflected forms, is guaranteed from the large size of frequency lexicons. The differences indicated in Table 3 (cf. Paragraph 3.2.2) are evidence of the fact that there exist different structural elements for each kind of language (political, press, standard, spoken).

It is possible to find, for the occurrences, an expressive range that goes from the more formal language (the political language) to the more informal (spoken language), with an intermediate register in the middle (the language of the press and standard language). It is possible to summarize this tendency as follows: an increasing usage of verbs (from 19% in the political language to 30% in spoken language), a substantial stability for nouns, a decreasing usage of adjectives (from 8.5% in political language to 4% in spoken language) and a greater preference for adverbs (from 3% in political language to 5% in spoken language).

Regarding verb persons and personal pronouns, Figures 5 give further evidence for the existing distinction between "informal" languages (spoken and standard) and "formal" ones (press and political). With a few exceptions, the former are characterized by a wider use of the first and second person (singular and plural), whereas the latter is characterized by the use of the third person is important.

If we organize this logic of measurement and comparison, it will be possible to define the imprinting of reference for each language typology. These characteristics could be useful also for the automatic classification of texts, in so much as this is based on the similarity with the *imprinting*. Such a possibility is suggested in a study (Koppel et al. (2002)) which was carried out in order to recognize the gender of the author by analyzing some structural characteristics of a text.

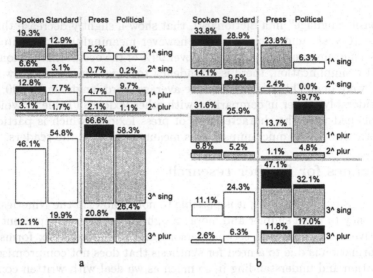

Fig. 5. Verb persons (a) and personal pronouns (b) in lexicons

References

BALBI, S., BOLASCO, S., VERDE R. (2002): *Text Mining on Elementary Forms in Complex Lexical Structures.* In A. Morin and P. Sebillot (eds.) (2002), vol. 1, 89-100.

BOLASCO, S. (2002): Integrazione statistico-linguistica nell'analisi del contenuto. In: B. Mazzara (ed.): *Metodi qualitativi in psicologia sociale.* Carocci Ed., Roma, 329-342.

BOLASCO, S. and CANZONETTI, A. (2003): *Text mining (TM) as key to reading the Nineties' language in the daily "La Repubblica".* SIS Scientific Convention, Napoli.

BOLASCO, S., VERDE, R., BALBI, S. (2002): *Outils de Text Mining pour l'analyse de structures lexicales à éléments variables.* In: A. Morin e P. Sebillot (eds.) (2002), vol. 1, 197-208.

CHIARI, I. (2002): *Ridondanza e linguaggio.* Carocci, Roma.

DELLARATTA, F. (2003): Automatic texts' classification on the basis of evaluative dictionary. In AA.VV.: *Book of short papers.* Cladag2003, CLUEB, Bologna, 155-158.

GAETA, L. (2001): *Sviluppi recenti dell'analisi quantitativa della produttivit morfologica.* Seminary at Institute of Psycology, CNR, Roma.

GIORDANO, R. and VOGHERA, M. (2002): *Verb system and verb usage in spoken and written italian.* In A. Morin e P. Sebillot (eds), vol. 1, 289-300.

KOPPEL, M., ARGAMON, S., SHIMONI, (2002): Automatic categorization of written text by author gender. *Literary and Linguistic Computing, vol 17, n 4, 401-412.*

MORIN, A. and SEBILLOT, P.(eds.) (2002): *JADT 2002.* St Malo, IRISA-INRIA, 2 voll.

SULLIVAN, D. (2001): *Document Warehousing and Text Mining: Techniques for Improving Business Operations, Marketing, and Sales.* Wiley, N.Y.

Evaluating Undergraduate Education Through Multiple Choice Tests

Franca Crippa

Dipartimento di Statistica,
Università di Milano–Bicocca, Italy
franca.crippa@unimib.it

Abstract. Multiple choice tests have been recently introduced in Italian Universities as an instrument for evaluating students' performance. In our paper we appraise the objectiveness of such a classification, adopting a Dichotomous Rasch Model (RM, Rasch (1960)) that transforms, *via* a Simple Logistic Model (SLM), test scores into the general structure of correct and incorrect answers. As widely understood, measurement requires that the quantification assigned to the construct be independent of both the observer and the sample of respondents. Subsequently, we extend the analysis to the polytomous answers, by means of a Partial Credit Model (PCM, Masters (1982)), in order to further distinguish different levels of incorrectness, between the classification of the errors above.

1 Introduction

Quality assurance in testing involves many aspects of what is known in statistics as quality control procedures, while requiring the respect of the specific nature of the data. This paper fits into such an analytical framework, as it aims to verify the adequacy of multiple-choice tests, recently introduced in Italian Universities, as a means of objectively evaluating -and hence classifying- undergraduate students' ability to master a scientific subject. In truth, outcomes consist in the evidence of the ability of scientific reasoning, the latter being a non observable or latent variable. Moreover, classical theories definitions of the difficulty of items as the mere distribution of successes and failures is highly unsatisfactory in an educational processes. Indeed, as results so obtained rely on the respondents, they do not necessarily take into account the full ability in completing professional tasks. This approach does not seem consistent with the purposes of academic institutional duties, as a candidate is considered competent or proficient if fully able to perform professional and/or scientific tasks. For instance, a surgeon or an chemist who would learn to systematically skip some steps of her/his job would be socially unacceptable, despite the degree of relevance of the skipped steps themselves.

2 Methods and materials

In grading, only the correct answers is highlighted, regardless the fact that in each item distractors may not always be equally wrong. Therefore, the multiple-choice format is considered a special test construction in which the answers are to be recoded and transformed into a dichotomous scoring function. 'Fail' and 'pass' are the response alternatives and the probabilistic Dichotomous Rasch Model (RM, Rash (1960)) is applied. On the teaching side, though, such a model is required to provide substantive insights in the students' developments not always expressed effectively by the grades. As a matter of fact, in the progress toward competence, students make mistakes at different levels and to different degrees. The mere concept of failure might provide an incomplete feedback, as it does not inform on the nature of the errors in reasoning and, subsequently, on the pathway of the improvements, in case they are possible. These considerations lead to the analysis of outcomes by means of a Partial Credit Model (PCM, Masters (1982)): the multiple-choice structure sometimes presents an inner item-specific hierarchy, not necessarily shared by the various items. The resulting classification of the inadequacy levels could be useful in defining the kind of educational counselling needed and the type of effort asked on the students' side to meet the required standards. The sample is drawn from results of final examinations in a section of the course in General Psychology at the Faculty of Psychology at the University of Milano–Bicocca, and it consists of 149 undergraduates, mainly females (75.2%). Hereafter, for sake of simplicity, items labels are omitted and substituted by numerical codes, the test being composed of 30 questions on memory, learning and motivations.

3 The internal structure of the outcomes assessment

3.1 A measurement model for classifying performances

The simplest response format records only two levels of performance on an item, a pair of exhaustive and mutually exclusive response alternatives. It is the most frequently used format for scoring outcomes of educational tests: it gives no credit for partially correct solutions. Such Rasch Dichotomous Model can be written as:

$$\Pr(X_{ni} = 1|\beta_n, \delta_i) = \pi_{ni} = \frac{\exp(\beta_n - \delta_i)}{1 + \exp(\beta_n - \delta_i)} \tag{1}$$

for $n = 1, \ldots, N$ and $i = 1, \ldots, I$. Expression (1), the Simple Logistic Model (SLM), gives the probability of a correct answer x_{ni} by the n-th subject when replying to the i-th item. Both the item difficulty δ_i and the person's ability β_n are measured along a shared continuum. Due to sufficiency properties, the estimation of the parameters β_n is independent of the hardness of the exam (*test free*) and conversely the estimation of the parameters δ_n is independent of the ability of each subject (*sample free*). Our response matrix is subjected to the dichotomous analysis through the WINSTEP software (Linacre (1991-2003)).

We limit hereinafter the discussion to few diagnostic aspects, as an accurate reference to the extremely high number of testing procedures goes beyond the aims of our paper. The problem of evaluating model fit is solved in RM within the framework of the general multinomial model (Fischer and Molenaar (1995)). In particular, we are interested in chi-square fit statistics (Wright and Masters (1982)). The infit statistic is an information-weighted sum of the standardized residuals. In a RM the information relative to an observation is given by its variance; if the observation is not extreme, then the variance tends to increase, otherwise it falls. The infit of an item is a weighted sum across subjects:

$$\text{infit} = \sum_{n=1}^{N} Z_{ni}^2 W_{ni} / \sum_{n=1}^{N} W_{ni} \qquad (2)$$

where Z_{ni}^2 are the squared standardized residuals for subject n replying to item i, and W_{ni} are the individual variances of residuals. The weighting operation lessens the impact of the unexpected responses that are farthest and enhances the ones that are closest to the persons' or item measure.

The outfit is the unweighted sum of the squared residuals:

$$\text{outfit} = \sum_{n=1}^{N} Z_{ni} / N \qquad (3)$$

and, oppositely to the previous diagnostic, gives relatively more importance to distant unexpected responses rather than to close ones (correspondingly, the infit and the outfit for each person are summed across items). In our sample, we adopt a rigorous criteria and decide to remove from the model and to devote a special attention to items and subjects not strictly respecting the requirements. Such an attitude is maintained even when in RM routine more attention is paid to aberrant infit statistics, causing more concern than large outfit ones (Bond (2001)), the reason being the relevance of the task of grading undergraduates. Both the items and the subjects' removals from the database meet other studies standard (Tesio and Cantagallo (1998)). Six items, equally split between the 'easy' and the 'difficult' questions, are to be excused as misfitting. Their outfit statistic is always positive; therefore, they arise almost systematically unexpected responses, since some of most able students (also due to idiosyncrasies) fail them and/or, on the other hand, they are passed by the least able subjects. Among these troublesome items, 3 do not match even the infit statistics: anomalous items are the most common source of large infit indexes and this seems the case in our sample. Multiple-choice answers are sometimes constructed with semantic biases, in order to verify the ability of avoiding them, but this structure may turn out in a trap. Large infit statistics may, in fact, highlight items that sound ambiguous, representing an extraneous domain and capturing some peculiarity of the subjects' sample. As far as diagnostic procedures on persons are involved, we remove 38 students from the original 149 persons. As shown in Table 1, some students show an infit statistic larger than 2 in absolute value with an adequate outfit, as subjects number 48 and 56. Both students seem to be quite unsuccessful at a group of questions that are below in measure their ability levels, respectively +0.41 and +0.73; in other words they fail the easiest questions. The investigation of the individual problems in the scientific matter requires a diagnostic evaluation of the map of each student and deeper qualitative inspection to find out the reasons of gaps in fundamental concepts, if this turns out to be the case. Student 88 has an ability measure of -1.71. The standardized infit index, equal to 1.2, indicates a pattern of performance that closely approximates the predicted RM response pattern based on the student's ability estimate, since the expected value of the infit statistics is 1, whereas the outfit index exceeds the cut-off value of approximately 2. In this case, some of the few unexpected correct responses were obtained with a bit of guessing.

Subject Number	Raw Score	Measure	Error	Infit Zstd	Outfit Zstd	Subject Number	Raw Score	Measure	Error	Infit Zstd	Outfit Zstd
4	14	-0.12	0.41	0.3	2.1	88	6	-1.71	0.51	1.2	2.4
39	15	0.05	0.41	-2.4	-2.0	89	10	-0.83	0.44	1.3	0.7
48	18	0.55	0.41	-2.3	-1.6	97	10	-0.83	0.44	1.3	1.1
53	13	-0.29	0.42	1.9	1.4	105	10	-0.83	0.44	0.9	0.9
56	19	0.73	0.42	-2.3	-1.5	107	10	-0.83	0.44	0.8	1.0
61	3	-2.70	0.67	0.2	2.5	111	13	-0.29	0.42	0.0	1.2
63	17	0.38	0.41	1.7	1.1	146	8	-1.24	0.46	1.7	2.6
75	12	-0.47	0.42	1.5	1.0	149	20	0.90	0.43	1.6	3.6

Table 1. Measures of ability, infit and outfit statistics, residuals relative to some misfitting students

3.2 Evaluating the adequacy of the examination test

The group's average ability estimate, in logits equal to +0.16, is the first indicator that this exam is rather well-matched, being the value close to 0 for a perfectly designed test. (An analogous piece of information is gathered on the whole sample of items and students, misfitting included, since the mean value is 0.05). The standard deviation of 1.22 for person estimates indicates smaller variation than the one with item measures, being the overall standard deviation equal to 1.77. The fitting items and students' measures are illustrated in Figure 1: the measures, in true interval logit units of the subjects' ability, share almost the same domain on the continuum as the measures pertaining the items. The evenly spread of questions along the variable (the vertical axis), with few gaps, indicates a linear, rather well defined or tested variable; in addition, subjects follow almost a bell-shaped distribution, as few of them gain either a low or a high score and the most part get an intermediate score. Person and item separation indexes are computed, defined as the ratios of the true spread of the measurement (i.e. the standard deviation of the estimates after subtracting from their observed variance the error variance attributable to their standard error of measurement) with their measurement error.

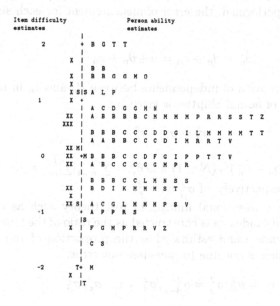

Fig. 1. Item-person map for the analysis of the multiple-choice test in General Psychology assessment, section on Learning and Memory.

3.3 The differentiating power of the test among candidates of different abilities

The requirement of internal consistency in latent trait theory, to which the measurement of an ability belongs, consists in the items in a test reflecting all the same unobservable variable. The counterpart of internal consistency on the subjects' side is unidimensionality. The latter is a single individual characteristic, the very one of interest, expressed by a unique value on a unique latent continuum (Andrich (2003)). It then follows that, in such a probabilistic model as SLM, consistency on the persons' side is even more important, since the ordering of the subjects may be influenced only by the unique non observed dimension the test aims to measure. Therefore reliability is a separation reliability, whereas conventional indexes such as Cronbach Alfa take merely into account the variance of the subjects' total scores, as the greater this factor the greater the index.

Let the mean and variance of the latent trait, the true ability in the studied scientific matter, be μ and σ_β^2 in the population. For each person, the ability can be written as:

$$\beta_n = \mu + \theta_n \tag{4}$$

where θ_n represents the individual departure from the population average. Once estimation is performed, the error of measurement for each subject ε_n can be added in (4):

$$\hat{\beta}_n = \beta_n + \varepsilon_n = \mu + \theta_n + \varepsilon_n \tag{5}$$

and, under the assumption of independence between β_n and ε_n in the population, the variance of actual abilities is given by:

$$\sigma_{\hat\beta}^2 = \sigma_{\beta}^2 + \sigma_{\varepsilon}^2 \tag{6}$$

where $\hat\sigma_{\beta}^2 = \sum_{n=1}^{N}(\hat\beta_n - \hat\beta_n^-)^2/(N-1)$ and $\hat\sigma_{\varepsilon}^2 = \sum_{n=1}^{N}[\sum_{i=1}^{I}\hat\pi_{ni}(1-\hat\pi_{ni})]^{-1}$ are the estimates, respectively, of σ_{β}^2 and σ_{ε}^2.

In analogy with conventional indexes in test theory such as Cronbach Alpha, SLM reliability index r_β is constructed as the ratio of the true variance to the observed variance and estimated as the proportion of the observed sample variance which is not due to measurement error:

$$r_\beta = \sigma_\beta^2/\sigma_{\hat\beta}^2 = \sigma_{\hat\beta-\varepsilon}^2/\sigma_{\hat\beta}^2 = 1 - \sigma_\varepsilon^2/\sigma_{\hat\beta}^2 \tag{7}$$

This expression gives the proportion of dispersion reproducible by the model itself, that is the reliability as generally understood.

On the other hand, the ratio:

$$g_\beta = \sigma_\beta/\sigma_\varepsilon = \sigma_{\hat\beta-\varepsilon}/\sigma_\varepsilon \tag{8}$$

represents the standard deviation of the sample in standard error units. It allows to calculate, through appropriate algebraic transformations, the number of statistically distinct person strata identified by the examination (Wright and Master (1982)). In our sample, person reliability and person separation coefficient are respectively equal to 0.78 and 1.87. The spread of the person measure is fairly wide, and the students are classified in three group with distinct levels of ability. On the item side, Rasch separation coefficient is 3.63, reliability 0.93; the greater the separation, the wider is the range of ability which can be measured by the scale and transformed into grades.

4 An insight in conceptualisation problems: the Partial Credit Model

The similiarities or the elements of truth in several of the replies to a question in the test may confuse to a different extent a less than perfectly prepared student and the kind of educational counselling needed may vary accordingly. As a matter of fact, it is explained above how responses in multiple-choice tests may be incorrect, but still indicate some knowledge; therefore they are given partial credit towards a correct response. The amount of partial correctness varies across items. It follows that a straightforward extension of 'right or wrong' scoring is the identification, in our case, of one intermediate level of performance on each item; such an intermediate step is awarded partial credit for reaching it. Three ordered levels of performance are identified in each item, labelled 0 (no o 'absurd' response), 1 (incorrect answer but with some elements of knowledge) and 2 (appropriate answer).

In order to understand a certain concept -and subsequently reply correctly- the students need to have completed the steps from level 0 to 1, and from the latter to 2, in their studying towards the final examination. A general expression for the probability for the subject n scoring x on item i, developed from (1), may be written as:

$$\Pr(X_{nix} = 1|\beta_n, \delta_i) = \pi_{nix} = \frac{\exp\left[\sum_{j=0}^{x}(\beta_n - \delta_{ij})\right]}{\sum_{k=0}^{m_i}\exp\left[\sum_{j=0}^{x}(\beta_n - \delta_{ij})\right]} \tag{9}$$

for $x = 0, 1, \ldots, m_i$. The observation x in (9) is the count of the completed item steps. The numerator contains the difficulties of these completed steps, $\delta_{i1}, \delta_{i2}, \ldots, \delta_{ix}$, while the denominator is the sum of all possible m_i+1 possible numerators. The response matrix is submitted to the Partial Credit diagnos-

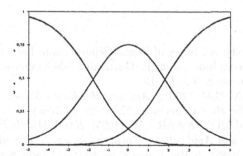

Fig. 2. Probability curves for a well-functioning two-steps item, where the first step is still an incomplete level of competence, but with some sounds elements of truth. The distinction is valid for educational counseling only.

tic procedure, through the same software mentioned above; due to misfitting statistics, only two items (namely 19 and 21) are to be excused. It should be noticed that they are a subset of the six items removed in the dichotomous study. A premise to the diagnostic interpretation should be posed: the Partial Credit Model points towards a 'mischievous' path taken during the students' conceptualisation process, since a partially correct answer implies elements of proper knowledge mixed up with completely extraneous domains of information. The parameters are estimated for the difficulties of each step of every item, as there are no shared rating scales (Wright, Masters, (1982)). The results show that, in 13 items out of 28, the progression from level 0 to 1 is easier than the one from 1 to 2 ($\delta_{11} < \delta_{12}$); in 2 items it is the same, while in the remaining 13 items the relation is the reverse ($\delta_{11} > \delta_{12}$). The implication is that in 50% of the questions difficulties arise from grasping the subject, in the remaining cases from a 'superimposition' of information that are not logically set in place. These results are relevant, nonetheless providing an incomplete understanding, as they do not convey the source and the type of setback in gaining competence. An improvement can be obtained from extending the scale for each item, i.e. allowing at least one more step in the multiple choice test structure, in case confounding causes are identifiable. Rasch item separation coefficient is 4.35, corresponding to 6 strata, reliability 0.95. On the students' ability side, the separation coefficient is equal to 2.02, identifying 3 strata, reliability 0.82. The troublesome point in the diagnostic procedure here is that the 37 misfitting subjects do not always coincide with the ones in the dichotomous analysis. In conclusion, the students are satisfactorily classified by the items, provided they fit, as a relevant number (at least 37 out of 149 in both models) do not. The grading systems holds and the weak point of the learning/teaching process is clearly identified, indicating that the latter needs to be pinpointed with far higher precision, relying on the flexibility of the multiple choice structure and on other analytical instruments.

References

ANDRICH, D. (2003): An Index of Person Separation in Latent Trait Theory, the Traditional KR-20 Index, and the Guttman Scale Response Pattern. *Eucation Research Perspective, 9:1, 90–10.*

BOND, T. and FOX, C.M. (2001): *Applying the Rasch Model. Fundamental Measurements in the Human Sciences,* Erlbaum, Mahawa.

FISCHER, G.H. and MOLENAAR, I.W. (1995): *Rasch Models.Foundations, Recent Developments, and Applications.* Springer-Verlag, New York.

MASTERS, G.N. (1982): A Rasch model for Partial Credit Scoreing. *Psychometrica, 47, 149–174.*

RASCH, G. (1960): *Probabilistic Models for some intellingence and attainment tests.* [Danish Institute of Educational Research 1960, University of Chicago MESA Press 1980, MESA Press 1993], MESA Press, Chicago.

TESIO L. and CANTAGALLO A. (1998): The Functional Assessment Measure (FAM) in closed traumatic brain injury outpatients: A Rasch-based psychometric study. *Journal of Outcome Measurement, 2(2),79-96.*

WRIGHT, B.D. and MASTERS, G.N. (1982): *Rating Scale Analysis.* Mesa Press, Chicago.

A New Approach in Business Travel Survey: Multivariate Techniques for Strata Design

Andrea Guizzardi

Dipartimento di Scienze Statistiche
Università di Bologna, Italy
guizzard@stat.unibo.it

Abstract. Business travel demand in official statistics is often measured by means of households/travellers survey. Such approach produces very little evidence about expenditure and demand structure because for that purpose others statistical units should be sampled. Enterprises - that actually buy business travels - are rarely interviewed. The application of CHAID technique to data from an explorative sampling survey on the Italian enterprises shows statistically significant relationships among business travel expenditure, enterprise size and economic sector. The multivariate analysis allows to derive the definition of the optimal strata design for survey on business travel through enterprises interviews.

1 Measuring the role of tourism in economies

Tourism is an important part of modern life-style and plays a crucial role in the world economy. In Europe, the tourism sector employs around 7 million people directly, which account for about 5% of total employment. Almost three times as many are indirectly involved through business connections with other related sectors. About 7% of total SMEs in Europe belongs to the tourism industry and 6.5% of the total turnover of European SMEs is generated by the tourism industry (source http://europa.eu.int/comm/enterprise /services/tourism/tourismeu.htm). Tourism is a demand-side concept involving a wide range of activities and different motivations to consume, mainly leisure or business but the hospitality should also consider training purposes (i.e. visiting students; see Tassinari 1994) and others travel motivations. Developed economies are generally mature markets for leisure tourism, therefore attention is gradually shifting towards business travels. The latter reduce seasonality, it is more valuable than leisure tourism and - because of business trends in management, market globalization and training activities - it shows a rate of growth that generally exceeds the overall tourism growth rate.

Despite the sector importance, present-day statistics on tourism do not provide sufficient business information, as pointed out in several official reports (see among others OECD 2001). This lack of information is a consequence of Eurostat (2000) suggestion to use household surveys for data collection. Such approach produces no or very little relevant data about business travels structure and costs limiting the possibility to evaluate indirect GDP, business policy effects, employment consequences or to prepare a satellite account. The critical point is the tourism demand definition. Households represent only final demand; therefore they are not the optimal statistical units when the focus is on travel as an intermediate goods. The decision to buy business travel is not generally taken by travellers themselves but by company managers (enterprises), who are the only subjects knowledgeable about travel costs, purchasing processes or travel policies. In order to provide a more complete statistical picture for this important sector it is necessary to collect information from both household and business surveys. Current official surveys on enterprises, monitors production costs but do not focus on travel cost. Following the 2002-2004 Italian National Statistics Programme directives, a new survey on production costs is being carried out (periodical but more detailed). It collects information on enterprises travel expenditures but, actually, the only available information is the adopted questionnaire (see www.istat.it, key search: "rilevazione sulla struttura dei costi").

There are in fact substantial differences between techniques used for business surveys and those used for household surveys. Surveys of firms are designed as one-stage stratified simple random samples; techniques such as two-stage sampling, which minimize the costs of enumeration, are not required. Stratification usually has two dimensions: size and type of activity. However, businesses are extremely heterogeneous compared with households. The largest businesses employ many thousands people and contribute enormously to economic activity; so they are usually included in the take all or completely enumerated strata. In addition businesses undertake activities which have very differentiated characteristics (from agriculture to public administration), thus showing very different behaviors.

It should be clear by now that referring to survey based on households or travellers in order to study business travel is theoretically not founded and technically inefficient. Taking enterprises as the population to be investigated has at least three advantages. First, the households/travellers' population is wider and less known than the enterprises' population. Second, enterprises are more informed about business trips and their real costs, which can be retrieved from business accountings. Finally, enterprises are generally more used to interact with statistical offices and can provide more reliable information. A better picture of the tourism sector can be obtained if leisure and business travels are considered separately, the first being a final consumption and the latter an intermediate consumption. Business travel should thus be investigated by surveying public and private organizations. A first step in this direction could be adding questions about business travel in current business surveys. However, there is little evidence for business travel expenditure dependence on enterprise's structural variables. Therefore it is not clear if the stratification variables used in current surveys on GDP and other production costs, are suitable as stratification variables for investigating travel costs.

This work attempts to provide a preliminary answer to such question, by applying the CHAID technique to the results of an explorative survey on private enterprises business travel expenditures. The first goal is to model travel expenditure with respect to business etherogeneity evaluating the relationship between travel expenditure and a set of structural variables commonly used as stratification variables in the national sampling survey of enterprises. CHAID build a tree which splits enterprises business travel expenditure into final nodes leading to a statistically significant discrimination. These nodes can be seen as the optimal (post)stratification of a survey on business travel expenditure; with this perspective it is possible to evaluate whether Italian business surveys can be efficiently extended to survey business travel as a production cost. Finally a new approach to business travel survey, coherent with the intrinsic nature of the object studied (that is a productive input) is suggested.

2 Data and stratification technique

Data on business travel expenditure used in the present work were collected in November 2002 through a direct survey of Italian enterprises. Only enterprises with more than 4 employees (in the service sector) and more than 9 employees (in the industrial sector) were included in the study. Most small enterprises (e.g. shops or farms) have a productive process where business travel expenditure is very marginal. Agriculture and the public sector are not considered. agriculture. The resulting set was of 371,100 enterprises, a 10% share of the total 3.8 million Italian enterprises which accounts for 55% of the total number of employees in Italy (data from the national archive of enterprises ASIA 2000). The selection was based on two different random samples; one among large enterprises (with more than 100 employees) and another among SME. In each sample the probability of selection was proportional to the size. Mail, fax and e-mail questionnaires were sent to a sample of 1,600 firms, 1/3 of which were selected among SME and 2/3 among big enterprises to have a better coverage of the more relevants units. The statistical units list was the "annuario SEAT ed. 2001", which covers almost two thirds of large enterprises population. In both samples the final response rate was 13% (206 completed questionnaires after telephone recall.

CHAID methodology (Kass 1980) was employed in order to identify heterogeneity across enterprises total expenditure in business travel (dependent variable) defined as all the costs recorded in company accounts as travel costs. This partition tree method was used to study the relationships with a set of possible predictor variables that may interact among themselves. These potential variables (splitting variables) have been chosen among those used in the Italian GDP survey. The number of employees (punctual), the ATECO 1991 two-digit classification (NACE Rev. 1 section-class), the 2 macro-sectors (industry and construction; services) and the geographical areas (4 macro regions) have been analysed.

CHAID allows to see whether a sample splitting based on these predictors leads to a statistically significant discrimination in the dependent measure. At the end of the tree building process a set of maximally different groups in terms of overall travel expenditure is derived. Intervals (splits) are determined optimally for the independent variables so as to maximize the ability to explain the business travel expenditure in terms of variance components. Therefore we propose to see CHAID results as the optimal stratification (based on predicting variables) for a survey on business travel expenditure. Statistical F-tests are carried out in order to evaluate splits significance. Tests are corrected conservatively for the fact that many possible ways of splitting the data at one time are examined. However, since some descriptive indications can be obtained from the tree structure, we allow for segmentation with a p-value less than 0,2.

3 Results

Results (see figure 1) show that enterprise size is the most important variable for describing differences in business travel expenditure. The partition found is significant at a very low p-value. Enterprises are split in 5 classes; as expected, average travel expenditure increases with enterprises size. The average business travel expenditure goes from 79.000 euro for the small size enterprises group up to 3 million euro for large enterprises. It is interesting to note that small expenditure enterprises have a size threshold of 90 employees which can be consider the optimal splitting point in a two strata sampling design. The value is very close to the enterprise size that in the national GDP survey represents the threshold between the sample survey and the total survey. This group, as well as the group of large enterprises (with more than 687 employees), has a sample expenditure variability that - given the sample size - does not allow for other significant splits. For medium size enterprises there is enough empirical evidence to show significant effects of the productive sector (ATECO) on travel expenditure. A general pattern is that, for a given enterprise size, services have a higher travel expenditure than industries. In particular, activities in R&D, computer and renting (ATECO sub-section k) show the higher average expenditure, while retail and wholesale (sub-section g) show the lowest, because of the high frequency of short trips. In the industrial sector, the higher expenditure is in the sub-sections da "food drink and tobacco" and dk "Machinery construction, installation and maintenance". No significant effects were found for geographical location. In purely descriptive terms, southern enterprises expenditure is on average lower than that of other areas, for almost all sizes and ATECO classes.

Although limited sample size does not allow for a very detailed analysis, results provide sufficient evidence to counter the frequently advanced hypothesis of indipendence between productive sector and business travel expenditure (i.e. the fixed proportions between travel expenditures and enterprises size; see amongst others G. Woollett, et al. 2002). The amount of expenditure varies also across sectors reflecting the fact that different productive processes need different kinds of business travel. Therefore the means of transport, the length of stay and the travel frequency vary across sectors. This information is relevant for business studies and for structural analysis of

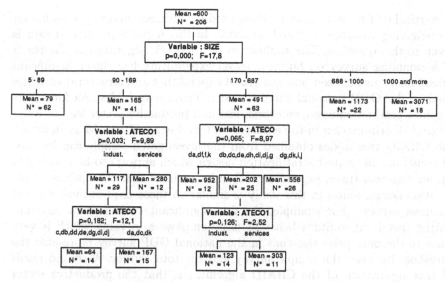

Fig. 1. The CHAID tree for business travel expenditure (Euro x 1000)

business travel expenditure especially in order to assess tourisms direct and indirect cross-sector impact.

Official statistics should no longer ignore or downplay the role of the business travel as part of tourism sector. In order to provide a fuller picture, business travel costs should be considered among other production costs in official surveys to enterprises. This paper shows that this is feasible, at least from a technical point of view: the sampling design that appears to be optimal to survey business travel expenditure is indeed similar to those used in most current business surveys.

4 Final remark

Most surveys on enterprises' expenditure don't include travel as one of the investigated variables. At the same time, European statistics are not adequate for identifying the role of business travel as part of the tourism sector. In fact, such statistics do not differentiate between travel as final consumption (leisure travel) and travel as an intermediate consumption (business travel). This is because most surveys on travel behavior are made by interviewing travellers or households, which are asked about their leisure and business travels. The paper shows that the correct statistical units to measure business travel volume and cost are the enterprises themselves. Choosing an inadequate statistical unit leads to inaccurate measures.

A significant improvement may thus be obtained including questions about business travel in current business surveys on production costs. However, there was no evidence so far that this would be statistically "optimal" and in particular if present stratifications used in business surveys are viable for investigating enterprises' travel behavior. In this paper a positive answer is given to this question. The application of a CHAID algorithm to the result of a sampling survey on business travel expenditure has shown significant causal relations between business travel expenditure and structural variables used in the GDP national survey as stratification variables. As for others business production costs, enterprise size and productive sector lead to a significant discrimination in the enterprise's travel expenditure. More in detail, the CHAID tree nodes obtained from the investigated sample can be used to construct an ex-post stratification design which appears to be optimal to survey business travel expenditure. Results indicate that the optimal stratification design found in this study is similar to those used in most current business surveys. For example, the first significant cut off point discriminating travel expenditure behavior is 90 employees, a value which is very close to the enterprise size that in the national GDP survey represents the threshold between the sample survey and the total survey. A second result of this application of the CHAID algorhitm is that the productive sector in the ATECO classification appears to be a significant discriminating variable in business travel expenditure behavior. Different productive processes seem to need different kinds of business travel - a result that contradicts the frequently advanced hypothesis that travel expenditure and enterprises size vary in fixed proportions across economic sectors. Business travel is a sector with an increasing importance in most developed countries, given its sustainability, its high profitability and its lower seasonality compared to leisure travel. Although limited sample size does not allow for a very detailed analysis, the CHAID results of this study provide sufficient evidence to suggest that business travel expenditure could be easily included among other production costs in official business surveys. This development would provide a more adequate picture of the tourism and travel market, and a more detailed account of enterprises' production costs.

References

EUROSTAT (2000): Balance of Payments Working Party executive summary *Technical group travel report*. Kirchberg, Luxembourg.

KASS, G.V. (1980): An exploratory technique for investigating large quantities of categorical data. Applied Statistics, 29, 119-127.

OECD (2001): Measuring the Role of Tourism in OECD Economies *The OECD manual on tourism satellite accounts and employement, enterprise, industry and service*. OECD, Paris.

TASSINARI, F. (1994): Turismo culturale e turismo di studio, *Rivista italiana di economia demografia e statistica*, vol. XLVIII, 1-2.

WOOLLETT, G. and TOWSEND, J. and WATTS, G. (2002): Development of QGEM-T - a Computable General Equilibrium Model of Tourism, *Office of Economic and Statistical Research working paper*. Queensland Treasury, Australia.

Value-Orientations and Partnership

Rossella Miglio, Lucia Pasquini, Alessandra Samoggia, and Gabriele Soffritti

Dipartimento di Scienze Statistiche
Università di Bologna, Italy
{miglio, pasquini, samoggia, soffritt}@stat.unibo.it

Abstract. The aim of the paper is to analyze, for both men and women, the role played by value orientation and social condition in the choice of the various forms of partnership (marriage and cohabitation) in some European countries that represent the varying diffusion of cohabitation and are characterized by different ideational dimensions. The data analyzed using classification trees were obtained from the European Fertility and Family Surveys; the trees, identified separately for men and women in each country, were compared using a modified version of a recently proposed proximity measure, aimed at evaluating whether decisional processes differ between genders and whether they are specific to the nations examined.

1 Foreword

Since the nineteen-sixties, family models in the industrialized world have changed radically; in particular, albeit with different intensities and time frames, cohabitation has become far more common, due to both an increase in the period spent studying and therefore a delay in acquiring economic independence and the increased individual ethic, religious and political autonomy (Preston 1986). The importance of considering ideational factors as well as economic ones in an explanatory phase was discussed at length and demonstrated for a number of central European countries by Lesthaege and Moors (1996). Taking inspiration from Lesthaege and Moors, in this paper we aim to analyze, for both men and women, the role played by human capital and value orientation on the choice of the various forms of partnership (marriage and cohabitation) in certain European countries. In particular, cohabitation will be assumed to represent a type of partnership that, at least theoretically, is associated to a reduction in gender differences: the absence of pre-set roles should, in fact, make the relationship between partners more equal and free (Pasquini and Samoggia 2003a).

2 Couples and values

In order to examine the reasons that cause men and women to choose to live together outside marriage, it was believed opportune to study only those countries in which cohabitation is not yet the norm as this makes it possible to identify the circumstances that motivate unconventional choices (Kiernan 2000). Moreover, because ideal orientation is believed to be one of the most important factors in dictating the type of partnership, we decided to select the countries to be analyzed from the areas identified by Inglehart (1997), which are similar with regards to value orientation; within these areas the following nations were chosen: Italy, Spain, Switzerland, Slovenia, Hungary and Latvia (Pasquini and Samoggia 2003b). It goes without say that the six countries chosen are not representative of the area they belong to if considered singly, neither are they representative of Europe as a whole. They simply constitute a range of situations that we intend to investigate and compare with one another. Later in the paper reference will be made to the countries in the West and countries in the East; the former refers to Italy, Spain and Switzerland, the latter to Slovenia, Hungary and Latvia. The data derive from the Fertility and Family Surveys conducted in the 1990s (Table 1).

	Italy	Spain	Switzerland	Slovenia	Hungary	Latvia
Men	3.6	8.4	25.5	17.1	7.6	12.9
Women	3.9	6.9	21.2	14.8	6.9	12.1

Table 1. Incidence of cohabitation (100 couples).

As far as the variables used to define the set of values are concerned, reference was made to the materialism/post-materialism (national goals to strive for; 4 items), tradition/innovation (importance of marriage, of family and motherhood outside a stable partnership; 3 items), the reasons for splitting up (8 items) and the ethics of abortion (5 items), the sense of responsibility towards one's children (3 items) and religiosity (2 items).

The analysis of the subject values and the type of partnership highlighted a stark difference between women and men. The former show more conservative behavior (they more frequently practice their faith, adhere to materialist values and attribute greater importance to marriage and the family), however, they also show signs of a greater openness to change: the more widespread acceptance of birth outside a stable partnership and abortion indicate how in the countries analyzed a common female ideal model is forming, still strongly characterized by the presence of the principal conventional values, but with more innovative elements than those of their male counterparts.

With regards to the partnership between value-orientations and the family form adopted, it can be said that certain values are so strongly rooted (importance of the institution of marriage, the family and children) that they set aside the type of partnership chosen. Certain other values are associated to the various family types with a very clear bond in western countries and less evident ones in the East, due to the effect of both the weaker value model that characterizes these nations and the different meaning assumed by cohabitation: indeed, as is known, in the East the decision to live together outside marriage often derives from the economic impossibility to get married. However, in the West it is clear that partners who merely live together have ideals and behavior less closely linked to tradition. For a more detailed description of these results, including figures, see Pasquini and Samoggia (2003b).

3 The ideational dimension

Multiple correspondence analysis was used to summarize the information concerning values. The variables considered active in the analysis are those relating to religiosity, materialism/post-materialism and opinions. The modalities of certain context variables were then projected into the factorial space in order to better interpret the meaning of the new dimensions identified. Multiple correspondence analysis was performed separately on the countries examined in the study because, as shown by the descriptive analysis, active variables play different roles in the various situations. The exceptions are Italy and Spain, which are considered together as they appeared to be permeated by the same ideational context. Within each country or cultural area, the analysis was conducted jointly for the two sexes as the cultural context within which the individuals live is characterized by the same value-orientation, regardless of the fact that it can influence men and womens orientation in different ways. On the basis of the multiple correspondences' results, the representation of subspace was defined as that identified by the first three factorial axes, which account for approximately 90% of the overall inertia. The results are synthesized in Table 2.

Italy and Spain		Switzerland		Slovenia		Hungary		Latvia	
Axes	r.i.	Axes	r.i.	Axes	r.i.	Axes	r.i.	Axes	r.i.
Religiosity	64,4	Religiosity	53,6	Certainty	56,1	Certainty	68,5	Certainty	58,7
Dogmatism	20,6	Dogmatism	25,5	Tradition	32,3	Tradition	15,9	Tradition	23,5
Tradition	6,0	Tradition	8,8	Religiosity	5,5	Religiosity	7,1	Sentimental	6,3

Table 2. Axes identified by multiple correspondence analysis for each country, and revaluated inertia (r.i., expressed in %).

It is interesting to observe how in the analyzed countries the axes were characterized by a meaning that was in part common to all (albeit of varying importance) and in part specific to each nation. The defined "religiosity" axis contrasts the typical positions of a rigid religious ethic with secular values. This axis is the most important in Italy, Spain and Switzerland, whereas in Slovenia and Hungary, where the religious tradition is less widespread, it only occupies the third place and in Latvia it does not figure at all. The second most important dimension in Italy, Spain and Switzerland defined as "dogmatism" contrasts the ability to express an opinion to the questions posed with the incapacity to do so. A more detailed analysis, which made it possible to further investigate the meaning of the axis, revealed that the set of subjects who were unsure of their opinion seems to be constituted by individuals who believe that certain practical situations cannot be judged *a priori*, but rather must be put into context before it is possible to express an opinion on the subject. It would therefore appear to be an axis that contrasts possibilism, in other words the absence of stereotypes, with a sort of dogmatism. The "certainty" axis, which was the most important in Slovenia, Hungary and Latvia, contrasts those subjects who have already matured a well-established opinion with those who, on the contrary, having yet to conclude the process, are more uncertain. Subjects who were unable to answer do not appear to be characterized in any specific way by the illustrative variables considered and therefore for them the conflict between ideology and opinions detected amongst the doubtful in other countries does not appear to exist. This factor could be connected to a phenomenon of presentification, that refers to an exclusive interest in the present, which results in the inability to express opinions on matters with which one is not directly involved. The "tradition" axis, which was present for all countries, clearly contrasts the more traditional values with innovative ones. This factor is the third most important in Italy, Spain and Switzerland and the second most important in other countries. In Latvia, multiple correspondence analysis identified an axis that seems to be determined almost exclusively by opinions on the reasons for splitting up and the acceptance of abortion. This axis contrasts the more material reasons with sentimental ones. It therefore appears to represent the vision of a partnership intended on the one hand, as a sort of well-defined contract, that does not permit exceptions and, on the other, as a sharing of feelings. On the basis of these findings, it was defined the "sentimental" axis.

In order to analyze how all these different aspects influence the choice between cohabitation and marriage in the considered countries, we have used classification trees (Breiman et al. 1984). The analysis has been performed separately not only by country but also by gender to highlight different decisional processes between males and females. The comparison between classifications trees has been performed using the dissimilarity measure proposed by Miglio and Soffritti (2004), which has been slightly modified so as to take into account the differences among predicted class probabilities.

4 Proximity measures between classification trees

The solutions proposed in the statistical literature to measure the proximity between classification trees differ on the features of a tree that they take into account; in fact, the comparison can be based on one or more of the following aspects: the partitions associated to the trees, their predictions and their structures.

The distance proposed by Shannon and Banks (1999) measures the amount of rearrangement needed to change one of the trees so that they have an identical structure; this distance considers only tree topology, and does not take into explicit consideration the partitions of the units and the predictions associated to each observed tree. Other measures have been proposed which compare classifiers with respect to their predictions (Cohen 1960) or the partitions induced by the trees (Chipman et al. 2001) or both aspects (Miglio and Soffritti 2004). When two classification trees have to be compared, all the previously considered aspects (the structure, the partition and the predictive power) should be simultaneously considered. In fact, trees having the same distance with respect to their structures can show a very different predictive power. On the other hand, trees with the same predictive power can have very different structures. For this reason, a dissimilarity measure which considers the structure and the predictive power at the same time has been proposed (Miglio and Soffritti 2004). It is defined as follows:

$$\delta(T_i, T_j) = \sum_{h=1}^{H} \alpha_{ih}(1 - s_{ih})\frac{m_{h0}}{n} + \sum_{k=1}^{K} \alpha_{jk}(1 - s_{jk})\frac{m_{0k}}{n}, \tag{1}$$

where m_{h0} and m_{0k} denote the number of units which belong to the h-th leaf of T_i and to the k-th leaf of T_j, respectively; the introduction of the relative frequency of each leaf weights the discrepancies proportionally to the number of their observations. α_{ih} and α_{jk} measure the dissimilarities between the paths of the two trees; s_{ih} and s_{jk} are similarity coefficients whose values synthesize the similarities s_{hk} between the leaves of T_i and those of T_j, defined so as to take into account the partitions and the predictive powers of the trees; for instance, a possible definition for s_{ih} is $s_{ih} = max\{s_{hk}, k = 1, \ldots, K\}$, where

$$s_{hk} = \frac{m_{hk}c_{hk}}{\sqrt{m_{h0}m_{0k}}}, \quad h = 1, \ldots, H, \; k = 1, \ldots, K; \tag{2}$$

m_{hk} is the number of objects which belong both to the h-th leaf of T_i and to the k-th leaf of T_j; $c_{hk} = 1$ if the h-th leaf of T_i has the same class label as the k-th leaf of T_j, and $c_{hk} = 0$ otherwise.

The coefficient defined by equation (2) can be slightly modified to take into account the difference among predicted class probabilities instead of class labels. This result can be obtained simply by changing the definition of the c_{hk} term as follows: $c_{hk} = 1 - f_{hk}$, where f_{hk} is a normalized dissimilarity index that compares the response variable frequency distributions of the h-th leaf of T_i and the k-th leaf of T_j, respectively (Leti 1983, p. 529). Measure (1) has been also normalized (for more details see Miglio and Soffritti 2004).

Except for the distance proposed by Shannon and Banks, all the solutions for the comparison between classification trees described in this Section have to be applied to a single data set D: in fact they compare the partitions of the same set of units and/or the associated predictions. When two trees are obtained from two independent data sets containing the same predictors and class variables, it could be useful to compute the proximities between trees using each data set and to compare the so obtained results.

5 Factors determining the choice of the type of partnership

The results obtained are extremely interesting and highlight that decision making processes are strongly different between genders and specific to the various countries. It should also be pointed out that all the variables analyzed offer a considerable contribution in the explanatory phase.

The variable that proved to be of greatest importance in the choice of the type of partnership is age: in fact it occupies a forefront position in the situations observed almost always for men and often for women, with the exception of Italy and Spain, where the main role is played by the value-orientation. Cohabitation therefore appears as a mainly juvenile phenomenon that has only become common in recent generations. As with age, values also seem to exert a strong influence on decision making processes, appearing in almost all the classification trees analyzed. Religious spirit assumes a primary role in countries belonging to the Catholic area, Italy and Spain (where men are also influenced by the traditional mentality), and to a lesser extent in Switzerland. The ideational system also exerts its influence, albeit to a lesser extent, in the other nations examined. Exceptions include, on one hand, Hungarian and Latvian men who are not guided by any value, on the other, Latvian women who are noticeably conditioned by tradition. Human capital (education and professional activities) often appears among the explanatory variables and is always present in the observed subsets with the exceptions of Slovenians and Swiss men. However, the influence exerted on the choice of partnership differs. For Swiss women, their professional life is the most important variable, showing how work and the consequential economic independence, permits them to opt for cohabitation if they desire. Although it plays a lesser role, human capital has the same effect on Italian and Spanish women. Its influence in Hungary and Latvia is completely different, as those who are less well educated and do not work, or only work occasionally, tend to form free partnerships more frequently.

Overall it can be concluded that in all the nations examined, cohabitation assumes the connotations of a juvenile phenomenon, but its meaning differs in the eastern and western countries examined. In the West, it mainly involves the more secularized, the less conventional and women with a high human capital, thus representing an innovative type of partnership that precedes or replaces marriage. In the East, on the other hand, partnerships outside marriage are associated with a value-orientation that has less weight and is frequently in possession of a modest human capital: here they loose their innovative meaning, often appearing to be the fruit of a forced choice connected to situations of particular social unease.

The diversity in mens and womens decisional processes has been quantified through the proximity measure between classification trees described in the previous Section. Two trees have been built for each country, one for each gender, using the CHAID algorithm (Kass 1980) constrained to produce binary trees. The samples used to grow each tree have different sizes, so the minimum dimension of each leaf in a tree has been set proportional to the corresponding sample size. In order to highlight possible different decision processes by gender in each country, the trees obtained from the analysis of male and female samples (D_M and D_F, respectively) have been compared, within the same country, by computing measure (1) and using the modified definition of the c_{hk} term given in the previous Section, as the proportion of marriages is much higher than cohabitations in each analyzed country. As each tree has been obtained from a different data set, the comparison between trees based on measure (1) has been performed considering each data set used to grow the compared trees. In this way it is possible to compare each pair of trees by means of two data sets. The so obtained results are summarized in Table 3.

	Italy and Spain	Switzerland	Slovenia	Hungary	Latvia
By using D_M	0.252	0.259	0.297	0.513	0.320
By using D_F	0.244	0.482	0.336	0.533	0.294

Table 3. Values of $D(T_F, T_M)$ computed for each country by using both data sets.

The least differences are detected in Italy and Spain, where the dissimilarity between males and females trees has resulted equal to 0.252 using the male sample, and equal to 0.244 using the female one. These results mean that the tree built to describe the female behavior offers a discrete description of the male one, and vice versa the tree built to describe the male behavior offers a discrete description of the female one. Thus in this area the importance of the religious spirit has such an important influence on the behavior of men and women as to mitigate gender differences, which do however subsist, as shown by the varying influence of human capital.

Different results have been obtained for instance from the analysis of the Switzerland data. When the comparison between males and females trees is performed by using the male sample the value of the dissimilarity is 0.259, while the same dissimilarity evaluated with respect to the females data set has resulted equal to 0.482. This is due to the fact that in Switzerland male and female trees give different indications. In the female classification tree the variable with the strongest influence is occupation, which divides the collective data in two subsets characterized by different decisional processes.

The reduced distance observed in correspondence with the adoption of this tree for the male data set is justified by the fact that most Swiss men are employed and that the structure of the male tree is very similar to that of the subtree of employed women. On the contrary, the structure of the branch of unemployed women has a different form. Among the Eastern European countries, Slovenia and Latvia show very close distances: here men and women are influenced by different value systems, which are instead completely non-existent for Latvian men. Lastly, Hungary records the greatest difference between the behavior of men and women; the latter being more sensitive to both values and human capital, both irrelevant for men.

Acknowledgments

This research has been financially supported by MURST ex 40% "Gender and demography in developed countries", coordinated by A. Pinnelli, Roma.

References

BREIMAN, L., FRIEDMAN, J. H., OLSHEN, R. A. and STONE, C. J. (1984): *Classification and Regressione Trees*. Wadsworth, Belmont, California.

CHIPMAN, H. A., GEORGE, E. I. and McCULLOCH, R. E. (2001): Managing multiple models. In: T. Jaakola and T. Richardson T. (Eds.): *Artificial Intelligence and Statistics 2001*. ProBook, Denver, 11-18.

COHEN, J. (1960): A coefficient for agreement for nominal scales. *Educational and Psychological Measurement, 20, 37-46*.

INGLEHART, R. (1997): *Modernization and Postmodernization. Cultural, Economic and Political Change in 43 Societies*. Princeton Univ. Press, Princeton.

KASS, G. V. (1980): An exploratory technique for investigating large quantities of categorical data. *Applied Statistics, 29, 119-127*.

KIERNAN, K. (2000): The state of European Unions: an Analysis of FFS Data on Partnership Formation and Dissolution. Flagship Conference, Brussels.

LESTHAEGHE, R. and MOORS, G. (1996): Living arrangements, socio economic position, and values among young adults: a pattern description for France, West Germany, Belgium, and the Netherlands. In: D. Coleman (Ed.): *Europe's Population in the 1990's*. Oxford University Press, Oxford, 163-222.

LETI, G. (1983): *Statistica Descrittiva*. Il Mulino, Bologna.

MIGLIO, R. and SOFFRITTI, G. (2004): The comparison between classification trees through proximity measures. *Computational Statistics and Data Analysis, 45, 577-593*.

PASQUINI, L. and SAMOGGIA, A. (2003a): Sistema ideazionale e scelte di vita di coppia. In: A. Pinnelli et al. (Eds.): *Genere e demografia*. Il Mulino, Bologna, 253-280.

PASQUINI, L. and SAMOGGIA, A. (2003b): Sistema di valori e forme di vita familiare in alcune realtà europee. In: A. Angeli et al. (Eds.): *Nuovi comportamenti familiari, nuovi modelli. Italia ed Europa a confronto*. Clueb, Bologna, 1-53.

PRESTON, S. H. (1986): Changing values and falling birth rates. *Population and Development Review, supp. n.12, 176-195*.

SHANNON W. D., BANKS D. (1999): Combining classification trees using MLE. *Statistics in Medicine, 18, 727-740*.

An Item Response Theory Model for Student Ability Evaluation Using Computer-Automated Test Results

Stefania Mignani[1], Silvia Cagnone[1], Giorgio Casadei[2], and Antonella Carbonaro[2]

[1] Dipartimento di Scienze Statistiche,
Università di Bologna, Italy
[2] Dip. Scienze dell'Informazione,
Università di Bologna, Italy

Abstract. The aim of this paper is to evaluate the student learning about Computer Science subjects. A questionnaire based on ordinal scored items has been submitted to the students through a computer automated system. The data collected have been analyzed by using a latent variable model for ordinal data within the Item Response Theory framework. The scores obtained from the model allow to classify the students according to the reached competence.

1 Introduction

Evaluation of students' learning and competence about a subject can be obtained by submitting them a test that contains a set of items related to some facets of the particular subject of interest. The analysis of the responses given by the examinees allows to evaluate their level of learning. The procedure of evaluation requires two different important steps. The first one consists of designing the test to be submitted to the students. The second one is dedicated to the evaluation of the student's ability considered as a latent construct. To this aim a model that expresses the latent construct in function of the item of the test can be determined.

In this work we have analyzed the results of a computer test delivery in order to evaluate the ability of students of the Economics Faculty - Bologna University - in solving Computer Science problems by using an Item Response Theory model. From the results obtained we can classify the students by giving them a vote ranging from 18 to 30+.

2 Assessing student ability

2.1 Test delivery and data collection

In the experimental results so far executed, data have been collected through a testing system that consists of a web application. In this way, different exams can be created according to the different sessions. Each question has been assigned at random and the student could read every question twice before answering. One answer for each question could be given.

As for the test delivering, different areas of Computer Science have been involved. In particular, the test sessions have been organized by using a database that contains five different arguments: *Glossary* (computer science glossary), *Fundaments* (computability elements), *Prolog* (programming capability), *Prolog1* (the knowledge of syntax), *Prolog2* (competence in problem formalization). Problems with different levels of complexity have been included in each argument (item). More in detail, the problem solving process contains a finite number of steps so that the ability of a student can be evaluated on the basis of the step achieved, namely, higher steps achieved are related to higher ability. In this way, for the i-th item an ordinal score m_i is assigned to the examinee who successfully completes up to step m_i but fails to complete the step $m_i + 1$. Following this procedure, a score ranging from 1 to 4 is assigned to each examinee for each item with respect to the solving level achieved (1= no correct answers, 2= correct answers only for preliminary problems, 3= correct answers also for intermediate problems, 4= all correct answers). Such a technique of assigning a score doesn't allow to get missing data.

2.2 The methodology

The methodology used for evaluating an individual ability is the Item Response Theory (IRT) (Lord and Novick, 1968). It has been introduced in educational test field to deal with the case in which a single latent variable (students ability) is measured by means of a test consisting of a set of item. The main feature of IRT is that it allows to evaluate, simultaneously, the characteristics of the item, the difficulty and the discrimination power, and the students performance. The item difficulty parameter represents the point on the latent scale where a person has a 50% chance of responding positively to the scale item. The discrimination parameter describes the strength of an item's capability to distinguish between people with trait levels below and above the difficulty parameter. That is, IRT takes into consideration if an item is answered correctly and utilizes the difficulty and discrimination parameters of the items when estimating ability levels. Thus, unlike the classical test theory in which an aggregate of item responses, the test score, is computed, the basic concept of IRT is the individual items so that people with the same summed score but different response patterns may have different IRT estimated ability. A variety of probabilistic models have been developed within the IRT approach with the aim to formalize the relationships between the latent variable, also called latent trait, and the manifest variables. In this work we apply a particular IRT model called Proportional Odds model introduced to treat the case of ordinal observed variables. The model is illustrated in Section 3.

3 Model specification

Let $x_1, x_2, \ldots, x_p$ be p ordinal observed variables representing the items of a questionnaire and let m_i denote the number of categories for the i-th variable. The m_i ordered categories have probabilities $\pi_{i1}(z), \pi_{i2}(z), \ldots, \pi_{im_i}(z)$, which are function of z, the latent factor representing the individual's ability. They are known as *category response functions*. Indicating with $\mathbf{x}_r = (x_1, x_2, \ldots, x_p)$ the complete response pattern of the r-th individual examined, we can define the unconditional probability of $\mathbf{x}_r$ as:

$$\pi_r = \int_{-\infty}^{+\infty} \ldots \int_{-\infty}^{+\infty} \pi_r(z) h(z) dz \tag{1}$$

where $h(z)$ is assumed to be a standard normal and $\pi_r(z)$ is the conditional probability $g(\mathbf{x}|z)$. For g the conditional independence is assumed, that is when the latent variable is held fixed, the p observed variables are independent. In the case of ordinal observed variables it is defined as:

$$g(\mathbf{x}|z) = \pi_r(z) = \prod_{s=1}^{m_i} \pi_{is}(z)^{x_{is}} = \prod_{s=1}^{m_i} (\gamma_{is} - \gamma_{is-1})^{x_{is}} \tag{2}$$

where $x_{is} = 1$ if a randomly selected person responds in category s of the i-th item and $x_{is} = 0$ otherwise and $\gamma_{is} = \pi_{i1}(z) + \pi_{i2}(z) + \ldots + \pi_{is}(z)$ is the probability of a response in category s or lower on the variable i. γ_{is} is known as *cumulative response function*. The model is defined in terms of a logit function of γ_{is} and can be expressed in a general form within the generalized linear models framework as Moustaki (2000):

$$\ln \left[\frac{\gamma_{is}(z)}{1 - \gamma_{is}(z)} \right] = \alpha_{is} - \beta_i z, \quad s = 1, 2, \ldots, m_i - 1 \tag{3}$$

The model so defined is called Proportional Odds Models (POM) and is very similar to the well known Graded Response Model by Samejima (1969). It ensures that the higher the value of an individual on the latent variable, the higher the probability that individual belonging in the higher categories of an item. The intercept parameter α_{is} can be interpreted as the item *difficulty* parameter whereas β_{ij} can be interpreted as the *discrimination* power parameter. To define ordinality properly, the condition $\alpha_{i1} < \alpha_{i2} < \ldots < \alpha_{im_i}$ must hold. The parameters of the model are estimated using the maximum likelihood estimation by an E-M algorithm. At the step M of the algorithm a Newton-Raphson iterative scheme is used to solve the non-linear maximum likelihood equation.

To score the individuals on the latent dimension we can refer to the mean of the posterior distribution of z defined as:

$$E(z|\mathbf{x}_h) = \int zh(z|\mathbf{x}_h)\mathrm{d}z \qquad (4)$$

where $h = 1, \ldots, n$ and n is the sample size. These values are normally distributed as given by the previous assumptions.

4 Analysis and results

4.1 Data description

We have considered a sample of 256 students who have sustained the exam of Computer Science. As for the description of the computer test results, Table 1 shows the percentage and cumulative percentage distributions for each argument.

Categories	Fundam		Glossary		Prolog		Prolog1		Prolog2	
	%	cum%	%	cum%	%	cum%	%	cum%	%	cum%
1	4	4	7	7	8	8	4	4	13	13
2	16	20	30	37	47	55	50	54	57	70
3	33	52	32	69	36	92	42	96	20	91
4	47	1	31	1	9	1	4	1	10	1

Table 1. Percentage and Cumulative percentage distributions

We can notice that *Fundam* and *Glossary* present the highest percentages in correspondence of the scores greater or equal to 3. On the contrary, for the three arguments concerning *Prolog* (that is *Prolog*, *Prolog1*, *Prolog2*) the most frequent score is 2. It is interesting to notice that the 48% and the 31% of the students get the highest score (equal to 4) for, respectively, *Fundam* and *Glossary*, whereas for the arguments about *Prolog* less than the 10% of the students gets a score equal to 4. These exploratory results seem to highlight that the items that assess the programming capability and the problem formalization are more complex to solve than the items related to the basic knowledge.

4.2 Model results

The model estimated has 20 parameters, 3 difficulty parameters for each item and 5 discrimination parameters. The difficulty and discrimination parameter estimates for each item are reported in Table 2. We can notice that the items that tend to be more difficult are *Prolog1* and *Prolog2* since their difficulty parameters have very different values among the 3 categories and present the highest absolute values. This indicates that for the items *Prolog1* and *Prolog2* it is very difficult for a student to get a high score and hence to have a good performance. On the other side, the item that seems to have the lower difficulty is *Glossary* for the opposite reasons listed above. Furthermore we can observe that the item that presents the highest parameter discrimination is *Prolog2* (1.740) followed by *Prolog1* (1.068). Conversely, *Fundam* is the item with the lowest discrimination value (0.491).

Item	category	α_{is}	s.e
Fundam	1	-2.51	1.48
	2	0.23	0.35
	3	2.58	0.31
Glossary	1	-3.31	1.38
	2	-1.49	0.69
	3	0.09	0.56
Prolog	1	-2.81	1.33
	2	-0.60	0.40
	3	0.87	0.35
Prolog1	1	-3.68	3.70
	2	0.21	0.44
	3	3.83	0.45
Prolog2	1	-2.78	1.75
	2	1.25	0.31
	3	3.27	0.56

Item	β_i	s.e
Fundam	0.49	0.20
Glossary	0.51	0.25
Prolog	0.63	0.20
Prolog1	1.07	0.27
Prolog2	1.74	0.49

Table 2. Classification of students according to their performance

As for the goodness of fit assessment, we can look at Table 3, that contains the frequency distribution of the response patterns.

We can notice the data are sparse because, although the number of possible response patterns are 256, only 145 response patterns are present in the data. Furthermore, 87 of them occur once, 35 occur twice and only 1 occurs 9 times. For this reason, it is not feasible to carry out a global test. Instead, we have referred to the fits of the bivariate margins (Jöreskog and Moustaki, 2001) comparing the observed and expected frequencies (residuals) for each pair of responses. The residuals are not independent and so not a formal test can be applied. Nevertheless, if the model is correct, the residual in a single cell would have a chi-square distribution with one degree of freedom so that

Frequency	No of response patterns	No of cases
1	87	87
2	35	70
3	10	30
4	5	20
5	4	20
6	1	6
7	2	14
9	1	9
Total	145	256

Table 3. Frequency distribution of the response patterns

a value greater than about 4 would indicate a poor fit. Thus, we can consider the sum of these residuals over all the cells of the two-way marginal table S_{ij} and we can refer to the rule of thumb by which if:

$$S_{ij} > (4 \times m_i \times m_j)$$

where m_i and m_j are, respectively, the categories of the variables i and j, then we get a bad fit for the $m_i \times m_j$ marginal table. As we can observe in Table 4, all the residuals present values less than 64 ($4 \times 4 \times 4$) so that the model gives an adequate description of the data for each couple of items.

Items	2	3	4	5
1	12.78	17.92	7.30	26.67
2		17.37	7.82	16.26
3			11.71	15.67
4				10.17

Table 4. Sum of Chi-square values for a pair of items from the two-way marginals

Following this rule, we can build also an overall measurement of fit (Jöreskog and Moustaki, 2001) given by the average of all the fit indices reported in Table 4 (we can consider the simple average of the fit indices because the number of categories is the same for all the variables). This value is equal to 14.37 so that it seems to indicate a good fit of the model to the data.

4.3 Student classification

The students can be classified by obtaining a vote according to the different levels of ability $E(z|\mathbf{x})$. The votes are assigned by fixing two extreme values that indicate, respectively, the lowest level of ability to pass the exam and the highest level of ability. The range between these extreme values is divided into intervals of equal width. A ranked vote is associated to each of them.

On the basis of the indications derived by the expert (the professor of the subject analyzed) from the previous exams, we decide that the student doesn't pass the exam if $E(z|\mathbf{x})$ is smaller than -0.85 ($\Phi(z) = 0.20$ where Φ is the normal distribution function) and we assign the maximum score (30+) to the students that get a value equal or greater than 1.65 ($1 - \Phi(z) = 0.05$). The remaining votes are given by dividing the range from -0.85 to 1.65 into 12 intervals of equal width and by associating them a score graduated from 18 to 30. In this way we can get a rule for student classification that is not influenced by the performance of specific groups of students in different sessions. That is, the vote the student receives is independent from the votes given to the rest of the students so that it is possible that all the students in a session don't pass the exam and viceversa.

In Table 5 the frequency distribution of the votes are reported. We can notice that in this session only almost 10% of the student don't pass the exam whereas the 2% of them get the maximum score. Looking at Figure 1 we can also notice that the distribution of the votes shows a slight negative skewness, to indicate that the students who get a vote ranging from 18 to 23 are the most part.

$E(z|x)$	Vote	n_i
< -0.85	< 18	24
$-0.85 \vdash -0.61$	18	18
$-0.61 \vdash -0.40$	19	37
$-0.40 \vdash -0.19$	20	26
$-0.19 \vdash 0.02$	21	37
$0.02 \vdash 0.22$	22	26
$0.22 \vdash 0.43$	23	21
$0.43 \vdash 0.64$	24	15
$0.64 \vdash 0.85$	25	21
$0.85 \vdash 1.05$	26	5
$1.05 \vdash 1.26$	27	10
$1.26 \vdash 1.47$	28	6
$1.47 \vdash 1.65$	29	5
≥ 1.65	30+	5
		256

Table 5. Classification of students according to their performance

5 Conclusions

The analysis presented in this paper has allowed to obtain an evaluation of student ability concerning Computer Science problems by using a computer test delivery. An IRT model for ordinal observed variables (POM) has been

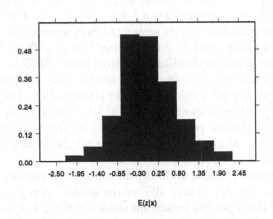

Fig. 1. Histogram of the expected posterior $E(z|\mathbf{x})$

used with the aim to formalize the increasing level of complexity related to the test submitted to the students. Model estimation has highlighted inequalities among the arguments involved in, both in term of difficulty and discrimination. This inequalities have led to evidence different levels of ability among the students analyzed. A student classification is also proposed based on both the values of the latent variable ability estimated through the model and the judge of the expert, the professor of the subject analyzed.

This is a first analysis of student ability evaluation. Further developments can be considered by improving some aspects of the IRT model, like the goodness of fit problem, and by referring to different data sets in order to consolidate the results. Also a self-evaluation test can be introduced in the analysis.

References

LORD, F. M. and NOVICK, M.E. (1968): *Statistical theories of mental test scores.* Addison-Wesley Publishing Co.

JÖRESKOG, K. and MOUSTAKI, I. (2001): Factor Analysis of Ordinal Variables: A Comparison of three Approaches. *Multivariate Behavioral Research, 36, 347-387.*

MOUSTAKI, I.(2000): A Latent Variable Model for Ordinal Variables. *Applied Psychological Measurement, 24, 211-223.*

SAMEJIMA, F. (1969): Estimation of ability using a response pattern of graded scores.*Psychometrika Monograph, 17.*

Functional Cluster Analysis
of Financial Time Series

Andrea Cerioli, Fabrizio Laurini, and Aldo Corbellini

Dipartimento di Economia
Università di Parma, Italy
andrea.cerioli@unipr.it – flaurini@stat.unipd.it – aldo.corbellini@unipr.it

Abstract. In this paper we address the problem of clustering functional data. In our applications functional data are continuous trajectories evolving over time. Our proposal is to cluster these trajectories according to their sequence of local extrema (maxima or minima). For this purpose, we suggest a new dissimilarity measure for functional data. We apply our clustering technique to the trajectories of the shares composing the MIB30 stock index computed at the Milan Stock Exchange Market, paralleling the contribution of Ingrassia and Costanzo in this Volume.

1 Introduction

Functional data analysis (FDA, for short) concerns the statistical analysis of data which come in the form of continuous functions, usually smooth curves. Let $\mu_i(t)$, $i = 1, \ldots, n$, be one of such functions. In our application t denotes time, although it might have a more general meaning. In practice, we collect information about $\mu_i(t)$ at a finite number of points, say T_i, and observe the data vector $y_i = (y_{i1}, \ldots, y_{iT_i})'$. FDA works under the basic statistical model

$$y_{ij} = \mu_i(t_{ij}) + \epsilon_i(t_{ij}) \qquad i = 1, \ldots, n; j = 1, \ldots, T_i, \tag{1}$$

where t_{ij} is the time value at which observation j is taken for function i. The independent disturbance terms $\epsilon_i(t_{ij})$ are responsible for roughness in y_i.

Although the goals of FDA are essentially the same as those of any statistical analysis (including data description, dimension reduction and study of relationships), its tools are much different. Basically, in FDA each data function is seen as a single entity, rather than a collection of individual observations. In this spirit the observed data vector y_i is first converted into an estimate of its true functional form $\mu_i(t)$, which then becomes the input for subsequent analyses. Neither the observation times t_{ij} nor their number T_i need to be the same for all subjects. This makes FDA very different from both multivariate and multiway data analysis. Ramsay and Silverman (1997, 2002) give a broad account of the theory and applications of FDA.

In this paper we address the problem of clustering functional data, that is of detecting hidden group structures within a functional dataset. For this purpose we suggest a new dissimilarity measure between functional data, based on the time values at which the extremal points, that is local maxima or minima, of each curve occur. Local extrema are also called "landmarks" or "structural points" of a curve.

The issue of measuring the similarity between time trajectories is not a new one. In the time series literature, for instance, Piccolo (1990) suggests a metric based on the fitting of ARIMA models. We refer to Corduas (2003) for an overview of this and other related approaches. However, we do not follow this line because a parametric time series model imposes a much stronger structure than the basic functional model (1). Also the familiar L_2 distance of functional analysis (Hall and Heckman (2002); Abraham et al. (2003)),

$$d_2 = \left[\int \{\mu_i(t) - \mu_l(t)\}^2 dt \right]^{1/2} \qquad i, l = 1, \ldots, n, \qquad (2)$$

is not appropriate in the present context, as it does not take curve shape into account. Indeed, it is not difficult to show that (2) provides a sensible criterion for clustering the functions $\mu_1(t), \ldots, \mu_n(t)$ only when they have approximately the same shape.

Nonparametric clustering algorithms that allow for trajectory shapes are considered by Chiodi (1989) and by D'Urso and Vichi (1998) in the context of three-way data analysis. Chiodi (1991) and Heckman and Zamar (2000) suggest more general methods that can be applied when observation times may differ from unit to unit, as is the case in model (1). Our approach is different in that it rests on the landmark description of each curve and it shares some ideas with the growing field of symbolic data analysis (Billard and Diday (2003)). In this respect, our dissimilarity measure extends the one proposed by Ingrassia et al. (2003), where time is not considered explicitly.

As shown by Gasser and Kneip (1995), landmarks are important tools for identifying the shape of a curve. Focusing on landmarks has some practical advantages too. First, it seems a natural approach for the purpose of describing curves with oscillatory behaviour, such as many of those in our stock market dataset of §2, in contrast to the analysis of monotone growth curves. Second, it puts less emphasis on the rather delicate process of derivative estimation, which affects our dissimilarity measure only through the identification of local extrema. An additional bonus is that it is possible to attach an uncertainty measure to each landmark estimate. This allows the distinction between "true" and "spurious" extrema. Such inferential statements are admittedly difficult in other clustering approaches, such as the one of Heckman and Zamar (2000). The extension to include inflection points is straightforward, but it is not considered here.

This paper is organized as follows. In §2 we give a brief overview of the Milan Stock Exchange dataset. Our dissimilarity measure for functional data is described in §3. In §4 we show this measure in action: the first application is to a simulated dataset with known clusters and the second one is to the Milan Stock Exchange dataset.

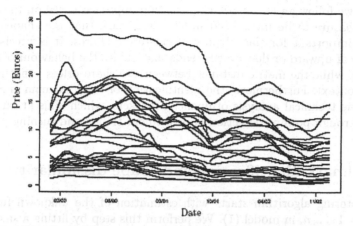

Fig. 1. Milan Stock Exchange dataset. Estimated trajectories of share prices.

2 The Milan Stock Exchange dataset

In §4 we apply our clustering technique to the trajectories of the shares composing the MIB30 stock index computed at the Milan Stock Exchange Market[1], which is made up of the 30 most capitalized and traded companies on the Stock Market list. We consider share prices in the time interval starting on January 3rd, 2000, and ending on December 30th, 2002. The MIB30 basket varies periodically according to changes in the ranking of shares, so the actual sample size is greater than 30. We refer to the work of Ingrassia and Costanzo in this Volume, and to the web site www.borsaitalia.it, for more details about the MIB30 basket. We exclude from the dataset the shares that have very limited permanence in the basket, as well as those present only at the beginning and at the end of the period. An additional problem is company incorporation during the observation period. We connect the trajectories of the shares of incorporating companies and we report them under the same heading. As a result, in our application $n = 35$ and $199 \leq T_i \leq 758$, where T_i is the number of days of permanence of share i in the MIB30 basket.

Although the available data are recorded daily at the closing time of the Stock Exchange Market, we think of share prices as continuous functions of time. This is quite reasonable since the exchange flow for the shares making up the MIB30 index is virtually continuous all over the day, and actual prices react almost immediately to such exchanges. Figure 1 shows the estimated smooth trajectories corresponding to the available sample of shares.

Our focus is on clustering, that is on detecting unknown groups of similar curves. Figure 1 looks messy, apart from a general decrease in prices following the shock of September 2001. Hence visual inspection is not of great help.

---

[1]The authors are grateful to Research & Development DBMS (Borsa Italiana) for supplying the data.

Instead, we follow an automatic classification approach based on the dissimilarity measure to be introduced in §3. We remark that the shape of each curve is important for the purpose of clustering shares. It is precisely the existence of upward or downward trends that guides the behaviour of market investors, while the metric distance between two share prices is not relevant in this context. Furthermore, the identification of local extrema is a major tool in the technical analysis of financial markets, which aims at improving profits through prompt detection of investment trends and turning points.

3 Landmark identification and shape dissimilarity

Our clustering algorithm starts with estimation of the unknown functions $\mu_i(t)$, $i = 1 \ldots, n$, in model (1). We perform this step by fitting a smoothing p-spline curve $\widehat{\mu}_i(t)$, for $t \in [t_{i1}, t_{iT_i}]$, to each data vector y_i (Ramsay and Silverman (1997, p. 60)). These estimated curves are the smooth functions shown in Figure 1. Smoothing p-splines satisfy the penalized residual sum of squares criterion

$$\sum_{j=1}^{T_i} \{y_{ij} - \mu_i(t_{ij})\}^2 + \lambda \int \{D^p \mu_i(t)\}^2 dt, \tag{3}$$

where λ is a smoothing parameter and the penalty involves the pth order derivative of $\mu_i(t)$. For instance, popular cubic smoothing spline functions are p-splines of order 2, penalizing the second derivative $D^2 \mu_i(t) \equiv \mu_i''(t)$. We choose to fit smoothing p-spline curves of order 4 because this leads to an estimate of $\mu_i(t)$ with smooth first and second derivatives. In the applications of §4 the smoothing parameter λ is specified by fixing the number of degrees of freedom that are implicit in the smoothing procedure.

The R function predict.smooth.Pspline provides the first derivative of $\widehat{\mu}_i(t)$, say $\widehat{\mu}_i'(t)$. This information is used to obtain the landmarks of $\mu_i(t)$. An ancillary but potentially useful step is to eliminate spurious extrema, that is the zeros of $\widehat{\mu}_i'(t)$ which can be attributed to estimation error in model (1). For this purpose we compute an approximate 95% pointwise confidence interval for each value $\mu_i'(t_{ij})$ as follows. First, we recognize that $\mu_i'(t)$ is a linear functional of $\mu_i(t)$. The high order penalty of the p-spline fitting described in (3) implies that this functional is itself smooth. Hence, we can approximate it in the interval $[t_{i1}, t_{iT_i}]$ by regressing the estimates $\widehat{\mu}_i'(t_{ij})$ on a reduced number of basis functions. In the applications of §4 the basis dimension is obtained by retaining one time point out of 15, corresponding approximately to one day every three working weeks. Following Silverman (1985), we then apply standard least-squares theory and the central limit theorem to compute the required asymptotic confidence interval for $\mu_i'(t_{ij})$, $j = 1, \ldots, T_i$. If the lower bound of this interval is greater than zero, we have confidence that $\mu_i(t)$ is actually increasing at time t_{ij}. Similarly, we treat $\mu_i(t)$ as decreasing

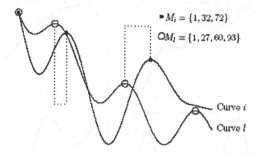

$\bullet M_i = \{1, 32, 72\}$

$\bigcirc M_l = \{1, 27, 60, 93\}$

Curve i

Curve l

Fig. 2. Exemplification of (4). In this case $d_{il} = (|1-1|+|32-27|+|72-60|)/3 = 5.7$.

when the upper bound of the confidence interval is negative. We have a local maximum when the derivative changes from positive to negative. The maximum is set equal to the largest value of $\widehat{\mu}_i'(t)$ in the period where this change occurs. A similar reasoning applies to the detection of local minima.

For simplicity, in what follows we consider only the information provided by maxima. Let $M_i = \{\tau_1^{(i)}, \ldots, \tau_{m_i}^{(i)}\}$ be the collection of time points where the estimated curve $\widehat{\mu}_i(t)$ has a local maximum, possibly after the exclusion of spurious ones. The number of such maxima is m_i. We deal with boundary points by setting $\tau_1^{(i)} = t_{i1}$ if $\mu_i(t)$ is decreasing after the first observation time, and $\tau_{m_i}^{(i)} = t_{iT_i}$ if $\mu_i(t)$ is increasing before the last observation time. Under this assumption $m_i > 0$ even if $\widehat{\mu}_i(t)$ is a monotone function.

We define a dissimilarity measure between two smooth curves $\mu_i(t)$ and $\mu_l(t)$ by comparing the two sets M_i and M_l. Let $\tau_{*j}^{(l)}$ be the element of M_l which is closest to $\tau_j^{(i)}$, i.e.

$$\tau_{*j}^{(l)} = \{\tau_{j'}^{(l)} : |\tau_j^{(i)} - \tau_{j'}^{(l)}| = \min\} \qquad j = 1, \ldots, m_i.$$

We then suggest computing the average distance

$$d_{il} = \sum_{j=1}^{m_i} \frac{|\tau_j^{(i)} - \tau_{*j}^{(l)}|}{m_i} \qquad i, l = 1, \ldots, n. \tag{4}$$

Figure 2 describes how (4) is computed in a simple example with $m_i = 3$. Obviously, $d_{il} = 0$ if $\mu_i(t)$ and $\mu_l(t)$ have the same shape (implying that $T_i = T_l$), so also $d_{ii} = 0$. Finally, we adjust formula (4) for symmetry by taking

$$\delta_{il} = (d_{il} + d_{li})/2 \tag{5}$$

as our dissimilarity measure.

Alternatively, a scaled dissimilarity measure can be obtained by noting that $d_{il} = t_{iT_i} - t_{i1}$ when both i and l are monotone curves, but with opposite trends. Hence, we may standardize δ_{il} by replacing d_{il} in (5) with $d_{il}^* = d_{il}/(t_{iT_i} - t_{i1})$, and similarly for d_{li}.

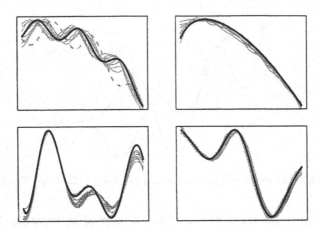

Fig. 3. Simulated dataset with four clusters of 10 curves. Each panel corresponds to a cluster (numbered clockwise). Black lines: template curves for the clusters; grey lines: estimated trajectories through the p-spline method.

4 Applications

4.1 Simulated curves with four clusters

Before reverting to our main application in §4.2, we check the performance of the dissimilarity index (5) in a simulated dataset with four known clusters of curves. Figure 3 summarizes this dataset. The black lines show the template curves representing the four clusters. These lines are chosen to mimic the behaviour of share prices in the Milan Stock Exchange dataset. Ten observation vectors for each cluster are then obtained by adding Gaussian random noise at $T_i = 900$ equally spaced time points in accordance to model (1), after random displacement of the local extrema of the corresponding template curve. The grey lines are the resulting smooth trajectories estimated through the smoothing p-spline criterion (3). Clusters are numbered clockwise.

We focus on maxima, as in the application of §4.2. Figure 4 shows the average linkage dendrogram, using dissimilarity (5). The four existing clusters clearly appear from the dendrogram, with only one mis-classified unit (Curve 8 from Group 1, labelled as GR.1.C.8 in the picture). This unit is the dashed grey trajectory in the top left panel of Figure 3. Random perturbation has made the shape of this curve rather different from the rest of its cluster: the curve decreases at the beginning of the period and its local maxima are located very close to those of the curves belonging to Group 4 (bottom left panel of Figure 3). Hence, mis-classification is not surprising for it. We conclude that our method reassuringly detects the underlying group structure we have introduced in the data.

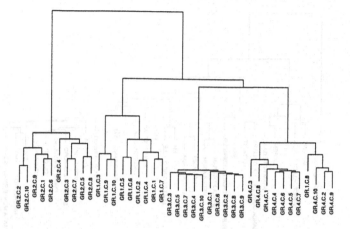

Fig. 4. Simulated curves with four clusters. Average linkage dendrogram using dissimilarity (5).

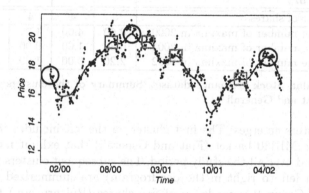

Fig. 5. Estimated smooth trajectory of the share price of Rolo Banca, with "spurious" (squares) and "true" (circles) local maxima.

4.2 Milan Stock Exchange data

We apply our clustering algorithm to the Milan Stock Exchange dataset, introduced in §2. We focus on local maxima since we aim at reducing the effect of the shock of September 11th, 2001. The first step of the algorithm identifies local maxima in the estimated smooth trajectories of Figure 1. We discriminate between "true" and "spurious" maxima through the inferential procedure sketched in §3. For instance, Figure 5 shows the details for Rolo Banca, a bank that belongs to the MIB30 basket up to June 2002.

Figure 6 is the resulting average linkage dendrogram, when the dissimilarity measure (5) is used as input. Now a broad structure with five fairly

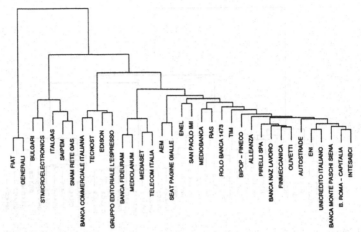

Fig. 6. Milan Stock Exchange dataset. Average linkage dendrogram using (5).

Group Summary	2	3	4	5
Number of shares	5	4	4	20
Average number of maxima in 2000	0.60	4.00	1.75	1.70
Average number of maxima in 2001	0.80	1.00	0.00	1.25
Average number of maxima in 2002	2.20	0.00	1.00	1.60

Table 1. Milan Stock Exchange dataset. Summary of the clusters in Figure 6, excluding Fiat and Generali.

distinct clusters emerges. The first cluster on the left includes the only two shares in the MIB30 basket (Fiat and Generali) that exhibit monotone decreasing trend over all the study period. The subsequent clusters (numbering follows from left to right in the dendrogram) are summarized in Table 1. Specifically, Group 2 is made up of five shares (Bulgari, etc.) that have a relatively large number of price maxima in 2002, while the opposite is true for the shares belonging to Group 3 (B. Commerciale Italiana, etc.). Then we observe a cluster of four shares (B. Fideuram, etc.) that exhibit positive behaviour at the beginning of the period, followed by a steady decrease interrupted by some bumps in 2002. Finally, the largest cluster is composed by shares showing more volatility, with a general decrease in prices after the shock of September 2001, but also with a number of maxima before and later.

5 Concluding remarks

This paper suggests a new dissimilarity measure between functional data, which can be used as input for hierarchical clustering algorithms. Our measure is specifically intended to capture the similarity of function shapes, through the landmark description of each curve. This feature makes our approach appealing when clustering financial time series, since trend detection and identification of local extrema lead the behaviour of market investors.

An additional bonus is inference on estimated landmarks. Here inference is performed through pointwise asymptotic confidence intervals for the first derivative. However, the actual coverage of these intervals might be affected by the specified amount of smoothing. Better approximations to the true landmark description are currently under investigation.

References

ABRAHAM, C., CORNILLON, P.A., MATZNER-LØBER, E. and MOLINARI, N. (2003): Unsupervised curve clustering using B-splines, *Scandinavian Journal of Statistics, 30, 581-595.*

BILLARD, L. and DIDAY, E. (2003): From the statistics of data to the statistics of knowledge: symbolic data analysis. *Journal of the American Statistical Association, 98, 470-487.*

CHIODI, M. (1989): The clustering of longitudinal multivariate data when time series are short. In: R. Coppi and S. Bolasco (Eds.): *Multiway Data Analysis.* Elsevier, Amsterdam, 445-453.

CHIODI, M. (1991): The clustering of longitudinal multivariate data with growth curves of different shapes and different time lags. *Third Conference of the IFCS. Abstracts.* Heriot-Watt University, Edinburgh.

CORDUAS, M. (2003): Il confronto tra serie storiche nell'analisi statistica di dati dinamici. In: *Analisi statistica multivariata per le scienze economico-sociali, le scienze naturali e la tecnologia,* Società Italiana di Statistica, RCE Edizioni, Napoli, 213-224.

D'URSO, P. and VICHI, M. (1998): Dissimilarities between trajectories of a three-way longitudinal data set. In: A. Rizzi, M. Vichi and H.H. Bock (Eds.): *Advances in Data Science and Classification.* Springer, Berlin, 585–592.

GASSER, T. and KNEIP, A. (1995): Searching for Structure in Curve Samples. *Journal of the American Statistical Association, 90, 1179-1188.*

HALL, P. and HECKMAN, N. (2002): Estimating and depicting the structure of a distribution of random functions. *Biometrika, 89, 145-158.*

HECKMAN, N. and ZAMAR, R. (2000): Comparing the shapes of regression functions. *Biometrika, 87, 135-144.*

INGRASSIA, S., CERIOLI, A. and CORBELLINI, A. (2003): Some issues on clustering of functional data. In: M. Schader, W. Gaul and M. Vichi (Eds.): *Between Data Science and Applied Data Analysis,* Springer, Berlin, 49–56.

PICCOLO, D. (1990): A distance measure for classifying ARIMA models. *Journal of Time Series Analysis, 11, 153-164.*

RAMSAY, J.O. and SILVERMAN, B.W. (1997): *Functional Data Analysis.* Springer, New York.

RAMSAY, J.O. and SILVERMAN, B.W. (2002): *Applied Functional Data Analysis. Methods and Case Studies.* Springer, New York.

SILVERMAN, B.W. (1985): Some aspects of the spline smoothing approach to non-parametric regression curve fitting. *Journal of the Royal Statistical Society B, 47, 1-52.*

The Role of the Normal Distribution in Financial Markets

Michele Costa, Giuseppe Cavaliere, and Stefano Iezzi

Dipartimento di Scienze Statistiche,
Università di Bologna, Italy
costa@stat.unibo.it
cavaliere@stat.unibo.it
iezzi@stat.unibo.it

Abstract. The hypothesis that financial variables are normally distributed is often rejected in both theoretical studies and extremely specific cases. In the "real" world of financial investors – where risk averse agents mainly hold government bonds, a few equities and do not hold derivatives – the normal distribution still plays a lead role. To show this result, in this paper we focus on a number of efficient portfolios subject to several constraints which make them close to the portfolios held by most of financial agents. A multivariate approach is proposed, which refers to the case of a financial asset manager who cannot only pay attention to the average return of all of his portfolios, but must evaluate the risks associated to each of his portfolios jointly.

1 Introduction

Since Fama's (1965) seminal work the financial markets literature has been overflowed by studies about skewness, kurtosis and tail-fatness in the distribution of financial returns (Affleck-Graves and McDonald, 1989; Campbell et al., 1997; Dufour et. al, 2003; Jondeau and Rockinger, 2003; Szego, 2002; Tokat et al., 2003). The unanimous conclusion states that financial returns are not normally distributed. This is an extremely relevant result since normal distribution represents the key assumption of the traditional (mean-variance) portfolio theory by Markowitz (1952) and of the usual measures of systematic risk by means of the β coefficient (Sharpe, 1964; Lintner, 1965).

The purpose of the paper is to evaluate to what extent departure from normal distribution can influence risk management strategies. In particular our concern refers to the usual trading activity of a common investor, who does not usually hold oversold accounts or derivatives, but mainly Treasury Bills and a few equities. Therefore we want to analyze the role of normal distribution for a "normal" investor.

The first step of the study concerns the univariate analysis of portfolio returns, by considering the global position of an investor or an asset manager. In the latter case, however, a multivariate extension is of great interest, since it allows to consider the global portfolio not as a whole, but as a combination of many single portfolios, all managed by the same decision unit. The asset manager cannot operate on the basis of the mean return of the global portfolio, but is constrained to consider all single positions. The statistical consequence is moving from a univariate analysis of a global portfolio to a multivariate analysis of single portfolios.

The paper is organized as follows. The statistical approach is illustrated in Section 2; specifically, Section 2.1 deals with the univariate analysis which is generalized to multivariate portfolio analysis in Section 2.2. The empirical assessment of the validity of the normality hypothesis is carried out on Italian data in Section 3. Section 4 concludes.

2 The basic set-up

Let $\mathbf{R} = (R_1, ..., R_i, ..., R_n)'$ be the vector of the random returns on n financial variables. Our goal is to analyze the implications of the departure from the normal distribution (i.e. $\mathbf{R} \sim N(\mu, \Sigma)$ in the multivariate case – $R_i \sim N(\mu_i, \sigma_i^2)$, $i = 1, 2, ..., n$, in the univariate case), with particular emphasis on the left tail of the distribution.

Instead of focusing on the normality of n single returns, the first step of our analysis is to move from n individual financial variables to a mean-variance efficient portfolio $R_p = \sum_{i=1}^{n} R_i \cdot x_i$, where the fractions $x_1, x_2, ..., x_n$ of the initial capital invested in assets $1, 2, ..., n$ are obtained by solving the portfolio optimization problem

$$\min_{\{\mathbf{x} \in \mathbb{X}^A\}} \sigma_p^2 = V(R_p) = \sum_{i,j=1,...,m} x_i x_j Cov(R_i, R_j) \tag{1}$$

$$\mathbb{X}^A = \left\{ (x_1, x_2, ..., x_n)' \in \mathbb{R}^n : \sum_{i=1}^{n} x_i = 1, x_i \geq 0, i = 1, 2, ..., n \right\} \tag{2}$$

under the constraint

$$E(R_p) = \sum_{i=1}^{n} E(R_i) \cdot x_i = \mu_p, \text{ given.} \tag{3}$$

Note that the (realistic) non-negativity restriction on the weights $x_1, x_2, ..., x_n$ rules out the possibility of *short positions*. In order to compare our analysis with the existing studies we also consider portfolio weights $x_1, x_2, ..., x_n$ chosen within the set

$$\mathbb{X}^B = \left\{ (x_1, x_2, ..., x_n)' \in \mathbb{R}^n : \sum_{i=1}^{n} x_i = 1 \right\} \tag{4}$$

$x_i \geq 0$, $i = 1, 2, ..., n$, which allow oversold positions[1]. In the following, an efficient portfolio with weights belonging to the convex polyhedron $\mathbb{X}^A$ ($\mathbb{X}^B$) is denoted as 'portfolio A' ('portfolio B').

---

[1]Our approach can easily be generalized in order to include other types of asset allocations. As suggested by Ruszczyński and Vanderbei (2003), one could also limit

3 Methodology

3.1 Univariate framework

As stressed in the previous section, our aim is to analyze departure from normality not with respect to original financial variables, but by referring to efficient portfolios. This choice represents a key issue since an analysis of the normality assumption performed on the basis of a set of individual assets is unlikely to provide useful results.

Initially, we consider an asset manager who holds a set of m efficient portfolios and needs to evaluate risks associated to a specific portfolio. Hence, the normality assumption corresponds to

$$R_{p_j} \sim N(\mu_{p_j}, \sigma_{p_j}^2) \text{ for } 1 \leq j \leq m. \tag{5}$$

Together with the assessment of the departure from normality by means of standard (univariate) tests, we need to consider to which extent, in the case of financial variables, departure from normality is relevant when related to the *left tail* of the distribution, as in the framework of Value-at-risk measurement. In order to perform risk control we compare empirical frequencies to the expected values under normal distribution by measuring

$$P_{\nu_j} = Prob\left\{ R_{p_j} < R_{\nu_j} \,\middle|\, R_{p_j} \sim N(\mu_{p_j}, \sigma_{p_j}^2) \right\} \tag{6}$$

where R_{ν_j} represents the νth percentile of the empirical distribution of R_{p_j}.

P_{ν_j} measures the probability that a normally distributed asset return is smaller than the νth percentile of the asset return empirical distribution. Therefore, if $P_{\nu_j} > \nu$, normal distribution leads to overestimate the risk, while, for $P_{\nu_j} < \nu$, normal distribution underestimates the risk.

3.2 Multivariate framework

Now, we evaluate the case of an asset manager who holds a set of m efficient portfolios and needs to evaluate the related risks simultaneously. This implies generalizing the analysis to a multivariate context

$$\mathbf{R}_p = (R_{p_1}, ..., R_{p_j}, ..., R_{p_m})' \sim N(\mu_p, \Sigma_p) \tag{7}$$

In the multivariate framework, an important criterion for assessing deviations from normality is represented by the multivariate extension of the Jarque and Bera test (1987) proposed by Kilian and Demiroglu (2000).

---

the exposure to particular assets by placing upper bounds on the x_i's. Similarly, one could force at least a fraction x of the initial capital into a given group of assets (e.g. treasury bills). For space constraints we leave these extensions to future research.

Let $\mathbf{R}_p$ be a $T \times m$ matrix of T observations on returns of m efficient portfolios and let $\mathbf{W} = \mathbf{R}_p \cdot \mathbf{S}^{-1}$ where $\mathbf{S}$ is the Cholesky factor of $\mathbf{R}'_p\mathbf{R}_p$. Clearly, $\mathbf{W}$ may be interpreted as a standardized form of $\mathbf{R}_p$. Now consider the following multivariate extensions of the skewness and kurtosis statistics, respectively:

$$SK_{KD} = (sk_1, ..., sk_m)'(sk_1, ..., sk_m), \tag{8}$$

$$KU_{KD} = (ku_1 - 3, ..., ku_m - 3)'(ku_1 - 3, ..., ku_m - 3), \tag{9}$$

$$sk_j = \frac{T^{-1}\sum_{t=1}^{T} W_{jt}^3}{\left(T^{-1}\sum_{t=1}^{T} W_{jt}^2\right)^{3/2}}, \quad ku_j = \frac{T^{-1}\sum_{t=1}^{T} W_{jt}^4}{\left(T^{-1}\sum_{t=1}^{T} W_{jt}^2\right)^2}, \quad j = 1, 2, ..., m, \tag{10}$$

where W_{jt} denotes the elements of the matrix $\mathbf{W}$ defined above; sk_j and ku_j are the skewness and kurtosis measures for the individual efficient portfolios, based on the standardized data matrix.

The Jarque-Bera multinormality test is:

$$JB = \frac{T}{6}SK_{KD} + \frac{T}{24}KU_{KD} \underset{T\to\infty}{\sim} \chi^2(2m) \tag{11}$$

Furthermore, also in the multivariate context the left tail of the empirical distribution is compared to the left tail of the normal distribution in order to evaluate the reliability of risk measures related to normal distribution. In the multivariate framework the measure corresponding to (6) is

$$PT_\nu = Prob\left\{(R_{p_1} < R_{\nu_1}) \cap ... \cap (R_{p_m} < R_{\nu_m}) | \mathbf{R}_p \sim N(\mu_p, \mathbf{\Sigma}_p)\right\} \tag{12}$$

for R_{ν_j} equal to the νth percentile of the empirical distribution of R_{p_j}.

Quantities PT_ν measure, under the hypothesis of multinormality, the probability to observe that, at the same time, m portfolio returns are $R_{p_j} < R_{\nu_j} \; \forall j$.

Moreover, multivariate extension also allows to evaluate a further relevant risk indicator

$$P1_\nu = Prob\left\{(R_{p_1} < R_{\nu_1}) \cup ... \cup (R_{p_m} < R_{\nu_m}) | \mathbf{R}_p \sim N(\mu_p, \mathbf{\Sigma}_p)\right\} \tag{13}$$

which, under the hypothesis of multinormality, measures the probability of observing in the m portfolios at least one return $R_{p_j} < R_{\nu_j}$, $j = 1, ..., m$.

Quantities $P1_\nu$ are of the greatest importance for the asset manager, who basically is not interested in the mean return of his global portfolio, but is rather concerned with all single positions of his clients.

In order to control the risk of the m portfolios, we compare $P1_\nu$ and PT_ν to the empirical frequencies, $f1_\nu$ and fT_ν, to observe, respectively, at least one return $R_{p_j} < R_{\nu_j}$, $j = 1, ..., m$ and, at the same time, the m portfolio returns $R_{p_j} < R_{\nu_j} \; \forall j$. If $P1_\nu > f1_\nu$, or $PT_\nu > fT_\nu$, normal distribution leads to overestimate the risk, while, for $P1_\nu < f1_\nu$, or $PT_\nu < fT_\nu$, normal distribution underestimates the risk.

| Annual | | Efficient A | | | Efficient B | |
return		Daily	Weekly	Monthly	Daily	Weekly	Monthly
8%	μ	0.031	0.154	0.667	0.031	0.154	0.667
	σ	0.042	0.121	0.353	0.018	0.078	0.300
	JB	1588	44.95	1.699	21.50	25.63	5.902
	p	0.000	0.000	0.428	0.000	0.000	0.052
12%	μ	0.046	0.231	1.000	0.046	0.231	1.000
	σ	0.780	1.802	3.846	0.186	0.421	0.774
	JB	2766	83.50	1.469	1169	1.221	1.302
	p	0.000	0.000	0.480	0.000	0.543	0.521
16%	μ	0.061	0.308	1.333	0.061	0.308	1.333
	σ	1.522	3.507	7.525	0.361	0.809	1.451
	JB	2771	80.73	1.326	1224	1.790	0.390
	p	0.000	0.000	0.515	0.000	0.409	0.823

Table 1. Univariate analysis. Asset manager portfolio returns: mean, standard deviation, Jarque-Bera normality test.

4 Empirical analysis and results

According to Section 2, the study of the distribution of the efficient portfolios is partitioned into two classes, A and B, where portfolios A are obtained under the constraints $\sum_{i=1}^{n} x_i = 1$ and $x_i \geq 0$, while portfolios B are subject to $\sum_{i=1}^{n} x_i = 1$ only.

The data refer to 27 Italian stock returns over the January 1990–June 2003 period. The sample contains the main Italian equities as well as some smaller companies, randomly chosen[2]. Finally, 3-month Treasury Bills are considered as the risk-free asset.

In order to take account of the relevance of data frequency in order to study normality in financial variables, daily, weekly and monthly data are used. The set of m efficient portfolios which compose the global asset manager portfolio, see Sections 2 and 3, are chosen by referring to investors with different degrees of risk aversion.

Table 1 summarizes the results related to the univariate analysis on different types of asset manager portfolios (efficient A and B; daily, weekly and monthly data) having an annual expected return of 8%, 12% and 16%. Since in the 1990-2003 period the average annual return of the 3-month Treasury Bills is equal to 7.77%, an efficient portfolio having an annual return of 8% is almost entirely composed of the so-called risk free asset.

---

[2] Acque potabili, Acquedotto De Ferrari, Aedes, Alleanza, Autostrada TO-MI, Capitalia, Banca Intesa, Bastogi, Bonifiche Ferraresi, Brioschi, Cementir, Unicredito italiano, FIAT, Generali, IFIL, Mediobanca, Milano assicurazioni, Olcese, Olivetti, Perlier, Pirelli & CO., Pirelli S.p.A., Fondiaria-SAI, SMI, Snia, Telecom Italia, Banca Finnat.

| Annual | | Efficient A | | | Efficient B | | |
return	Percentile	Daily	Weekly	Monthly	Daily	Weekly	Monthly
	1st	R_1	−0.082	−0.141	−0.145	−0.006	0.012	0.080
		P_1	0.358	0.733	1.070	1.962	3.451	2.532
8%	5th	R_5	−0.032	−0.017	0.143	0.004	0.041	0.243
		P_5	6.788	7.847	6.885	6.542	7.401	7.894
	10th	R_{10}	−0.016	0.018	0.198	0.008	0.059	0.280
		P_{10}	12.997	13.000	9.205	10.549	11.251	9.871
	1st	R_1	−2.184	−4.572	−9.669	−0.422	−0.826	−0.828
		P_1	0.214	0.384	0.277	0.595	0.601	0.910
12%	5th	R_5	−1.100	−2.547	−5.082	−0.255	−0.459	−0.176
		P_5	7.100	6.156	5.691	5.303	5.055	6.430
	10th	R_{10}	−0.792	−1.827	−3.220	−0.176	−0.307	−0.005
		P_{10}	14.149	12.667	13.630	11.589	10.050	9.720
	1st	R_1	−4.274	−8.981	−19.448	−0.849	−1.731	−2.025
		P_1	0.219	0.404	0.288	0.591	0.586	1.032
16%	5th	R_5	−2.168	−5.057	−10.754	−0.525	−1.014	−0.997
		P_5	7.144	6.302	5.410	5.247	5.113	5.415
	10th	R_{10}	−1.565	−3.724	−7.086	−0.366	−0.697	−0.592
		P_{10}	14.259	12.514	13.162	11.852	10.717	9.232

Table 2. Univariate analysis. Asset manager portfolio returns: left tail analysis, percentage values.

From Table 1 it is worth noting that univariate analysis detects departure from normality, as widely known in the financial market literature: on daily data the normality assumption is strongly rejected, while weekly data play an intermediate role and monthly data are generally normally distributed.

Table 2 illustrates a further element of interest, which is given by the analysis of the left tail of the distribution, developed on the basis of R_1, R_5, and R_{10}, the 1st, 5th and 10th percentile of the empirical distribution of the efficient portfolio, as well as on the basis of the probabilities $P_{\nu_j} = Prob\{R_{p_j} < R_{\nu_j}|R_{p_j} \sim N(\mu_{p_j}, \sigma^2_{p_j})\}$.

Only the values for the 1st percentile show the presence of a fat left tail, since $P_1 < 1.00$, while results for the 5th and 10th percentiles indicate that the normal distribution leads to a slight overestimation of the risk associated to the asset manager portfolio.

In the multivariate framework, the asset manager portfolios are not considered as a whole, but as a combination of the m portfolios. We set $m = 3$, thus identifying three classes of risk aversion, where the first class is 'near risk free', with an annual return of 8%, while the second and the third class have an average annual return of 12% and of 16%, respectively. In the following, the global asset manager portfolio is equally composed of the three classes,

Efficient	Frequency	fT_1	PT_1	$f1_1$	$P1_1$	fT_5	PT_5	$f1_5$	$P1_5$	JB	p-value
	Daily	0.881	0.156	1.108	0.422	3.864	5.046	6.136	8.886	393.2	0.000
A	Weekly	0.850	0.176	1.133	0.961	2.660	3.616	7.648	10.53	339.2	0.000
	Monthly	0.617	0.048	0.617	1.310	1.852	1.505	8.025	10.79	51.77	0.000
	Daily	0.511	0.175	1.477	2.378	2.528	1.775	7.472	10.01	924.8	0.000
B	Weekly	0.425	0.122	1.558	3.915	1.133	1.194	8.782	11.32	125.7	0.000
	Monthly	0.000	0.087	1.235	3.478	0.617	0.904	9.259	12.41	11.85	0.065

Table 3. Multivariate analysis. Asset manager portfolio returns: left tail analysis on the basis of probabilities (12) and (13), percentage values; Jarque-Bera multinormality test.

but different combinations are quite simple to obtain and do not require any further assumption.

Table 3 shows how, differently from the univariate case, the multivariate Jarque-Bera test reveals departure from normality also for monthly data. The only exception is represented by the monthly efficient type B portfolio.

However, even if the asset manager portfolios are not jointly normal, the Gaussian law provides an useful tool for risk control. Values PT_ν, (i.e. the probability that $R_{p_j} < R_{\nu_j}$ for all $j = 1, 2, ..., m$), are, for the 5th percentile, generally higher than the respective empirical values, fT_ν. Multinormality, therefore, allows to correctly measure financial risk at the 95% confidence level, but seems to encounter some problems at the 99% level.

Furthermore, the multivariate framework also allows to obtain important information related to the single position of an individual investor: $P1_\nu$ (i.e. the probability that $R_{p_j} < R_{\nu_j}$ for at least one $j = 1, 2, ..., m$) measures the risk associated to one single investor and represents a more correct and adequate decision criterion. It is interesting to observe that $P1_\nu$ is generally higher than the corresponding empirical values ($f1_\nu$) also for the 1st percentile, thus suggesting the irrelevance of left tail fatness.

5 Conclusion

Although in the last three decades its validity has been widely rejected because of the strong leptokurtosis of financial variables, the normal distribution is still the assumption underlying most of the methods used in empirical finance.

To overcome this contradictory fact, in this paper we propose a multivariate statistical framework for evaluating whether departures from normality actually matter to 'normal' investors, i.e. agents who do not resort to derivatives or to particularly risky asset management strategies.

Surprisingly, the results of the paper clearly show that even when simple standard mean-variance diversification techniques are used the normal distribution remains an important reliable and useful statistical tool for managing financial risks. Moreover, the empirical analysis shows that the normal distribution has a relevant role not only when one-week and one-month horizons matter to the asset manager, but even when there is a need for risk evaluation and asset management at daily frequency.

References

AFFLECK-GRAVES, J. and McDONALD, B. (1989): Nonnormalities and Tests of Asset Pricing Theories. *Journal of Finance, 44, 889-908.*

CAMPBELL, J.Y., LO, A.W. and MacKINLAY, A.C. (1997): *The Econometrics of Financial Markets*, Princeton University Press, New Jersey.

DUFOUR, J.M., KHALAF, L. and BEAULIEU, M.C. (2003): Exact Skewness-Kurtosis Tests for Multivariate Normality and Goodness-of-Fit in Multivariate Regressions with Application to Asset Pricing Models. *CIRANO Working Papers n. 33, Montreal.*

FAMA, E. (1965): The Behavior of Stock Market Prices. *Journal of Business, 38, 34-105.*

JARQUE, C. M. and BERA, A. K. (1987): A Test for Normality of Observations and Regression Residuals. *International Statistical Review, 55, 163-172.*

JONDEAU, E. and ROCKINGER, M. (2003): Conditional Volatility, Skewness and Kurtosis: Existence, Persistence, and Comovements. *Journal of Economic Dynamics and Control, 27, 1699-1737.*

KILIAN, L. and DEMIROGLU, U. (2000): Residual-Based Tests for Normality in Autoregressions: Asymptotic Theory and Simulation Evidence. *Journal of Business and Economic Statistics, 18, 40-50.*

LINTNER, J. (1965): The Valuation of Risk Assets and the Selection of Risky Investments in Stock Portfolios and Capital Budgets. *Review of Economics and Statistics, 47, 13-37.*

MARKOVITZ, H. (1952): Portfolio Selection. *Journal of Finance, 7, 77-91.*

RUSZCZYSKI A. and VANDERBEI R. (2003): Frontiers of stochastically nondominated portfolios, *Econometrica 71, 1287-1297.*

SHARPE, W. F. (1964): Capital Asset Prices: a Theory of Market Equilibrium under Conditions of Risk. *Journal of Finance, 19, 237-260.*

SZEGO, G. (2002): Measures of Risk. *Journal of Banking and Finance, 26, 1253-1272.*

TOKAT, Y., RACHEV, S.T. and SCHWARTZ E.S. (2003): The Stable Non-Gaussian Asset Allocation: a Comparison with the Classical Gaussian Approach. *Journal of Economic Dynamics and Control, 27, 937-969.*

Functional Principal Component Analysis of Financial Time Series

Salvatore Ingrassia and G. Damiana Costanzo

Dipartimento di Economia e Statistica,
Università della Calabria, Italy
s.ingrassia@unical.it, dm.costanzo@unical.it

Abstract. We introduce functional principal component techniques for the statistical analysis of a set of financial time series from an explorative point of view. We show that this approach highlights some relevant statistical features of such related datasets. A case study is here considered concerning the daily traded volumes of the shares in the MIB30 basket from January 3rd, 2000 to December 30th, 2002. Moreover, since the first functional principal component accounts for the 89.4% of the whole variabilitity, this approach suggests the construction of new financial indices based on functional indicators.

1 Introduction

Functional domain supports many recent methodologies for statistical analysis of data coming from measurements concerning continuous phenomena; such techniques constitute nowadays a new branch of statistics named *functional data analysis*, see Ramsay and Silverman (1997, 2002). Financial markets offer an appealing field of application since the phase of dealing is continuous and then the share prices, as well as other related quantities, are updated with a very high frequency.

This paper focuses on functional principal component based approach to the statistical analysis of financial data. In finance principal component based techniques have been considered sometimes e.g. for construction of uncorrelated indices in multi-index models, see Elton and Gruber (1973); moreover they have been suggested in high frequency trading models by Dunis et al. (1998). Here we show that the functional version provides an useful tool for the statistical analysis of a set of financial series from an explorative perspective. Furthermore we point out as this approach suggests the possibility of the construction of stock market indices based on functional indicators.

The analysis is here illustrated by considering the data concerning the daily traded volumes of the 30 shares listed in the MIB30 basket in the period January 3rd, 2000 - December 30th, 2002.

The rest of the paper is organised as follows. In the next section we outline functional data modeling and give some details about functional principal component analysis; in Section 3 we introduce the MIB30 basket dataset and present the main results of our analysis; finally in Section 4 we discuss further methodological aspects and open a problem concerning the construction of new stock market indices on the ground of the obtained results.

2 Functional PCA

Functional data are essentially curves and trajectories, the basic rationale is that we should think of observed data functions as single entities rather than merely a sequence of individual observations. Even though functional data analysis often deals with temporal data, its scope and objectives are quite different from time series analysis. While time series analysis focuses mainly on modeling data, or in predicting future observations, the techniques developed in FDA are essentially exploratory in nature: the emphasis is on trajectories and shapes; moreover unequally-spaced and/or different number of observations can be taken into account as well as series of observations with missing values.

From a practical point of view, functional data are usually observed and recorded discretely. Let $\{\omega_1, \ldots, \omega_n\}$ be a set of n units and let $\mathbf{y}_i = (y_i(t_1), \ldots, y_i(t_p))$ be a sample of measurements of a variable Y taken at p times $t_1, \ldots, t_p \in \mathcal{T} = [a, b]$ in the i-th unit ω_i, $(i = 1, \ldots, n)$. As remarked above, such data $\mathbf{y}_i$ $(i = 1, \ldots, n)$ are regarded as *functional* because they are considered as single entities rather than merely sequences of individual observations, so they are called *raw functional data*; indeed the term functional refers to the intrinsic structure of the data rather than to their explicit form. In order to convert raw functional data into a suitable functional form, a smooth function $x_i(t)$ is assumed to lie behind $\mathbf{y}_i$ which is referred to as the *true functional form*; this implies, in principle, that we can evaluate x at any point $t \in \mathcal{T}$. The set $\mathcal{X}_{\mathcal{T}} = \{x_1(t), \ldots, x_n(t)\}_{t \in \mathcal{T}}$ is the *functional dataset*.

In functional data analysis the statistical techniques posit a vector space of real-valued functions defined on a closed interval for which the integral of their squares is finite. If attention is confined to functions having finite norms, then the resulting space is a Hilbert space; however often we require a stronger assumption so we assume $\mathcal{H}$ be a *reproducing kernel Hilbert space* (r.k.h.s.), see Wahba (1990), which is a Hilbert space of real-valued functions on $\mathcal{T}$ with the property that, for each $t \in \mathcal{T}$, the evaluation functional L_t, which associates f with $f(t)$, $L_t f \to f(t)$, is a bounded linear functional.

In such spaces the objective in principal component analysis of functional data is the orthogonal decomposition of the variance function:

$$v(t, u) := \frac{1}{n-1} \sum_{i=1}^{n} \{x_i(t) - \bar{x}(t)\}\{x_i(u) - \bar{x}(u)\} \tag{1}$$

(which is the counterpart of the covariance matrix of a multidimensional dataset) in order to isolate the dominant components of functional variation, see e.g. also Pezzulli (1994).

In analogy with the multivariate case, the functional PCA problem is characterized by the following decomposition of the variance function:

$$v(t, u) = \sum_j \lambda_j \xi_j(t) \xi_j(u) \tag{2}$$

where $\lambda_j, \xi_j(t)$ satisfy the eigenequation:

$$\langle v(s,), \xi_j \rangle_h = \lambda_j \xi_j(u) . \tag{3}$$

and the eigenvalues:

$$\lambda_j := \int_T \xi_j(t) v(t, u) \xi_j(u) dt \, du$$

are positive and non decreasing while the eigenfunctions must satisfy the constraints:

$$\int_T \xi_j^2(t) dt = 1 \qquad \text{and} \qquad \int_T \xi_j \xi_i(t) dt = 0 \qquad (i < j).$$

The ξ_j's are usually called *principal component weight functions*. Finally the principal component scores (of $\xi(t)$) of the units in the dataset are the values w_i given by:

$$w_i^{(j)} := \langle x_i, \xi_j \rangle = \int_T \xi(t) x_i(t) dt . \tag{4}$$

The decomposition (2) defined by the eigenequation (3) permits a reduced rank least squares approximation to the covariance function v. Thus, the leading eigenfunctions ξ define the principal components of variation among the sample functions x_i.

3 An explorative analysis of the MIB30 basket dataset

Data considered here consist of the total value of the traded volumes of the shares composing the MIB30 index in the period January 3rd, 2000 - December 30th, 2002, see also Costanzo (2003) for details. An important characteristic of this basket is that it is "open" in that the composition of the index is normally updated twice a year, in the months of March and September (ordinary revisions). However, in response to extraordinary events, or for technical reasons ordinary revisions may be brought forward or postponed with respect to the scheduled date; furthermore, in the interval between two consecutive revisions, the shares in the basket may be excluded due to particular reasons, see the website *www.borsaitalia.it* for further details.

Raw data have been collected in a 30 × 758 matrix. There are 21 companies which have remaining in the basket for the three years: Alleanza, Autostrade, Banca Fideuram, Banca Monte Paschi Siena, Banca Naz. Lavoro,

Enel, Eni, Fiat, Finmeccanica, Generali, Mediaset, Mediobanca, Mediolanum, Olivetti, Pirelli Spa, Ras, San Paolo Imi, Seat Pagine Gialle, Telecom Italia, Tim, Unicredito Italiano; the other 9 places in the basket have been shared by a set of other companies which have been remaining in the basket for shorter periods. Such mixed trajectories will be called here *homogeneous piecewise components* of the functional data set and they will be referred as $T_1, \ldots, T_9$. An example, concerning T_1, T_2, T_3 is given in Table 1. Due to the connection

Date	T1	T2	T3
03/01/2000	AEM	Banca Commerciale Italiana	Banca di Roma
04/04/2000	AEM	Banca Commerciale Italiana	Banca di Roma
18/09/2000	AEM	Banca Commerciale Italiana	Banca di Roma
02/01/2001	AEM	Banca Commerciale Italiana	Banca di Roma
19/03/2001	AEM	Italgas	Banca di Roma
02/05/2001	AEM	Italgas	Banca di Roma
24/08/2001	AEM	Italgas	Banca di Roma
24/09/2001	AEM	Italgas	Banca di Roma
18/03/2002	Snam Rete Gas	Italgas	Banca di Roma
01/07/2002	AEM	Italgas	Capitalia
15/07/2002	AEM	Italgas	Capitalia
23/09/2002	Banca Antonveneta	Italgas	Capitalia
04/12/2002	Banca Antonveneta	Italgas	Capitalia

Table 1. The homogeneous piecewise components T_1, T_2, T_3.

among the international financial markets, data concerning the closing days (as week-ends and holidays) are regarded here as missing data.

In literature functional PCA is usual performed from the original data (x_{ij}); here we preferred to work on the daily standardized raw functional data:

$$z_{ij} := \frac{x_{ij} - \bar{x}_j}{s_j} \qquad (i = 1, \ldots, 30, \quad j = 1, \ldots, 758), \qquad (5)$$

where $\bar{x}_j$ and s_j are respectively the daily mean and standard deviation of the e.e.v of the shares in the basket. We shall exhibit later how such transformation can gain an insight into the PC trajectories understanding. The functional dataset has been obtained from such data according to the procedure illustrated in Ramsay (2001).

The trajectories of the first two functional principal components are plotted in Figure 1; they show the way in which such set of functional data varies from its mean, and, in terms of these modes of variability, quantifies the discrepancy from the mean of each individual functional datum. The analysis showed that the first PC alone accounts for the 89.4% and the second PC accounts for the 6.9% of the whole variability.

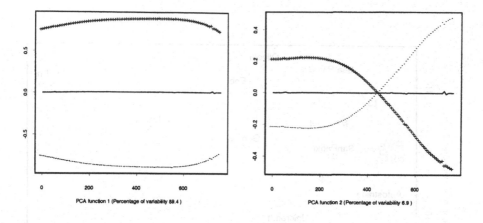

Fig. 1. Plot of the first 2 functional principal components.

The meaning of functional principal component analysis is a more complicated task than the usual multidimensional analysis, however here it emerges the following interpretation:

i. The first functional PC is always positive, then shares with large scores of this component during the considered period have a large traded volume as compared with the mean value on the basket; it can be interpreted as a *long term trend component*.

ii. The second functional PC changes sign at $t = 431$ which corresponds to September 11th, 2001 and the final values, in absolute value, are greater than the initial values: this means that shares having good (bad) performances before the September 11th, 2001 have been going down(rising) after this date; it can be interpreted as a *shock component*.

This interpretation is confirmed by the following analysis of the raw data. As it concerns the first PC, for each company we considered its minimum standardized value over the three years $z_i^{(min)} = \min_{j=1,\dots,758} z_{ij}$ ($i = 1,\dots,30$). In particular $z_i^{(min)}$ is positive (negative) when the traded volumes of the i-th share are always greater (less) than the mean value of the MIB30 basket during the three years.

As for the second PC, let $\bar{x}_{Bi}$ be the average of the traded volumes of the ith company over the days: 1,...,431 (i.e. before September 11th, 2001) and $\bar{x}_{Ai}$ be the corresponding mean value after September 11th, 2001. Let us consider the variation per cent:

$$\delta_i := \frac{\bar{x}_{Ai} - \bar{x}_{Bi}}{\bar{x}_{Bi}} 100\% \qquad i = 1,\dots,30 .$$

If δ_i is positive (negative) then the ith company increased (decreased) its mean e.e.v. after the September 11, 2001. Finally consider the scores on the

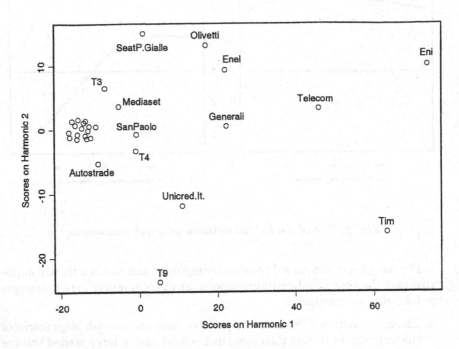

Fig. 2. Scores on the two first harmonics

two first PCs given in (4), respectively $\mathbf{w}_i^{(1)}$ and $\mathbf{w}_i^{(2)}$ (see Figure 2). We observe that : i) companies with large positive (negative) value $\mathbf{w}_j^{(1)}$ present a large (small) value than the mean during the entire considered period, i.e. of $z_i^{(min)}$, see Table 2; ii) companies with large positive (negative) value $\mathbf{w}_i^{(2)}$ show a large decrement (increment) after September 11th, 2001 (Day=431), i.e. of δ_i, see Table 3. Further details are given in Costanzo and Ingrassia (2004).

4 Further remarks and methodological perspectives

The results illustrate the capability of functional PCs to highlight statistical features of a set of financial time series as the subsequent analysis on the raw data has been also confirmed.

As we remarked above, the functional data set has been here constructed using the standardized data (z_{ij}) defined in (5) rather than the original data (x_{ij}); Figure 1 shows how this approach clarifies the contribute of the PC trajectories with respect to the mean trajectory. For the sake of completeness, we point out that the first two PCs computed on the non standardized data (x_{ij}) explained respectively the 88.9% and the 7.1% of the whole variability;

$z_i^{(min)}$	Company	$w_i^{(1)}$
0.3294	Eni	73.743
0.0579	Telecom	46.118
0.0566	Tim	63.311
−0.2197	Enel	21.967
−0.2770	Generali	22.375
−0.5360	Olivetti	17.086
−0.5554	Unicredito	10.970
−0.6404	T_4	−0.881
−0.6552	Mediaset	−5.232
−0.7511	Seat Pagine Gialle	0.997

Table 2. Comparison between $z_i^{(min)}$ and $w_i^{(1)}$ for some companies.

δ_j	Company	$w_j^{(2)}$
−80.20%	Seat Pagine Gialle	14.998
−58.50%	Olivetti	13.149
−47.08%	Enel	9.283
63.21%	Unicredito	−11.900
83.10%	Autostrade	−5.273
133.79%	T9	−23.748

Table 3. Comparison between δ_i and $w_i^{(2)}$ for some companies.

the plot of the scores on such two harmonics is practically the same of the one given in Figure 2.

In our opinion, the obtained results open some methodological perspectives for the construction of new financial indices having some suitable statistical properties. As a matter of fact, the construction of some existing stock market indices has been criticized by several authors, see e.g. Elton and Gruber (1995). For example, it is well known that the famous U.S. Dow Jones presents some statistical flaws, but, despite these drawbacks in the methodology used in their computation, it continues to be widely employed.

In Italy, the MIB30 share basket is summarized by the MIB30 index which is calculated according to the formula:

$$MIB30 = 10000 \left(\sum_{i=1}^{30} \frac{p_{it}}{p_{i0}} w_{i0} \right) r_0 \quad \text{with} \quad w_{i0} = \frac{p_{i0} q_{i0}}{\sum_{i=1}^{30} p_{i0} q_{i0}} \quad (6)$$

where p_{it} is the current price of the i-th share at time t; p_{i0} is the base price of the i-th share which is the opening price on the day on which the updating of the index takes effect (multiplied, where appropriate, by an adjustment coefficient calculated by the Italian Exchange in the event of actions involving the i-th company's capital); q_{i0} is the base number of the shares in circulation of the i-th stock. The weight w_{i0} of the i-th share in (6) is given by the ratio of the company's market capitalisation to the market capitalisation of all the companies in the basket. Finally r_0 is a factor with the base set equal to one, used to maintain the continuity of the index when the basket is updated and the value 10,000 is the base of the index on December 31st, 1992.

However such indices don't take into account the variability of the share prices (or of the traded volumes, or other related quantities) during any time interval (e.g. between two consecutive updating of the basket composition). Due to the resulted presented above, the shares scores on this harmonic seem constitute a good ingredient for a new family of financial indices trying to capture as most as possible of the variability of the prices in the share basket. This provides ideas for further developments of functional principal component techniques in the financial field.

Acknowledgments

Dataset used in this paper have been collected by the Italian Stock Exchange. The authors thank Research & Development DBMS (Borsa Italiana).

References

CERIOLI, A., LAURINI, F. and CORBELLINI, A. (2003): Functional cluster analysis of financial time series. In: M. Vichi and P. Monari (Eds.): *Book of Short Paper of Cladag 2003*.

COSTANZO, G.D. (2003): A graphical analysis of the dynamics of the MIB30 index in the period 2000-2002 by a functional data approach. In: *Atti Riunione Scientifica SIS 2003*, Rocco Curto Editore, Napoli.

COSTANZO, G.D., INGRASSIA, S. (2004): Analysis of the MIB30 basket in the period 2000-2002 by functional PC's. In: J. Antoch (Ed.): *Proceedings of Compstat 2004*, Prague August 23-27, 2004.

DUNIS, C., GAVRIDIS, M., HARRIS, A., LEONG, S. and NACASKUL P. (1998): An application of genetic algorithms to high frequence trading models: a case study. In: C. Dunis and B. Zhou (Eds.): *Nonlinear Modeling of High Frequency Financial Time Series*. John Wiley & Sons, New York, 247-278.

ELTON , E.J. and GRUBER, M.J. (1973): Estimating the dependence structure of share prices. Implications for portfolio, *Journal of Finance, 1203-1232*.

ELTON , E.J. and GRUBER, M.J. (1995): *Modern Portfolio Theory and Investment Analysis*. John Wiley & Sons, New York.

PEZZULLI, S. (1994): *L'analisi delle componenti principali quando i dati sono funzioni*, Tesi di Dottorato.

RAMSAY, J.O. (2001): *Matlab and S-PLUS functions for Functional Data Analysis*, McGill University.

RAMSAY, J.O. and SILVERMAN, B.W. (1997): *Functional Data Analysis*. Springer-Verlag, New York.

RAMSAY, J.O. and SILVERMAN, B.W. (2002): *Applied Functional Data Analysis*. Springer-Verlag, New York.

WAHBA, G. (1990): *Spline Models for Observational Data*. CBMS-NSF Regional Conference Series in Applied Mathematics, SIAM, Philadelphia.

Elliptically Symmetric Distributions: A Review of Achieved Results and Open Issues

Fiorella Romito

Dipartimento di Scienze Statistiche e Matematiche "Silvio Vianelli",
Università degli Studi di Palermo, Italy
romito@dssm.unipa.it

Abstract. The spherically and elliptically symmetrical distributions are used in different statistical areas for different purposes such as the description of multivariate data, in order to find alternatives to the normal distribution in multinormality tests and in the creation of statistical models in which the usual assumption of normality is not realistic. Some achieved results, open issues and some proposals for their use in applications, especially in the financial area, are here presented.

1 Introduction

Recently, a great attention has been devoted to the class of spherically and elliptically symmetrical distributions by statistical literature, both in the applied and the theoretical fields. In this paper some of the main results achieved for such class of distributions are presented. We will see as the spherically and elliptically symmetrical distributions are used in different statistical areas for different purposes such as the description of multivariate data, in order to find alternatives to the normal distribution in multinormality tests and in the creation of statistical models in which the usual assumption of normality is not realistic. At last, an application of Capital Asset Pricing Model (CAPM) with elliptic errors is compared to a CAPM with normal errors.

2 Basic principles of the elliptically symmetric distributions

A $d \times 1$ random vector $\mathbf{X} = (X_1, X_2, \ldots, X_d)'$ is said to have an elliptically symmetric distribution if its characteristic function is:

$$\exp(it'\mu)\phi(t'\Sigma t)$$

where $\mu_{d \times 1}$, $\Sigma_{d \times d} \geq 0$ and ϕ are its parameters and it is written as

$$\mathbf{X} \sim EC_d(\mu, \Sigma, \phi).$$

In particular, when $\mu_{d\times 1} = 0_d$ and $\Sigma_{d\times d} = I_d$, $X \sim EC_d(0, I_d, \phi)$ it is called spherical distribution and it is written as $X \sim S_d(\phi)$. Its stochastic representation is:

$$X = \mu + RA'U^{(d)}$$

where R is the random variable with $R \sim F(r)$ in $[0, \infty)$ called the generating variate and $F(\cdot)$ is called the generating c.d.f.. $U^{(d)}$ is a random vector uniformly distributed on the unit spherical surface in $\mathbb{R}^d$ called uniform base of the elliptical distribution, R and $U^{(d)}$ are independent and $A'A = \Sigma$. In general, a given random vector $X \sim EC_d(\mu, \Sigma, \phi)$ does not necessarily possess a density. However, if density of X exists it must be of the form:

$$|\Sigma|^{-1/2} f\left((X - \mu)' \Sigma^{-1}(X - \mu)\right) \tag{1}$$

for some nonnegative function $f(\cdot)$ of a scalar variable.

When $f(x) = (2\pi)^{-n/2} exp\{-x/2\}$, X has a multivariate normal distribution. Many of the characteristics and properties of the elliptically symmetric distributions can be found in Fang and Zhang (1990).

The class of elliptical distributions includes various distributions such as symmetric Kotz type distribution, symmetric multivariate Pearson type VII and symmetric multivariate stable law (Fang et al. (1989)). Examples below provide some subclasses of elliptical distributions.

Example 1 (Symmetric Kotz type distribution) *Let* X *be distributed according to a symmetric Kotz type distribution with density:*

$$C_d|\Sigma|^{-1/2}[(x - \mu)'\Sigma^{-1}(x - \mu)]^{N-1} exp\{-r[(x - \mu)'\Sigma^{-1}(x - \mu)]^s\}$$

where C_d *is a normalizing constant,* $r, s > 0$, $2N + d > 2$ *are parameters. When* $N = s = 1$ *and* $r = 1/2$, *the distribution reduces to a multivariate normal distribution and when* $N = 1$ *and* $r = 1/2$ *the distribution reduces to a multivariate power exponential distribution. This family of distributions was found to be useful in constructing models in which the usual normality assumption is not applicable.*

Example 2 (Symmetric multivariate Pearson type VII distribution) *Let* X *be distributed according to a symmetric multivariate Pearson type VII distribution with density:*

$$C_d\{1 + [(x - \mu)'\Sigma^{-1}(x - \mu)]/m\}^{-N}$$

where C_d *is a normalizing constant,* $N > d/2$, $m > 0$ *are parameters. This subclass includes a number of important distributions as the multivariate t-distribution for* $N = (d + m)/2$ *and the multivariate Cauchy distribution for* $m = 1$ *and* $N = (d + 1)/2$.

3 Tests of multivariate normality

The tests to verify the multivariate normality are very important since many of the techniques of statistical inference are based on the hypothesis of multivariate normality.

One of the relatively simpler and mathematically tractable way to find a support for the assumption of multivariate normality is by using the tests based on Mardia's multivariate skewness and kurtosis measures:

$$\beta_{1,d} = E\left\{(y - \mu)'\Sigma^{-1}(x - \mu)\right\}^3, \qquad \beta_{2,d} = E\left\{(y - \mu)'\Sigma^{-1}(y - \mu)\right\}^4$$

provided that the expectations in the expression of $\beta_{1,d}$ and $\beta_{2,d}$ exist. For the multivariate normal distribution $\beta_{1,d} = 0$ and $\beta_{2,d} = d(d+2)$. The quantities $\hat{\beta}_{1,d}$ and $\hat{\beta}_{2,d}$ can be used to detect departure from multivariate normality. Mardia (1970) has shown that for large samples $k_1 = n\hat{\beta}_{1,d}/6$ follows a chi-square distribution with degrees of freedom $d(d+1)(d+2)/6$, and $k_2 = \{\hat{\beta}_{2,d} - d(d+2)\}/\{8d(d(d+2)/n\}^{1/2}$ follows a standard normal distribution. In order to deduce the limit distribution of Mardia's multivariate skewness and kurtosis measures many different methods have been used. Baringhaus and Henze (1992) show that in the peculiar case of an elliptical distribution the limit law of Mardia skewness measure is a weighted sum of two independent chi-square distributions. Klar (2002) gives a unified treatment of the limit laws of skewness measures and other statistics like multivariate kurtosis which are closely related to components of the Neyman's smooth test of fit for multivariate normality. For assessing deviations from multivariate normality, Kilian and Demiroglu (2000) suggest a multivariate extension of Jarque-Bera test, obtained by combining skewness and kurtosis measures. Let $\mathbf{Y}_{n \times d}$ matrix of observation and let $\mathbf{W} = \mathbf{Y}\mathbf{S}^{-1}$ where $\mathbf{S}$ is the Cholesky factor of $\mathbf{Y}'\mathbf{Y}$. The multivariate extensions of the skewness and kurtosis statistics are respectively:

$$SK_{KD} = (sk_1, \ldots, sk_d)'(sk_1, \ldots, sk_d)$$

$$KU_{KD} = (ku_1, \ldots, ku_d)'(ku_1, \ldots, ku_d)$$

$$sk_j = \frac{n^{-1}\sum_{i=1}^n W_{ij}^3}{\left(n^{-1}\sum_{i=1}^n W_{ij}^2\right)^{3/2}}, \quad i = 1, \ldots, n$$

$$ku_j = \frac{n^{-1}\sum_{i=1}^n W_{ij}^4}{\left(n^{-1}\sum_{i=1}^n W_{ij}^2\right)^2}, \quad i = 1, \ldots, n$$

where W_{ij} denotes the elements of the matrix $\mathbf{W}$ defined above; in other words sk_j and ku_j are the individual skewness and kurtosis based on the standardized residuals matrix. The Jarque-Bera multinormality test is:

$$MJB = \frac{n}{6}SK_{KD} + \frac{n}{24}KU_{KD} \overset{n \to \infty}{\sim} \chi_{2d}^2$$

Many tests for multinormality have been proposed and some of them were summarized by Fattorini (2000). Kuwana and Kariya (1991) using the symmetric Kotz type distribution with $N = 1$, and $r = 1/2$ (that is the multivariate exponential power distribution) verify the tests of multinormality: $H_0 : s = 1$ vs $H_1 : 0 < s < 1$ or $H_1 : s > 1$, where the alternative hypotheses correspond respectively to thicker and thinner tailed distribution compared to the normal distribution and from it derives the unvaried locally best test both in the case in which μ is known and in the cases μ or not, but with Σ always unknown. Naito (1999) infers a formula of approximation for the power of the test of multinormality against elliptically symmetrical distribution and he gives examples for the symmetric Kotz type distribution, the Pearson type II and VII distribution. Manzotti et al. (2002) present and study a procedure for testing the null hypothesis of multivariate elliptically symmetry independently on the parameters that characterize the underling elliptically symmetric law. The procedure is based on the averages of some spherical harmonics over the projections of the scaled residual of the d-dimensional data on the unit sphere of $\mathbb{R}^d$. The proposed statistic Z_n^2 has as limit distribution a χ^2 independently by the parameters which define the underlying elliptical distribution.

4 Multivariate non normal models

The normal distribution has had an important role in the development of many techniques of multivariate modelling. It is well known that we often assume as true the multivariate normality of data. The elliptically symmetric distributions are an alternative to analyze multivariate data. Gomez et al. (2002) study a generalization of the dynamic linear model from the Bayesian point of view, which has been created using an elliptical joint distribution for the parameters and the errors of the model. In particular, the multivariate exponential power distribution is used. Solaro and Ferrari (2003) as well use a multilevel model assuming that the random consequences follow a multivariate exponential power distribution. Moreover, the strength of iterative procedures of estimate of maximum likelihood is studied, using a simulation technique which exploits the stochastic representation of elliptical symmetric distributions. Consider the d-equation Seemingly Unrelated Regression model

$$Y_i = \alpha + X_i\beta + \varepsilon_i; \qquad E(\varepsilon_i) = 0, \qquad cov(\varepsilon_i) = \Sigma, \qquad i = 1, \ldots, n$$

where Y_i is a $d \times 1$ vector of responses, X_i is a $d \times q$ design matrix of explanatory variables for every i, β is a $q \times 1$ vector of regression coefficients, ε_i is a $d \times 1$ error vector, and Σ is the $d \times d$ covariance matrix. We assume that $(X_1', \ldots, X_d')$ is of full rank and X_i is of the form

$$\begin{pmatrix} x_{i1} & 0 & \cdots & 0 \\ 0 & x_{i2} & \cdots & 0 \\ \vdots & \vdots & \ddots & \vdots \\ 0 & 0 & 0 & x_{id} \end{pmatrix}$$

where x_{ij} is a $q_j \times 1$ vector of explanatory variables for the response j for every i and $q = \sum_{j=1}^{d} q_j$. Ng (2002) assumes that $(\varepsilon_1, \ldots \varepsilon_n))$ have a joint elliptically symmetric distribution with probability density function given by (1). The CAPM implemented in next section falls within this class.

5 Applications

The multivariate normality is largely inadequate in the financial data of returns, largely due to tail thickness. For example the Capital Asset Pricing Model, originally derived under the assumption of normality, is prevalently refused as a correct model of returns. The CAPM is formalized in the following equation:

$$E[R_i] = r_f + \beta_i \left(E[R_M] - r_f \right) \tag{2}$$

where R_i is the random rate return on asset i, $\beta_i = cov[R_i, R_M]/var[R_M]$, R_M is the rate on the market portfolio and r_f is the risk-free rate. Defining $r_i = E[R_i] - r_f$, equation (2) can be written as $r_i = \beta_i r_M$.

In this section CAPM assuming that the errors follow a multivariate exponential power distribution is compared with a CAPM under normality assuntion. We create three efficient portfolios in mean-variance sense using daily data on Italian stock returns observed from January 2000 to June 2001, while 3 months BOT are considered as the risk-free rate.

In applying the CAPM, some care should be taken regarding the possibility of conditional heteroskedasticity in regression disturbances. A solution would be to correct $r_{i,t}^* = r^t/\hat{\sigma}_{it}$ for the conditional heteroskedasticity in preliminary estimation step. We use a Garch(1,1) model. Table(1) and (3) report the results of estimating of CAPM:

$$r_t = \alpha + \beta r_{Mt} + \varepsilon_t \tag{3}$$

where r_t is the 3-vector of portfolio excess returns, α and β are 3-dimensional parameter vectors, $r_{M,t}$ is the excess market return and ε_t is a 3-vector of errors, using unweighted and weighted excess returns under normal errors assumption. Table(2) and (4) test the null hypothesis of normality for residuals using the Mardia's multivariate skewness, kurtosis and Jarque-Bera test statistic. We find that estimates of α and β are lower using GARCH(1,1) conditional standard deviations weighted excess returns also relative their standard errors. Mardia's multivariate skewness Jarque-Bera test statistic of multinormality are not reject but is reject Mardia's multivariate kurtosis both unweighted and weighted excess returns. Table(4) and (5) report the results of estimating of CAPM using unweighted and weighted excess returns under multivariate exponential power distribution assumption for errors. We do not find substantial differences except for portfolio 3 under GARCH(1,1) conditional standard deviations weighted excess returns.

U nweighted Excess Returns

	α_i	Std.Error	β_i	Std.Error
Portfolio 1	0.8474	0.3729	0.73	0.1189
Portfolio 2	1.53833	0.21674	0.51021	0.6909
Portfolio 3	-3.3882	1.3352	2.0807	0.4252

Table 1. Results of estimation of CAMP under normal errors assumption.

U nweighted Excess Returns

	Skewness test	Kurtosis test	Jarque-Bera test
Measure	8755.229	1682.4023	1247871
P-value	1	0	1

Table 2. Tests the null of normality for residuals using the Mardia's multivariate skewness, kurtosis and Jarque-Bera test statistic.

G ARCH(1,1)conditional standard deviations weighted excess returns

	α_i	Std.Error	β_i	Std.Error
Portfolio 1	0.18572	0.23039	0.25209	0.07344
Portfolio 2	0.41846	0.09712	0.17717	0.03096
Portfolio 3	-0.49455	0.12772	0.46834	0.04071

Table 3. Results of estimation of CAMP under normal errors assumption.

G ARCH(1,1)conditional standard deviations weighted excess returns

	Skewness test	Kurtosis test	Jarque-Bera test
Measure	35185.77	1374.125	2898419
P-value	1	0	1

Table 4. Tests the null of normality for residuals using the Mardia's multivariate skewness, kurtosis and Jarque-Bera test statistic.

Unweighted Excess Returns

	α_i	Std.Error	β_i	Std.Error
Portfolio 1	0.8474	0.3729	0.73	0.1189
Portfolio 2	1.53855	0.21771	0.50970	0.6921
Portfolio 3	-3.2347	1.3388	2.0283	0.4268

Table 5. Results of estimation of CAMP under elliptical errors assumption.

GARCH(1,1)conditional standard deviations weighted excess returns

	α_i	Std.Error	β_i	Std.Error
Portfolio 1	0.18650	0.23041	0.25174	0.07345
Portfolio 2	0.41843	0.9714	0.17711	0.03096
Portfolio 3	1.09425	0.23330	-0.03757	0.07437

Table 6. Results of estimation of CAMP under elliptical errors assumption.

6 Conclusion

In conclusion, we can say that the elliptically symmetric distributions can be used in different statistical areas and for different purposes as, for instance, the description of multivariate data, in order to show alternatives to multivariate normal distribution in normality test and in the creation of statistic models in which the usual hypothesis of normality is not realistic.

In this section CAPM assuming that the errors follow a multivariate exponential power distribution is compared with a CAPM under normality assumption. The standard estimator of this model is ordinary least squares which will be full efficient under normality, but not be full efficient if normality fails. Various methods have been suggested to estimate the parameters when hypothesis of normality is rejected. In future work we will development MLEs using non-linear optimization algorithm.

References

BARINGHAUS, L. and HENZE, N. (1992): Limited Distribution for Mardia's Measure of Multivariate Skewness. *Ann. Statist., 20, 1889–1902.*

HODGSON, D.J., LINTON, O. and VORKING, K. (2001): Testing the Capital Asset Pricing Model Efficiently under Elliptical Symmetry: A Semiparametric Approach. *www.unites.uquam.ca/eco/CREFE/cahiers/cach143.pdf.*

FANG, K.T., KOTZ, S. and NG, K.W. (1989): *Symmetric Multivariate and Related Distributions.* Chapman and Hall, London.

FANG, K.T. and ZHANG, Y.T. (1990): *Generalized Multivariate Analysis.* Springer-Verlag, Berlin.

FATTORINI, L. (2000): On the Assessment of Multivariate Normality. *Atti della XL Riunione Scientifica della SIS, Firenze.*

GOMEZ, E., GOMEZ-VILLAGAS, M.A. and MARIN, J.M. (2002): Continuous Elliptical and Exponential Power Linear Dynamic Models. *Journal of Multivariate Analysis, 83, 22–36.*

KILIAN, L. and DEMIROGLU, U. (2000): Residuals-Based Test for Normality in Autoregressions: Asyntotic Theory and Simulation Evidence. *Journal of Business and Economic Statistics, 18, 40–50.*

KLAR, B. (2002): A Treatment of Multivariate Skewness, Kurtosis and Related Statistic. *Journal of Multivariate Analysis, 83, 141-165*

KRZANOWSKI, W.J. and MARRIOTT, F.H.C. (1994): *Multivariate Analysis, Part1: Distributions, Ordinations and Inference.* Edward Arnold, London.

KOTZ, S. and OSTROVSKII, I. (1994): Characteristic Functions of a Class of Elliptical Distributions. *Journal of Multivariate Analysis, 49, 164–178.*

KUWANA, Y. and KARIYA, T. (1991): LBI Test for Multivariate Normality in Exponential Power Distributions. *Journal of Multivariate Analysis, 39, 117–134.*

MANZOTTI, A., PREZ, F.J. and QUIROZ, A.J. (2002): Statistic for Testing the Null Hypothesis of Elliptical Symmetry. *Journal of Multivariate Analysis, 81, 274-285.*

MARDIA, K.V. (1970): Measures of Multivariate Skewness and Kurtosis with Applications. *Biometrika, 57, 519-530.*

NAITO, K. (1998): Approximation of the Power of Kurtosis for Mutinormality. *Journal of Multivariate Analysis, 65, 166–180.*

NG, V.M. (2002): Robust Bayesian Inference for Seemingly Unrelated Regression with Elliptically Error. *Journal of Multivariate Analysis, 83, 409–414.*

SOLARO, N. and FERRARI, P.A. (2003): Robustezza della Procedura di Stima dei Parametri nei Modelli Multilivello. *Atti del Convegno Scientifico Intermedio SIS, Napoli.*

Author and Subject Index

Printing: Strauss GmbH, Mörlenbach
Binding: Schäffer, Grünstadt